WATER IN ENGLAND

Also by Dorothy Hartley, and published by Macdonald and Jane's

FOOD IN ENGLAND

DOROTHY HARTLEY

WATER IN ENGLAND

MACDONALD AND JANE'S · LONDON

First published 1964
This edition published 1978 by
Macdonald and Jane's Publishers Ltd.
Paulton House, 8 Shepherdess Walk, London, N1 7LW

ISBN 0 354 04048 0
ISBN 0 354 04048 0

Made and printed in Great Britain by
Richard Clay (The Chaucer Press) Ltd, Bungay, Suffolk

CONTENTS

LIST OF PLATES

PREFACE

When I wrote FOOD IN ENGLAND I studied only the plain food of the land, cooked on local fuels and eaten by everyone, kings and commoners—because it was all the food they had.

This study is of WATER IN ENGLAND: the plain water everyone uses because it's all we have.

Our water was always important. Before roads were built it was our travel guide and map-maker. We caught it running, kept it static, conducted it about and made it work for us. We washed in it (homesick Romans built Bath for it); we even drank it sometimes. Our saints made it miraculous, minerals made it medical.

All our green and pleasant land depends on our rainwater. Visitors sometimes consider we supply too much of it, but even a short dry season is devastating. I hope some good English hostess will find this book of use in amusing her visitors during a thoroughly wet week.

Dorothy Hartley, 1978

INTRODUCTION

ANCIENT WATER

SOME IDEAS ABOUT WATER

"And God made the firmament, and He divided the waters which were under the firmament from the waters which were above the firmament."

GENESIS.

We believe the earth round, with water in it, on it, and round about it. Most mediæval people believed the earth flat, with water above and below.

This was reasonable; water fell down from above, and welled up from below.

Mediæval water ran down, ran off, or "went through" the earth. This they could see was true, so they believed it cheerfully.

Those living in limestone districts saw springs "burst up from the rock" and "sink down through the ground". Chalk-land streams came and went by seasons. Mediæval people, who journeyed on foot or horseback, were guided by streams and when crossing the hill divides had a very close study of springs and streams, so early travellers commented at once on any spring or well that behaved eccentrically. Thus ebbing and flowing wells showed that something (or somebody) *was tampering with the waters from below.* Some springs came up hot, and others not only came up hot but smelling of sulphur. Which fact proved you went *down* to Hell if you did not go up to Heaven.

It's all so reasonable once seen through the mediæval eye. Transparent ice was earthly frozen water.

So precious stones (ice hard, cold and clear, lovely and everlasting) were a sort of heavenly ice, the solidified waters of Paradise. It was thought that many jewels were found in eastern rivers and the rivers flowed out of Paradise. (Some said the tears of Adam and Eve ran those rivers.)

Crystal

"Crystal is a bright stone and clear. . . . Men trowe that it is of snow or ice made hard in space of many years. This stone set in the sun taketh fire, insomuch if dry tow be put thereto, it setteth the tow on fire. That crystal materially is made of water, Gregory on Ezekiel i. saith: 'Water is of itself fleeting but by strength of cold it is turned and made steadfast crystal.' "

Now these rivers came from the east and the sun rose in the east, so somewhere in the east there was the old garden of Paradise. The mediæval thought is crystal clear when understood.

Any child could see that earthly water crystallized in earthly rocks (perhaps the white spar had once been snow?), so Paradise crystals were real and wonderfully precious, and some were so heavenly precious that they even cured earthly ills.

That there existed this "land of Paradise" there could be no doubt.

Rivers of Paradise

"Paradyse is a place in the partyes of the East. Therein groweth all manner of trees and all manner of trees bere apples. Therein is the tree of lyfe. In the middel thereof spryngeth a well, that findeth water inoughe to that place. That welle is parted in four stremes and ryvers, (but) the way thereto is stopped and unknowe to mankynde after the synne of the fyrste man.

[Paradise] is departed from londes that men dwellen in with Occean and mountayne—that is moost fere, and stretcheth as hyghe as it were to the cercle of the moone.

Tygris is a ryver of Mesopotamis and cometh out of Paradise and Eyprates is a ryver of Mespoltamia and cometh out of *Paradise and is most copyous in gemmes and precious stones.*"

BART. ANGLICUS

Birds of Paradise were brought from there; they had no feet (since they flew under heaven) and ate only honey dew and heavenly fragrance, since their lovely bodies held nothing but the spices with which the Indian merchants had stuffed the skins!

Paradise, and the Water of Paradise were a fact. They existed on this flat earth and were accessible to mediæval people, as outer space is to people today—that is "accessible in theory": people had been there, otherwise how did they know.

A REALLY SCIENTIFIC VIEW TAKEN FROM AN ENCYCLOPAEDIA OF A.D. 1300

"Water is called Aqua, as it were Equa—for it resteth never in moving till one side thereof be even as the other.

Also Constantin sayeth, that water is a colde element and moyste and more subtyl than earth, and bright and clean, and will not hold in with his own markes and boundes, for water should all to shed and fall to nought, be that [unless] he was stopped and holden in, with other bonds than his owen.

And Water composeth with vapours, and flyeth up on hygh, and chalengyth heven. And water is cause of all bread, and breedeth corn and fruit, and bringeth forth trees, herbs and grass. And water washeth away filth and giveth drink to man and beaste. Also, water taking changing and likeness of colour and flavour, and places by whom he passeth. And, therefore, water is sometimes salt and sometimes fresh, now clear, now troublous, now thick, now thin, for water of itself hath no determinate qualitie nor colour of itself.

Also, water taketh the lyghte of the Soun [sun]-Beemes, and reboundeth it again towards heaven; so he hath the part of a mirror.

And there be many diveise waters, for water springeth, and cometh of the air as rain water, and, for that this is heavens water;[1] it is most profitable to things that grow in earth. Other waters spring and wellen out of thin parts of the earth, as well water and springs, and some waters passeth and runneth over the earth as the water of rivers.

And some water byclypteth the sydes of the earthe—as the see of Occean and of the mydle earth."

BART. ANGLICUS

WATER AS WE KNOW IT

COLD WATER

"O ye ice and snow, bless ye the Lord,
Praise Him and magnify Him for ever."

H_2O. Water becomes ice at 32° Fahrenheit: on cooling it shrinks till 39°F. is reached, after which it expands. This irregular behaviour causes burst pipes, cleared ponds, racking of wines, "waters stilled at eve", and other phenomena.

The explanation lies in the change of weight caused by the change in density. Expansion makes it lighter, contraction heavier (for its smaller bulk). The surface of the water being exposed to cold air contracts and becomes heavier and sinks down through the warmer water below. This causes a current that sweeps downward any particles held in suspension in the water (exactly as a sideways current in a stream sweeps sand and pebbles sideways). It is this steady downward current that *clears* the pond, so that the still cold water is cleaned and the bottom of the pond is seen to be covered with a film of mud lying as slightly as dust. Racking:

[1] *Thunder (rain)water.* "We praise Rain Water, and amongst all rain water, that which falleth in a thunderstorm, for the movement of the thunder smitheth the vapours, and maketh the water subtle and clere, and pure and clene. Water of melted snow is not good, for it smitheth the stomack, and setteth the teeth on edge."

the same movement takes place invisibly in casks and tubs, the cloudy debris of fermentation is carried down and lies as a thick sediment at the bottom of the cask so that the fine clear liquid can be drawn off. For wines, this change of weight and substance is sometimes artificially produced by the introduction of isinglas or other "finings".

When the whole of the water, or a proportionate depth of it, is all reduced to the uniform 39°F., then ice forms rapidly. Long needles of ice shoot across the surface, and the first thin top ice thickens downwards until the very thickness of the covering prevents further cooling. This is why deep ponds seldom freeze right down to the bottom, and fish survive in the cold but unfrozen water below, getting oxygen from the small "air-lock" that forms between the ice and the water. Fish often seem to swim up, to gaze earnestly at skaters above, but it is more likely they are depending on the spring of the elastic surface after the skaters have passed to give them a greater depth of air and less chance of a stubbed nose.

The air space below thick ice may be much increased if (as in mountain lakes) the lower outlet streams continue to run after the inlet streams far higher up the mountain have frozen up. In some lakes the water may be almost drained away below the ice, then the tension holding the frozen

surface taut breaks suddenly and the whole wide surface of the lake drops down "ponk" like a struck drum skin. And like an enormous drum the vibration shakes the air above, beats against the ear and gives a sensation of a pale lightning flash. The loud cracks, thundering and rumbling noises and sometimes musical sounds and slight swift winds, give delight to those who adventure among mountains in winter.

This "talking ice" is mentioned by our oldest mountain travellers. It is heard also in the Fen districts.

Talking ice

"In the winter, when the lake is frozen over, the surface of the water is converted into a shell of ice. It emits a horrible sound, resembling the moans of many animals collected together. This may be occasioned by the sudden bursting of the shell (of ice) or the gradual passing of the air (out) through imperceptible channels."

GIRALDUS CAMBRENSIS, A.D. 1199.

PILLARS OF ICE

Pillars of ice that rise up from a level surface of water have caused wonder for centuries. In mediæval days they were surely ascribed to magic. This example is taken from a periodical of 1859–60.

This wooden tub, with its strange phenomena, is an epitome of the great ice pillars forced up under Arctic conditions, and remarked upon by all voyagers to the Arctic seas. The explanation is that the water, freezing rapidly *in a confined space*, becomes solid ice before the lower water has completed its expansion. Therefore, the pressure below forces a break through the ice, and shoots its freezing-point water upwards in a jet, which freezes as it rises up into the cold air. This example shows so well the force of expanding water. The wonder of wind-curved snow, the crystals hung on trees and the silver-musical pipes, sounding in the wind around a frozen waterfall, these show so well the beauty of cold water.

HOT WATER

"O ye fire and heat, bless ye the Lord,
Praise Him and magnify Him for ever."

Water boils at 212°F., the temperature rising steadily to 200° and jumping the last degrees more swiftly. (Which is why tea must be made with absolutely boiling water.) Vapour is dispersed water, and invisible, rising from the face of the waters; its heat, altering the density of the air, may give that trembling appearance which is also seen at the spout of the kettle, but when the vapour is cooled, beyond the kettle's spout, then it is visible, as in the clouds, floating in the sky. When it is cold enough the vapour becomes water again, distilled water, absolutely pure, as its soluble minerals and suspended particles have been "dropped out" while it passed through its vapour form. This is why rain water is soft and pure. The force of water expanded by heat was a "power" discovered very early by mankind, probably as soon as he did any cooking, when he found that hot water would split pots.

In Ireland, the great rocks they clear away to make their small fields are embedded in fire of brushwood and then water soaked, and "it breaks the heart of them entirely". Every quarry man knows the water trick, and workers in slate learn to guard against it, for a damp slate which has dried around the edges, or is set into a fire so that the damp in the centre layers becomes imprisoned, will "fly", shivered into thin shattered pieces sharp as glass, which can be dangerous.

Water power, even when adopted to the peaceful domestic hot bath, deserves respect and consideration.

WATER RUNNING

"That joined brooks to dales, to hills fresh water springs,
With rivers sweet along the meads, to profit many things."
TUSSER

SPRINGS IN GREAT VARIETY

"Fountain", "springs", and "welles" can be confusing. Old records use the words loosely, and a "spring" which gushes out like a "fountain" may also be a "well". Curiously, minerals provide a similar anomaly. In most countries the term for the substance is the constant. Only in English the same substance can be quarried above ground and mined below ground. For example, you can have a slate quarry underground in a mine, but it remains a slate quarry.

In fortresses and castles during a siege, water was often the crux of the battle and, as the castle was usually built on a hill, some of the old castle wells are incredibly deep. In other districts pressure raises the water, so that curious syphon effects produce shallow wells in high courtyards.

On the land, villages and farms were built near streams or springs, and though wells were dug (and many are ancient and deep) the convenient spring was much easier.

Towns and cities were set on rivers (the county towns of England are each situated on their river) and used the river water for all main supplies of trade.

As most cities expanded *parallel* with the river, along the banks, the houses could usually rely on finding good water at not much below river level and the water seeping through was reasonably clear. This is shown by multiplicity of wells all over any old city plans, and accounts for the sudden cave-in of old house floors, and many damp cellars.

After the Fire of London plans were made to throw back a wide river frontage, with easy access to the Thames and sites for quays, but before the plans were carried out the houses and small yards had swept back to the water's edge. The streams that ran through the city, and the hundreds of small private wells, remained for years as the city's water supply and drainage (*see* page 136).

It is an effort to visualize a swampy osier hope where Westminster School now stands, and to think of the Fleet river as running down between stone banks in Bridge Street. Yet the lie of the land is there. Aldgate Pump and Tottenham Well are still landmarks. The "marshes" keep their name and character, though the flat moors around Bartholomew's old hospital and Smithfield are built over, and few of the Essex mud flats remember sheep grazing, potash burners and lime vats.

In the country, before increased population required official laid-on water supplies, there were serious water problems. Sometimes a water supply failed, and then the village simply moved away (*see* page 258). Some of the "lost" Midland villages became derelict because the population increased beyond the water supply; or the water, finding a lower level, left the village high and dry. Air survey shows a number of such "lost" villages and their positions are of interest to geologists. An air survey of almost any city shows it centred on its original water supply. The village pump and the village pond have ceased to be used, but the residential pattern they enforced still remains.

Because springs and wells are set so closely all over England, one must make a wide general classification before one can even begin to study their infinite variety. In desperation I have taken a few old springs each representing a distinct type. The close study of these should serve to explain some thousands of others of similar types.

So if the reader feels these single descriptions too laboured, please will he realize that it is not one small muddy spring he wades through, but whole centuries of springs that may, hereafter, flow more clearly before him.

AN ORDINARY ANCIENT VILLAGE SPRING

A Welsh spring with steps leading down to it on either side, a front slab, and overhung lintel above, is more properly a pent-up spring than a well in the English sense of the word. The diagram shows the usual

Typical Welsh village spring

layout, the depth of the water depending on the height of the retaining slab. The water was scooped out into pails, often carried away in pairs on a wooden shoulder yoke. These springs are found all over the principality, and were the common source of drinking water, even if the village community relied upon stream, river, canal, or rainwater tubs for the softer washing water.

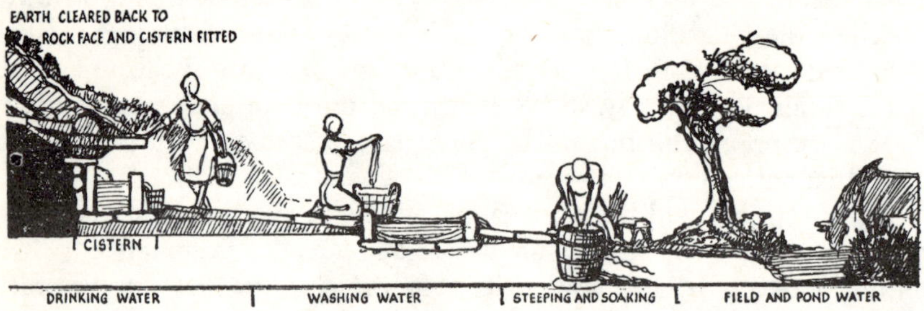

The diagram shows the normal sequence of a Welsh spring where the water is normally reasonably soft and serves all purposes.

A slate or stone gulley led away the overflow to a wash place, often set beyond a slate cistern, where wool or feathers could be washed, churns and barrels put to soak, and ordinary domestic jobs done in the running water, without fear of fouling the drinking water above. In lowland Scotland this place was called "the wring" (*see* note on laundry).

Beyond this clean-edged pool the water, especially on farm lands, would flow through a "soak" and supply a pond for watering cattle. Stevens, in his nineteenth-century book on farm work, condemns this for drinking if this pond is used for washing the hooves and fetlocks of the farm horses and insists there should be a proper watering trough raised up above the trampling of horses and cattle. (One can see the reason for his disapproval.)

In many Welsh towns today the sequence of the original well can be traced, though often the water has been piped away to the mains, and the steps now lead down to a dry spring set below the wall of a busy highway, as in the following drawing of Llangollen.

The end of such an ancient spring

This stream still supplies some very ancient leather works lower down. The stream itself marked the turn of a footpath up to a grange of the local abbey, and by following it across the watershed, you cross the pass and come down into the adjoining valley.

The spring, at a very early period, may have supplied a few huts, and a custodian's cell. (A reliable resident at this spot would be a wise arrangement, for the Cistercian monks had cause to keep tally of all wool brought down off the hills.) The few early Cistercians, like the hard-headed French peasantry from which they evolved, let no one with wool to trade miss their Abbey. So well marked were the devious mountainous bridle paths that the place is still called "the Valley of the Cross". The great stone bases into which the shaft of the cross was dowelled are still found at strategic points all around the district. This well almost certainly provided the water of baptism for the earliest church of St. Collen.

Now the water lies under the main high road with a garage on one side of it and has long ceased to be a well, being dry and deep in refuse. The edge of the old slate trough can just be seen, though the rest is buried under the earth. The "spout" of the spring is gone and the round cement tank of the new Water Board is built into the bank.

THE TAVERN SPRING

For the solitary dweller one little reliable spring sufficed; but for a community, or hostel, or inn, an extra outside water supply was more urgent. Abbeys, monasteries, and nearly all communities have a second spring, usually at a little distance from the building, as well as one within the walls. Any old abbey—there is the well in the cloister, and also a holy well outside.

In any old inn yard there is the outside pump site, though now the horses are gone, the stone trough may hold geraniums!

Because these outside wells later took the name of a patron saint it did not prevent their being entirely utilitarian in origin. Sometimes an abbey or hospice was built by an already established saint's well, but more often than not it was the other way round. Nor, because the water was sanctified, was it less excellent for washing or brewing good ale.

We give St. Peter's Well as an example of the decline and fall of a once important mediæval tavern spring. Today St. Peter's Well has almost vanished. It is little more than a muddy stream, meandering across rough pasture below Ruthin Hill. Here and there, from various causes, both ancient and modern, the stream spreads out into small pools and patches of bog where, deeply embedded in the mud, lie shaped stones (both ancient and modern). In summer the stream runs sluggishly over the flat ground, and the trampling cattle and passing travellers have left the water distinctly unblessed. But the field is still called White Friars Field, and over it pass tracks to Mold and Chester on the east, to Ruthin Town on the west. Llanwryst, St. Asaph and the monastic fishing grounds at Rhos on Sea lie due north, and Vale Crucis lies over the pass due south.

Site of an old tavern spring

The field around the spring shows the humps and hollows of ancient buildings, and there is little doubt that St. Peter's Well once supplied a busy mediæval hostelry (such as flourished near most crossroads on any trade route). For centuries "Ffynon Bedr" was probably the meeting-place, left luggage office, news room and exchange-and-mart for all the passing traffic up and down the country. There would be space around for tethered pack trains, sheds for riding horses, hitching posts and watering troughs, stores for man and beast, cauldrons and tubs for footbaths and ale brewing, and a smithy of sorts. In short, the water would supply a busy mediæval settlement, *but the spring belonged to the inn*

It was probably under the jurisdiction of some monastic order and may have been part of a regular grange. It would be a source of considerable income, and probably supported a chapel dedicated to St. Peter—the name White Friars suggests this. In those bygone days, the stream must have been much larger and far better utilized. There are old inhabitants in Ruthin today who can remember the spring as a clear, clean washing place that was used by the lower cottages for all domestic purposes, but now a railway cutting and a new road serving a modern housing estate, have altered all. Only some long large flat stones set across the morass suggest that at one time the traffic across the stream warranted a clapper bridge. The site would surely reward further exploration, but it is only one example of the hundreds and hundreds of such tavern springs that have almost perished and will soon be forgotten.

SPRING WATER SUPPLY INDOORS

> "The brethren helped him (St. Cuthbert) to build his tiny dwelling (a cell) surrounding it with a ditch . . . and such essential (out) buildings as an oratory and a communal shelter (?). He then directed the brethren *to dig a well in the floor of the dwelling* although the ground was hard and stony, and there seemed no hope whatever of finding a spring. . . . But they did so . . . and it was found full of water next day . . . and this spring still provides an ample supply for those who come."
>
> BEDE

All very sensible; the outer ditch was probably filled with loose stones to form a land drain and keep the house dry (*see* page 125) and water was available at no great depth inside. The hazard of an overflow in extremely wet weather was no greater than the hazard of a burst pipe in extreme frost. (And probably far better provided for.)

A single cell was often built to enclose its spring, especially when a rock face was incorporated in the structure of one wall.

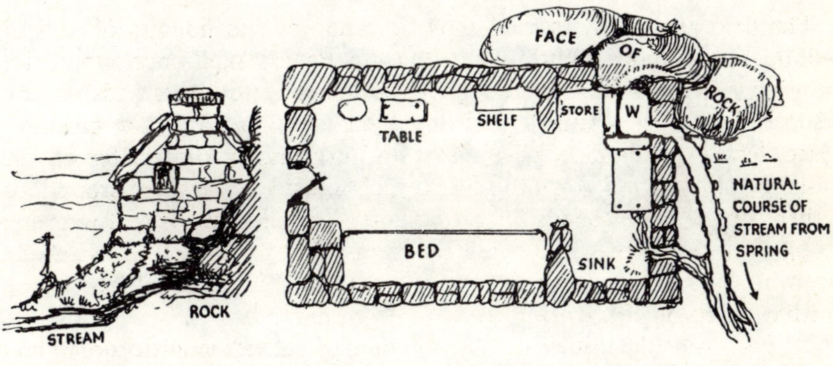

The diagram was made from the remains of an old hut near Llanwryst. A second sluice shows where an overflow had been arranged. (Possibly this was for a latrine, as it emptied into the natural run of the stream lower down the hillside.)

It is comparatively easy labour to excavate and pull down earth and rock, so most small hand-made huts are built on a slope. The diagram shows how the excavated earth rolls down to form a platform and allows for water drainage.

St. Trillo's spring is a well-known landmark near Colwyn Bay and is an excellent example of an ordinary caretaker's cell built around its own small indoor spring (*see* plate 28).

The stone hut is just long enough to take a bed, table and seat, and was probably the simple dwelling of the man who guarded the adjacent fish trap. His cooking hearth would be built outside under what was then a sheltering cliff. Because of its position, his cell became a port of call for travellers using the coast line, or crossing behind the Great Orme.

Probably the shallow estuary water was bedded over to retain the silt and refuse carried downstream into the bay. The Conway fisheries, adjoining the district, have the tradition of a patron saint, who, as she crossed the mountain, picked green rushes and threw them into the water, where, by a miracle, they became a shoal of fish. The explanation is simple. This artificial sieving of river water in estuaries by floating down shallow mats of reeds is an age-old trick. The reeds retain the refuse and give breeding shelter to the small water creatures that form a natural ground-bait for the fish. It is interesting to note that the refuse of a mediæval industrial town supplied good fish fodder and encouraged fish to swim up rivers. Today, the drainage from our industrial towns and chemical factories destroys fish life in the rivers. The remains of the old fishing ground at Rhos-on-Sea are still traceable, and the old cell has become a very lovely small chapel in the care of the National Trust. At what date this utilitarian hut and its single caretaker became "St. Trillo and his holy well" is uncertain.

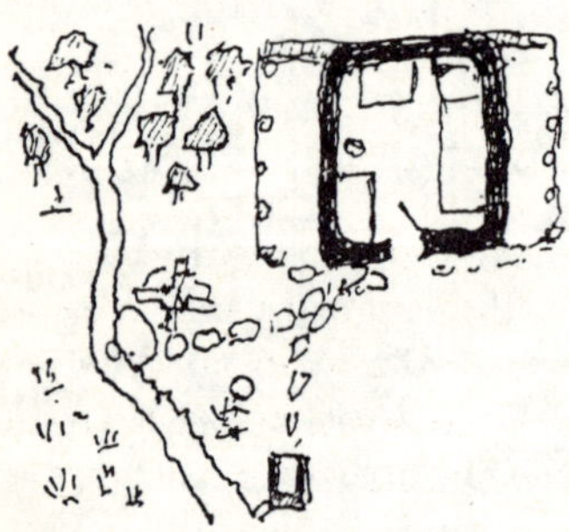

Map of site

Outside spring. This was St. Anthony's

Exactly the same sensible arrangement is found wherever a solitary worker, or small householder, settled down. If the hut was wattle and daub the spring was usually outside.

Huts and small houses have a way of continuing on the same site for centuries, the debris of each century forming the foundation of the next building, so that many of the streams that now run *under* old cottages were very likely the original spring *over* which the first hut or cell was built. Many of the small "spring houses" on farms were the original small cells built on the spot, long before the farm came into existence.

SPRING WATER SUPPLY JUST OUTSIDE THE DOOR

This spring, at Penmor, Anglesey, is chosen as an example because it is called officially, "the well of St. Seirol" and the adjoining stone circle within the shelter of rock is the "saint's cell". The small dwelling, set by its convenient natural spring, was probably exactly like a thousand others, and the saint may have used the water to baptise his early converts as well as boil his oats. Later, when there was a monastic settlement on the site, the spring would be their water supply. As the establishment grew, the way to the spring would be paved and the spring itself built around more conveniently. It may then have been arranged as a foot-bath for travellers, and for the working brothers to clean up after coming in from a dusty field or muddy shore. The shape reproduces so exactly the foot pools common outside buildings all around the Eastern Mediterranean,

St. Seirol's Well

that one has to think of pilgrims and crusaders, though the design may be only the coincidence of materials. Later, the Augustinian monks built a new wash house and warming room nearer to the main building (though still on the east side), and after that the "old wash house near the fish pond" might be turned into the laundry. The shelves outside are a convenient height to take wooden buck tubs, and a quantity of soapwort still grows wild in the locality. The stones may have been part of an early sweating house, from which the bathers could step out into the pool and sluice themselves with cold water, resting their behinds on the narrow slate ledges, so reminiscent of miserecord seats.

Disregarding the brickwork, which is definitely eighteenth-century, the slate "slabbing" may also have been rearranged for later usage. They would make good dairy shelves for cooling butter and churning. (There were good small farms on Anglesey at that period.) *It was a continuously useful spring*. Because any spring correctly and officially labelled as used for one purpose is often accepted by a docile public as "to be used for that one

purpose only" (thereby losing a mass of historical interest), we choose this example for a spring outside a cell.

"St. Seirol's spring" could, in its time, have been used for baptism, foot-washing, bathing, shaving tonsures, salting fish, cooling buttermilk and doing the monastic laundry. It still keeps up to date. This summer, it was filling Thermos flasks and replenishing the radiators of cars.

SULPHUR SPRING

Though accepted as curative for skin troubles, including leprosy, sulphur springs are seldom officially sanctified, thus providing a good argument for the belief that most Holy Wells were originally ordinary domesticated waters, since no one was likely to domesticate a sulphur spring for his regular drinking water.

Spring in brickyard district, water delivered through earthenware pipe into stoneware sink and taken away in pottery jug.

Spring in stone and iron district, water delivered through metal tap into pail set upon an iron waste grid.

STAND TAPS REPLACE SPRINGS

These stand taps were frequently put up by landlords for their grouped cottages. In some cases they piped the water from some distance, and raised the tap over a grated drain. This drain, in time, washed out new channels, which in the course of years, appeared a natural stream. This caused confusion when Rural District Councils took over, as after mains water was laid on into the cottages, the old stand taps perished and disappeared. Privately raised stand taps in the country were usually the old lead pipe and turn tap, only where manufacturers built "squares" of houses for their work people was it worth while to order mass produced iron standards.

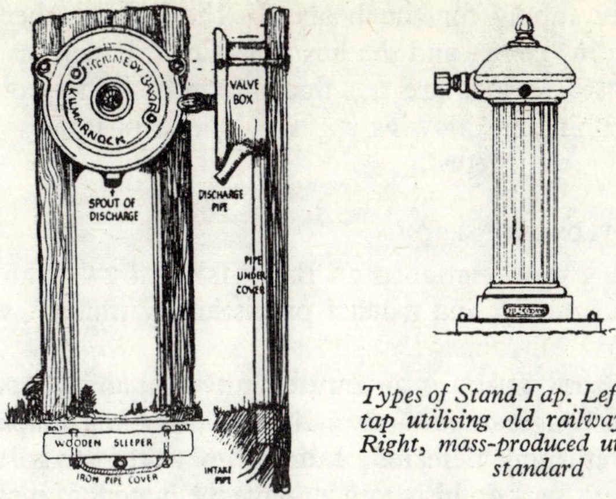

Types of Stand Tap. Left, country tap utilising old railway sleeper. Right, mass-produced urban iron standard

THE FIELD SPRING

The field spring, cleared for watering flocks and herds, was sometimes covered to prevent cattle fouling the source, or arranged to make easy filling of buckets. One drawing is reproduced from Spenser's "Shepherd's Calendar" of the sixteenth century and the other is contemporary.

Ancient

Modern

Many of these springs have degenerated into muddy field ponds or swampy places that show only as dark patches on a dry newly-ploughed field (*see* ponds, page 87). Many have been purposely drained away from the open field to the ditch at the lower side to facilitate the passing of the tractor. Many near villages once supplied small fish ponds or (below the village) hemp ponds. Sometimes, where two or three boulders still remain near the spring (alien stones that had been rolled into position) there was once a wattle and daub hut that housed some workman. The stones may show old scars of his fire.

A SEA SPRING OF FRESH WATER

St. Mary's Well at Aberdaron is set below tide level. It was considered miraculous because, after being submerged by the sea, it immediately ran fresh again. Pilgrims to the monastery on Bardsey Island used it with veneration. The small chapel at St. Mary's nearby was where travellers obtained absolution before embarking on the rough crossing, and the well was the water supply for the boats. In those days Aberdaron was an important trading centre and the hostelry (Cegin Faur) was large and well used. These sea springs are not uncommon around a rocky coast line, but like the ebbing and flowing springs dependent upon tide water, they always caused great interest.

EBBING AND FLOWING SPRINGS

Such a spring was mentioned on Barry Island by Giraldus Cambrensis in the twelfth century, and when I painstakingly walked over his route I tried to find it.

Nowadays Barry Island is an amusement park, and hunting a vanished hermit's cell among garages and modern housing was dispiriting. It was dusk when, returning defeated, I met two workmen going home; one with a plumber's sack on his shoulder gave me hope for one last try. They listened carefully while I described this spring with its fluctuating output, so many gallons one day, so many less the next, etc. I gave the position it ought to be in, and assured them it *had* existed once. . . . There was a curious pause, then one spoke: "It's that leak back of the new council houses, Bill". As I returned to tea with Bill through the gathering twilight he explained about a mysterious leak that No. 1 council house complained about, "and when we got there it wasn't". Next day No. 10 council house had a cellar flooded "and before we got to *that* it was gone!" Apparently the old spring had provided almost as much mystery as it had done in the eleventh century. We located it next day. Some of the old stone work was still intact below the deep ash and cement of a new car park (which only goes to show the diverse uses of history).

THE SPRING HOUSE

The "Spring House" of New England had its counterpart in the small spring houses (sometimes built outside as a dairy) that utilized the spring water of a farmstead. Often it was an offset from the main water force that turned the mill wheel, and could be geared onto the churn, or chaff cutter, or other mechanical contrivance.

In these small spring houses the butter was set to cool, the milk and buttermilk to "keep", and sometimes it housed the salting troughs. We have studied many old houses where this spring house was incorporated in the main building; the small stream, passing along slate troughs through the larder and dairy, formed a very adaptable natural refrigerator service. Slate, split by the grain, is absolutely waterproof, and therefore no more dampness resulted from this contrivance than from piped water.

Often after leaving the house the same stream crossed the garden, pausing to provide for the hens and bees, and finally formed a sort of water closet as it ran below the outside "privy".

THE SPRING AS MEETING PLACE

"... him I'll desire
To meet me at the consecrated fount
A league below the city, and from thence
By cold gradation, and well balanced form
We shall proceed with Angio."

Measure for Measure

The holy well (or consecrated fount) has always been a well-known meeting-place, because everyone went there to fetch water. The enforced wait while water runs, or buckets fill, the exchange of help in lifting the heavy bucket or adjusting a tub to the head or yoke or cowstail to the shoulder, all give excuse to pause by the water. Even gathering a few leaves to float on top of the water to prevent splashing, made a small delay and gave the "drawers of water" time to talk. What better place to hold a meeting, and settle a small official matter, openly, in "well-balanced form". For travellers the spring or well would be a convenient meeting-place. For riders from a distance it offered refreshment for man and beast while waiting, and Shakespeare's strolling players would quite naturally "get together there" while they decided upon the yard or inn or show ground where they were to act and what play they intended to produce.

That this city was Venice and the duke disguised as a monk made the "consecration" of the fount even more suitable, but it would probably be at a fount somewhere just outside the city, if not at the market cross.

SPA SPRINGS AND THE HOLY WELLS

"As Satan was flying over Harrogate wells
His senses were charmed by the heat and the smells!
Said he 'I don't know in what region I roam,
But I guess from the smell—that I'm not far from home!'
An old Biddy called after him 'Satan, I say!
You seem mightily pleased with your journey today.
Pray stay till I've done, and we'll both go together—
For I'm heartily tired of this changeable weather.'
But Satan well knew if for Biddy he stayed—
His journey home going would long be delayed,
For Harrogate waters such wonders can do
That the Devil himself is oft robbed of his due!"

Without irreverence one may consider the spa as the descendant of the ancient holy well. There were medical cures at both, for the custodian at the holy well was probably far more advanced in medical knowledge than his patients. If he found his special spring possessed certain properties that helped skin troubles, or acted as a natural aperient, he'd have no hesitation in attributing the fact (and the cure) to a patron saint. From every diplomatic angle it was safer to make the saint's goodness responsible for the cure, and the patients' crimes responsible for the disease. But, apart from these considerations, there are many small details of holy administrations that suggest commonsense in the use of the "spa" (or spring) and instructions to the patients at the "spring" (or spa) that were sound and sensible (whether given by priest or doctor). In the twelfth century infection was little understood, but contagion was obvious, so sometimes, a patient having used the water, sufficient prayers had to be said to allow time for that water to run clear again, before another patient got in. Or, if the water was sufficiently cold, and quick flowing, for many to use it simultaneously, there were processions around it, and a tactful sorting of the "cases" beforehand. Realize also the effect that a good bath and rub down, followed by a gift of hot food, a warm rest, and perhaps clean clothing, would have on sickly lice-infested beggars. For them, indeed, it would be a Holy Well, and rightly they would praise the saint who had led them to it. So, with the rich, corpulent and over-fed patient, judicious fasting, and long walks to a nicely-selected line of shrines, would reduce his weight, improve his circulation, and increase his faith, and again he could give thanks to heaven with good cause. In the same way, many spas had charities from over-fed and hard-drinking patients, cured by restricted diets and copious cold water. In all spa cases, the mineral content of the water was there, and so undoubtedly were the cures. It was not till the chemist provided the same, and even more interesting medicines, that most of the later spas fell into disuse. Now the few large spas still active do good work, but still depend largely on *the way the "waters" are used, and how the patients react to the treatment* (which is exactly what *all* holy wells and spas have been doing ever since their waters first began to flow).

A FEW SPA SPRINGS

At the height of the Spa period in the early nineteenth century, the springs are as often listed by the new minerals as their old saints. Many never had been "holy" (in that their virtues were believed supernatural) and the great length and diversity of the lists reflects the gradual improvement in road surfaces, making travel more general, and also the new interest in chemicals (fostered by the German influence of the Prince Consort).

It would be tedious to give the full lists, but this short selection restricted to "some spas and springs in Wales" shows the variety and research that went into the subject, and there were even more springs and spas in England.

Aberagon, 16 miles from Aberystwyth. Chalybeate.

Aberhavesp, 4 miles from Newtown. Black Well. Local reputation for scrofulous diseases.

Abersock, Caernarvon. Ffynon Fyew had 2 baths surrounded by a wall 2 yards high and 1 yard thick, enclosed by a massive oak door.

Aberystwyth. Chalybeate.

Amloch. St. Eleth's. For rheumatism.

Bettws Garmon, 5 miles from Caernarvon. All skin troubles.

Cayo, Carmarthen. 8 miles from Llandovey. For rheumatism.

Bryn Nant and Dolcothy. A double spring of strong sulphur.

Pump Saint. Chalybeate.

Cemaes, Borthwen. St. Patrick's. For eyes and indigestion.

Cilcen, Flint. 4 miles from Mold. Used for rheumatism.

Convil, Carmarthen. 7 miles from "Fossanafos Sana". An iron spring.

Corwen, close to Rug. St. Julien's. Rheumatism.

Cwm Dau, Radnor. Sulphur.

Egleysilan, Glamorgan. Notable spring now buried.

Festiniog, Merioneth. St. Michael's spring. For rheumatism. (Probably ice cold under slate, and effective by temperature.)

Fishguard. A mineral spring used for cramp.

Glascomb, 8 miles from Builth. Two springs of strong sulphur for skin troubles. (These, the researcher notes, are very fine springs, but the surrounding scenery and bad lodgings locally retard the process of a "spa".)

Hope, Flint. On the banks of the River Alyn, 5 miles from Wrexham. Had muriate of soda springs.

Little Newcastle, Pembroke. Has a golden well that depends on the tides of St. George's Channel (ebbing and flowing). Properties "are yet unknown but are good for eyes".

Llanaethaiarn, Caernarvon. ¼ mile from the Parish Church; an old enclosed bath filled from St. Aelpaian's spring.

Llangllgo, Anglesey. A sulphate of lime spring. A chapel-of-the-well shows this to have been very old.

Llanano, 12 miles from Knighton. Has a "New Well", a spring of sulphur.

Llanarthng, Carmarthen. A privately owned spring in the Myddleton Hall grounds. A chalybeate spring (carbon, acid gas, carbonate of lime, carbonate of iron, muriate of soda, and sulphurated lime). This spring was commercialized and hot and cold baths built over it.

Llanbadam, Fawr, Radnor, near Penybont. A spring used for skin troubles.

Llanbediog, Caernarvon. "God's Well" (did the Welsh Saints dispute ownership?). Has been enclosed and a place made where people may go free and drink for rheumatic troubles.

Llanberis, Caernarvon. Near the church of St. Peris; seems to have been one of the ordinary village wells under the benediction of the local saint.

Llanbister, 12 miles from Knighton. Has several mineral springs of black and red waters. Copper dipped into one becomes white and silver yellow. The springs are within 10 yards of each other in the same small meadow.

Llandefally, Brecknock. Sulphur and salt.

Llandeglay, Radnor. A sulphur spring so strong it could be exported to Hereford and Worcester for sale.

Llandilo, 5 miles south of Towyn. Chalybeate.

Llandyfrydog, Anglesey. On a farm called Clorach are the springs of Gybi and Seirol. These are on an old route. There was constant communication between the old Penmon Priory, Holyhead, and the main land. These would be ordinary, utility springs.

Llandyrnog, Denbigh. A chalybeate spring.

Llanegryn, Merioneth. Mineral spring.

Llanerchoedlan. Close to Builth, had a small "pump house" with a "bath house" and spring for eye troubles. (All these local springs and small spas now come under the general name of "Builth Wells".)

Llanerfyl, Montgomery, 10 miles from Dinas Mawddwy. Has a well by the church supposed to be Roman, as an old Roman road crosses the river Banwy very near it.

Llanfair Caerinion, Montgomery. On the 8 miles of high road towards Shrewsbury are many springs, but few good medical ones. From their position these probably marked the usual watering posts of any drover route that was forced to leave the river side, and drive cattle along main roads. The stone troughs by the high roads developed for horses in the posting and coaching periods, but driven cattle needed longer drinking space to avoid stampedes and overcrowding. (The recent stampede of cattle between a railway depot and the River Trent shows what cattle drovers had to circumvent to prevent thirsty beasts from breaking out of control to reach water.) (*See* drovers' water.)

Llanfihangel. Chalybeate.

Llangadfan, Montgomery. Spring of curative value called St. Cadvans was built over as a bathing-place but was in ruins (1767).

Llangybi, Caernarvon. St. Gybis well had stone seats and in 1767 Dr. Linden, M.D., proved the water so good for eyes and nerves "that it could vie with any continental resort".

Llanllower, Pembroke. A spring on the mountainside that cured ague "but is now neglected". (1850).

Llanlleonpel, Brecknock. A sulphur spring on church property.

Llanrhidan, 11 miles from Swansea. A spring on a salt marsh, strong of iron and sulphur.

Llanrhudd, Denbigh, near Ruthin. Chalybeate.

Mallwyd, Cae Gwyn. Spring, good for eyes.

Meifod, 14 miles from Oswestry and Teirtref. Is a spring and well with a cupola built over it. Was a "divination" spring (but had no special mineral interest), but at Groftydd very near there was a sulphur well in a wood near a spring, *Pistyll y Clawdd*, which had real medicinal value. A shed was built over it and instructions on the walls for using the water. This was probably an old fairy well, for on the eighth Sunday after Easter "there was a gathering and drinking of the water and dancing around till nightfall".

Penmon, 4 miles from Beaumaris. Sulphate of lime.

Pentrevolas, 14 miles from Denbigh. Chalybeate.

Rhayader, 4 miles from Cardiff. The "bright waterspout", very cold, used for sprains and recovery of strength after injury.

Ruthin. At the south end of a field called White Friars, St. Peter's well, chalybeate, but now disused. (This is described as one of the typical examples of a tavern or hospice well.)

St. Asaph. A lime water spring with canopy and carved pillars.

Swansea. A spa depending on a tidal spring (similar to that at Aberavon).

Talyllyn, 8 miles from Dolgelly, a well for rheumatism.

Tefid. A thermal spring (showing Roman masonry) near Cardiff.

Towyn, 16 miles from Dolgelly. A spring, originally dedicated to St. Cadvan, in a field below the church, has been enclosed and a very commodious bath-house erected. (There seems to have been a rival spring at Rhydyromen near by that was free for all!)

This list from various guides about 1850–1900, gives only the "Notable Springs" in one small locality, many of which have almost vanished, so the reader will realize the difficulty in selecting springs as fair examples of different types.

A FEW OTHER INTERESTING SPRING WATERS FROM VARIOUS SOURCES

Moffat, in Scotland, had a water with a great reputation for ulcers (internal). "Ten quarts a day might be drunk safely, but a glass of wine taken beforehand often helps a weak stomach and prevents an inclination to sleep!" (Some brave souls drank the water five seasons running, and it was thought to have "no equal in Colics of every kind".)

Arncliffe, 3 miles from Wigan. Had a well through which gas issued that would take fire if lighted, and burn all day, "so that eggs might be boiled over the flame—though the water remained cold". This was undoubtedly gas from an adjoining coal mine.

Codsall Wood, Staffordshire. Has a spring "one can smell 20 yards off".

In *Dorset*, near Weymouth. A spring that "smells like boiled eggs, and will turn a silver shilling yellow in a few minutes".

At *Brosely*, near Wenlock, 7 miles north of Bridgnorth. A well that bubbled a gas "far hotter than any common fire, and broiled mutton chops and rashers of bacon with an excellent flavour". (Unfortunately an earthquake stopped up this well in 1752).

Tilbury water "was taken from a hill top 2 miles from the Thames; it was straw-coloured, and made excellent "Punch" (and extremely good tea, being soft and drawing out the strength of the leaves well). At the current price of tea (1780) this was a great recommendation.

Witham, Essex. Had a "ferruginous spring that was good for nerves, appetites, and asthmas, and improved all lowness of spirits".

Glastonbury. Water in 1751 cured "a certain sufferer from asthma". But, as the water was proved absolutely pure the cure was claimed as a miracle, caused by the water "having filtered through the graves of the blessed in the Abbey grave yard". This claim cured the popularity of the spring.

It is thought that this well was the one used by the monks in their brew house. A cider barrel is among the interesting stone carvings found near the well.

What a stream of interest we lost when we had water "laid on", blended, ready mixed and chemically purified!

SOME DISCOVERIES AND DEVELOPMENTS OF MEDICAL SPRINGS AND BATHS

At Llanwrtyd a sulphurous spring was discovered by the Reverend Evans of Llangamach. It was called "Ffynon Drewllyd", for indeed it stank like the devil. A report says that in 1752 the "Reverend Sufferer" was "near to leprosy with the scurvy". On being told by some old folk in the district that the water was good for skin trouble, the Rev. Evans went to see it . . . but when he smelt it, retreated to an adjacent stone, and sat down, watching the bubbling water very sorrowfully, when a fine fat frog popped out, looking so cheerful that he took courage and drank a pint. As the water stayed down, after half an hour he drank another pint, and on returning home felt so much better that he took the plunge, and bathed in the water and drank it for two months. "By which time he was completely cured and lived hereafter 35 years, dying in 1767 aged 73." It is interesting that the word "leprosy" is used by Mr. Evans, for it was most probably the word suggested to him by the old folk of the district. Tradition lasts long, and though they did not know it, that same water had been renowned in mediaeval times for the treatment of leprosy.

Fifteen miles from Llandovery, the Llangemarch Spa had a barium and calcium spring, which caused a notable hotel to be built for the bathers, together with an assembly room and concerts. The place was reported to have "the only barium spring outside Germany, and the water cured goitres and glandular complaints". This spring was discovered by a pig. In 1820 the bed of the Irvon river ran dry, and a cottager on the banks saw his pig wallowing in one of the muddy pools where there seemed to be a spring rising within the bed of the river. The cottager tried the water, hoping to be able to use it, but spat it out and proceeded to barricade off the spring from the rest of the river bed. This spring was taken very seriously by the medical papers of the period. *The Lancet* reported the water as exceptionally pure and good. *The Medical Annual* of 1890 stated that barium chloride was being used as a cardiac tonic, and to alleviate pains in the cardiac region. After that the hotel economized on concerts and employed a physician who was acquainted with the methods in use at Nanhiem to come and lecture to bathers between June and October.

The more scientific analysis so popular in the late nineteenth century shows in their Advertisement of 1880: "The hydro-sulphuric acid gas is beneficial in cutaneous eruptions, and the lime, so often the cause of calculi is absent. In fact its [the water's] natural saponaceous quality, proves a dissolvent for the sabulous matter that forms stone in kidneys."

TREFRIEW, AN ANCIENT SPA OF INDUSTRIAL ORIGIN, STILL IN USE

Today, facing the main road to Conway, motorists pass a small Victorian building set primly in a neat garden behind a huge hydrangea of the most

Old Bath House at Trefriew

Cyclopean Building

astonishing blue. In the windows are rows of medicine bottles, as the spa now carries on a postal trade. Hidden behind this modern façade, unknown and unshown, are two far earlier springs of intense interest, both well worth exploration.

No one knows when the minerals in the rocks above were first mined. The Conway river was fished for pearls by the Romans, and one of their guard houses was adjacent, so it is reasonable to suppose the Romans worked the mines with native labour, but this is conjectural. We do know that the lead above was worked in the 1700's and that the workers used the water from the spring below as an antidote to lead poisoning. It was one of these old miners, a man of 90, who reported it to Robert Owen, mining agent to Lord Willoughby. The old man said the spring ran from an old horizontal shaft that had been "driven for sulphur", and the whole place was now buried under the debris of this sulphur mine.

Mr. Owen had the debris cleared away, and the old shaft was found with three distinct springs, each of slightly different mineral content. This proved they had come diverse ways through the matrix of ore-bearing rock above. These springs filled rock basins in the entrance cave and were, from 1833 onwards, used by workers from miles around.

So efficacious was the water that in 1863 Lord Willoughby took the matter seriously, and, at his own expense, built a handsome bath house of native rock.

This neglected bath house is one of the finest examples of cyclopean quarry architecture in existence.

The blocks of stone are an average of 4 to 6 ft. long and up to 4 ft square. The roof is spanned by four single slabs of solid stone and the twin doors of oak are iron bound. It stands firm as a rock, and is very like a rock, and is a testimony to the strength and skill of the Welsh quarry men who used nothing but simple gravity hoists and the jumper drills and wedges of their own skilled trade.

The present use of this noble old bath house as a reservoir to supply small bottling taps, is surely unwarranted. It should be preserved as testimony to the skill of the Welsh rockman.

Today, this old bath house is overgrown with trees and almost unknown. A small wooden notice reads:

ORIGINAL BATH HOUSE

ERRECTED 1863 AD by LORD WILLOUGHBY DE ERESBY

Built to provide more suitable accommodation for patients who prior to this time at great inconvenience had bathed in the rock hewn basins in the cave.

"Analyst" in *The Lancet*, 1874, gives "protosulphate of iron, magnesia, soda of lime and sulphur from the three combined springs", and recommends that the water should be drunk fresh, as the sulphate of iron decomposes in the air.

To experts it is interesting to note that scleroderma verrycosom (the earth ball) fungus grows in the vicinity of the spring, smelling, as one fungus expert said, "like hell of sulphur"!

AN EXCELLENT "SLATE" SPA. NOW COMPLETELY RUINOUS

Near Caernarvon, there was a spring called Ffynon Begin Arthur (the Kitchen of King Arthur). This spring was on a farm near Dinas Dinoric (in the slate district) and during the summer a coach drove twice a day from Port Dinoric, taking patients to bathe in the slate tanks built around the water. The rockmen said that there was a bed of iron ore, far down, and the water percolating slowly, and being charged with carbonic acid, dissolved the iron salts, which it carried up. Camden reports that the remains of the baths were still there when he visited the district. The closing of Port Dinoric changed the way of life in the district, though the waters were used by local people for some time. We know the spring continued in use, because medical treatment was studied in the district by Dr. Wyn Williams, M.D., 1858, who used the water for the bone complaints prevalent in that enclosed valley. Dr. Williams treated his patients to the water, internally and externally, but as he supplemented the treatment with iodine of potassium and cod liver oil, he was probably

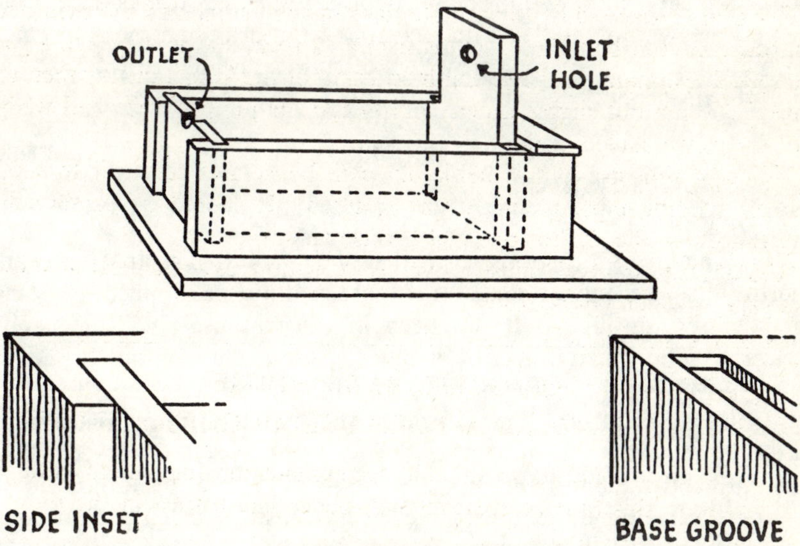

Construction of a Slate bath

dealing with a deficiency of diet among his poorer patients. He also used the water for kidney trouble, half a pint into an empty stomach before breakfast, and "*walk to the well* and drink it as it bubbles from the source". His overweight patients must do this daily for three weeks (and take aperients of Epsom salts or Glauber, *not* brimstone and treacle). In a period of deep drinking and overfeeding among the rich, Dr. Williams must have been successful if not popular.

THE "TREATMENT" SIDE DEVELOPED

Doctors at most spas—and many other doctors—insisted upon "exercise and healthy interests". Just as the earlier pilgrimage might be a cure for bodily ills, as well as spiritual ones, so with the later pilgrimages to spas. The following "correspondence" upon spas dates from the late nineteenth century:

"The chronic patient, having been supplied almost hourly with gilded pills and phials of choicest liquids, by Dr. Bolus" consults yet another doctor, who, "having heard and ruminated upon the matter, says, 'Sir, it is in my power to pick your pocket of many fees, but I scorn so mercenary a procedure, so take your horse, and hasten to Scarborough, or Harrogate, or Cheltenham. It is my opinion *any* of these waters will recover you.'" So with great fatigue he trots down to the first of those places (giving his liver a good shake up as he trots), "intent to try *all* of them, if necessary". "With great expense, he abides at Harrogate for the usual time, and from the use of the waters his humours were, in some measure, checked." (You cannot imbibe unlimited drinks and "take more water with it".) "But the delights of the place and the amusement of the company gave him a new flow of spirits, and he returned to town full of satisfaction."

A CURATIVE SPRING DEPENDING ON TEMPERATURE ONLY, NOW ABSORBED BY A WATER BOARD

The Orog

The volume of this spring rivals that of St. Winifred's. It arises on the north side of a mountain range, is icy cold, and it once supplied the grange of a Cistercian abbey. It has been in constant use since the twelfth century. The waters have, by a miracle, escaped canonisation. At the time of writing, the spring is being taken over by a water board but was still used for restoring sprains, lesions, and "strengthening broken bones after the removal of the plaster". The wife of a brickyard worker told me her husband went to bathe his shoulder, stiff from a dislocation, in the spring several times. She explained, very sensibly, that the firm gentle pounding of the falling water, combined with its icy coldness, restored the circulation. "You hold your joint under the water till it's so cold you can't feel it, and then take it out and rub and work it till it's warm again, and do it several times. Then wrap it up warm with flannel and when you get home you'll feel it all glowing hot, and you must keep it wrapped up warm, and, as you can feel the blood pushing back, you must keep moving it gently, and keep it warm till next morning. It's the finest cure for any stiff joint."

The spring seems originally to have broken out higher up the hillside at the side of an old foot track along the base of the rocks, and by an old building whose foundation was perhaps an outlying part of the Cistercian grange below.

Plas y Pentre, the adjacent twelfth-century building, is almost submerged under the later Tudor superstructure. Some worked stones are visible in the foundations of a later Georgian brick hall (Trevor Hall). In the "spa" period, or perhaps earlier, there may have been a regular outdoor bath house on this higher site. Sixty years ago it was still flooded. A slab 1643, with initials, is incorporated in a slovenly superstructure erected on the earlier cyclopean foundation. (Such "outdoor bath houses" were fashionable in the seventeenth century.) My brother remembers it being called "the old bath house" and having a splash in the shallow water that still filled it in 1920.

At Malvern Spa, they reduced a patient so successfully he was accidentally wrung out in his own wet sheet.

A SHORT NOTE ON THE LORDLY SPA OF BATH

An Epistle from Bath, 1817

"This morning at the York Hotel
I found myself alive and well
And having got my breakfast down

I sallied forth, to see the town.
The folks are odd! The streets uneven,
The belles, the fairest under heaven.
The Pump Room, is extremely spacious;
The waters—very efficacious!

Here doctors conscientiously contrive,
By daily calls, to keep their friends alive.
All systems change, and physic, like the rest
When newly fashioned operates the best.
Thus each practitioner his system draws
From some internal over-lying cause
And laying former doctrines on the shelf
Cures by a mode, peculiar to himself.

One feels your pulse and portently observes
All your complaints originate in nerves.
One says the stomach is the tainted part,
One says the head's at fault—and one the heart.
One undertakes to set you up with ease
And swears that bile occasions your disease.

* * * * *

In May or in June, all the world goes away
To dip in the ocean and pickle their clay.
At Cheltenham, remove constitutional faults
By drinking the waters and swallowing salts.
For though Bath in the winter with fashion is full
Yet, Bath in the summer is dreadfully dull!" "Q"

In the 1800's the fashion, wit, and social life that collected during the "Bath Season" had political influences. The social life in London was changing. As the new industrial element developed, the necessity for posting mail between London and Bath (for the diplomats, courtiers and merchants) did much to inaugurate new and better road services, and this brought Bristol and the West Country back into the important position they had held in the earlier Elizabethan days.

The position was convenient for the new Irish lords at Westminster. The surrounding West Country produced all that was rich for the "sumptuous repasts" (that well defeated the use of the waters), and altogether the Bath Spa had much influence on English social life during the eighteenth and nineteenth centuries.

By the end of the century Bath had lost much of its glamour, and took itself more seriously. For nearly a century it had been the meeting place of French and English doctors, and continental theorists (good and bad), but by the early twentieth century the treatments had settled down into steady English routine. The Pulteney had a reputation for expensive, respectable comfort. There was little gaiety and few visited Bath Spa without genuine cause, or interest in Roman remains. Long brochures, published about 1890, give a fair description of the change from the old treatments to the new.

There are dozens of ways of "using the waters". Douching is most stimulating—previous to the (new) pumping process, "bucketing" was the mode. Two of the tallest and strongest guides stood in the bath over the prostrate patient with buckets from which they poured the water down upon him with great force.

"When the waters are used as a bath the bather is advised to let the vapour that has collected during the preparation of the baths escape first. The bather should then descend gradually into the bath and, on leaving it, be enveloped in a warm sheet, covered with a warm blanket. The sheet, aided by gentle friction, absorbs the moisture from his body. When this has been done, it should be allowed to slip down, the warm blanket pressed around the person, and the bather may then return to the dressing-room where he submits to a vigorous rubbing with warm towels."

N.B. The same nineteenth-century pamphlet states that "all linen is found free by the Bath authorities".

In that hard drinking period, gout was a fashionable complaint and its treatment most sympathetic. "The utmost candour will be observed with regard to the vapour treatment of acute gout. The timid, whatever their preconceived notions on the treatment, need have no fear of the gout flying to other parts as a result. Nothing can be more reprehensible than the laxity and recklessness sometimes shown in the treatment of gout. A patient is often told that a hot bath will 'bring it out'. This is down-right empiricism, as well as cruelty—the effect being to bring out all over, an attack that ought to have been confined to one locality." So cases are treated locally with waterproof sheeting.

"Persons suffering from Adiposes to whom diminishment of weight is important may resort to the Berthollet system," by which "A gentleman rider, under treatment whilst engaged in his ordinary pursuits, reduced his weight 7 lb. in five days".[1]

The Bath Chair

"Where the chill wretch, creeping like a snail
And fearful lest his tottering limbs should fail
And staggering at a sudden puff of wind
Orders a *chair* to following close behind."

"Q"

[1] All medical treatment at spas reflects the social history of the times and horse racing as a lucrative sport was just coming into fashion.

No description of Bath Spa would be possible without the Bath chair, that relic of the old Sedan chair, that was pulled before and pushed behind by bath chair men, or, more considerately, by docile ponies. At the first period of the safety bicycle adaptations of these canework chairs were turned into trailers and pulled behind by pedal pushers, the front handle fitting into the back of the rider's saddle.

THE LORDLY SPA OF LATER DATE AND MORE COMMUNAL OUTLOOK

"A description of the wonderful vertue of the Bathes of Buck Stone.

"Of the origine of the name, I neyther could reade it in any author nor heare as yet.

"Howbeit many years past it was frequented for the health of thousands by bathing them, as well as it is in these our days. For between it (Buck Stone) and Burghe there is an high way forced over the moores, all paved, of such antiquity as none can expresse, called the Bath Gate (Gait?).

"It is not unlikely that stagges and buckes wounded, would take soil (assoile?) there, and the foresters of the forest called it Bucks land—as for the 'inuentious' about St. Anne founding the well, or the water set free from Flood Jordan. I recke not them worthy the recital."

DR. J. JONES, 1572

Buck Stone—Buxton—included diet treatments

This rather curious choice of an example shows the continual change in the human attitude towards water, while water continues to run on unchanged.

Dr. Jones wrote in 1570; his book reprinted in the late eighteenth century, and all the changes bubble out between the lines.

Older Bath has the stability of its Roman foundations. Bath survived a period of affluent fashion, and continues as a grave, respectable, static and residential spa with a good equable climate. Perhaps, because Buckstone has a more bracing air (being blown down upon, by cold blasts from the peak), this later spa has a more active and changeable mediæval character. Today, there are junketings at the hotels at Christmas very reminiscent of the old "Lord of Misrule", and parties of disreputable wet walkers that arrive, snow-driven, from the uplands by Flash, are not unlike weary old packhorse travellers.

The doctor may have been right about his wounded deer (which could have staggered from the margins of any illuminated MS. of the twelfth century), but a Bucking Stone, or washing place between the river and the spring, seems more likely, and his "modern scientific explanation" is a century removed from the Reformation that closed so many holy wells.

"Natural Baths be those that flow through the entralles of the earthe, taking their effect of such thinges as they runne throu and receyne power by", and this strictly earthly power "is for many infirmities most available". This simple statement does not discredit Artistotle or the ancient ideas of water as an element, and it almost accepts its ceaseless struggle to maintain its allotted position between earth and air (and below the outer element of fire) but the idea of the water attracting and repelling and absorbing other substances is accepted with the cheerful authority of a much later chemistry, Again, the juxtaposition of hot and cold water being so varied, that as "myne one foote shoulde steppe on the hot spring and the other on a cold" is only stated as a matter of interest. The same phenomena in the fourteenth century would have been considered a "marvel".

The old bath house that Dr. Jones saw in 1572 was being renovated, and later one finds his Elizabethan great hall embedded in the new erection, which is admired with all the eighteenth-century flair for domestic architecture. "Joyning the cheefe spring, between the river and the bathe, a very goodly house. Four square, and four stories hye, and so well compacte, with houses of office beneath and with a great chamber (was this the old hall retained within its new shell?) and other goodly lodging, to the number of thirty. It is, and will be (for it is still under construction), a bewty to behold and very notable to accommodate the honourable and worshipful . . . as also for others, yea, the poorest shall have lodging and beds, hard by for their use only."

Here is shown the new form of charitable consideration for the "poor and needy", which began during Queen Elizabeth's reign, and by which civil authorities were gradually constrained to take over the indiscriminate benevolence of the feudal lords and decadent Church. By the seventeenth century the providing of these "lodgings hard by" has become a social duty, though the social status of the doctor's "honourable and worshipful" patients is becoming even more important, for "the bathes are so bewtified, with seats round about, defended from the ambyent aye and chimneys for fyre to ayre your garmintes in the bathes side, and other necessaries most decent".

The arrangements for the "poor and needy" are only stone seats around the walls of the bath house, and all open to the "ambyent ayre", (so continuing the ancient architecture of the old holy wells). Yet, even here, one senses the new civic responsibility for the body that is replacing the mediæval religious responsibility for the soul.

This later, almost scientific, study of spa water, now includes a study of the food to accompany the drink.

Travellers, on foot or horse, do not carry more weight than necessary, and so must rely on the provisions obtainable near the spa. So, gradually between the sixteenth and eighteenth centuries, diet treatment develops with the water cures, and the everlasting arguments over the white loaf begin. "Some countrys make bread of cleane wheate [i.e. entirely of wheat] as in Somersette shyre, Kent, Lincolne and Norfolk [this is new, only before small loaves and the holy wafer of the Mass had been made of all white wheat], some of beanes and pease, as Leycesstre shyre and Nottingham shyre". (The new wool values and the "enclosure" troubles are outlined as clearly as the change in soil.) "Stafford shyre of Rye", and "Lanckashyre Cumberland and Westmorland and Cornewall use otes". "Some of the Shyres use tares and French wheat, as for rustickes". Thus all the new detailed domestic interest develops, and the notes that gather around the "diet for spa treatment" describe cookery methods—"some backe in frying pans, some yrouns like wafrons [wafer irons], some in round cakes a bysket for ships" (a very topical subject; long-distance voyages make important the study of storing fresh water and bread).

The whole example shows the development of a spa, as a definite "treatment" rather than a cure that relied on the water only. Finally, the doctor epitomises the cause for most medical treatments for all time: "We will all eat what is preferred before that which is best for us."

GAMES—AT BUCKSTONE BATHS

Dr. Jones' old thesis upon these baths mentions that in wet weather the "ladyes and gentle women wyves and maydes" used to play a type of hole ball "rolling balls through eleven holes at the end of a long board".

Several Bath houses had specialized amusements just as they provided special dainties and special music.

Bath specialized in food, hence Bath buns, Bath chaps, etc. Buckstone today still specializes in gay amusement in contrast to the solemnity of Bath.

DERBYSHIRE WATERS

"Who would believe that there were mountaineers,
Dew-lapped like bulls, whose throats had hanging at them wallets of flesh."

THE TEMPEST

Not all waters were beneficial, so it is curious that the popular Buckstone spa was close to the Derbyshire dales, where the water was supposed to be the cause of goitre or "Derbyshire neck". Though from the context Shakespeare probably referred to the cold Alpine valleys.

THE SPA THAT FAILED (*See* plate 30)

For years the almond trees have shed their fruit ungathered, drifts of dried nuts have lain on the rough grass under the trees, the soft green leaves have brushed the old gold stone, and the sunlight and shadow have danced on the gracious portico, but the lovely spacious ruin has been derelict for years, and the beautiful design has been overtaken by hideous ugly commercial sheds. The "baths" are now an untidy garage. Further back is a beast market, and on either side lie the dustbins and debris of back doors.

The architect is unknown, except by his name. The builder was a mine-owning marquis, through whose coal pits flooded a copious saline spring. It was the period of spa popularity, Ashby-de-la-Zouch was the centre of a hunting county, the nearest spa was Leamington, so a new spa in the east seemed a sound speculation. But it failed completely. Perhaps fashion was moving westwards. Perhaps the medical advertisements were unprepossessing? Gout indicated an ancestral wine cellar, but "scrophula and scurvy", "chilblains and carbuncles" were plebeian. Contributing excuses were plentiful, but the basic fault was that *there was no spring*.

The water ran a thousand feet underground at the coal face and had to be pumped up and carried in tanks by rail. The spa was the act of man, not the act of God, so vast expense and skilled engineering were all to no purpose.

This forlorn derelict of wasted beauty should have a moral somewhere.

PUMP ROOMS AND TABLE WATERS

By the end of the nineteenth century the most popular spas still in use seem to have been:

Droitwich	Gilsland in Cumberland
Bath	Trefriew
Buxton	Harrogate
Builth	Leamington
Clifton near Bristol	Llandrindod

Margate (for sea baths), Malvern and Ingleborrow, Llanwrtyd and a few others, continued to have small seasons. The larger spas such as Bath and Buxton and Harrogate already depended as much upon their concerts and social attractions as their pump rooms. Malvern water, having been proved to be "exceptionally pure", carried on a while on that recommendation, and St. Anne's Well is still preserved, but already a long trade list of "English bottled spa waters" and a longer list of foreign spa waters, show the interesting new fashion for continental travel. These travel routes to the continental spas follow, curiously, the old pilgrimage routes to holy wells.

There is also a new scientific assessment of the mineral contents of the waters, a new impressive display of chemistry and geological pattern. The movement from the source of the spring to the homely dining-room sideboard, and thus onwards to the chemist's shop has begun. (And the glass-bottle works increase in number!)

WATERS SOLD BOTTLED

Malvern Water. "Bottled at the spring." A table water of the highest class. Remarkably pure, containing only 6½ grains of minerals to the Imperial gallon. This 6½ grains is chiefly carbonate of soda, lime, magnesia, chloride of sodium, and a minute quantity of iodine of sodium. This water has long been celebrated for its curative properties in rheumatism, gout, scrofula and affections of the liver and kidneys. Its methodical use is calculated to prevent the formation of morbid concretions and deposits.

Langammarch water is saline barium and advisable for glandular, epilepsy, and heart disorders.

Buxton water is saline and advised for gout and arthritis (this is a new-fashioned complaint).

Flintwick water is chalybeate, and may be drunk for neuralgia, indigestion, debility, etc. (The advertisement does not sound convincing!)

Harrogate waters are definitely medical, being sulphurous and advised for cutaneous affections, lead and mercurial poisoning, syphilis and deterioration of the blood arising from gouty diathesia, chorea, chlorosis, anaemia and indigestion.

Leamington water is saline, and advised for haemorrhoids, sciatica, lead poisoning, scrofulas, lymphatic glandular enlargements, cutaneous affections and jaundice.

Aqua sulis (Bath). This well-known water is alkaline and gaseous, and should be taken for dyspepsia, anorexia and "impaired mobility of the stomach".

Woodhall water is bromo-iodised and has a list of "advised for" as long as the rest, but finishes, "also for goitre and fibrous tumours".

All these waters are supplied bottled (and also as dried salts) by

Ingram & Royle,
St. Paul's Wharf,
London, Liverpool and Bristol.

Thus the "spa" declines, the "mineral water" arrives and the "bottle of medicine" is on the way.

AN INDUSTRIAL EXAMPLE

Mineral waters were gradually explored for industrial use; for example: Parry's Mountain in Anglesey had the largest output of copper before the Rhodesian mines were worked. It was opencast, and Queen Elizabeth I granted a charter for the workings.

In 1762 water flooded the workings, which lapsed, being worked in connection with mines in Caernarvonshire. Later, streams of water from the workings were followed up, drains (natural and constructed) were made, and the streams from the mountain were, in the 1920's, used to decompose tin waste carried from Liverpool and Manchester to settling ponds. The output of chromium was dependent upon the mineral content of the water from the old workings.

HOLY WATER

Miracles

"Many a wax candle hangs a record of a miracle,
But all the world knows well, that miracle is none.
It profiteth your purses, and ye prelates suffer it.
That men should live and die and believe, in their ignorance
And all the world is worse for this your covetise."

PIERS PLOWMAN

Holy water is used today in Roman Catholic chapels and households. The water is blessed each year, before the Easter midnight Mass, using the ancient liturgy of the Holy Saturday ceremonies. The water is then placed in holy water stoups, set in the chancel, and porches, and near small side altars. It is also carried away to fill small stoups in Catholic households, that the devout may cross themselves with it, before and after prayers.

Holy water is also used at ceremonies such as baptisms, weddings and funerals, and to exorcise evil spirits, lay ghosts and consecrate buildings. In processions, the water was carried before a priest, who, using a soft whisk of white horsehair set into a delicate jewelled holder, gently sprinkled the water over the bowed heads of the devout. With mediæval humour the warrior's grim scourge of spiked iron balls, made after the shape of horse chestnut burrs and chained loosely to an iron handle, was called a "holy water sprinkler".

The crusaders used to bring back phials of Jordan water,[1] and long after the Reformation many old protestant families used to store a bottle of Jordan water for their baptismal ceremonies, though probably more in a spirit of ancestor worship than in hope of special spiritual efficiency.

The misuses of holy water figure sadly in early witch-hunting records, as, for example, when an unsuspecting black cat, suddenly sprinkled with cold holy water, exploded in blasphemous wrath, and was seriously accused of "demoniacal possession", rather than "reasonable feline expostulation". In the twelfth century one note describing a poltergeist says that "holy water could not purge the place, in fact the priests themselves were attacked".

THE "HOLY SPA" AND THE "HOLY WELL"

We may call medicinal those in which the water has definite mineral content; but for water where no natural curative element can be found, the cures must be attributed to the supernatural. This is the only division possible. Medically, the enforced cleansing of the body, and the attitude of mind induced, are capable of making any water holy and blessed, and only the icy coldness of the water and the special providence of the custodians can have prevented many of the most crowded wells from spreading more infection than ever they cured. The laws for lepers, that enforced drinking from their own bowls, washing downstream, and keeping outside churches, and away from all shrines where others worshipped, were sound hygiene, and though we can find no direct evidence, there was every opportunity for the custodian to "asperge" the waters with some simple purifying substance, such as lime (we know they used charcoal), or in case of suppurating sores use a saline solution. The puff ball dust, used to staunch bleeding, is not so far from some modern treatments. The same loving combination of medical aid, with divine instruction, is used by medical missionaries today, so one can be sure earlier missionaries would use the same heavenly kindness with understanding.

In the spirit of compromise we offer Holywell, in Flintshire, as the example of an ancient "holy well" and "Prayres for use at Baths" from an ancient "medical well".

AN EXAMPLE OF A HOLY WELL STILL IN USE—SAINT WINIFRED'S HOLY WELL

> "There is a wel in Wales called Saynte Wenefrydes Well. Walshe men sayth that if a man doth caste a cope or staffe or a napkyn in the wel it wyll be full of droppes of frakiles [freckles? flicks?], redysshe like bloude. The whyche is false for I have proved it contrary in sondry tyme".
>
> *Boke of the Introduction of Knowledge, dedicated to Lady Mary, daughter of Kyng Henry the eyght.*

[1]See Butler's *Way of all Flesh.*

This is an example of a holy well, that never claimed medical properties but entirely miraculous ones.

St. Winifred's (Welsh *Gwenfrwddi*) Well is an example of a holy well that still remains in use after 1,300 years. History reports that St. Winifred's father was a wealthy man, and her mother a sister of St. Breuno, who lived near them, and taught his niece the Christianity of his own mission. Caradoc, a young chieftain of Harwarden, desired her, but the girl was determined to become a nun. One day, on her way to the little chapel built by St. Breuno, Caradoc pursued her and, so the tale went, slashed off her head! Robert of Shrewsbury (one source of the story) says that "instantly the earth opened and swallowed up Caradoc, and a copious fountain burst forth where the severed head hit the ground", and, to add to the wonder, St. Breuno restored St. Winifred to life by picking up and replacing the head upon her neck, where it grew again, leaving only a slight scar! What is the true history? St. Winifred certainly existed, and so did Caradoc, and being a lover and a Welshman he would pursue his love on her way to chapel. It is reasonable that she fell, or was felled, at the church door, hitting her head a bang upon the hard stones, where she lay unconscious, "as if dead". (And instantly we are sure Caradoc *did* wish the earth would open and swallow him up and probably said so!) Falls and concussion were common in those days of horse travel, and St. Breuno, as a sensible man, would have the girl's apparently lifeless body lifted into the building, and laid down flat on the rush matting, and would bid the crowd to "stand back and give her air". So the wondering crowd probably watched her "come to", while St. Breuno's hands were still gently feeling around her head for a cracked skull. And, if Caradoc had clutched her throat, the same gentle hands would probable be seen laying a cold water bandage round the bruised throat. Then surely St. Breuno would be experienced enough to turn out the chattering crowd, and let the girl sleep and rest, flat on the floor, in the quiet of his little stone chapel. So the crowd drifts slowly away, talking and comparing notes, and quickly retailing "what they saw St. Breuno do with their own eyes" (as every crowd at every accident has always done). So it is easy to see how the mediæval miracle piled up over "the sad incident, between two such nice young people, both so well known locally"!

St. Winifred recovered (from concussion and shock), and went to recuperate at her desired convent, where she became a nun, and later abbess. Her body was buried in the abbey, but in 1138 it was dug up, and carried to the Benedictine Abbey at Shrewsbury. In 1398 "Canterbury" ordered her feast to be kept on November 3rd, and St. Winifred's Well has continued as a holy well and place of pilgrimage ever since. The "well town" of "Holywell" was on the main route from Bardsey, Anglesey, and Penmon, past Basinwerk Abbey, to the fords across the Dee to

Chester and St. Johns, so that pilgrims carried the gossip and the fame of the well increased rapidly. In 1629 it is reported that fourteen thousand pilgrims and one hundred and fifty priests attended St. Winifred's feast (it was a very appropriate period historically).

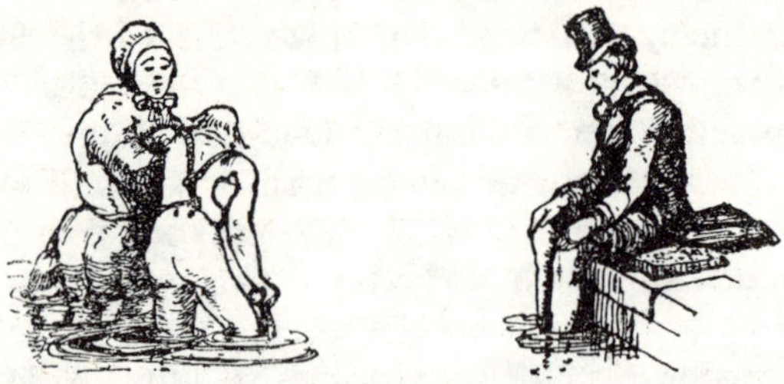

Taken from Roscoe's guide to N. Wales in 1886. The bathwomen who assisted the infirm bathers seem to have been upholstered in white Welsh blanket cloth and wore linen caps.

In 1774 Dr. Johnson reported bathers at the well, "the water icy cold and cures frequent". The original bath and spring house were first built by Margaret, mother of Henry VII, and other Welsh nobles added to it, so the present building has a conglomerately Gothic architecture. There are hotels for pilgrims in the town, and services in the chapel.

The Jesuits owned the place for some years, and there is today a steady flow of pilgrims from Cheshire and Lancashire Roman Catholic communities. In 1917 mining operations in the adjoining Halkyn mountains drained the spring, and a law suit was brought by the Church against the mining company who, by arrangement (*see* footnote), agreed to return the water, which still rises as freely as do the prayers of the devout.

During the thirteenth and fourteenth centuries, when the long bridle path passed the door of the chapel, the small Gothic building must have hung like a stone nest in the branch of the green glen. Now, a metalled motor road has buried the door twenty feet deep below ground level. Earth, sliding down from graveyards above, clustering houses, and hideous Victorian Gothic enlargements and turnstiles, enclose the ugly outer bath.

The earlier building was a graceful octagonal enclosure around the water, which welled up from a white stone floor, and flowed out through a shallow balustrade, very delicately carved, so that the strong water fell in silver curves to the small bath with stone steps on either side. Behind the white stone tracery of the shrine the walls were hung with old crutches and splints, more devout than lovely. But now all the stone tracery is broken away, and only worn stumps of stone are left, above an ugly iron rail.

At present the spring house is undergoing restoration and it will be a modern miracle if engineers can stop and clear away the ever-falling earth of centuries and control that powerful bursting water.

Broken portions of the stone work seem to lie in the well, and the exquisite fan vaulting (so like that of the Henry VII chapel at Westminster), is flaking badly. Most of the carved bosses have perished, as have the mediæval animals scrambling round under the broken eaves. One surviving deep pendant boss that told the story in coloured low relief, hung centrally, so that the unlettered could watch the story unfold as they circled around it, pacing the shrine with eyes raised to heaven.

At Holywell today the sale of "shrine tokens", flasks in which to carry away the water, and all the clustering commercial encumbrances of "accommodation for pilgrims", reproduce exactly the more sordid activities of an old mediæval shrine. That the present owners of this holy well may restore their small stone gem, in its green setting, to its earliest simplicity of design is the devout prayer of this pilgrim.[1]

A MEDICAL WELL—MADE HOLY

A Sermon at Bath (A.D. 1692)

> "I cannot do better than to send you to that Angel, who, according to St. John, flies in the midst of Heaven, . . . saying with a loud voice, Fear God, and give glory to Him, and worship Him that made Heaven and earth and the sea and the fountains of waters, Rev. xiv. 6, 7, and I beseech you to observe how often . . . he particularly mentions springs and fountains of waters as a very wonderful part of creation, for out of the dark places of the earth, through passages and from causes unknown to the wisest of men, God makes sweet and fresh springs to rise."

This sermon, of great length, then advises the bather to give place to the Physician, "for the Lord hath created him, and there is a time, when in their hands, there is good success", and after many more quotations, ends with an exhortation to begin their "cure" by "reading devotional books on the subject of which (Blessed be God!) there are good store".

AN INFERNAL SPA OR UNHOLY WELL

The phenomenon of gas escaping through water, giving the effect of water burning, is fairly common in old records. Around coal-mining districts it was probably more common before the legalized ventilation of modern mechanized workings.

[1] It was reported that the Mines Company offered to return the spring "Hot or Cold". Curiously, Giraldus the Welshman, who passed that way to Basinwerk, makes no mention of the well.

In some cases there seems to have been a spout of inflammable oil; and, if the present oil boring in Ireland succeeds, it may clear up a twelfth-century miracle. For there was, at that date, a cave on an island on a lake, which belched forth sulphurous fumes and burning flames, so that it was seriously suggested as an entrance to hell! (As a child I was told, most seriously, by an old Irish nun that "there used to be an entrance to purgatory through a deep cave in Ireland, but it had been closed".)

A similar inflammable gas seems to have burnt for centuries in a cave in Europe, and the early Irish Church probably knew of this, and took over its lucrative scenic effects. Kindly Saint Patrick may have used the isolated place to lay the comfort of an earthly penance upon some sinner, but his lock was soon broken, and by the twelfth century the burning spring of St. Patrick's purgatory was going full blast! An Englishman, Henry of Huntingdon (1152), wrote a lurid account of the place, and one of King Stephen's knights crossed the waters and reached the brink of hell there. All through the thirteenth century, to the end of the fourteenth century, the fame of that infernal "spa" grew and spread. It became a place of expensive pilgrimage. Edward III granted passes for noble Hungarians and Lombards to go there, and signed testimonies guaranteeing that they had "faithfully performed" the pilgrimage. Richard II gave safe conduct to "a Knight of Rhodes, with 20 men and 30 horses". To go there became an exciting religious high adventure (and, as Piers Plowman put it, "they had leave to lie thereafter").[1]

It was only a few years before the fifteenth century (about 1495) that a solid Dutchman from Eymstadt plodded over to see for himself. Seriously he went through the fifteen days' preparation, and steadfastly he sat out the night in the cave, expecting devils that did not come, so he plodded back home and stated the fact solidly. In 1497 the Pope ordered the purgatory to be destroyed and the cave closed.

Now, if there had been a hot spring and a vent of inflammable gas on the isle, then letting in the water from the lake would provide the clouds of mist and vapour, and all the heat that was used to scald and impress the pilgrims. This explanation of the spa is suggested in converse between Froissart, the reliable chronicler, and Sir Wyllyam Lysle, the experienced soldier, two men of the world, out riding together. One can almost hear the bridles clink as they walk their horses through the pleasant weald of Kent. Sir Lysle has been to see this purgatory, and Froissart asks him "What think you of it?" "It's a hole, and it stinks," says the soldier, "and certain

[1] "Many a wax candle hangs a record of a miracle,
But all the world knows well, that miracle is none.
It profiteth your purses, and ye prelates suffer it.
That men should live and die and believe, in their ignorance
And all the world is worse for this your covetise."
PIERS PLOWMAN

hot vapours rose against us, and it was so hot that we slept—and dreampt", but in the morning they had forgotten their dreams, so "thought the matter a phantasy" . . .

It is, perhaps, stretching a point to include this "unholy hole" among medicinal spas and gentle holy wells, *but it illustrates the strength of the old illusions that could be worked up around anything unusual or unnatural.*

One regrets broken shrines and ruined wells, but today, when engineers are our miracle workers, "may the saints preserve" the few little blessed springs that still seep through the green mosses among the primroses.

BOTTLED HOLY WATER AND SOME CURIOUS USES AND CAUSES

The filling of flasks and "taking away for use at home" of bottles of holy water, follows the same usage as that of medical spa water. (Payment in each case is "on the bottle", and in some cases this is returnable.) But the laying of articles in sanctified water to become sanctified was restricted to holy water only, and is of very ancient usage. This caused reasonable derision during the Reformation, especially in cases where the water became holy accidentally. The following is an example of this:

> "After King Oswald's death, his niece, the Queen, and her husband Ethelred, wished his bones to be reinterred at the Monastery at Bardney (Lincolnshire). When the wagon carrying the bones arrived towards evening the monks were reluctant to admit it. Though they acknowledged Oswald's holiness, they were prejudiced against him because he originally came from a different province and had ruled them as an alien king. So the king's bones remained outside the gates all night, with a large cover spread over the wagon on which they lay."

But a sign from heaven showed them their error, for "a shaft of light shone from the wagon all night". "Accordingly the bones were washed and laid in a casket, and placed in the church, and the water in which the bones had been washed was poured away in a corner and from that time the very earth that received this venerated water had power to expel devils."

The story goes on to tell how holy Abbess Ethelhilda collected a little bagful of this holy earth and used it to good purpose.

In this connection one must recall the old bones and cods' heads that for centuries have been used by fisherfolk to shine in the dark and mark out a narrow footpath. All old countrymen must have known this phosphorescent light and accepted it as natural when it shone on the bones of a dead fish. Could they believe it supernatural when it shone on the bones of a dead saint? How much the mediæval peasant accepted spiritual explanations diplomatically is the historian's insoluble problem. The peasant was sane and knowledgeable in the things of the earth. How much did he believe what the scholars told him of the unearthly?

Commercially the facts were indisputable! Any saints' relics were an acquisition to a religious community, and were used by them for all manner of charms and cures. So that the water that had washed saints' bones was valuable. This was intensified in the case of St. Blaise, whose bones were so valued that they were used for making holy water.[1] As a contemporary poet wrote:

> "I divers barrels oft have seene, drawne out of water cleare,
> Through one small blessed bone, of this same Martyr; bear
> And carried thence; to other towns; and cities far away . . ."

We must judge the brutal honesty of this poetic indictment in its own Reformation period. Today, one might hesitate to remove the comfort of very *un*blessed water from some pious believer, as one might hesitate to remove any useless medicine from an invalid who had faith in it. For if there is a cure, it is of the mind; and the mind may turn to a cure through the body, and both be blessed.

So, slowly, it seems, truth seeps down through the centuries to water the roots of that tree whose fruit is the knowledge of good and evil.

THE ODOUR OF SANCTITY AND BONE WASHING

This washing of bones and reliques was but the belated washing of the dead, always carried out with religious care. It was this Jewish tradition that brought the women early in the morning to the tomb of Christ. The grave bands, the incense, ointments and herbs, were sensible when saintly remains had to be venerated as long as possible, or conveyed some distance for appropriate disposal. The volatile oils of rosemary, spike oil and balm supplemented the spices, gums, and rock salts that were used. The length of time such a pot-pourri mixture will retain and develop fragrance, when kept closely covered, could well account for the "waft of heavenly fragrance" commented upon, when some old shrine was unclosed, or the stiff waxed grave clothes stirred! The devout could believe the evidence of their senses. The scent of such a paradise garden is an odour of sanctity, but the piety of uncleanliness is a mediæval perplexity! The acceptance of poverty and dirt and privations was revered for holy administrations. In this strange Christianity, Christ washing the feet of his disciples is an "ensample" of piety far beyond ordinary hospitality. By deduction in reverse, the worse the dirt the greater the

[1] In the same manner as the ham bone of the economical community was hired out to flavour broth! One stir for ½*d.*—a good wallop for 1*d.*

humility and the more magnificent the cleanliness, the greater the virtue. An "ensample" from the thirteenth century:

> "There was a pious lady who took pity on a leper faint with the hot sun and did off his shoes and washed him, foot and body, and layde hym in her bed, and her owne softe pylowere under his head, and schett the dore and went her way . . . and the Knight her husband (when he returned) entered the room wondyr wherewyth she had made the chambyr so swete wyth spycerye and smellyth as it were paradyse."

But the leper "was go" and the lady "wepyng for Ioje told her Lord how she had do".

Now this sort of story is the romantic equivalent of the pious Victorian tract, that was written to inculcate piety by showing the reward of virtue, or, at a later date, one might even liken it to the advertising story of the popular women's weeklies, which induce a pathetic belief, in some "marvellous scented ointment", which produces "alluring loveliness overnight". They are no less silly than the mediæval lady who believed that if she gave the "softe pylowere" and total service in this impossible situation, she too might have her "chambyr smelling as if it were paradise". Study of this example, and many others, illuminate the mentality of the period. So much that seems impossible and extraordinary sorts itself out as quite rational behaviour, if the mental attitude of the time is understood.

WATER OF THE FONT

"Nine times about the Font they marche and on the Saintes call,
Then still at length they stand, and straight the Priest begins withall.
And thrice the Water doth he touch, to crosses thereon make.
And Bigge and Barbrous words he speaks, to make the Devill quake!
And the holsome water conjuireth, and foolishly doth addresse,
Supposing holier to make, what God himself did blesse!"

THOMAS NAVGEORGUS, *Trans. by Barnabe Googe*

The font used to be filled once a year, usually at Easter, with ceremoniously blessed water (which partly accounted for the size of the font), but like everything connected with the Church, from church bell grease to candle wax, the water used to be stolen and used sacrilegiously. So from 1236 locked font covers were compulsory. Sometimes in old stone fonts the staple holes can be found that once took an iron padlock. For others the covers were of wood, too heavy to lift singlehanded.

THE WATERS OF BAPTISM

"Thou askest . . .
What spirits are these? . . .
. . . They sinned not, for they had not Baptism, which is the portal of the faith that thou believest. For no other fault are we lost and only so far afflicted that, without hope, we live in desire."

DANTE

Pre-Reformation teaching held that a baby dying unbaptized could not enter heaven but must be detained in Limbo, a place where the souls of the just who died before Christ were detained, till Christ had opened the gates of heaven. It was all part of the complicated reasoning that made every man the inheritor of Adam's original sin, from which baptism cleansed him. Therefore, though baptism was the prerogative of the priest, in an emergency anyone could baptize an infant likely to die, with any sort of water out of any sort of dish.

In those days, when childbirth was a real peril and infant mortality high, a large percentage of babies were baptized with the washtub water or water in a silver bowl, hurriedly brought up from the dining-table. Midwives, when giving the new born its first cleansing, were, if they saw it in peril of death, instantly to turn the bathwater into the water of baptism by "saying the words over it" and so ensure the child had a blessed soul before it left this earth, and could therefore go to heaven. Hence, this warning to Mydwyfes by Robert le Brunne:

"Y shal you telle of a mydwyfe that loste a chylde both soule and lyfe. When she sawe that hyt should dye she began loude for to crye and moan and sayd 'God and seynt joune crysten this child both flesshe and bone.'
The prest asked the mydwyfe
If hyt were cristenede when it had liffe?
And who hyt cristened? And on what manere?
And what was seyde that any myght here? (*for a witness was desirable*).
The mydwyfe seyde unto the prest,
'This herde they? That stood me next.
That God Almighty and Sent Joune
Give the child Cristendom in flesshe and boune.'

Then seyd the prest 'God and Sent Joune
Give thee both sorrow and shame
In evyi time were you y bore
For yn thy defaulte a soule is lorn';

She was commanded she should no more
Come elfesones where chyllyn were y bore.
(*The Prest then instructed that if*)
Thou see a chylle yn swyche perel
That none may save hyt wyth no wylle
Say thou thus—'Give thou in haste
Y crysten thee yn the name of the
Fadr and Sone and Holy Gast'
And gyve what thou wylt hyt a name
And kast on water on hyts frame
Mydwyves! That wyth wymman wone
Alle these pyntes behove thou kone."

RIVER BAPTISM

"During the period he (Bishop Paulinius) did nothing from dawn to dusk but proclaim Christ's saving message to the people who gathered from all the surrounding countryside . . . and when he had instructed them he washed them in the cleansing waters of Baptism in the nearby River Glen."

BEDE, A.D. 627

In 625 Paulinius was consecrated bishop and sent with the Kentish Princess Ethelburga to Northumbria, where she was to marry and possibly convert the pagan King Eadwine. Paulinius did well, and in a couple of years baptized the king in the wooden church of St. Peter at York. (This king subsequently built the church of stone at York.) Paulinius made constant missionary journeys up over the passes and down the dales, where the rivers made natural track ways through the Pennines. Converts were baptized on the spot in their own rivers, there being no churches. Also, as the converts were dependent for water on the rivers, which were constantly before their doors, the site would serve to remind them of their conversion.

During the religious revival at the turn of this century, several river bathing places were used for mass baptisms. Many people of other religious sects attended, though the Baptists were the most forward to do so. The revival was very strong in the country places in Wales, and young people collected picture postcards of their favourite ministers with the zeal that young people today collect photos of their film favourites. One glossy card showing "*Evan Roberts smiling while preaching*" was a great favourite and I remember seeing it pinned up in several bathrooms, because, the maidens explained, it "put them in mind of being baptized".

My mother was fortunate enough to see one of the great baptisms held in the river Dee. She described to me, how, from the very early dawn "the roads were black with people pouring down from the villages around to gather on the river bank".

The bank on one side was high and wooded above the clear water. She said "a thick fringe of riding horses and ponies and donkeys and small carts and farm traps were tied to the trees at the top of the bank, and all down the bank were people, tiered in rows as on some vast grandstand. Some climbed up into the trees, some crawled out onto rocky ledges; as far as eye could see up the riverside were people, and farther than eye could see you could hear them singing". She said that you could hear the music in the far distance, "coming downstream, mixed with the sound of the rushing water and the wind in the trees—till, as the sound came closer the massed voices, singing in Welsh, drowned the sounds of the river, and other voices coming down from the chapels above joined in". The men and women awaiting baptism were gathered in flocks—black and white—on the further side. When I saw a later baptism, there were far fewer people riding than on foot, but the roadway was blocked with cars and the ceremony was carried out in the same way. The women all wore long white dresses, and one showed me how the hem was weighed down with little stones so that the skirt would not float up in the water. (She said her mother, who had been at the previous baptism, had advised this.) The men, wore cycle clips around their ankles to hold their trousers down.

All were huddled together tightly in groups, and their friends stood back a little. Then a small black figure walked out, deep into the river pool, and between him and the waiting groups on the bank stood one or two helpers, making a human chain. The running water banked up in ripples behind their backs as they faced downstream. Another song, and then silence, as the candidates came, one at a time, down to the brink, paused a moment, and then there was a small splash as they stepped in and waded to the outstretched hand of the first helper, who passed them to the minister. Quickly, he dipped them under the water, and up again, and at once passed them across to the second helper who led them back to the bank, where they scrambled up and stood dripping, dazed and wet, till gently collected and moved off down the road, to the fold where dry clothing and a hot drink awaited them. When all had been bathed, the crowd melted away, and one heard the singing break out again in the distance. It was a most reverent impressive ceremony, deeply religious, and the more so for being carried out with the simplicity and despatch of shepherds at a sheep dipping.

RIVERS

"Tyme passeth as water in a ryvere
No mortall man can it revoke agayne
Dethe, with his daitis unwarely doth apere
It is the ende of every man certayne."
Shyp of Fooles, 1509

THE THREE RIVERS OF ENGLAND

"England is a wel good land, it were of each land best
It is set in the end of the world; afar in the west
And England is full enough of fruit and of treen—
Of woodes and of parks, that joy it is to seen
Of foules and of bestes; both wild and tame also
Of salt fishe; and fayre rivers thereto.
Of welles swete, and colde snow; of leafen and of meade
Of felner ore, and of gold; of tyn and of lead
Of stele, and iron, and of bras, and of good corn great wonder
And of the white wool good, betere n'er may be noe other.
Water she has eke good enough—before all others three
Out of the land, into the sea, armes as they be
Whereby the ships move, that come from far and wende
And bring our land goods enough, aboute in each ende
Severne and Themes; Homber it is the pride
Of where it is, as it were set, the land amid.
Homber bringeth by the north, much good and wide
Severne by the west and south, the Themes by the east side
So that of goods enough, that other lands has
They cometh to England, by no default ways."

THE RIVER FOR TRAVEL (*see* plate 17)

"Diversum is a bendyng of the way and Byurticulum is a branching off from the way, but Bivium is two ways, of which one lyeth on the ryght hand, the other on the left hand and is ofte a perylous place and suspecte, for in such places—the cominalty ben afte robbed—and is a dowtefull place, for men dowbte which of those wayes they shall take, wherefore ymages and crosses benne sette in such wayes that the men thereby may know which they shall take."

BART. ANGLICUS

Only by walking can one appreciate the accurate guidance of old river maps. The scale of the water course is deliberately exaggerated, but the directions are correct, and so is the position of the watershed from which the rivers take their source. Every walker learns the elementary guide for getting across mountains—"Set your face to the right point of the compass, and follow the streams up and down. It may be rough going, and you will detour bogs and rocks, but once you reach the top of the pass if you find any stream *that is flowing the other way* it is bound to get you down into the valley on the other side."

The increasing maze of roads, rails, and boundaries that have crowded maps since the seventeenth century, confuse this simple water guidance and only an expert can visualize the distant landfall from the contour lines. Yet today, if you make the experiment and set out from any old valley church and walk across country to a fold in the hills ahead, you will soon find a river at your side. Remember, that regardless of the volume of water, it is the main stream which keeps its direction, the tributary which changes direction to join it. So if you follow the main stream, you will find your old map understandable, and presently it will lead you to the exact tarn, pass, or hilltop it shows so clearly (and often graphically).

We speak from experience, having walked all about England for years. Moreover, guided by these old maps, you will be led past a surprising number of forgotten crosses, direction stones, and small derelict cells and chapels. By all ferries and landing places, there will be traces of the old hospices and taverns that once sheltered wayfarers like yourself. On these old ways you will find the traveller's plants. The iris at the fords, the horseradish (whose juice made so good an embrocation for stiffness), comfrey, or boneset (to foment a saddle sore or set a broken leg).

The river routes were well trodden of old, and the chance of hearing news, learning the latest market price, or consulting traveller's merchants, gave excuse for a great many of the granges and rest houses belonging to abbeys, or other large estates, to be strategically placed. Frequently a watchman had his cell (and smallholding of goats and poultry) high up by a mountain pass, where he supplemented a hard living by giving succour to the weary or stormbound. But it was on the main track routes that most danger was feared.

THE CITY RIVERS FOR INDUSTRY

Although individual springs and wells were used by special industries, the disposal of all used industrial water commonly depended upon the river that ran through a city. Even today, when the dispersal of industry and the long-distance piping of water from artificial dams blurs its outline, the fundamental flow of industry can be traced to its water supply. The diagram has been compiled from many rivers, and centuries of industrial enterprise. Industries are not placed haphazard, and though modern transport, and economic outlook, place some of them in unexpected places because of available local labour or cheap building costs, etc., the position of fundamental industries that depend upon water supplies remain remarkably static.

The inflow of clean water is not more important than a good outlet of fouled water. Disposal and intake must balance. Now work downstream on the diagram (as if working down through past centuries).

High up, where the clean stream flows most swiftly (very likely where the contour line causes a fall, or where springs emerge from an exposed strata), the corn mills and brewing suggest malt houses and cooper work, and transport downstream to the city. These industries have over-lapped, though licence laws and commercial brewing have replaced the private brewing of ale. To the north, the cattle roads need watering streams for the droves of animals. Below the city, the slaughter yards are adjacent to the leather vats which, in turn, require access to the lime-burning industry. On the north side of the diagram, we place the influx of tanning barks from timber yards. These may use oak bark, from the wood used in smelting iron (pre-seventeenth century) or willow strippings from the osier beds along the waterside. (The salicylic acid of the "sally willow" being specially used for water-proofed leathers.)

The tan yards require water to fill tanks in which the hides soak in lime water to remove the hairs. Then the hair and skin grease are recovered and water is required to cleanse both of these separately. The recovered hair is used in making fibrous plaster for builders, and sometimes for upholstery, though in Queen Elizabeth I's reign this was strictly illegal, since "mattresses and upholstery made of hair that has been wrought in grease, if foul, give out, by the heat of a man's body, a savour so abominable and contagious that many are destroyed thereby".

The wool washing of the sheep is upstream, as are the fulling mills, weaving sheds and tenting yards, for the water required for the washing, dying and dressing of woollen cloth must flow swiftly.

To the south side of the diagram the more level lands require slower water for inundating water meadows.

The south side of the diagram shows fertile lowlands, the water irrigating the gardens and fruit orchards that always lie near any city, to supply the fruit and vegetable markets. Bees were such general stock everywhere (till sugar became cheap) that we need only consider the honey industry in connection with the offal trades, for beeswax was needed, with tallow, by the chandlers. Their industry coincided with that of the soap boilers, whose use of water has required a complete chapter to itself.

The horn and hoof dealers would use the water of the main river, and by law they worked below the city. The glue boilers required more water than one would expect, as much soaking and setting and cleansing had to be done before the pure colloidal solution could be dried off into

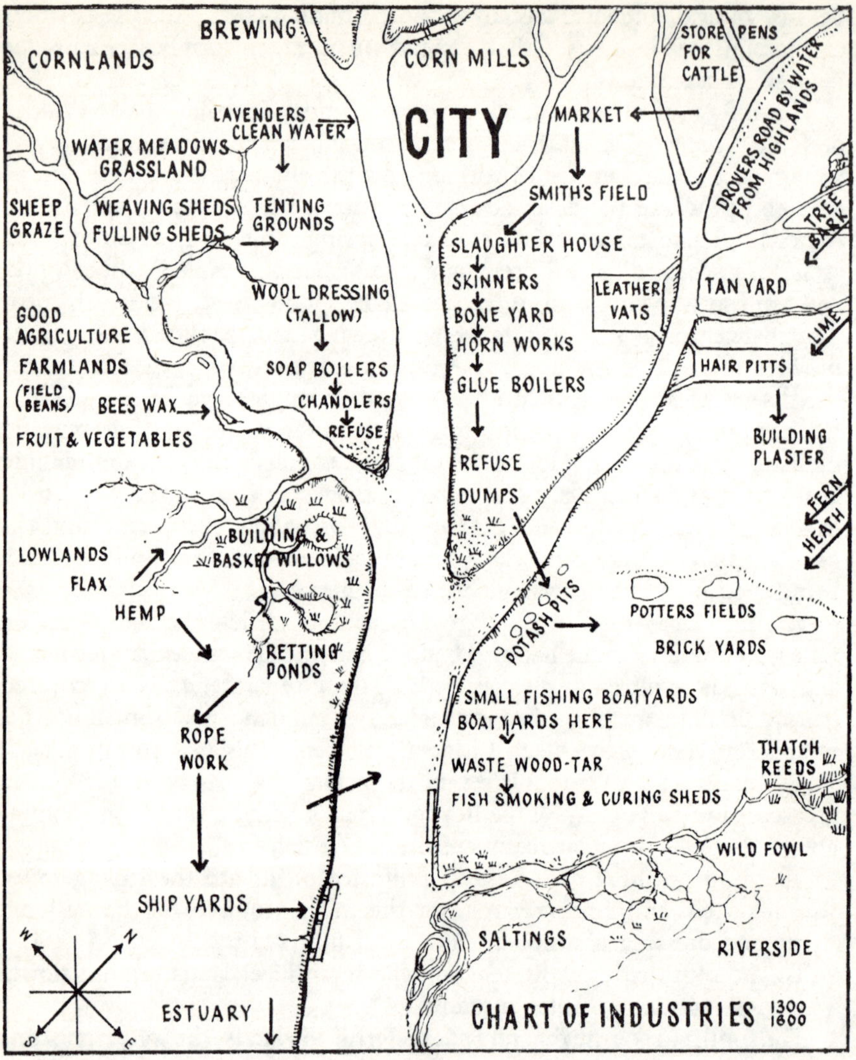

This diagram of a city's water, as needed for a city's industries can be used as basic study for students doing industrial research. In past centuries the utilising of waste products was so *stream-lined* that there remained *no* waste product! All was used, even the last water-borne particles were absorbed into the fishing industry and (being purified by the fish) returned on Fridays to the mediæval "board meeting"— smoked and salted.

industrial glue (some mediæval glue had the quality of fine amber). By the time these slaughter-yard products had drained into the river, it was full of animal refuse, and the befouled and littered banks became excellent fishing grounds.

The rougher debris along the water line was collected by professional beachcombers, and others scavenged the countryside for refuse to burn in the potash pits which supplied the potters and tile-makers with glaze. Anyone curious to do so, can trace this sequel of water-borne industry down the Thames, past Bow Bridge to the refuse tips of Tilbury, and the old Kentish brick and tile works at Faversham and Oare. Even the old potash pits can be traced on the Essex coast, fishing and shrimping boats still ply off Gravesend and cockle shells from Leigh-on-Sea used to be burnt for lime.

On the south bank of the diagram the hemp and flax industries, together with the willows, use an enormous amount of *static* water. Their water disposal problem has been difficult ever since hemp was first retted, as hemp rot is very foul. Tusser, in 1560, warns against setting flax and hemp to rot in water near farms and dwellings, lest it "harm people and cattle with stink". The deep brown-stained water where hemp is laid to rot (to get rid of the outer husk) is quite definitely harmful to cattle and, as it cannot be purified, ponds, swamps, and "waste marsh" are a corollary of the hemp industry. As the old sailing ships used miles of rope rigging and acres of sailcloth, the rope works would be adjacent to flats near the river. (Even such an inland rope walk as that of Nottingham was adjacent to the river Trent.)

In the diagram we have completed the industrial water sequence by indicating a tidal estuary and saltings. The city refuse, the reed ponds and fishing and slaughter offal, would attract wild fowl, and the waste wood of the ship-building, the waste tar products, would support fish curing and smoking sheds. Mediæval dried and smoked eels still dangle in the East End of London. The cockle shells of Southend are no longer burnt for lime, but the long trails of blue smoke, from burning weed and reed, still drift over the river downstream from the City of London, and, as the shallow lapping edge of the tide creeps to our feet, we may voyage back to the far lands of long ago, that sleep so quietly around us.

Transport by Thames

The Frost Fair broadsheet is well known, and deals with the sports and fun that were carried on the frozen Thames. This THAW broadsheet is less well known, and shows well the river transport that was as regular in the seventeenth century as the bus services are now. The Watermen were the regular "Taxi cabs" of the period, each had his special stand, at certain "Steps" along the embankment, or small "Hard" up or down river—

and unless you were a Man-about-Town, and kept your own Coach and Barge for your family use—you "went by river" as the easiest way to travel. Westward Ho! or Eastward Ho! were regular Watermen's cries—and reclaiming their "regulars" reconditioning their boats, and many other interesting transport notes will be found in the Thaw poem. . . .

The THAMES Uncas'd:

OR,

The Watermans Song upon the Thaw.

To the Tune of Hey Boys up go we. 18. feb. 168 4/3

THE THAW

The Thaw that followed the great Frost was also berhymed, and gives many interesting sidelights on the seventeenth-century London river usages.

1. Come, ye merry men all
Of Watermans-hall,
Lets hoiſt out our Boats and careen;
The Thames it does melt,
And the Cold is ſcarce felt,
Not an Icicle's now to be ſeen
Let's pull down each Skull
That hung up in Hall,
Like Weapon ſo ruſty, and row:
Let's cheerly fall to't,
If we've not forgot; how to do it!
For the Froſt is over now.

2. Let's ſet up our Maſts
That ſtood like Poſts,
As Props to our Tents on the Thames,
Or Signe-poſts made,
With an antient diſplai'd,
While our oars were the great Croſs beams.
Let's hoiſe up our Sail
That was a ſide-Vail
To hide Doll when with Brandy ſhe'd glow;
Or a Roof compos'd,
You might elſe have been froz'd,
Though the Froſt be over now.

3. We'll no longer ſtand
With a Tapſters hand,
With the Spigot in hand for an Oar,
Crying out, Our Trade is cold,
Here's four gallons in hold,
I have drawn out but half my ſtore.
Prithee Lads ſtand to't
And help it to go,
That the Veſſel once more may flow;
Then come again
With a thrifty train;
But the Froſt is over now.

4. Let's tune our Throats
To our uſual Notes
Of "Twitnam, Richmond", hey!
Sir, Skuller, Sir? Oars, Sir?

Loudly roar, Sir,
"Here's Dick, Sir, you won't paſs him by?"
Inftead of good Ale,
And Brandy-wine ſtale,
Let's cry out, "Weftward hoe!"
Shall we Moretlack, make,
Or for Brandford tack,
For the Froſt is over now?

5. We'll take no Boat
That once did float
And Fervice good had done,
And on his Keel
Clap Sledge for heel,
And inforce him like Traytor to run;
So to make him appear
Like a China Carr,
With a tawdry painted Prow,
And a tire or more
Of Potguns four;
For the Froſt is over now.

Verse 4: The watermen are suggesting that they can go either to Twickenham or Richmond, or Westward Ho! for Mortlake or Brentford.

Verse 5 is a topical note on the "Chinese" influence that showed in Chinese Chippendale and painted wallpapers. The design of the later Chinese Chippendale poster beds is interestingly suggestive of the shape made by four raised oars with sail drapery tied on at the notch (see illustration on page 66). This may have caught some contemporary's imagination.

FORDS AND BRIDGES

The building of fords and bridges was often a lucrative investment. The chapel-on-the-bridge usually had a bridge-keeper's cell and the owners kept in regular communication. Cash payments for use of the bridge were firmly collected.

There were regular bridge engineers (just as there were other specialized workers for cathedrals or mills), but hundreds of small bridges were put up by local workmen. Unfortunately it was so much an everyday job that there are few records. Sometimes the making of an old clapper bridge

1 and 2. Shrine tokens or travel souvenirs, the left one modern, the right one mediæval.

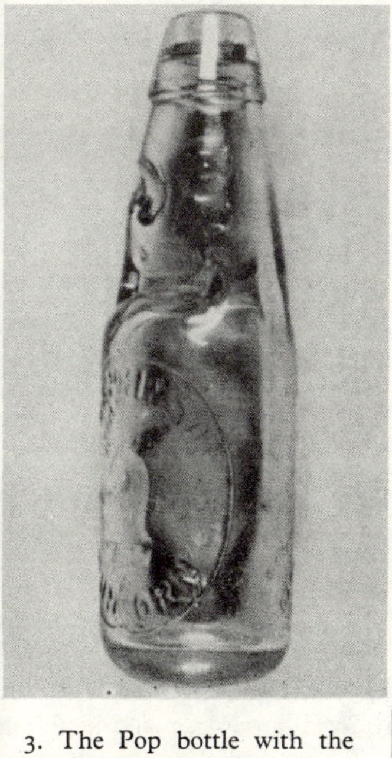

3. The Pop bottle with the glass stopper was secured by pressure from within against a rubber ring—a type now discontinued.

4. The Rajah's Well at Stoke Row in Buckinghamshire, available to the villagers from sunrise to sunset.

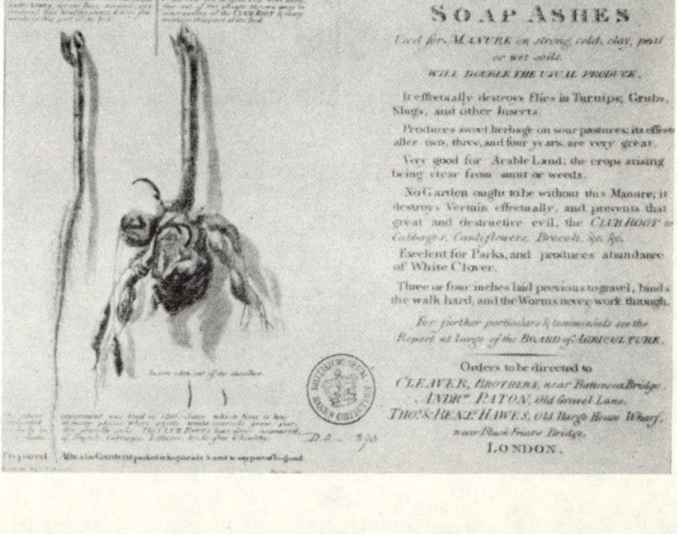

5. By-product of the soap-boiling industry; as a fertiliser it was effective against turnip fly and club root, etc.

6. These Elizabethan water-carriers hold forked staffs on which to rest the cowstal (pole) when changing shoulders or resting.

7. This 18th-century yoke has leather straps and wooden buckets.

8 and 9. London fire engine, an early Phoenix model. Note the watchman with police rattle lower left corner. *Right*, this 20th-century yoke has metal chains and galvanised-iron pails.

can be traced by the old iron quarry rails that had been used to bring the stone down, or there may be records of payment for extra labour or transport. Old bridges are usually too narrow for modern traffic, and the worn tracks of most fords remain the width of the old ironshod horse waggon.

Some small pack-horse bridges may have been paid for by pedlars and drovers. They were easily built by men used to working in stone, and the same thick wood frame for the arch could be horse-drawn across the hills and set up where needed to arch another stream.

We give descriptions of the old methods of building under water and setting about the job. It will be seen that all materials were easily available (willow and stones), etc., and experience taught the countryman how to let the stream do the work itself. Here is an abridged example, in verse, of communal bridge-building on a fairly large scale:

THE BUILDING OF OUR BRIDGE

"Of all werkys in the world, that ever were wrought
Holy Chirche is chefe; for there children been christened
And by baptism these bairns to blisse been brought
Through the grace of God and pryare refreshed.
Another blessed besiness, is Brigges to make
Where that pepul may not passe after gret showers
Dole it is to drawe a dede body oute of a lake
To found drowned in a fount a fellow of oures.

There lived here a ladde was a waterman longe
He helpe stop the streme till the work was afore
It was a solace to see, in the somer season!
300 werkmen, werking at onys!
4 and 4 relay'd by reson
To wit who wrought best, were set for the nonce.

The Peple proved their power with the pecoyfe (pickaxe)
The matok was man-handled right wele while
With spade and schovelis they made such a noise
That men myght here them thence a myle.

Wyves went out to wite how they wrought
Five score in a flok—it was a fayre sight
In bord clothes bright, white brede they brought
Cheese and chickens, clerelych dight

Thus wern the wyches i diged in ful harde grounde
And cast up to arere with the way
Sethen they were i set with a quik mownde
To hold in the bunkes for ever and ay."

The poem was written about 1458 and is preserved in its entirety at Christ Hospital at Abingdon. There was, as in most parochial enterprises, a considerable cross current of local feeling over the evaded toll! We wish we could give the entire poem but this short extract gives a perfect picture of a rural community "getting to work". First, the slowly aroused conviction that "something ought to be *done*" brought to a head, because "someone had got himself drowned". The bringing forward of an experienced old workman "who'd been a waterman longe" and so could put them in the right way to work. The gradual competitive feeling, "Reckon I could handle a pick as well as him". The fetching out of old tools, the dividing into small teams, and the betting against each other for time and length of dig.

A sluice had to be dug to carry the water aside, and the crucial moment came when the barrier had to be thrown across the current. This was probably a stone and hurdle blocking, and was a perilous part of the work, for if the restrained river burst its banks it might destroy the very site chosen for the bridge.

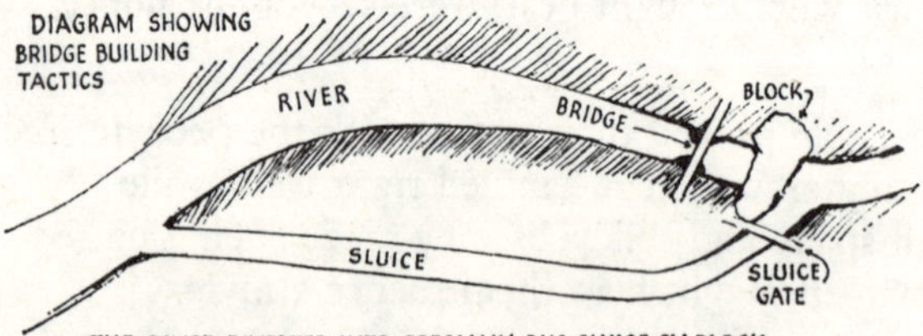

THE RIVER DIVERTED INTO SPECIALLY DUG SLUICE BY BLOCK, WHICH WAS THEN REMOVED TO CLOSE SLUICE

No wonder the "wives went forth in a flock to wit how they wrought", and what competition and pride among those wives! How foam-white those "borde cloths", how firm and succulent those cold roast chickens, how golden the bread and cheese! One derives so much pleasure from old bridges if one can picture the builders, trace the placing of the old sluices and understand the cunning way abutments have been built out from the banks. If you can see the *way* the work was done, then you may cross the centuries and meet these workers. You may glimpse the flap of a table cloth, see on the flowering elderberry bushes the "thick slices of white bread", and hear the echo of a pick axe, or a stone chat bird on the further bank.

Even today a pickaxe is a "matok" or a "pyckoyes, or a pyke as sume men says", and the names of English tools continue to be as diverse as the English workman.

CONSTRUCTION OF BRIDGE AND FORD. BUILDING UNDER WATER

> "I cannot describe the indignation and sorrow I felt at finding an art of such public utility—so shamefully neglected."
>
> SEMPLE

The whole subject of the bridges, fords and weirs built throughout the land by workmen, often with no guiding surveyor, is worthy of special study. It was not training, but thought and observation that gave the knowledge and skill to perform difficult engineering feats, using the simplest materials.

Anyone watching a river sees how sand, gravel and stones pile up in front of a fallen tree or boulder and how, *behind* the obstruction, the ground is hollowed out by the scooping drag of the waters. These facts the workmen utilized when building weirs or fords. A line of hurdles across the stream, loosely woven to let the water pass, and some bank clearing and rush cutting above, soon floated down enough debris to pile itself up against this barrier, till it collapsed and fell flat, causing the first slight ridge across the river bed. This process was repeated with the continuous help of stones, carried out in boats to consolidate the debris, and it soon raised a considerable underwater barrier. A cut in the middle of this barrier let the

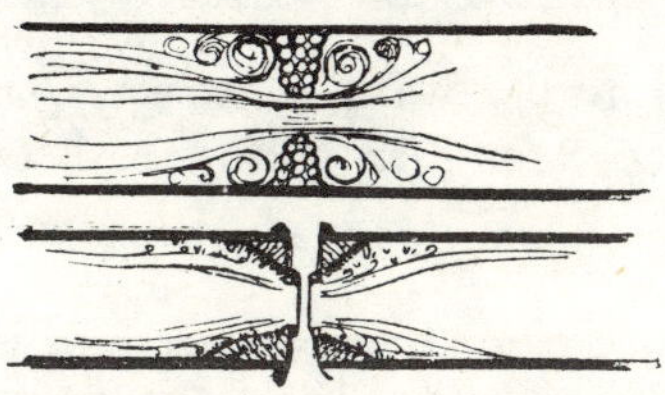

river through, thus deepening the *centre* of the bed, allowing the earth to accumulate at the *sides*. (This principle, that it is the back of the obstruction which requires strengthening, not the front, carries on through all elementary water building, and its effects can be traced by anyone walking along a water course and examining the old structures.)

For creating piers, or joining the water head at the end of a barrier, or the buttress of a weir or water dyke, the hurdle method was adapted in basket form. Large coarse baskets (kreels, kishes, keves or kiddles—the words overlap), woven of the willow growing by the river, were weighted with stones and sunk (from boats) into the position required. The boats then brought out more stones and filled up the anchored baskets to the brim. If a barrier was needed, the kishes were placed close in line and the debris allowed to silt up against them, spaces being left for the stress of the water to pass by. If the water was tidal, the waterproof willow rods held long enough for packings of small stones and gravel and mortar to be poured in during the low-water periods, but even if there was no change in the water level, the continued dumping of stones ultimately caused a block, *against which the river itself continued to build.*

This method, called Kesh work, was in use in Ireland when I was there in the 1920's and seems to have impressed Semple, who writes: "Kesh work is large baskets made of boughs and branches four or five feet square, sunk in rows, by throwing stones promiscuously into them till they grounded, and then filling them up till the water is almost knee deep, whereon they lay timber across, and so begin to build their piers, banking the Keshes all around, with stones and hard stuff." He goes on to say: "Keeve work is the same, but uses tubs (vessels) of red deal boards, hooped with iron and strong oak hoops. Chest work is the same, but using wooden chests twelve or fifteen feet square, and the French call this 'Caisson'."

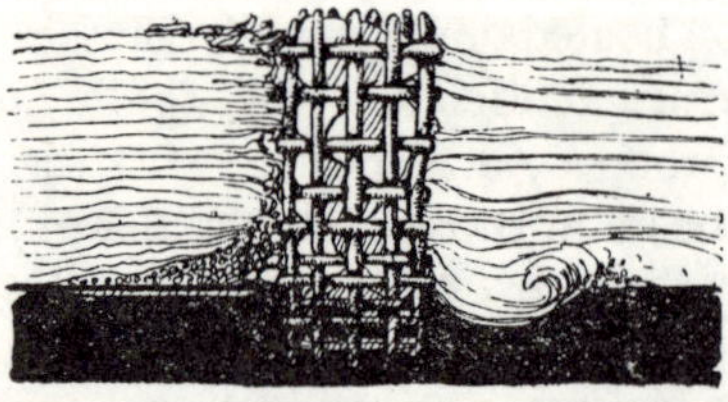

Many wide shallow fords, water causeways, and 'hards' have been built with no more apparatus than willow baskets filled with stones.

He then describes how the chest is sunk into the bed of the river by "drudging" out the floor within the "chest". The older form of this (centuries earlier when hand-sawn logs were prohibitively expensive) was to use the primitive Kesh baskets, sunk closely in circles, and packing and daubing the more closely woven interstices with spagnum, and other materials that would bind and swell, and make the *outer* circle of the Keshes waterproof. Again, working on the principle that it is the stern, not the prow, of a water break that is most vulnerable, the downstream half of the circle of baskets needed reinforcing with packed stone and rock. The circle within the ring of baskets could then be drudged out and filled up with stones and packed gravel, with mortar poured in as the work proceeded.

MORTAR

No one can be absolutely certain as to the "mortar" used in these old foundations, but there is strong opinion that unslaked lime was used, believing the heat would dry out the mortar. Certainly, some of the old mortars and cements are stone hard.

The trick of drying out mortar with quicklime seems to have been used in the thick walls of Edwardian castles. The outer and inner faces of the stone were raised ahead of the rubble that was filled in as the work progressed. Cavities show that the filling was poured in from above. Thus, once the outer wall face was breached, it was comparatively easy to mine through and push out the inner wall. Hence the mediæval strategy for brushing invaders off the walls with swinging tree trunks.

WATER FOR WAYFARERS

> "When they were outside the towns, her fellow travellers took off their clothes, and sitting naked, picked themselves [of lice] but she was ashamed to put off her clothes as her fellows did, and therefore had part of their vermin, and was bitten and stung full evil both day and night."
>
> *Journal of Margery Kemp*, 1436

Many mediæval travellers were lousy, and the straw, dust and crumbs accumulated on an earthen floor were ideal for fleas. Years ago, in an Irish cabin, where the littered earthen floor exactly reproduced mediæval conditions, I felt the springing, stinging, fleas "ping" against my bare ankles in their thousands. Every stirring of the straw released gusts of them, thick as a cloud of mosquitoes, and they massed, like shining brown treacle, in the hollows between the cobbles. The experience was rare, most cabins were clean, and an earth floor can be as smooth as cork lino, but it convinced me that mediæval authors were not exaggerating, and that when they state a place was "dirty and swarming with fleas" it must have been like that. Much depended on management. In wealthy establishments, where the owner kept open accommodation for guests as a matter of custom, his guests would be well attended riders, whose grooms and personal servants would be as clean and polished as their employers (perhaps more so). Even the rougher fellows with the luggage horses would be reasonably clean and trustworthy, and could sleep with their host's own servants in the open hall.

The hall was the charge of the steward of the hall, an important "personne", with servants under him and pages to instruct. It was his business to have the hall kept clean, order the floor rush renewed, the water flagons filled and the livery cupboard well stocked. He had to see the trestle tables taken down and fresh bedding straw issued to the sleepers in the hall (who guarded the door and kept the fire in). Now, though the lord and his guests dined apart on a raised dais at the far end of the hall, and some of the workers at the lower tables were decidedly "below the salt", *yet all of them would be people on the estate, known to each other, and known, at least by sight, to the hall steward.* So it is reasonable that they would have a rough wash and brush up outside after work, and before coming in to dinner. The house party and guests would certainly wash and change before the meal, for it was the social event of the day. During dinner they washed their hands between courses (very necessary when eating with the fingers). One simply turned sideways a little and the page poured from a flagon with one hand, while the other hand held the basin below to catch the water. (This was very difficult! When pages were very young, or the guests very important, one page took the flagon and another managed the basin.) Towels were provided lavishly; mediæval people were fond of well-laundered linen, and a guest at the castle might certainly ask for a hot bath.

TRAVELLERS AT A MONASTERY

"And it is grete curtisye
To give your alms hastylye
Not for to make long delay
To lete a wrecche stonde all day
Crying at thy gate in cold;
He loseth thy almes manifold
And therefore it is well doone
To give thy almes gladly and soone."

Instruction to the brother at the door

The well-found traveller arriving at a wealthy abbey was given much the same cleanliness he would expect in a secular establishment, and in simpler religious houses and hospices the arrangements seem to have been sensible. The diagram (page 72) is the layout I have found most usual.

There would be paddocks with water for the horses (and a lock-up for a too ardent stallion), a spring of running water and a trough for the grooms to wash and, for a consideration, a tub of hot water carried upstairs for the master. In large monasteries and abbeys, there would be a guest room for the noble traveller. "Hospitality for all" might be the rule, but the really dirty ones seem to have been given shelter in buildings outside the walls. For, when you measure the space within, it does not check up with the numbers reported to have been entertained. Also, the usage of removing huts to clean sites suggests this (*see* the note on sanitation, page 223).

It is not feasible to suppose charitable accommodation was entirely indiscriminate. Respectable traders, and occasional scholars and others, would also need hospitality, and this would be impossible for months after bedding had been used overnight by the lousy, infected, or leprous! Such extravagant gestures were the stock-in-trade of popula religious romances, which had as little contact with reality as romances have today.

The brothers were admonished to be courteous to the poor and keep no one waiting, but they were not forbidden suitable authority; and as it was they who had to keep the place clean and wash the blankets, very sensibly they'd insist on some form of delousing before entry.

N.B. The prevalence of fleabane growing wild around their ruined precincts is suggestive.

THE WATERSIDE, OR FERRY HOSTEL

An inn-keeper could not easily refuse entry to anyone able to pay, and even in the comparatively late sixteenth-century Tusser's "Posey for a Guest Room" does not give the casual traveller too good a character. Hostels on busy pilgrimage routes were, on the whole, well run. It was their source of income, and though each shrine was independent, they were to some extent "all under one management"—that is, on a well-known route the pilgrim could carry on from one shrine to the next. But other travellers went to some trouble to land among friends, or where they had heard there was good accommodation. This state of things continued, made somewhat worse after the closing of the already deteriorated monastic accommodation, till the early coaching days turned the small inns and taverns to hotels. Then post houses became important institutions (for the traveller able to pay), but vagabonds lay out under the sky, for the workhouse idea had only just begun.

When exploring remains of such buildings, position and measurements are the only constant. All are on a definite old route between established centres and near, or actually on, a river, and their size is a multiple of six feet. Just as the single cell is usually six feet by twelve feet or fourteen feet, so the larger hostel, allowing for sleepers against each wall, and a gangway down the middle, is usually about fourteen feet wide. The length varies enormously. Many old hostels have become lost, being used as quarry material for later builders. Some have been turned into barns built into farms, some have been taken over in later centuries by civic authorities and become tolbooths or almshouses, or turned into chapels. The new ordnance map of monastic foundations shows many, but hundreds remain unlocated. And any walker would find them interesting.

Water had to be plentiful because of the horse transport, and at least one spring for drinking water. In many cases, as in the cell examples, one spring is included in the building or under cover adjoining it. Where the coast requires it, traces of an old "hard" for landing may be discovered though this was frequently no more than a convenient rock.

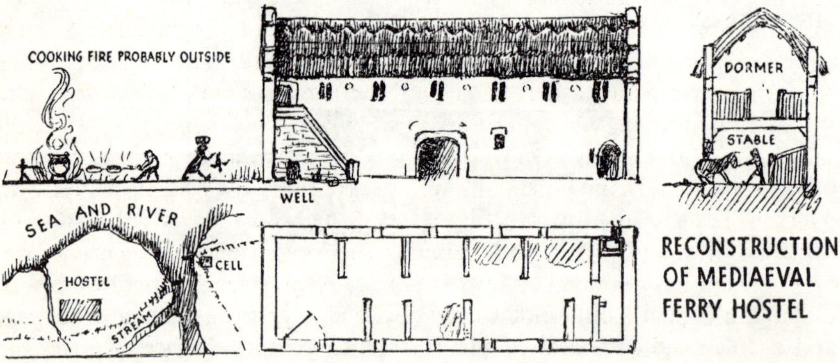

RECONSTRUCTION OF MEDIAEVAL FERRY HOSTEL

The illustration has been reconstructed from many examples, as no two hostels were alike. It is as difficult to average a mediæval hostel, as to average a modern inn.

Sometimes, if the hostel had direct connection with some monastic foundation the architecture is similar, but no religious claims prevented any hostel from becoming an excellent trading post, and centre of useful information on market prices. Hostels may have been good, bad, or indifferent, but MS. drawings usually show them as well built, and usually with a fire going, and something cooking. There would be paddocks for pack horses, and the ground-floor stable could be used for special mares, saddle horses, and grooms. The partitions of wood that turned the open dormitory above into separate sleeping quarters, were movable, and the "end place" (in all those I've examined) had an outdrain for water and traces of a wash place. The custodian usually had a separate room built on the lower floor, and here he doubtless kept the first-aid kit and stores, and collected fees, etc. There would be wooden tubs for washing feet and possibly clothes, and probably a little cultivated ground or even a small field for corn. There would be poultry, dried fish, and bacon and beans against emergency, for bad weather might keep travellers some time at a ferry hostel. Around these hostels still grow wild the standard herbs for man and horse, the horseradish for embrocation, and the comfrey or boneset for broken bones.

AN EXAMPLE OF A FERRY HOSTEL AT BIRKENHEAD

At Birkenhead from A.D. 1150 onwards a small establishment of Benedictine monks *owned* the monopoly of the ferry across the Mersey, and as currents and winds frequently held up travellers they ran a hostel or waiting-house. As with all such places it became a well-known Exchange and Mart, as the priory had storehouses in Liverpool where their own products in grain and wool and other goods could await sale.

Basinwerk Abbey was on the Welsh coast and commanded a busy overland trade route. The value of the ferry and hostel increased for three centuries, and when it passed into government hands after the dissolution, though its value had gone down considerably, it was still worth over £102 a year. On closing down the monks were given 40*s.* a year each, a new secular gown and allowed to take the tools of their trades with them. They remained in the district working, and reports say that many secular tradesmen were glad to employ the "experienced" men.

Tradition has it that they buried the monastic treasures before leaving, and the place, still called "Monksferry", is haunted by their hospitable ghosts.

TRAVELLERS' LAUNDRY

> "In the monastery was a brother named Bodudegn, who served in the guest house. All the brethren and guests testify that he was a very devout and religious man, who did his appointed task solely for the sake of a heavenly reward.
>
> One day he had washed the cloaks used in the guest house by the sea, and as he was returning homewards, he had a sudden seizure and fell to the ground . . . when at last he got up, he found one side

of his body paralysed from head to foot and made his way home with the greatest difficulty leaning on a stick."

(Condensed from Bede's account of the life of St. Cuthbert.)

BEDE, *Book IV*, *Chap.* 31 *Trans. by Sherley Price*

The brother recovered from his stroke by the intercession of St. Cuthbert and, to the great joy of his brethren, was able to return to his work in the guest house. These small sidelights illuminate the domestic life in a monastery much more vividly than the "Full Rule".

We know the "Rule" arranges for the monastic guest service, and that the brother in charge "must be gracious and not keep the poor waiting". Though details of service are left to individual judgment, we know there must have been regular daily sweeping, cleaning and preparing of bedding, and when travellers arrived soaked to the skin some provision must have been made to dry them out. They could hardly drip dry at the supper table, and if expected to attend chapel they could not do so naked.

The monks themselves would each have a change of habit; some orders changed into their second habit for sleeping each night (their arrangements were far more sensible than is usually supposed), but these gowns and habits were their religious uniform, and certainly would not be on loan to all and sundry travellers who arrived soaking wet.

Some contemporary MS. illuminations show armfuls of clothes and drapery being handed out at a convent gate, and though the illuminations are stylized and conventional they do give the impression that spare clothes were available. Indeed, one cannot see how they managed without them!

Facilities for medical attention were part of the regular monastic service to travellers, and must have included washing of clothes; and where any clothes washing is done, arrangements must be made for drying, or in a spell of wet weather the place becomes uninhabitable!

The "warming room" was for the monks' personal use, but it is reasonable to suppose that both warming room and kitchen were used overnight for drying out rain-soaked clothes, and that some form of cloak, or night gown (the equivalent to our dressing-gown or bathrobe) would be on hand.[1]

Another example of dry clothes for wet guests. In polite circles wet guests were assured of dry clothes, as testified by Sir Gawain when wandering through Wales in winter in search of the Green Knight.

[1] Very like the conglomeration of old overcoats and blankets that accumulate in a modern Youth Hostel, which the kindly warden keeps "in case you come in soaked through", or, like the "common denominator", a sort of wrap kept on hand in the casualty ward of a hospital.

"When the cold clear water from the clouds shed and froze ere it fell, he was near slain with the sleet among the naked rocks. They brought him to a bright bower where the bedding was noble, curtins of clene silk, with cler gold hems, covertures full curious, with comely panes of bright white fur, above embroidered sides. Curtins running on ropes on gold rings. Tapis[1] fixed to the walls.... There he was dispoiled of his birnie, rich robes readily the man brought for him to choose and have of the best." (Hope you can find something to fit you among this lot, sir?)

"The vair[2] (fur) and his face verily seemed all of one hue."

COMPARISON OF A MEDIÆVAL ESTABLISHMENT WITH A MODERN OFFICIAL HOSTEL FOR TRAMPS

Substituting the old government Work House for these mediæval establishments, the arrangements for the vagabond thirty years ago approximated very closely. In both monastery and workhouse admission was at nightfall, and the crowd of beggars waiting outside for the doors to open could have come out of any fourteenth-century MS. The porter signed in each one, "Where from?", "Where bound?" and, as most of the tramps could not write, they made their mark X like their predecessors. Both institutions kept tally of numbers. Money had to be handed over for safe keeping and a donation extorted if possible. Then—washing was enforced.

The workhouse wash rooms, soap, and fumigating sheds were an improvement on the mediæval, and all the best workhouses insisted on a thorough washing and inspection. Far from resenting this, the houses where "they don't let no filthy beggars get by" were highly commended by tramps, and a "good house" where you could get hot water, and borrow a clean shirt while you washed your own was popular with the men-on-the-roads. As one of my tramp friends explained: "In some *low* houses they lets them in anyhow, and then the beds soon gets lousy and the place unpopular." On the whole a clean workhouse was preferred to a common lodging house (much as a good mediæval charity was preferred to a bad mediæval inn). "Even if you had the money why spend it, when you can get better for nothing?" Also, the lodging house, or inn, could be "too rowdy to sleep". All this has its exact mediæval counterpart, as also the supply of hot broth and bread, and the compulsory bedtime and rising time.

The cleansing and management of the poor traveller has altered little in its essentials down the centuries. There are good and bad examples in every period, but the warden of the workhouse casual ward, and the

[1] "Tapis"=tapestry used to line stone walls.
[2] Heraldically "vair" is blazoned blanc—argent.

hospitaller of a mediæval Hospice, both dealt with the same human problem, and that was how to get the washing done. I believe they tackled it in very much the same way!

THE ELIZABETHAN LODGER, ACCORDING TO TUSSER, 1571

The sloven and the careless man,
the roughish, nothing nice
To lodge in chamber comely deckt
are seldom suffered twice
With curtains some make scabbard clean,
With coverlid their shoe
All dirt and mire some wallow-bed
as spaniels use to do.

Though boot and spurs be ne'er so foul
what passeth some thereon
What place they foul, what things they tear
by tumbling thereupon
Foul mail, some cast upon on faire board
be carpet ne'er so clean!
What manners, careless master hath,
by knave, his man is seen.

Some make the chimney, chamber pot, till smells
like filthy sink.
Yet who so bold so soon to say 'How these
old houses stink!'
They therefore such as make no force, what
comely things they spill
Must have a cabin like themselves, although against
their will.
But gentleness will gently do
Where gentleness is shew'd
Observing this, with love abide, or else
Hence! all be shrew'd!

TRAVELLER'S WATER ABOUT THE TWENTIETH CENTURY

The necessity of water for the horses throughout the foot and horse travel centuries carried on into the early days of horse power motoring, when engines boiled upon the slightest provocation, and in winter the kitchen kettle of boiling water was required to "start her up". On railways water tanks were carried and filled up during station stops till the "scoop" invention, which drives up refills of water from out of long troughs set between the rails, and enables an express to re-water without stopping. Now restaurant cars and luncheon boxes make the earlier travellers' own water flasks unnecessary. Their neat wickerwork luncheon baskets and the cane-covered tea baskets have reverted to the motor car, where they have become a leather case in which Thermos flasks replace the kettles. But in both stage coach and early railway periods, most travellers carried their own water supplies. They cleaned up with a damp sponge from a neat box in their dressing-case, and carried a towel. Hot water was obtained over spirit stoves incorporated with a kettle and flask.

Small shelf tables let down in the old railway coaches and on these the traveller's basket would be opened, suitable cold refreshments laid out, the small spirit stove set up, and the kettle filled from a water bottle. Or it was carried, filled beforehand, and carefully screwed up, together with another flask of methylated spirit. (No wonder the old emergency cords notices began: "In case of fire" . . . and ended "Penalty for improper use £5".)

A spirit kettle for travellers (*about* 1850)

In hotels and boarding houses, or to take upon the sea front, the picnic basket, with commodious water flask and spirit kettle, was most convenient, nay, quite indispensable, to the traveller.

WATER FOR POST HORSES AND STAGE COACHES, ETC.

The coming of the "post" (it was literally a post at first, you hitched your mount to it, and waited till the next rider met you there) caused water to be "laid on" along the new highways, and since the new "posts" were strictly timed, water had to be ready at the official stopping places. Where horses were "changed" the ostlers had the fresh team ready, the stable boys rushed out and released the old team (who clattered off to their baiting) and the new team was harnessed up within minutes. (We gather that there was barely time for the "inside" and "outside" travellers to liquor up and return to their seats, before they were off again.) Where the coach only stopped to "pick up" or "set down" a groom stood by with a leather bucket and gave the horses as much (or more usually as little) as the driver demanded (and if the horses were overheated this was a very small quantity and slightly warmed). Private carriages usually carried their own leather buckets (well polished, and adorned with a crest if available) and many people did this to guard against infection from a dirty bucket, as the dangers of "infection by water" were being actively explored during the post chaise period.

As a riding horse should be watered some little time before a journey, and allowed to cool off afterwards, the rider usually watered his horse at the water trough in the yard of the inn and took the opportunity to dismount and arrange for his own refreshment at the same time.

When in the stable, riding horses were offered water at least four times a day, but both riding horses and work horses obviously preferred to go to the pond, or to stand at a peaceful accustomed trough where they could take their time over their drinks, so in the days when everyone rode everywhere, rider and mount usually learnt to accommodate each other.

The main development was "clean water available every few miles along a main road and at all post houses and stopping places". It was soft running spring water for choice, as pump water from deep wells was liable to be icy cold and frequently hard, *and the water trough made long enough to take at least two horses simultaneously.*

DROVERS' WATER

In mediæval times the huge droves of cattle that were collected and driven down to the great autumn markets, set watering problems all along the route. When possible, the drovers used riverside routes, and across the hills many streams were banked back to form long drinking troughs. Where water had to be "laid on" for the cattle, wooden ducts and troughs were made, and the droves had to be thinned out into a longer line and "held back" so that they could be watered in lots. Otherwise a stampede of thirsty beasts trampled each other to death. Sometimes the heavy old stone and slate troughs on hill roads show where such a watering place was arranged, but the stone troughs themselves would be too small for the use of large droves and so where these troughs do not serve some ancient farmstead, they probably mark an old posting road or well-used bridle path. Not all stone troughs are for cattle, some are woollen-cleaning troughs, and some of the foul old sheds and derelict buildings by the water courses were once fulling sheds where fleeces could be trodden clean and home woven cloth "footed" in the running water. Drovers' roads are usually well marked, and anyone interested can track down the sorting pens and sometimes the old smithy which made the quantities of thin ox shoes. These were sent up to the pens to shoe the cattle before they left the soft grass pastures, and started off down the long stony roads that led to town, market and slaughter.

The "smithfield" was near the slaughter ground, as there these iron shoes were removed and the iron salvaged for use in the city.

Master drovers were rich and influential people since they collected the sale money and acted as bankers for the farming community. They usually rode on ahead and negotiated with the landowners for passage and water facilities. Sometimes the drover could induce an enlightened agriculturist to let the cattle cross his land for the value of the manure. Sometimes he could arrange an advantageous "short cut" (in the absence of the owner of an estate!) and sometimes there were pitched battles with cattle stealers. The cattle on the western routes suffered so much from depredation by the Welsh princes that an English king, desirous to keep a good supply of beef along the South Wales route to Ireland, arranged for the lord of a southern estate to deliver his peppercorn rent each year direct by a team of eight *white* oxen (the Welsh cattle were all black!).

N.B. Oxen are slow drinkers and to keep in condition require water twice daily. A large drove might be a thousand head of cattle, so this problem of water was a drover's first consideration.

A SHORT NOTE ON RIVER WATER AND FISHING

RIVER RIGHTS

> "St. Dogmael, a Norman knight, founded the Monastery of St. Dogmaels, and the fishery at St. Dogmaels, on the estuary of the Tevi river with the rights of timber for building, the right to erect water mills, and to build wears, wherever they pleased on that part of the river which belonged to them, given by King Henry of England, through the exhortation of Matilda in compassion for the poverty of the Monks of Tyrone residing on land in Wales."
>
> A.D. 1126

The involved rights of miller and fisher have ever been the cause of trouble which probably began long before this date.

A KIDDLE OF FISH

Kiddle—(the early form is Guidel probably from the Norman French GURDEAU)—covered any sort of stake net or current directed trap.

"A pretty kettle of fish" continues to express widespread trouble and confusion, for the original kiddle so depleted a river of all fish that its size and use were the basis of stringent laws and serious punishments. Finally, in some waters, the surveillance was so strict that if *any* kiddle was found the entire district was held to be responsible. This, of course, set one suspect against another, till the whole place was in an uproar.

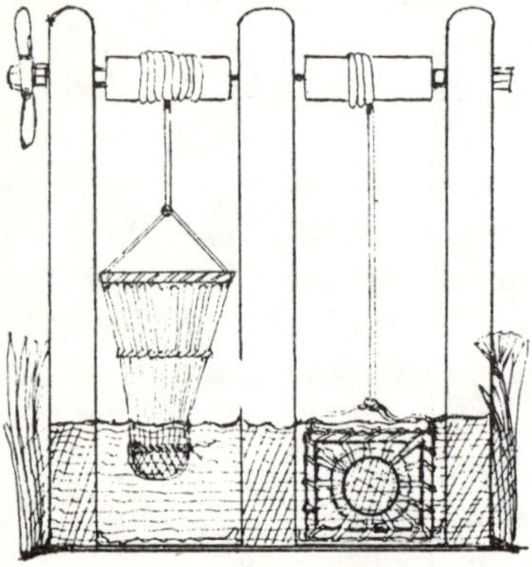

Diagram of double kiddle used for cleaning a fish run

Angling

NETS ON RIVERS

"When Wilfrid had first arrived in the province and found so much misery and famine, he taught the people to obtain food by fishing; for although fish were plentiful in the sea and rivers the people had no knowledge of fishing and caught only eels. So the bishop's men collected eel nets from all sides and cast them into the sea, where, by the aid of God's grace, they quickly caught three hundred fishes of various kinds—by this good turn the bishop won the hearts of all, and the people began to listen more readily to his teaching, hoping to obtain heavenly blessings through the ministry of one to whom they already owed their material benefits."

BEDE, *Translated by Sherley Price*

SPLASH FISHING

"No more dams I'll make for fish."

CALIBAN

Another method was the double dam. For this a dam is raised across a stream, leaving a spout or waterway too high for fish to leap up or a weir too shallow for a fish to swim through.

Having left this dam in place long enough for the disturbance to subside (and perhaps put down ground bait), the fishermen went some distance downstream, and splashing the water with rods or stones, drove all fish upstream till near this first barrier. They then either netted across or built a second light hurdle dam that let the water pass more freely

10. Fourteenth-century water-carriers. Note that the carrier pole is inset direct through the two elongated staves of the tub. A well with capstan, top right.

11. Tottenham pump, near the Swan Inn (note standing Swan sign) and Cross. The local water cart distributed the water to householders.

12. High bare rocks from which pure rain water drains down. Note the rapidly drying rock surface on the right and rapidly sinking water level.

13. Steep hillside. Rushing aerated white water passes swiftly downwards.

14. Water at lower level running slowly enough for insect and animal life to exist in it.

than the first dam. Thus the fish were penned for a time in water that grew shallow enough to make catching easy, and both dams could be demolished and carried downstream *leaving no evidence*!

The same method remained in use as the "splash net". The net was slung from bank to bank, or between two boats, and fish driven up into the hollow of the net, which could then be drawn up and carried away. Both splash net, and double dam, differ from the kiddle or trap, as they depended on *driving* the fish rather than taking them in the run of the water.

WATER MEASURE BY PIG TO RESTRICT THE TRAPPING OF FISH

We have mentioned the legislation over kiddles and the mesh sizes of fish nets, etc. There was also the more difficult matter of restricting the spacing of traps in rivers. It was useless to set a measurement for the net unless the measurement of the river bed was understood. A trap, well within the statute width, if set across the only *deep* channel, or across the special up and down channel of the tide, could still sieve out almost every fish of decent size. So each river had to be legislated for on its own water and the measured position of the trap readjusted as the channel altered, often by the residue and debris occasioned by the net itself. Here are some typical examples of legal ruling adapted for ministration by Local Authority, and carried out on the actual site of the trap. There were complaints of blocking the estuary of a Westmorland river, so it was ruled that a space must be left "wide enough for a sow and piglets to pass". The result was they found the thinnest sow possible, with two miserable runcklings, and squashed them past. So a new ruling was laid down, that the "owner of the sow" (and she a matron with fine pigs) was himself to conduct the lady, and responsible people on both banks were to attend the ceremony, to see there was no undue coercion! In another place, where kiddles had been ordered to be removed, they were as hurriedly replaced, so it was ruled that "12 men of the county, on oath", had to "gather together and see the nets, engines and kiddles *burnt* in their presence".

The variety of rulings over river water measurements are as many as the rivers, or more, for they varied down each reach of the water. In 1177 the King's Assize at Perth ruled that a "swine of 3 years old, and well fed, could not touch either side with head and tail". These measurements are not absurd, when it is realized that the statute-measurement-of-the-realm still varied in each district. Even the Imperial bushel was not established before 1826. Now the sizes of the pigs varied in each district, but *within that district each pig was about the same length*!

WATER WORM (LOB OR MUD)

One hesitates to include the lob, or mud worm, used by fishermen. It inhabits the salted mud of estuaries and is dug for locally. The worm is about four inches long, stretches to twelve inches and is seemingly full of juice. The worm relies upon water, and fishermen rely on the worm, so that quantities are dug and sold. Few fishermen dig their own worm, as regular "procurators of the worm" are more cognisant of its location. As they say "many get worms, but with some men, it's their calling".

RIVER WATER FOR PAPER POWER

With this new (still water-marked) paper, and printing, education was available. Probably the pseudo-religious science foisted upon the labourer which had caused the ridicule of Walter Mapes and others caused the ingrained suspicion retained even today by the agricultural labourer. He retains his medieval mistrust of the scientist; "they *say* it does some good" shows the same caution which enabled the medieval labourer to survive.

A water wheel (seen outside the window) driving a camshaft and trip-hammers in the pulping trough of a paper mill of 1564.

The "water mark" of paper depended upon the wires of the sieve in which the pulp was floated and drained. The fibres (originally of pulped linen) float in the water, but spread out flat as the water drains away. The process can be seen in the spread of fine seaweed as the tide withdraws and leaves it a flattened mat spread out upon the sand.

THE WATER OF THE RIVER MILL

MILLS

"Like a knitter drowsed
Whose fingers ply in skilled unmindfulness
The mill has woven with an absent heed
Since life first ran, and ever so will weave."
Thomas Hardy

To measure water speeds accurately requires mathematical knowledge, but the methods used by the old hoary-handed-sons-of-toil were simple and their calculations interesting.[1]

First they reckoned the speed of the stream by "log" timing, that is a float passing between two points at a measured distance. This was taken "at the fastest", in the middle of the stream. The float itself was first subject to trial, both for size, shape and substance, flat board, stick, cork or ball, etc., each being run separately by various people, and the average time arrived at. This gave the middle surface speed; but the rest of the water ran slower, being held back by rough banks and the stony bed. The varied depth and width of the stream made a lot of difference. This can easily be understood by watching autumn leaves carried downstream. The surface ones, especially in the middle of the current, by-pass the leaves below or near the banks. In practice this difference always had to be computed by experience, but the average was accepted as about a sixth loss of speed between the top middle of the stream and the stream taken as a whole.

So that (I give a farmer's figures) if, on a stream three feet wide and four inches deep, the surface best speed is one hundred feet in twenty seconds, then the whole stream would be three hundred feet in sixty seconds. But allowing one sixth off from the surface speed you get only two hundred and fifty cubic feet of water passing the points each minute. So you can expect about that speed at the spout.

THE WATER WHEEL

The paddle wheel or *undershot* requires a good force of water and is turned by direct pressure. The more usual type of bucket wheel turns more by weight. The problems involved in the height of the water drop, diameter of the wheel and width of the bucket or trough are mathematical and complicated, but anyone can see the problem by passing a glass slowly under a running water tap. Directly under the tap, the problem is

[1] If it was a slowish stream, so you couldn't rightly tell which part was fastest current, you could start a few frogs upstream with a duck after them; reckon they'd soon strike the slackest water for you, or downstream, the fastest! (It's these "home hints" that bring the job to life.)

only how long it takes to fill the glass before it must pass onwards. But down the circumference of the wheel, as it moves down, it also turns over, tilting and spilling part of its weight of water. If the foot of the glass is

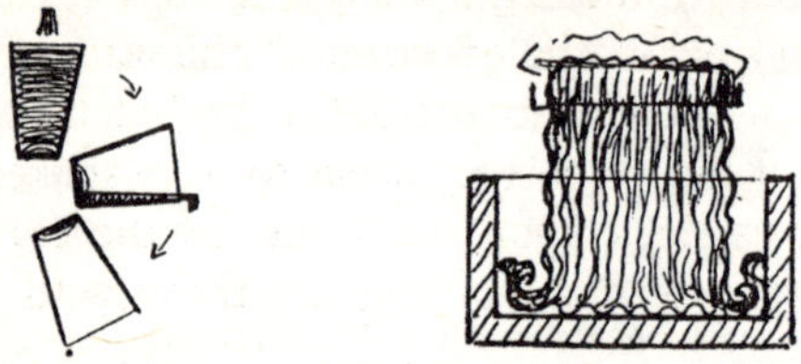

The fall of the water needs space to avoid an air block

turned inwards (as it would be if attached to a wheel), the lowest section of the rim (or on the wheel, the outside edge of the bucket) has the lost water pouring out over it. By raising this outer rim (or edge of the bucket) it will carry the water, unspilt, further down the circle. It must not be raised too high, or it will not have time to empty during the time taken to pass under the lower part of the wheel. Nor must it be able to scoop up any water on its return upwards towards the top. Clearance must be complete. Also, the top bucket must be filled slightly forward of the dead centre of the wheel, so that the turn is not checked, but carries around smoothly. This is another fine adjustment, so that there is far more calculation than people realize in the exact setting of a water wheel.

Water Wheels (Types)

The *breast* wheel was a plain paddle wheel, the weight of water being delivered on to the paddles when in the horizontal position, at right angles with the vertical diameter of the wheel. The power of this wheel depended upon the force of the fall hitting and pressing down the paddles.

Whereas the *undershot* paddle wheel *pushed* the wheel around from below, the *overshot* wheel required a bucket-type of wheel. This overshot wheel might turn in either direction, according to whether the weight of water fell to the front or back of the axle. The complete encasing of the wheel, either in brick or stone channel, or by an iron casting enclosing the

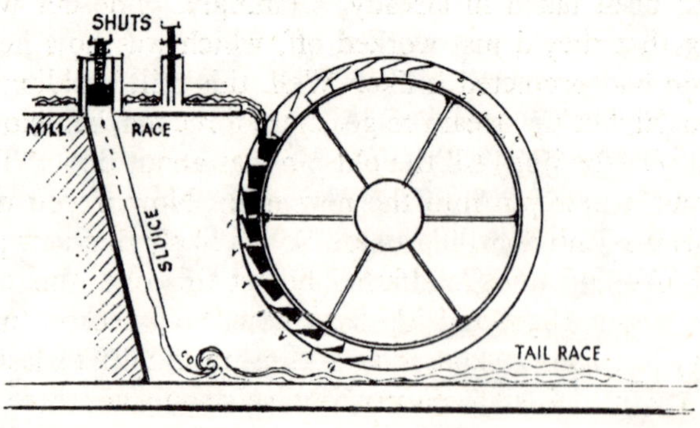

wheel, turned the whole into a type of turbine drive. Usually the mill wheel connected with a long shaft, one end of the shaft being the axle of the wheel, but there was one type that drove on a cog-wheel on the side of its circumference nearest to the mill, where the cogs engaged the driving wheel of the mill rather below the diameter of the water wheel.

The axle bearings of these water wheels needed to be but little longer than the thickness of the mill wall, which they seem to have shaken down frequently, cracking the iron castings upon the stones in the crash. So, generally speaking, the water mills still working are those with a long-shafted, solid *king-pin* axle.

The King-pin of a Water Mill

The king-pin of an old water mill required one entire tree trunk. The nice balance between the thick end outside, which formed the hub of the wheel, and the other end inside, which engaged the grinding gear, was extremely delicate.

The shaft must turn on a level bearing with the minimum of friction, as any overweight outside would cause the inside end to press upwards unduly, against the working gear. This inner end of the shaft wore out more quickly than the wheel end, so an extra length of shaft was allowed for outside, beyond the hub, which could later be *indrawn* into the mill. This extra length also required adjustment of balance. As I had the good fortune to see the last *king-pin* fitted to our local water mill, it is sensible to hand on the millwright's own explanation as it was given to me.

It was a quiet autumn day during the last war. The dismantled wheel hung jacked up and motionless, the old pin lay still, wet and dark in the green grass. On the pond above the *shuts* the mill ducks talked quietly among themselves, and the water slid by smoothly. Two millwrights where hand-shaping the new shaft to fit the old hub ring. I asked how long a *king-pin* lasted? "Well, when my grandfather was a lad he remembered coming to this mill with *his* father, and his father showed him the date 1750 cut on the shaft they drawed out then, and the cut was close in, so the shaft had been taken in already, seemingly. The cut was under the bearing ring that they'd just worked off, which was how he come to notice it, the iron had protected it like. Well, this mill building, she was moved here from higher up stream to get more force maybe. Now, they'd not likely move her (the mill) till the old pin was about done. They'd be most likely to put a new pin into the new mill. Now if you notice the date cut over this *new* mill door, it's 1640. So it's likely that new pin lasted from 1640 to 1740—and my grandfather he set this one, this one we've just drawed out, about 1850, and it's 1943 now. So I reckon (mind you, it's only my say, but I do reckon) that a king-pin ought to last about a hundred years, say, just about a century, but we've only got three centuries to go by yet. Maybe this pin we have just drawn out, she *might* have lasted a bit longer? But with Hitler like he is, we didn't want to delay, it seemed better that we even got a bit beforehand (with fuel going up). For this mill she runs by her own power, direct from the Almighty, as you might say, so—we're resetting this new pin *now*."

A Danside (=*Down side?*)

A wheel used for turning a verticle shaft was called a Danside. It was a spiral wheel, or wheels, enclosed within an inverted cone. The weight of the overshot water falling on the blades rotated the central shaft to which they were attached, the discharge being through the truncated apex of the cone, above the pivot base of the shaft.

The action was steady, but perforce restricted. It seems to have been adapted for use in early mine workings where the vertical shaft could turn a ventilating fan, but more usually for smaller work. It was not often adapted for mills.

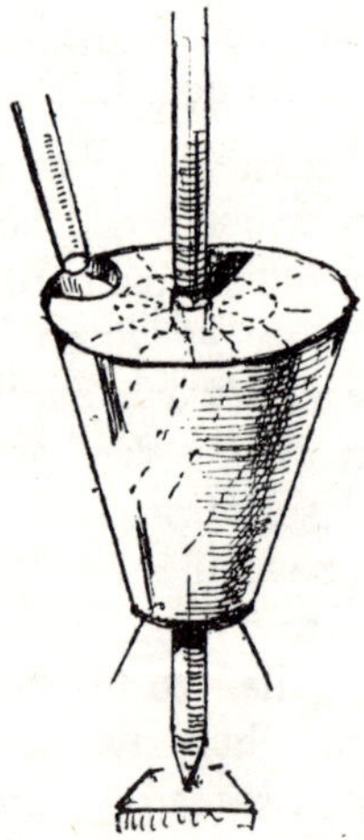

WATER STATIC

FARM PONDS

NATURAL AND ARTIFICIAL PONDS

> "On the night when Henry 1st expired two pools of no small extent, the one natural, the other artificial, suddenly burst their bonds, and, by precipitate course down declivities, emptied. The natural pool, with all its fish and contents, taking a (new) permanent situation in the valley."
>
> GERALDUS CAMBRENSIS

Artificial pools are a natural result of artificial waterways. The damming up of a hill stream would form the mill pond, or mill dam. Such a broken dam seems suggested by the above twelfth-century account. Leland confirms this, and places the pond near Lampeter, but this is controversial. The quotation describes exactly what must have happened fairly often, when an upland lake overflowed beyond the capacity of its artificial outlet and, cascading down the inadequate gully, swept out the dam, and probably the mill itself. The water then spreads out at lower level, mill house and all remaining submerged at the bottom of the new "lake". Presently, being forgotten, or wrapped into a legend, they became one of the underwater villages sunk for crime by witchcraft.

> "There is hardly a roadside pond or pool which has not as much landscape in it as above it."
>
> RUSKIN, *Modern Painters*

The horse pond, now almost obsolete, was near the farm. There the teams drank morning and evening. In dry weather the wooden farm waggons stood in the horse pond to soak and swell up the felloes of the iron bound wheels, shrunken in the heat. In Constable's "Haywain" that stands in the green farm pond, you can see the changed tone of the wood where the wheels have turned in the wet. The dog lies down, the waggoner drowses. One can hear the flies buzz as the horse drops his head to shake them off. But the men in the sunlit field beyond will have to wait another half hour before the waggon creaks across to them again.

In winter, when the ponds iced over, good ploughmen watered their teams by bucket from a trough left overnight in the warm stable. But some horses would have none of such coddling, and obstinately stamped down to the iced pond.

Cattle used field ponds, unless a stream ran through the grazing or a spring or tap was laid on to a trough. River watering of cattle, where banks are high, is not always simple. Also a river watering place must be fenced, for, if the water is shallow, the beasts will cross and wander[1]. One solution is to lay a cement or stone slope making a *hard* into the river. A pleasant summer sight is a herd of placid cattle, standing half asleep through the noonday in the shady shallow of a cool river. On the Mawdach estuary, where the tidal water foams up cool from the sea, the staid cows go splashing and paddling like heifers! If they happen to be on a high bank, when the smell of the tide reaches them, they canter along the bank prospecting for a jumping-down place, and splash in one after another and wade, udders-under, over to the opposite bank where they clamber up and do it all again, higher up, following the fresh of the tide.

CLEANING OUT PONDS

> "Also a welle amedyth [amendeth] the water of lakes and other standyng waters, as it were quyknynge [quickening] them with vertue . . . even a lytle spring makes a great water more holesome."
>
> 14th CEN.

A static pond is not healthy; it encourages flies and the water may become infected, especially where overstocking and trampling turns a shallow field pond into a marsh of green slime. This slime and mud get worse as the beasts move further in to reach drinking depth.

Therefore ponds used to be cleared out by hand labour, digging up the mud and loading it into carts. It was a filthy hard job, and the cattle had to be watered elsewhere for a week. So some years ago, when steam tractor ploughing was done, two engines with a cable between them pulled an eight-disc plough to and fro across the land. A Midland farm engineer adopted this arrangement for pond clearing. He fitted a scoop to the cable, lifted the mud up and drew it away across the field, where it spread a rich top dressing. This deep clearing of ponds unearthed some very interesting history. The puddled clay-over-straw that had been rammed down to form the pond basin was often curiously unbroken but, in the majority of cases, the centre of the pond when cleared, disclosed a well or a spring. This was often protected by a stone slab, and in many cases a regular stone-built "spring head" with a stone trough, showing the ponds had originally been running water. Had evaporation on the larger surface, and trees (which so often grew over the pond) prevented an overflow for centuries? Or had the sheer weight

[1] River water for cattle. "Encroachment made on Mitchley Marsh by cattle fording through old Barge River from Walthamstow Parish, proving a great grievance." A.D. 1781 *April, Vestry of Tottenham.*

of the sunken mud blocked up the welling water? Curiously, many of the ponds, after clearing, discharged such a strong stream that a run-away had to be arranged for future use.

We illustrate one such stone built watering trough that was discovered at the far side of a pond. It had been completely buried under accumulated earth, and the roots of an old pollard willow had clutched the old stones, which came at the end of a deep unsuspected old stone land drain.

WILLOWS AND PONDS

The willows that grew over field ponds and along ditches were necessary in the old days, for every farm provided its own baskets, creels and panniers, used willow spics for thatching, and built its own wattle-and-daub walls.[1] The strippings of the bark also had uses. Ponds and willows are complimentary, one needs the other, both for growth and also for "standing", i.e. weathering for use. Willow rods do not foul the water as hemp retting does, and the cut rods shoved down into the mud of the pond took root easily. Owls were very useful on farms, as they kept down rats and mice and they lived in the hollow tops of the pollard willows.

HEMP PONDS

(September)
"Now pluck up thy hemp and go beat out the seed
And afterwards water it, as ye see need:
But not in the river where cattle should drink
For poisoning them and the people will stink.
Hemp huswifely used, looks cleanly and bright
And selleth itself by its colour so white.
Some useth to water it; some do it not—
Be skilful in doing so—fear it do rot."

TUSSER

[1] "These chaires called Twiggen chairs because they are made of OWSIERIS and WITHEN twigs having round covers over the heads of them, like a CANAPY. These are principally used by sick or infirm people and such women as have bine lately brought to bed."

Henry VIII's navy was sadly short of cordage and rope for shipping. To encourage home manufactures the king discountenanced the importation of certain foreign goods:

> "amongst the which wares one kind of merchandise in great quantity, which is linen cloth of divers sorts made in divers countries beyond the sea, is daily conveyed into this Realm; . . . And also the people of this Realm, as well men as women, which should and might be set on work, by exercise of like policy and craft of spinning, weaving and making of cloth, lies now in idleness to the high displeasure of Almighty God, great diminution of the King's people, and extreme ruin, decay, and impoverishment of this Realm. Therefore, for reformation of these things, the King's most Royal Majesty . . . hath, by the advice and consent of his Lords and Commons in Parliament assembled, ordained and enacted that every person occupying land for tillage, shall for every sixty acres which he hath under the plough, sow one quarter of an acre in flax or hemp."
>
> (24 Henry VIII)

The retting (i.e. soaking or rotting of the hemp to free the fibres) caused the end of many pre-Reformation fish ponds.

A few willows would be grown nearby to supply packing binds (much as they were grown later in the Evesham valley to bind celery bales), and then the pond silted up later and became an osier hope for basket and creel making.

THE LIME POND

The banks that mark an old river meadow are usually unmistakable, but lower, smaller, banks by a stream may mark the site of old lime ponds. Not the small enclosures dug out near an old building, in which the quick lime for plaster, or brick and tile clays, were puddled. Liming ponds were made to take the stinking pelts of slaughtered beasts, and were located some distance away from habitation, down the lower run of the water.

These old lime ponds, or "vats", are now usually drained and dried. Only the raised enclosing bank, about two feet high, and often a slight change in the localized vegetation, show where centuries of intensive liming has altered the condition of the soil.

These small ponds were only for local use, by the castle, or manor, or village that slaughtered its own beasts each autumn. The local lime vat would not take the enormous number of hides that came from the great markets and fairs. Hides to be limed could not be laid too closely together, unless repeatedly changed over or stirred, but from September onwards, as the beasts were killed off, their pelts went into, and were withdrawn from, the lime ponds.

In spring the ponds were cleared of the fallen hair, which was used in the plaster of buildings. This greasy limed hair was also used to stuff harness collars, pad saddles and seats and mattresses, though commercially this last was illegal.

We found traces of such old lime ponds below the ancient castle of Long Buckby (Northants), and by it the small spring of clean water which the workers must have used for themselves, since the lime ponds and slaughter yards and offal pits must have made the working water too foul for use.

The position of the lime pond downstream usually provided the willow bark for tanning the hides, unless oak bark was brought in. The hair still remaining in the plaster of old walls and ceilings sometimes provides a clue as to the ancient breed of cattle in those parts, and their condition at slaughter time.

In some districts any long hair was treasured to weave mats for straining cider and weaving a coarse strong horsehair fabric.

PIT PONDS

Pit ponds are artificial and dangerous. These small, deep ponds are formed where old mine workings have been abandoned, and the open shaft has filled up with flood water and mud. Many old mine shafts are uncharted. The custom was to remove the pit-head gear, lid over the shaft with track timber and, once the grass or bog moss had grown over this, nothing could be seen but a green clearing among the heather or reed. Once the timber rots, the old shaft is open for anything to fall down or, if water filled, to sink in.

In some districts (Cornwall) they protected the open shaft by a low wall just high enough to trip you up and to shoot you down head first. When there is occasion to open old workings it is usual to find quite an accumulation of bones in the dib hole (the hole below the bottom of the shaft).

Quarry ponds form at the base of the worked rock face and also where stone has been quarried underground and caves have formed. After the workings are abandoned and the pumps cease to work, the water rises and forms a pond or ponds within the old workings. Old copper quarries, or where mineral veins are in the rock, are often brilliant clear blue and green, and usually icy cold.

DEW PONDS

These special ponds of the chalk downs are definitely artificial, being floored with straw, clay packing, rammed flints, etc. Their filling is still a matter of controversy, but probably it is condensation, working on the same principle as that of which the psalmist sings "who maketh the hard rock into a standing water and the flint stone into a springing well". Recent research has discovered rings of stone placed around plants and trees in desert lands that collected sufficient condensation water to keep the roots below watered. This study is outside the scope of this simple book on English water, but the filling of dew ponds has always aroused interest, and the craft is ancient.

PEAT PONDS

The peat pond is almost always artificial. Peat cutting rights are ancient and belong to the holding, much as wood rights belong to the manor. Shepherds with their crooks, workers with their weeding hooks, fern-cutters and herdsmen, servants of the estate, or owners of the holding, all had certain rights to fuel from the estate. The peat rights also carried rights of ingress and egress—the width of the peat sledge in a straight line to the nearest highway—similar to the right of egress claimed for minerals. The peat was cut in straight lines on a site

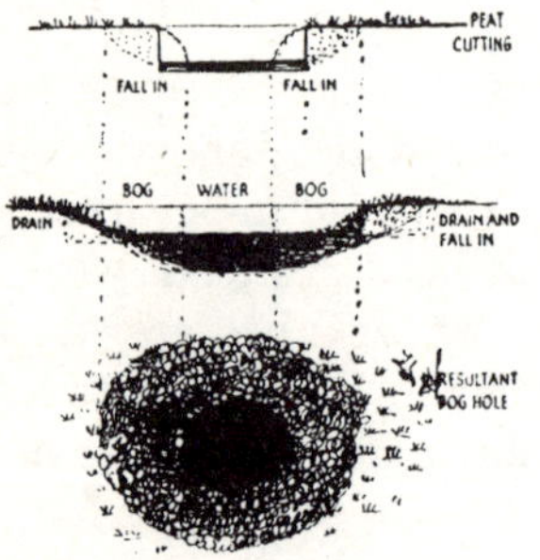

Squared peat cutting, resulting later in round pool

chosen for its drainage facilities. Therefore, once the peat was removed, the pit soon filled with bog water. The sides slid down, and that allowed the peat beyond to drain (*see* diagram). So that there formed a circular, or oblong, pond with a deep central "bog hole" and a wide margin of soft bog. Over the years the slight depression continues to drain the surrounding peat, which moves inwards till the hole is lost, and the round ponds of shallow bog water lie across the moorlands like bronze shields flung down after a battle of the gods.

THE MOAT

Was to all intents a circular pond surrounding a fortified dwelling. When all the refuse of that dwelling drained into the moat, the water must have been as offensive as defensive. Some moats were filled by tidal waters and others were supplied by rivers. In an old mediæval house-book "going boating on the moat" was suggested as pleasant pastime for bored ladies. (With a note that if wild fowl were afoot only really good shots were safe escorts!)

TARNS

These shallow mountain lakes are less ponds than delayed streams. They are filled by small mountain streams and usually discharge in the same way. Even the high circular pools of the "hollow hills", that are extinct crater pools, collect from above and discharge below. They are not usually brackish as are the peat ponds.

MERES, THE LOWLAND LAKES

Most shallow reedy meres, as individual in their different way as mountain tarns, are gradually being drained and the rich soil cultivated. A few new meres are formed by subsidence over mine workings, but their vegetation is completely different. In the Shropshire meres a curious effect happens in late summer. They "break" (the local term) and the clear water becomes thick and green with submerged vegetation. In Colemere, where there are underwater springs causing eddies, this loose green vegetation used to roll about in balls sometimes two feet in diameter. They could be seen from a boat, or caught in a net and lifted out. According to an old account, these balls were of two sorts: one of green moss, and the other, more firm and brown, being full of the pine needles from the trees on the south side of the lake. In the old days these meres used to be dredged and cleared, but now the "balls" are less noticeable. Old folk of the district remember where there used to be thousands of the balls, very visible, as they rolled along the clear bottom of the water, and parties went out in boats in August to watch the strange phenomena.

The damp land around the meres is still known locally as "the marshes" and the district has wonderful water plants. There used to be famous gardens of rare plants in the district before the old estates ceased to exist.

FRESH-WATER PONDS FOR FISH

> "A Ponde . . . is water gaderyd to fedynge of itself . . . the goodness of a ponde nedyth sadness of ground also it needeth the clennesse of water whyche rennyth thereto and contynuelly vennting and comyng.
>
> For, where as the grounde is fenny and myre, there well savouryd fysses maye not be nouryssed."
>
> BART. ANGLICUS

Mud fish could be kept in a still pond, but fresh-water fish from rivers needed some fresh water "contynually vennting and comyng". The ancient drains of many fish ponds have become blocked, but traces of them, or of conduits from a river or spring can usually be traced, though it might have been only a wooden sluice or aqueduct now completely perished. The monk's fish pond is accepted as part of any monastic establishment, but what is not so well realized is the general use of stored fish throughout mediæval times, and up to the end of the seventeenth century. To some extent the winter shortage of meat was responsible and, to some extent, religious restriction. But the main reason was not the shortage, but the abundance of fresh water fish throughout England.

The feuds between estates over fishing river rights, wars between millers and householders on the same estates, and the variety of fish traps, kiddles and river nets used, was only surpassed by the variety of the laws for and against their usage.

In some districts the flooding of water meadows complicated the issue, but in spite of all this there remained enough fish to stock hundreds of fish ponds. The general usage was to set fish traps and, after sorting the catch, convey the fish in open water casks to the establishment's pond, which was seldom far distant from the river road. Fish will survive in comparatively small water casks if the water is kept well aerated, and the splashing and shaking of pony transport over rough paths would ensure this. Fish breeding was carried out by a few individuals more for interest than to supply any large community with food.

The fish pond proper would be arranged with running water through it. (A castle moat was frequently too stagnant to provide any but mud fish and water rats.) Eels were, however, much enjoyed in mediæval days and when kept in clean water and fattened up were a better fish than the unfortunates that today squirm in tanks in the East End of London. The "Knight of the Tour" tells of a certain husband who had such a specially fed eel just about ready for table. Indeed, he had ridden off to fetch his friend to come over and share the treat, but while he was away his wife and her gossip decided they'd eat that eel, and made a pie of him. All might have passed off well, only, unfortunately, they had given the tame raven some of the savoury crust. And so, when the wife explained the absence of the eel by affirming "an otter hath eaten hym", the raven catching the word, hopped up and down croaking "Eel pie, eel pie!" This gave the show away and there "was a grete beating of the wyfe for the eating of the eel". Poor guilty raven—every time the smitten wife passed the wretched bird she would beat and pluck it and make the feathers fly, till the poor bird was quite bald! So ever after, if that raven saw a bald man, he would hop up to him and croak sadly, "Didst thou speke of an eel. Didst thou too speke of an eel?"

The family fish pond continued through the Middle Ages, but the great revival came in the years of Izaak Walton. It was the period of the private country house and the new fish pond was a serious architectural consideration. There are volumes of instruction for the owner of an estate on *The Situation and Making of Ponds*, or *The Proportions of Ponds*, or the *Conveying of Water into Ponds*, or *Renewing Olde Ponds* and *How a Thrifty Householder ought to have his Breeding Ponds*, and the *Advantages of Ponds* and how often they must be filled and stocked. There are separate volumes on the *Fish that Come to Ponds* and *Certain Opinions on the Voluntary Breeding of Pikes in Ponds*, and the *Instruments pertayning to Ponds*, etc. The seventeenth-century gentleman was apt to do things thoroughly and he went very deeply into his ponds![1]

THE VILLAGE FISH POND

Most records show communal village ponds, or parish ponds, run on the same lines as the private or monastic fish ponds, especially in Midland districts where transport of sea fish was almost impossible, and where local landowners had made local river fishing difficult.

These ponds were usually below the village, and being enriched by the domestic refuse the coarse fish therein did well. These ponds were usually small and three or four set close together—the fish being transferred from one to another for breeding and fattening up (as in fish hatcheries today). Some escaped destruction and the survival of the fittest thinned the numbers but increased the size of the inhabitants. A graphic description by a Northamptonshire villager in the 1880's was "when they did drain her there was carp as big as pig!"

THE GARDEN POND

Popular from the sixteenth century onwards—was an adapted or artificial lake replenished from the fountain. It served for bathing and feasting, and if large enough for small boats quite elaborate masques were held on it—with special music and lighting.

THE DECOY POND

Between the sixteenth and eighteenth centuries ducks and water fowl of many kinds were also bred in enclosed ponds. They were caught in decoys, and this description of an enclosed duck pond sounds like such a decoy adapted for use. "If you would preserve wild duck you must wall in a piece of ground in which there is a little pond or spring and cover the

[1] One wonders if the ancient tradition of having captive fish always on hand accounts for the ubiquitous modern fish-and-chip-shop-van?

These vans are now an English institution. They follow a regular course through our villages with their ice-stored fish and tanks of boiling oil. Exception being taken to the urban noise of its motor horn, our local fish van considerately changed his call to hooting like an owl. Now our owls are beginning to hoot like the fish-and-chip-shop-van. Where will this end?

top of it over with a strong net. The pond must be set with tufts of Oisiers and there must be secrete holes and cracks for the wild (water) fowl to make their delight and feed though imprisoned." The seventeenth-century note also described the setting of ducks' eggs under a competent and experienced hen.

WELLS

"Wells cometh of great waters and much-deal of the sea,
Through veins all under the earth, that to the sea wending be,
For there be as it were veins under the earth—many a one
That leadeth out of the sea—and anon springeth a well therefrom."

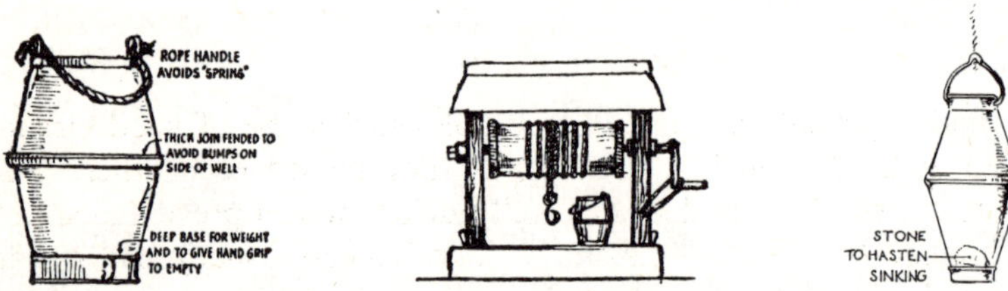

1 2 3

1. Typical well bucket. Shape: narrow and deep, with ridge join reinforced to fend off bumping against sides of brickwork. It has a deep base ring, easy to grip when emptying the bucket, and very usually a rope handle as it would be less likely to jerk and swing than a still metal one.

2. Simple essentials of a single-bucket well head. The loop at the side is to tether the handle when wound up, otherwise the weight of the bucket would unwind again as soon as the handle was released.

3. A "feather": a specially shaped bucket that did not damage the well's brickwork. ("A well, owned by one man, might be used by another *only if he put a feather down it.*")

The raising of water in districts dependent upon wells has developed so many arrangements that we can only study the most general and domestic of these.

The continental well-head with its long counter-weighted pole that is shown in so many landscapes by European artists, has never been common in England. We used the miner's windlass, usually the double winder that lowers the empty bucket down to the water while winding the full bucket up. This is the windlass that went to the New World and the cotton plantations. Uncle Remus tells the little English boy the delightful story of Brer Rabbit, who, having inadvertently gone *down* in the empty bucket, bamboozles Brer Fox to join him in the second bucket—"of course his weight drawed Brer Rabbit up and as he passed he sings out:

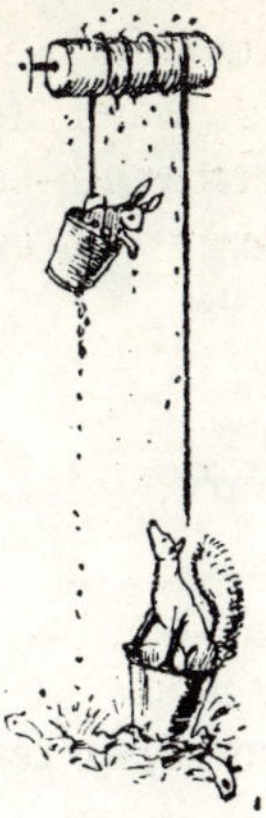

'Goodbye Brer Fox! Take care of your clothes!
For this is the way the world goes!
Some goes up while some goes down,
You'll get to the bottom all safe and soun'."

The winder (usually a rounded tree bole) had to be of good circumference to avoid the buckets clashing as they passed each other. This necessitated a wide well and special well buckets which prevented splashing were made by the local tinsmith. The buckets usually had a stone inside to make them sink into the water and not float on it.

When wells were deep, or the land too difficult for a wide well, a single bucket and narrow windlass was fitted over the narrow shaft. Many of these wells were later enclosed and fitted with pumps.

The pumps were very varied. The simplest shows an adaptation of the ship's bilge pump.

An ordinary "carried water" wash place, that could be set by an ancient well or used today.

A wooden bench holds large and small earthenware and wooden tubs, buckets to bring the clean water, and a drain or sink hole to pour it away after use.

THE WOODEN WATER BUCKET AND SPECIAL ROPE

The Bone of Discord, Apple of the War,
A brand new bucket, made of fatal Fir.
Low was the water, and the well profound,
The Pully dry, and broke, went hobling round,
Th' unlucky Hemp, Knotting, increased delay
And all their Hopes, hung dangling in Midway.
Some with still sighs the buckets absence mourn,
Other, impatient, curse its slow return.
At length it weeping comes, as if it knew
The Sanguinary work that was t' ensure.

Translation from the Italian (1248) *by Ozell,*
London, 1715

This imported poem is quoted for it so well describes the exasperation of "unlucky rope". Wet stiffens rope, and a well rope requires great pliancy and softness. A rope breaking under tension springs back into knots; a rope elastic, sways and bobs about. The selection of a good serviceable rope was most important and the rope should be kept uniformly damp. Alternate drying and wetting rots some ropes, as it does some timber. Wire ropes can be so springy and resilient that they will bounce all the water out of the bucket on the way up!

DIGGING A SIMPLE WELL

"Now Pat, who had never been put to a trade
But laboured away with a pick and a spade,
Got a job to perform which was no simple matter,
T'was to dig out a well, till he met with the watter."

JAMES THOMPSON, 1824

In country places shallow wells are sunk by hand, and the method probably has not changed in a thousand years. Compared with mechanical boring, the operation is peaceful and simple.

I was fortunate enough to watch a well being sunk through chalk in a Hampshire "bottom" in the 1900's, so this report is first-hand observation. No water diviner was required, the two workmen decided they "knew whereabouts to sink her".

They turned up on a Monday afternoon with two shovels, two buckets, one pick, and a piece of string. After courtesy greetings they walked to the place. One pushed a piece of stick into the ground, tied the string to it and scratched a circle. Then both brooded a bit. Then one laid a

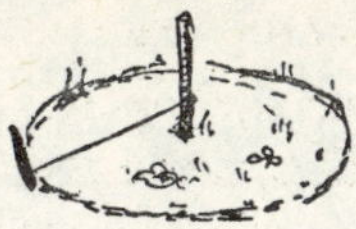

shovel across the circle and said "Hum?" The other slowly wound up the string, stowed it in his pocket and said, "She'll do." After this conversational outburst they proceeded in methodical silence and complete accord. Both got inside the circle and dug it out. They chucked the soil some distance away down hill. Both worked in the hole till it was so deep they crowded each other and could not lift the spadefuls to the surface. Then one man climbed out and the other carried on, while the top man thoughtfully tied the string to the bucket, and lowered it down for the bottom man to fill. After that they took turns; the top man taking away the full bucket, and lowering the empty one; the man in the well just dug. After a couple of days they brought a bit of rope to take the bucket, and the bottom man used the string to guide her away from the sides as she went up.

At first they climbed out—like chimney climbing—"walking up" and rolling out at the top—next day they brought a ladder.

Once, on the way down, they struck a soft place in the chalk and fetched a "brickie" to "brick her up thereabouts", and "let her set" before they went on below.

Soon "she began to fill" and after that it was a wet mucky job. They worked on till waist deep and then took time off while she cleared and "found her level".

They then cleared her out deeper and brickie was fetched back to build the coping, and a carpenter to fit a wooden cover and simple windlass. The rope, and specially shaped well bucket, were purchased and tied on and that was all. They said she should be used *through* the following winter, and cleared again next spring when "she'd have unbed herself loose and deeper", and they could use the windlass to lift the gravel that by then would be in her.

When I left the well was still in use, and should by these repeated clearings in a few years have become considerably deeper.[1]

MOUSE-WELL HILL

The water of this well once belonged to the dairy of a nunnery. It was a considerable resort of old, as a place of pilgrimage, its being "fabulouslie reported of a cure performed upon a King of Scots".

THE DEEP WELL AND THE WORKMAN

"Now should you have to uncover a well do not rush headlong into your grave by descending into a space filled with carbonic acid gas,

[1] There was not, to my knowledge, any Government Permit or Benefit of Water Board.

which cannot be seen, but will smother the strongest animal in the world. Always lower a lighted candle before you descend into any well—if the candle will burn, you are safe—if not, do not upon any consideration venture down till this deadly enemy is driven out. . . . Which is done by lowering anything to cause heat, so as to rarefy the air, or by blowing air from a blowing machine or by the use of hot water, a blacksmith's forge, or blow down pipes, which must reach down nearly to the water.

Sometimes the rising mains are made use of for pumping down fresh air" (i.e. using the pump pipes themselves as tubes).

In contrast to these simple examples of well digging, we give the sinking of a mine shaft, which had to be dug *under water* at Culross—date 1618.

". . . At low water the sea being ebb away, and a great part of the sand bare, upon this sand, mixed with rockes and cragges, did the master of this great worke build a rounde circular frame of stone, very thick and strong and joined together with glutinous and bitumous matter (*see* "Kesh work", page 68), so high withall, that the sea at the highest flood, or greatest storme, can neither dissolve the stones so well compacted, nor yet overflow the height of it.

"Within this round frame, he did set workmen to digge, with mattockes, pickaxe, and other instruments. They did dig 40 ft. downe, right through a rocke.

"At last they found that which they had expected, which was sea cole . . . (within 29 years, they had digged more than an English mile under the water, so that while men work below, the greatest ships of Britain may sail over their heads).

"The mine is cut (i.e. the gallery) so that a man may walke upright in most places. The travellers (Hume and Brown) report that at certain places the sea dothe leake in, and this water is all convayed to one *well* near the land, where the Engineer Sir George Bruce, hath a device like a horse mill, with 3 horses, and a great drain of iron, going downwards with 36 buckets fastned to the chain, of which 18 buckets goe downe still to be filled and 18 ascend up to be emptied, and do emptie themselves (without any mans labour) into a trough that conveyes the water into the sea again."

This 3 horse power chain pump would also act as a ventilating shaft (*see* 'Pumps', page 141). "The Mine did besides did make every week 99 to 100 tunnes of Salt."

WATER HELD AND CARRIED

THE WATER BUTT

Butts depend upon the local industries. Where tar barrels are discarded they are burnt out and used. Oil drums are used in other localities, and herring barrels, or clay tubs, or any sort of water-holding barrel will serve as a butt once it is cleaned out.

The barrel is mounted on bricks to prevent the base from rotting, and a cover with a hole to take the down spout is made to fit and it becomes a water butt.

All water butts should be covered to prevent accidents. A curious theory that *one* magpie living alone always drowned himself in the water butt arose from the indisputable fact that these birds are frequently found floating dead on the still water of the butt.

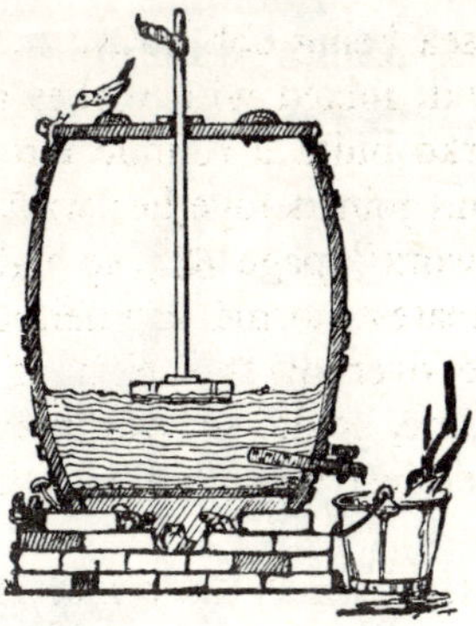

The long ash pole and wooden base of the churn plunger made a float indicator.

The best butts have taps below to draw off the water, but it's usually dipped up. (Illustration.)

Probably the bird saw his own reflection as he bent down to drink. The magpie's long tail tilts up as he peers down and the rim of the butt *is* narrow, and once in, he cannot rise to fly. Hedgehogs too have been known to run up and over the rim (they suffer badly from thirst in dry weather which reduces the number of juicy slugs and snails, their natural food), so all water butts should be kept closely covered.

The biggest water butt I ever knew belonged to some French nuns exiled in the West Yorkshire hills. Town water was laid on, but the laundry sisters sighed and "Mon Dieu'd!" for the soft water brooks of France. "The linen, the guimps! they perish!"

So (perhaps remembering their vineyards) the Mother Superior supplication made to the head of the large local brewery for "a cask of great size—but empty". With good humour, the jolly brewer sent them a gigantic old twenty-foot tunn. It took two men and a four-horse dray to convey it to the convent yard, where, amid much laughter, it was mounted upon a brick plinth and left looming high above the nuns' heads, omnipotent and vast.

The laundry sisters attended, ecstatic, and voluble, but . . . "The dear Saints!" "See, it was up-ended, it was superb, but, alas, it had not been scrubbed!" . . . Impasse. . . . And the dray-men had gone beyond recall!

After fearful agitation, old Grimes, the stolid Yorkshire gardener and general factotum to the convent, rose to the occasion; he would, he volunteered ("Ah! the brave one"), fetch a ladder and scrub inside it for them!

I can see him mount now and hear the awful clump of his clogs as he landed heavily within. Then was he the child of many prayers! "His safety—the brave one!" "Ah, hear him!" The little nuns clustered around like bees, while we heard, from within, the hollow thumping of his clogs as he scraped inside . . . Anon, his voice (de profundis), desiring "moar soappe" or "another paail o' watter".

Finally, little Sister Bernadette, holding anxious communication through the bung hole, announced "all clear". Grimes, restored, as they said, "like Jonah, from inside the whale", was hustled off to the kitchen door for a hot drink; the noble butt was fitted with a stop tap; and an ingenious water gauge was made, from the long handle of an old plunge churn, which rose upright through a hole in the cover after rain, and sank deeply after a heavy laundry day.

Luckily, there was always plenty of rain water in that wet northern climate, and the sisters' water butt continued a land-mark and an inspiration through generations of starched white laundry.

THE CISTERN

The cistern, tank and water butt all have their uses. The lead cisterns in the gardens of old houses were used to store rain water from the roof. Often the large squared "heads" that took the water from the gullies matched the same design of family coat of arms and date, the same plumber having made them all, under the eye of the same architect. Lead has curious expansion and contraction temperatures, so that it does not hold a very sharp casting impress, but it is very workable, and the raised designs are quite as much braces for the strengthening of the tank, as ornament. If you look at old lead cisterns you will see the thickened rims and braced corners, and "ties" of pattern across a flat expanse (where the water pressure might cause a bulge in the soft metal). The green deposit that soon formed on the inside of the tank was protective against the action of the water, though, as they were chiefly used for rain water, there would be little danger from mineral effects. A great many old lead tanks were melted down to recover the silver, as early lead had much in it.

The Underground Tank

These were probably more used in early centuries. Some of the unaccountable small cellars in old ruins may have been stores for ice or water, but there are few now listed as tanks earlier than 1700—when the brick-built tank seems to have been very common.

We had such a tank under our old house, of even earlier date. It filled from the roofs, and a few land drains also ran into it. The floor and walls were of close-set brick, the cover a slab of stone. The depth was eight feet and it was about ten feet square. It was like a small underground room, which makes me suspicious of some secret cellars which have been discovered around old buildings.

Our tank, with its later pump, was in a yard between the kitchen and the meat larder. This tall brick larder of 1700 had strong pulleys to the ventilated roof, iron hooks, and stone wall slabs, so it was probably used as a slaughter house for the spring lamb and the family pig, as well as to store the game.

Our underground tank was full of rain water all the year round, and in its dark depths swam bleached frogs, with blue lidded eyes. The wooden beams, that supported the slab cover, were already showing signs of decay, so by now the slab has probably fallen in, the pump perished, and another "underground passage" or "priest hole" may evolve.

A similar tank was discovered by a local resident who was correcting the slope of his new doorsteps. The bottom step fell inwards suddenly and crashed down into a brick cavity full of ancient bones. Research proved the house to have been an old butcher's shop. The butcher preferred water butts, so he used the old underground tank as a "bone bin". The house being on a sloping site, the tank had probably begun to leak. It was "bone dry" when discovered.

Here are builders' instructions for making brick or stone soft-water cisterns or tanks:

> "Build the outer wall of wet brick using soft mortar (for if the porous bricks were used dry, they might crack or stir when they became soaked). The inside wall should be set with a quick-lime mortar, so that the heat engendered will cement both together. If the cistern is to be stone-built the expanding quality of the dry brick dust seems to have been utilized, as the builder recommends a fourth part of dried powdered tile or brick dust mixed in with the mortar. The heat engendered by the lime might work differently on some stones and crack them. Dry quick lime shatters slate as soon as the slate becomes wet. The building of a waterproof cistern, capable of containing a considerable weight of water, was a very skilled job. Probably that was why so many large lead cisterns remained in use so long."
>
> *Old Builder's Journal, about* 1780

CISTERNS

> "Many things doth infect and putryfye and corrupteth the ayre, as the influence of sondry steues, standying waters, stynkyng mystes and marshes—and moch people in a smal rome lying unclenly, and beyng fylthe and sluthysse."
>
> A. BOORDE, 1400

London Water Cisterns of 1830

> "The Metropolis is at present divided amongst two large water companies, who are practically irresponsible for the quantity and quality of the water they supply. In 1830 it was stated to Parliament that the Capital invested for the supply of the Metropolis was

£3,310,342. Since that period extensive additions have been made to this capital, and still part of the dwellings of the poorer classes are either altogether without water or furnished with a very scanty supply, and 70,000 houses without any water whatever!

Suggestions are made for providing cisterns that could be filled from pumps, but 'The actual cost for butts, tanks and cisterns is estimated at two millions of money, and these receptacles are unnecessary, and pernicious'."

This followed the suggestion that until water could be laid on a supply of clean water might be delivered daily. But the cost of supplying each house with a receptacle was less prohibitive than the means of ensuring that the tenants would keep that receptacle for its clean purpose only. If used as the family piss-pot overnight it would be useless to fill it with drinking water next morning.

Report; on Town Water Bill by LORD LINCOLN

London Water Cisterns of 1866

"A paper on pure Water by Mr. E. Lancaster, extracted from a contemporary, which contains much information for the million, especially valuable just now, when great complaints are being made through the public press that our hospitals for fever patients are not what they ought to be as to accommodation and extent. How much water is a necessity of life, and therefore a preventive of disease, is beginning to be better understood now-a-days, and few know what a filthy supply of water is in the Metropolis better than that section of its inhabitants who have come up from some of our provincial towns, where attention has been paid to this great sanitary agent . . .

In this country few great cities and towns are worse supplied with water than is the greatest of them all, and this nearly every householder and working man in London is aware of. We have a double house in our mind's eye, in which there reside nine families, and where there are two shops—one a low-class butcher's—to which there is but one cistern, whose contents are under thirty gallons, and which from its defective condition is full seldom oftener than once a week. True, there is an underground cistern, which is in the cellar where the butcher keeps his bones and vile scrapings; that cistern has not been cleansed for thirty years, and yet six families draw their water supply from it, and the pump by which the water is drawn to the first floor is fastened up to the side of the only water closet on the premises. Our readers will not be surprised to hear that typhus held a levy here. . . .

And yet, this is London, the boast of the Empire, where typhus fever is claiming his victims in the month of January! This filthy water accommodation is sufficient to poison the best water supply in the world (which London has not by any means got). And this leaves us to observe that it is high time attention were paid to the fact that our water supply is growing less, whilst the population is growing larger. The main drainage, and other works, have dried up many wells, and so disturbed the water-bearing strata, as to have very much interfered with those which continue to yield a supply. The natural drainage falling into the Thames is also growing smaller, and if sewage should be utilized by being spread over the uplands, and lands which drain into the sources whence we draw our water in bulk, why, then, the sooner we think of going farther-a-field for the sparkling fluid, the better for all abstainers from ardent liquors. . . ."

Cisterns (*town water supplies*)

An outcry in Liverpool 1845 brought defensive praise of cisterns for water supply.

"If an elevated cistern be provided, a branch pipe from this cistern into each cottage will give an unceasing supply. In Kent Place (in Liverpool) are 54 houses each having a pipe from a capacious cistern, and the tenants enjoy the comfort of water always laid on."

The "Water Rate" was also commended. "A gentleman occupying a large House, remonstrated at the high charge upon him for water, having only a sister and two servants there. It was explained to him that thus he contributed to the supply of the lowly cottager, for, in effect a poor washerwoman, to whom a great quantity of water is requisite to obtain her livelihood, gets all she requires for three halfpence or twopence a week. While a House of Respectability would be charged more for such a quantity."

Water in cities, 1845

"Liverpool is supplied by 2 public companies, each having by Act of Parliament monopoly of supply. The Bootle Water Co. have their supplies from springs at Bootle, distant from the exchange 3 miles, and the Liverpool and Harrington Water Co. who have wells in various parts of the town. The original £100 shares in the Bootle Co., are now £380 and the Liverpool Harrington shares worth £610. The charge for supplying water for domestic use is 1*s*. in the £ rental. *And the water is usually supplied every other day.*

We have not in Liverpool a single public fountain, very few troughs for watering cattle. No stand pipes for cleaning foot walks, nor any reservoir for washing out public sewers."

Pamphlet by H. BANNER, 1845
(hotly disputed by the Companies concerned).

LEATHER

The Bouget, a leather water bag, is an heraldic device. It is common usage to sew the hides of animals into containers—such leather wineskins and water-skins are used all around the world. (Centuries ago, in Assyrian bas reliefs, they were shown inflated and used as swimming rafts.)

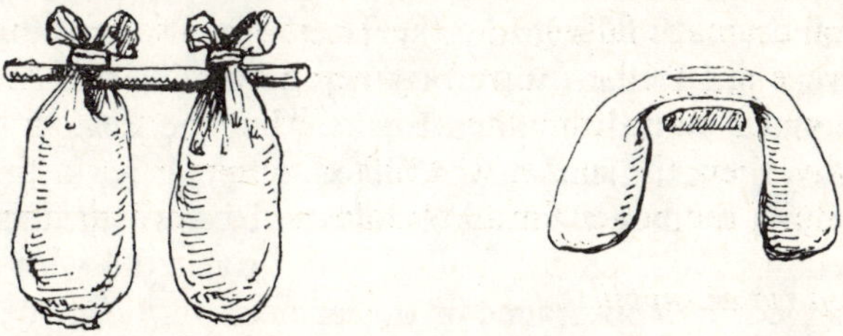

Water Bouget, a charge in heraldry, is conventionalised from the leather water bags (still used in many countries); in some designs it seems to be two bags slung from the cowstal (or shoulder pole) between two carriers; in other designs, the skin seems to have made one large bag slung like a bolster-shaped saddle bag.

Leather was standard usage for bags, pipes and containers of all variety —and the flabby leather bag was soon stiffened and adapted to convenient staple forms.

England specialized in the tall "leather botel", the "Jack Pot", the hoggin (a barrel-shaped bottle much used by the shepherd and field worker), and the bucket, leather stoupe and other shapes. Their flexibility was due to their leather texture, their stability to their construction.

The earliest forms depended only upon stitching construction; later, copper rivets were used and the leather itself was shrunk and hardened with boiling water and hot wax to form completely rigid bottles and jugs,

WATER CARRIERS

"A boket hyght Litula, for it accordeth to those that ben a thurste to drynke thereof. *Lithrasis is a bagge* or purse in the whiche wayfarynge menne carye bread and other trynges that theym nedethe in the way.

A Baskette (willow) hyght sporta, by cause therein is bredde corn and other thinges which nedeith to household . . . afte it is made of Roddes. (The willows used for basket-work are still classified as "Rods").

A Bacen hyghte Pelius and hath that name of Pellis the Skynne for in it is afte washe the skynne of fote and honde (and was made of leather).

Lebris is a vessel of Brasse to seethe fleshe in, and taketh blaknes of often brennynge and unclennesse and nedethe therefore oft scouringe and wypying.[1]

Cadus is a barrelle (cask).

Labathus is a baskette made of splyntes to beare fyshe therein. (Lath or splitwood is still used for fish boxes.)"

BART. ANGLICUS

[1] "No scouring for pride
Leave kettle whole side."—TUSSER

and the leather was sufficiently stiff to take silver mounts and rims. This craft of the leather "flagoner" is as old as leather itself, and it derived much from the "cuier boullier" of which much of the mediæval armour was made. This "boiled leather" armour could be worked, embossed and moulded in rich designs, and before firearms came into use was considered less handsome but better protection than plate armour, since it was resilient to the blows which dented metal armour and missiles tended to bounce back off a leather surface.

The Germans and Italians were better at decorating this boiled leather work than the mechanically-minded English, but the English flagons and drinking cups were excellently constructed.

It is interesting to note that a glossy slab of brown mediæval gingerbread studded with gilt clove "nails" and "rivetted" with round gilt box leaves, copied the appearance of this armour very exactly, and made it a very correct and knightly gift to a fair lady.

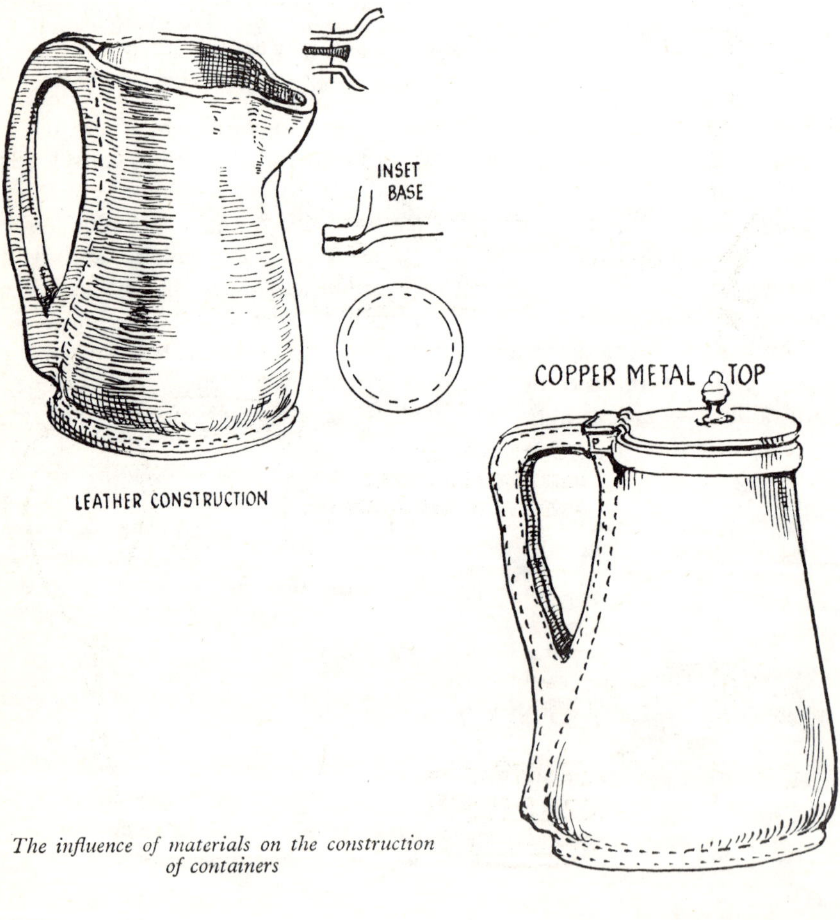

The influence of materials on the construction of containers

SILVER RIM
FULHAM STONEWARE JUG. ORNAMENT COPIES SCALLOPED LEATHER
POTTERY MADE LIKE A LEATHER JACK
METAL JUG REMINISCENT OF LEATHER CONSTRUCTION
SOLDERED METAL
PEWTER. TUDOR 1500 SOLID HINGE AND THUMB PIECE REMINISCENT OF WOOD CONSTRUCTION
EARTHERNWARE COPIES WOOD

TUBS, BUCKS, HANDYS, ETC.

Beyond the technicalities of cooperage the design of all tubs depends upon balance and humanity.

Obviously a tub to be carried by one person *using both hands* must be oval rather than circular, and less than 4 ft. of axis.

Any tub to be carried between two people must have handles at opposite sides and the slots must be wide enough to take all four fingers (the thumb doing balance on top). When carried between two people it must not be too deep to clear the knees when slung at straight arm's length. (*Note*.—The heavy creels and water tubs are slung on a pole, leaving walking space between the carriers (*see* plate 7).)

The shape of the tub remained unchanged for centuries, its design having been arrived at by experiments that involved the best angle to slope the sides to prevent the water from rocking, the size of the top opening for easy filling, and the weight and capacity for transportage.

These large transport tubs were filled up from the well bucket (also a carefully worked out shape) and each tub had a "float" to drop on top of the water to prevent splashing.[1]

If you look closely you will see the crossbar handle that engages with the pole is removable, to facilitate filling, and is designed to suspend the tub from the pole without swinging or twisting.

Earlier, common tubs show the pole passed direct through two handles arranged as part of the tub, by making holes in two elongated staves on either side. These elongated staves were vulnerable points of construction, since if one was snapped off it could only be replaced by taking the whole tub to pieces and inserting a new stave. The shortening of the "lift" staves was a great improvement in design.

The strong pole upon which the water tub is slung was called a "cow-stal". It had to be of solid splint wood, spoke-shaved and smoothed round, so that it took the weight without spring or bend, and if you look closely, some men carry long forked poles upon which they could rest the cowstal when they wished to stop and change shoulders. As it would be extremely heavy to raise the tub from the ground to shoulder height,

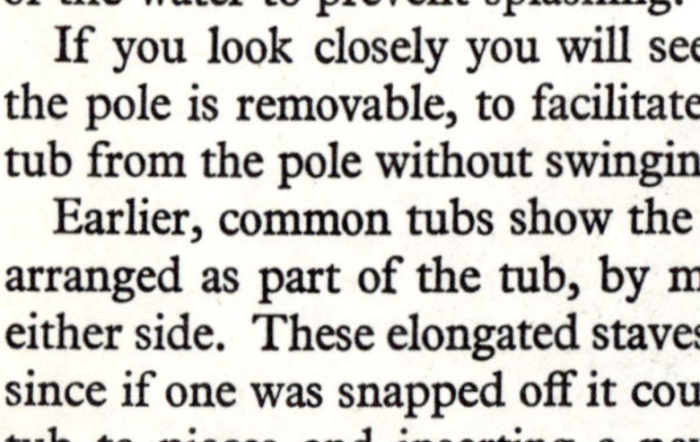

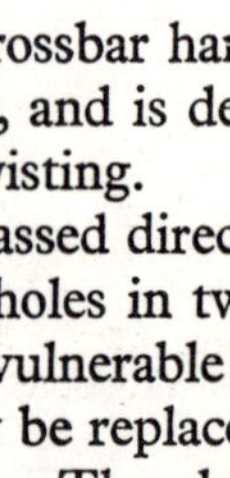

The cowlstaff or cowstal was the staff carried to support the weight of the pole when the bearers wanted to stop or change shoulders.

[1] The African women who carry water jars on their heads usually place a bunch of leaves to float atop for the same purpose.

some old wells have raised steps beside them, on which to stand the tub and from which to start walking away.

This basic water tub design continued in dairy milk pails and tubs, and the "under Buck" tubs continued to have two raised stave handles until the nineteenth century when metal tubs came into use.

The Scotch "handy" was a small interesting development. As the milkmaid tilted it forward under the cow and, as it was emptied after each cow, the lifting weight was never heavy, therefore the opposite handle was disused,[1] but the remaining handle grew longer and acquired a "grip top".

The small "handy" or little one-man tub could vary much in depth (according to use), but as it was usually carried at waist level, was seldom more than a foot deep. The handle varied with its use. As a milking pail or water dipper the handle was long. As a washing tub or feeding bowl for animals, a single small hole was sufficient and the low raised slat served to tilt the whole for drying out.

(Also when used to impound the broody hen, it did give the misguided female a chance to breathe!)

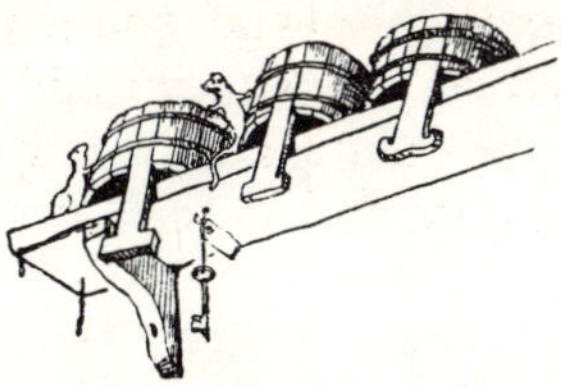

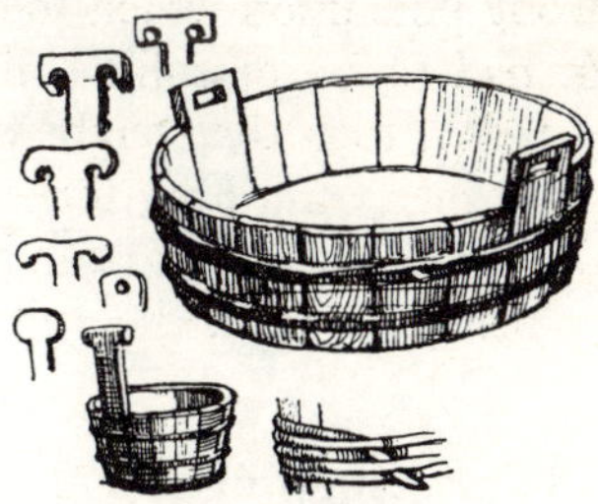

The evolution of the handy's "grip" is shown in the diagrams. Many quite complicated designs are the adaptations of accidents.

The left-hand sketch shows how milking pails were "shelved" like modern saucepans, handles down and sufficiently forward on the shelf to allow for the air to get inside.

[1] Also the tilted position under the udder would have made a second raised stave awkward.

For some usages the split withy binding was better than the newer metal hoops.

A "lade gawn" was a ladle holding about a gallon.

In brewing, a small handy with numerous holes in the base was filled with clean straw and used as a "Tap Wad" or strainer. The same idea was used to strain ley for soap.

There is no such thing as an inanimate object! Life and work shape all they touch, and the change in design of structural things is a continuous concurrent history.

Difficulty in filling buckets in shallow water

WATER CARTS

Water portage by pole and yoke carried on for centuries after wheeled water carts came into use. Even today the swinging weight of liquids in transport tanks is a problem for lorries, and the early water carts could only be used on reasonably level tracks.

The early water carts varied from strong old farm carts, adapted by having hogsheads secured on to them, which were set of necessity above the axle of the wheels and therefore extremely top heavy; or specially made farm water carts built on curved axles that allowed the weight of the water to swing between the wheels.

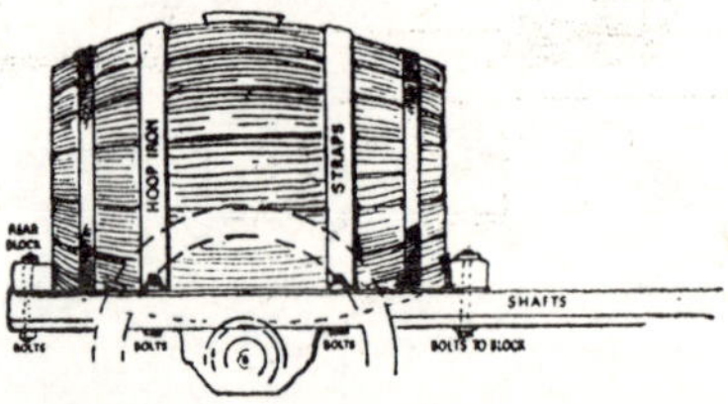

In the Tottenham print (plate 11), the bank by the pump is cut away to allow these top-heavy hogsheads to come level with the water runnels. If we can trust the artist, the strain when turning must have wrecked many an axle, and the least lilt in the track would throw all the weight onto one wheel cracking the spokes and forcing off the hub.

The detail of the filling funnel is important, as to cut one stave across completely would weaken the barrel tension. The opening had to be kept small to avoid this, and so a high, wide funnel had to be built up, surrounding the hole, to contain the water till it drained down into the barrel. This was more urgent for the dipper-filled barrel than the runnel-filled, but it is one of the details of construction impressed by the nature of water.

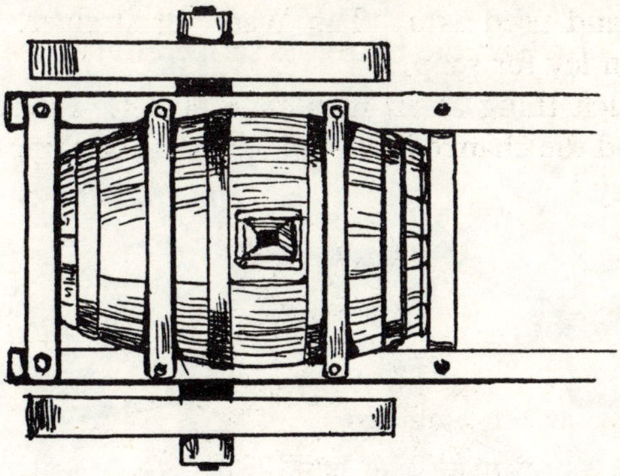

The shafts, about fourteen feet long, were connected by a fore and hind bar placed across at the exact distance to take the length of the cask. The width of the axle takes the diameter of the cask, and this axle is bent downwards into a semi-circle to accommodate the lower curve of the cask. The cask does not rest on the axle but is suspended, just clear of it, on two hoop iron slings secured to the shafts. Another pair of slings pass over the cask and are secured to the upper side of the shaft at the same place—so that the cask is carried clear, low down between the wheels, and prevented from slipping forward and backward by the crossbars.

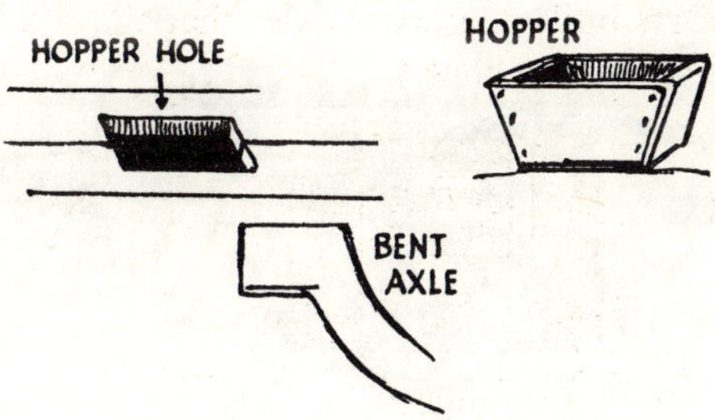

The size of the aperture cut into the cask must be restricted by the width of the staves. A spigot set low down at the back served out the water.

The water cart, used to lay the dust upon the roads, was a tank version of this barrel cart. The distributing pipe, set low behind, sprayed out the water like rain. In later models revolving wheels caught the water as it poured from the spigot and splashed it out sideways, covering a width greater than that of the cart itself.

The scoop or dipper needed to lift the water up and pour it into a water cart, required considerable technical skill to make and to use.

The handle had to be sufficiently long to reach from the pond or stream below, to the top of the cart above, *without the worker having to move*. That is, the worker was the centre of the circle of which the pole was a radius and of which the bucket described the arc.

Therefore, the position of the handle had to be calculated with care, so as to take the weight of the bucket a little below its centre of gravity. The angle of the handle with the bucket had to be calculated to give the angle of the lift, and the actual securing of the handle, obliquely through the bucket, was a technical difficulty (or the round wet pole turned in the holes and the upturned bucket doused the worker).

This apparently rough farm implement is a good example of the exquisite care and cunning of the old farm worker. Mathematical calculations so often corroborate the trial and error findings of the old farm labourer, that one realises it is the heritage of their hard-earned experience in these simple problems that lies behind the mechanical engineering of today.

HAND SCOOPS

WATER SCOOPS

1. The wooden scoop is cut from one solid block of wood and though the pattern varies the balanced wood handle usually has a hooked head that forms a stand to hold the bowl level when set down, or suspend it when hung up over the rim of a barrel. Much used in farmsteads as unbreakable and safe for use among animals. Also for brewing and pickling work where metal would corrode.

2. The common zinc dipper, usually with a wooden handle, is the laundrywoman and gardener's dipper. 3. The smaller, lighter version made in tin and called a "pan mug" holds about two or four pints and is used for scooping water into boilers or measuring water for mixing meal.

4. The pot mug, similar in size (2–4 pints), is usually glazed earthenware with solid thick handle and extra thick rim. It is used for all brewing, fermenting and pickling, and sometimes used in the laundry for preserving special starch hot (it chills rapidly in tin).

5. The old copper and brass dippers that scooped broth from the cauldron are seldom found in use now. This small shape also lifted hot water from the side boiler before it became general to fit taps.

THE WOODEN HOGGIN

These water vessels were in general use so long that it is easier to classify them by owners than periods.

The principle of non-conducting wood casing pre-dates the vacuum of the Thermos flask (both used by workers to carry their drinks to work). The wood had this advantage over the flask; it was almost unbreakable. In winter it kept the contents hot, in summer it kept them cold, because the hoggin was kept damp on the outside and allowed to swing in the air. Pilgrims are often shown with their gourds and water bottles slung to the top of their long pilgrim staffs. This applied the same principle as that used by motorists in the tropics, who sling their canvas water bags to the roof of the car. The continuous swinging in the dry air causes rapid evaporation and chills the water.

The pilgrim, in walking, held his tall staff low down, so that with every step the top of his staff swung in an arc backwards and forwards in the air above. Few who have noticed this, in old pictures, have realized the cause of that high-swung gourd.

The carter would use a heavier make of hoggin, and the rider would probably have a hoggin made of more resilient leather. The hoggins illustrated show a typical heavy waggoner's hoggin, a field labourer's hoggin, and a lighter poggin more convenient for a shepherd to carry.

Another interesting use for this wooden water vessel was the making (or should we call it brewing) of broth. The shepherd would put a handful of oatmeal into the hoggin and fill it up with water from some hillside

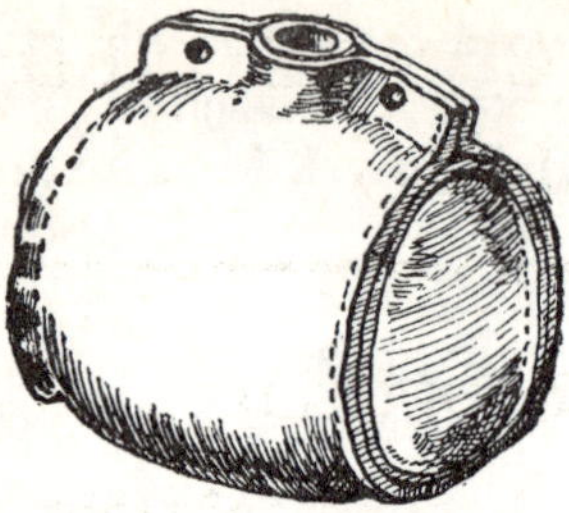

An ordinary leather bottle

The wooden hoggin: a heavy weight for a waggoner

brook before he started on his long miles of "sheep walk". A few hours later the continuous churning action, and probably some bacteria developed in the wood, caused a ferment, and a cool, slightly acid and aerated broth provided him with a sustaining meat and drink.

The light wooden hoggin for a shepherd to carry

The sailor's was oval: this took up less space

THREE HOGGINS COMBATANT

Three of these sturdy small barrels are preserved in the Leicestershire village of Hallaton, and are fought over between the Hallaton lads and those of the neighbouring village in a yearly battle that involves a huge hare pie, a handsome procession, and much strong ale! A church service has recently been added to this traditional holiday contest (of which nobody knows the exact origin). The hare was sacred to some pagan Saxons, and the event may commemorate an early insult when some hungry Christian ate one, but this is conjecture only.

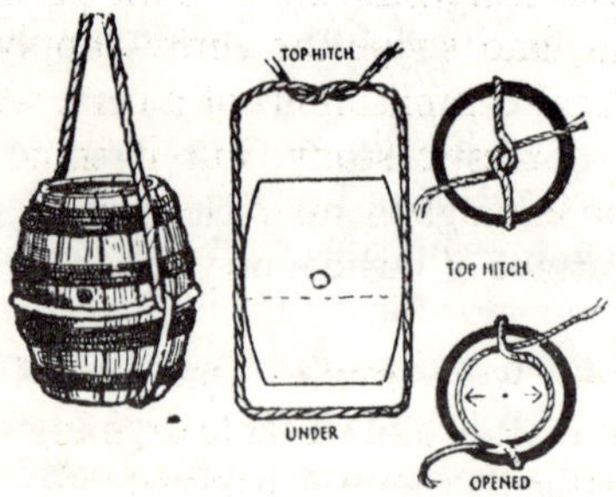

The barrel hoist, one of the simplest uses of the single knot, is opened and dropped down to encompass the barrel. The process may be repeated to make several holds on a longer barrel. And the same knotting secures rolled bacon.

WATER CAUGHT, AND CONDUCTED AND COMPELLED

WATER CAUGHT AND CONDUCTED

"Spring water can be ladde as hye in pypes as the place of y sprynge of the water—as from a well in the top of an hylle, ofte by pypes water is ladde to the same biznesse in another hylle."

BART. ANGLICUS

"Hydrostatics treat of the laws which govern the weight of fluids. The application of the physical pressure of fluids to the purposes of domestic economy and the wants of civilized life are extremely important, and afford some valuable objects of study to the mechanic and engineer, and with many of these it would be the interest of farmers to become acquainted."

H. STEPHEN, F.R.S.E., MDCCCLXXI

CATCHMENT WATER

The transition from private enterprise to mains and municipal water works still causes trouble, especially in districts where for centuries natural springs and small water courses have been channelled to form private water supplies. Sometimes a quarry, cutting back far into a hill, may alter the watershed of a whole district; or a mine gallery, tapping an underground spring, may stop the above-ground supply by throwing the water out in a different direction or at a different level. Recently, when so many old county estates have been purchased by new owners, who have immediately sold off the land attached, there has been a mass of trouble, because the new owners of the land, digging drains, tapping springs and putting streams underground, have completely altered old water supplies to lower houses. (In some cases, to the astonishment of both parties.) Or a rural district council may step in, and swipe the entire supply of water for some local enterprise. The legal complications of a rural water supply are beyond the scope of this domestic study, but if some air survey could X-ray down and show the entanglements of lead pipes and ancient drain pipes that lie under the surface of our countryside, it would be a political economy!

The old methods, for village or manor, were simple. One located the water above one's position, took pick and spade and suitable draining tiles (or pipes or tubing) and just ran the water to where it was wanted.

A deep quarry cutting off the water supply of these cottages

A good example of this is the long shallow "leet" that good Sir Francis Drake conducted all around Dartmoor to bring down fresh water for his ships at Plymouth. Almost any old Havod in the hills, or water mill in the valleys, will give you an example of individual catchment engineering. On raised banks or through sunk dykes they just brought the water along. No wonder that when canals were being built in the late 1700's there was a good supply of experienced labour. The head engineers may have done the surveying, and submitted the plans, but the average country man of that date understood the *job*.

For private houses the water was usually carried into the buildings through lead pipes. Lead was known to have a bad effect on some waters, but the old, heavy, cast-lead cisterns that now decorate so many gardens, were usually so well coated with a green deposit that the water hardly reached the metal. The same happened to many lead pipes which were constantly full of water. This is one reason why some lengths of lead pipe remained perfectly sound for a century, while other lengths of the same pipe crumbled to dry dust. Miles of old lead water pipes supply fountains and gardens all over the country, and road men, putting telegraph wires underground, or repairing gutters, may suddenly be flooded out of their excavations by a severed water pipe, spouting water up from some hitherto unknown source. (And next day the council offices will get an irate demand to know why the water supply has been cut off.) Catchment water is still a problem to many farmers and landowners.

The Fens are a study in cross-purpose drainage schemes by both Dutch and English experts. Among the many pockets of foreign settlement all over Britain, the East Anglian Dutch community is most interesting. Today, many public notices all across this district are printed in both Dutch and English. Wisbech could easily be in Holland, and a party of children competing in a local musical festival were half Dutch and half English.

An epitome of the fenlands can be studied on almost any waterlogged land where there have been extensive peat cuttings. The right to cut peat for fuel is covered by ancient laws, and the same laws give right of way from the peat cutting to the owner's hearth. (As with mineral rights, the line goes direct to the nearest highway, and the width of the road considers the necessity of the load.) On these old peat bogs the drainage is often in the line of the cuttings, and the sinking of the adjoining land, as the saturated peat drains into the cutting, gives a wide depression full of shallow water ending in a bog hole (*see* Ponds). Thus the curious effect of water having to be pumped *up* into a dyke that is now raised high above the fen it originally drained can also be seen on the moorlands, where water draining away has left the stones of a sunk drain now surfaced as a path. This "shrinking" of the bog brings to light the old ebon hard trunks of trees, and the remains of prehistoric Irish elk. They have not come up, it is the land that has sunk down.

But not all water in England is drained and dyked on this Fenland scale.

MARSH WALLS

> "What ever befall
> Amend the Marsh Wall."
>
> TUSSER

There are hundreds of smallholdings whereon one boundary of the land is a painstakingly raised and preserved marsh wall, holding the arable land safe from the tides of the estuary. Such a wall, made in the 1400's, can still be traced on the Stour, where Tusser farmed, though this is rapidly being destroyed by a more adequate commercial embankment.

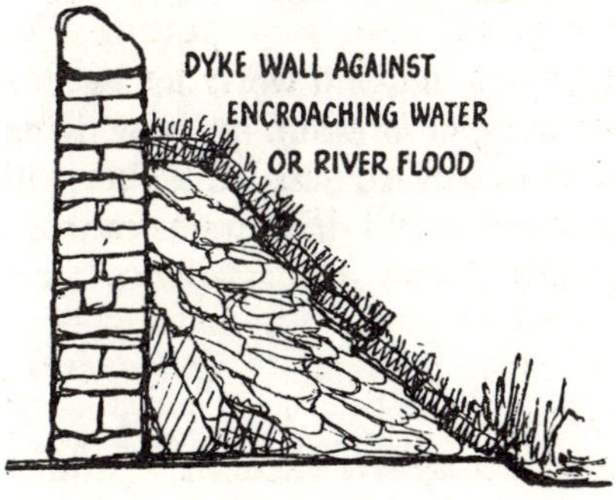

Stacked drain pipes

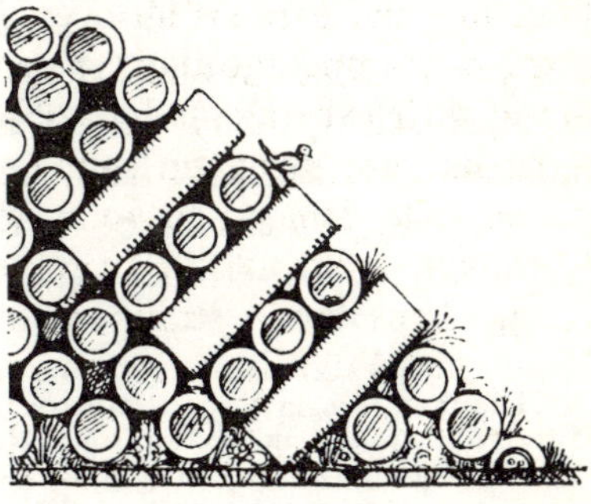

The foundation of the wall was built of rocks and stones, reinforced with wood and willow hurdles (*see* Kesh work). Each high tide the sand and mud was carefully plastered onto this foundation, and culverts were cut through, at an angle that would let the force of the water drive in easily, but drain out slowly. Thus, with constant care, a marsh wall grew more firm each season; but neglect at any one point, or a small breach unseen, could, in one flooding, undo the work of a century. The working principle was rather that of the water meadow, but the responsibility far more exacting. Marram grass could be used to consolidate sand dunes, but the marsh wall was not a sand dune, it had to be of a firm and constant texture. Clay was brought by sea as ship ballast, and the stones of ruined buildings and many other foreign bodies are found embedded in the marsh walls of old farmsteads. We ourselves have found a slab of Purbeck marble from a vanished fourteenth-century chapel washed out of a marsh wall near Cattawade Bridges.

LAND DRAINS

The porous drain pipe with two butt ends, used for field work, reverses the principle of the glazed household drain pipe, since it is designed to *let in* water along its entire length. Also, the laying is reversed. Mankind lays his household drain to convey water *where he wishes it to go*. Mankind laying land drains is at pains to discover where *the water wishes to go!*

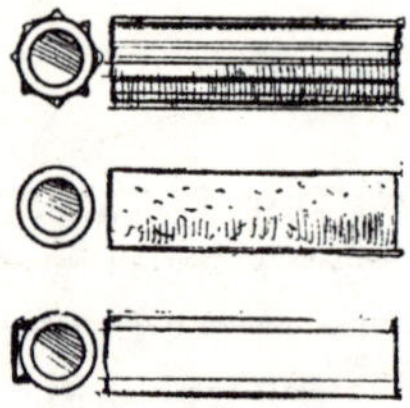

Porous drain pipes

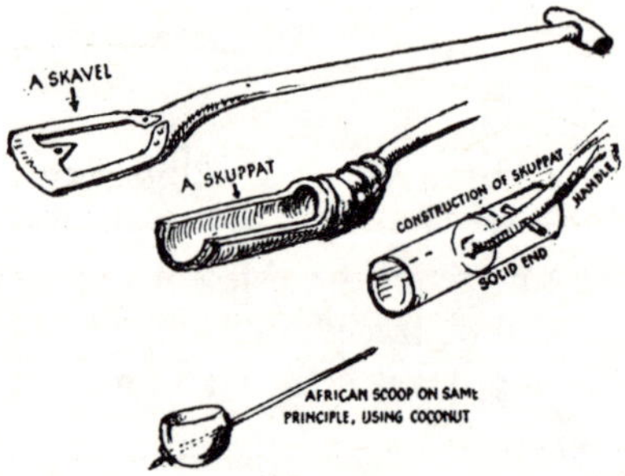

Early wooden tools

For water will always take the easiest way out, and will work downwards far more quickly than it will mount upwards by absorption. Anyone living on limestone, or chalk land, knows how swiftly streams sink down to lower levels. Water may be heard running below old dried water courses, and when the higher ones have ceased to run, fresh springs appear lower down.[1]

[1] The dried *dongas* of Central Africa could often provide water holes in the dry season if it were possible to sink wells through the empty river bed to the water still running below. Since writing this it is being done by game wardens to preserve animal life.

Water will also siphon underground through long and tortuous ways, till it levels out, so that in mountain work, draining a bog in one place may lower the level of a distant lake that seemed to be completely unconnected. Therefore in field or mountain the land drain is less a tube than a waterway arranged to let water run easily, and to this end all land drains are designed to follow the water's natural course as closely as possible.

A flat field with uniform tilt in one direction

A field tilted from end to end and sides to centre

In farm fields, the slope of the land and the tilt towards the discharge are comparatively slight. Where the field is tilted in one plane the parallel drain lines need never converge, and may be seen for centuries as wide rounded strips, often reminiscent of the earlier furrows of the plough (each furrow in itself a shallow surface drain line). On hill farms the field drains may have to vary in depth, and converge by devious ways to one discharge.[1]

The furrows of the plough were field drains themselves

Where observation and experiment were the farmer's only guide, the weight on the plough in winter, the colour of the straw in harvest, and the change of the weed in the stubble were his rules in setting his drains, and he used only the simplest survey levels.

The old land drains used to be made of local stone. Where layered stone (slate, lias, sandstone, etc.) was available, triangular drains were made. You see them, still firm today, where old farm lands are being bulldozed for housing estates. Where rounded river pebbles could be got, they were worth the cartage to make filled drains because the rounded surfaces never packed close, as broken stone was liable to do.

[1] Some of the undulations in pastures date from the period when the curved surface was considered to give more grazing space as well as extra drainage.

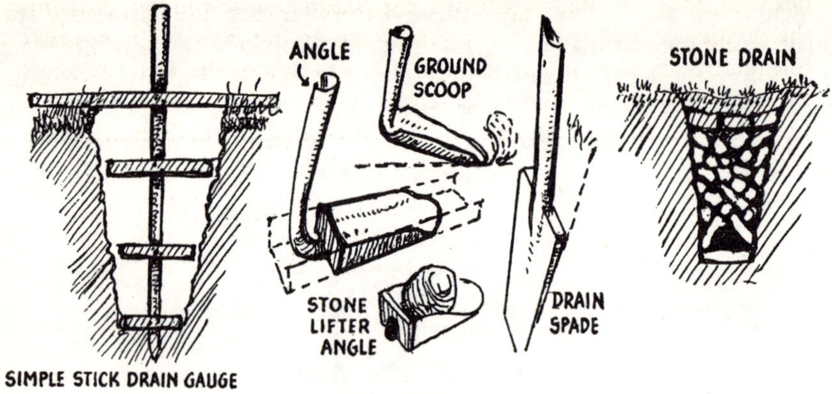

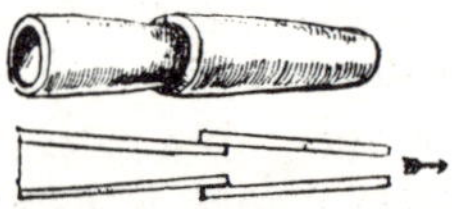

The tapered earthenware drain pipe followed the pattern of the wooden pipe

The earthenware "butt" pipe came into use later (on the whole about 1700, but this varied with the locality). The pipes were at first thought less efficient than the stone drain, but pipes were comparatively cheap and they were quickly laid.

Field-draining activity has always followed the rise and fall of wool prices, and lately there has been a redevelopment in mountain draining, since it was realized that liver fluke in sheep was carried by the small water snail. As the strange life cycle of that parasite required two different hosts, snail and sheep, the liver fluke could not attack sheep on dry pasture lacking in snails.

Curiously, the most simple and direct form of hill drain reproduces the outer and inner ditch of the ancient hill forts. We are told that the ancient earth works were for defence, but they were also a very comprehensive drainage system.

The diagram explains this "ring" drain very simply, but since few hills are as uniformly rounded as a pudding bowl, the actual working out of the ring, by contour line, can be complicated. Everyone who has crossed a mountain, following the streams up to the top, crossing the divide and following the stream down on the far side, knows that boggy stretch of no-man's-land at the top where the water collects till it decides which side to descend. Here, the drain must form a lip to the basin, or force a drain hole through near the bottom of the hollow.

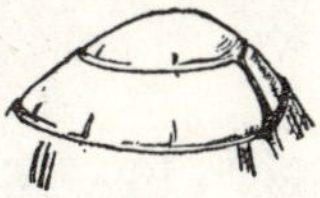

Hill-top drainage (man-made)

Natural drainage of volcanic lake crater

Volcanic hills often form their own basin and lip, and the crater lake discharges itself down its own water course.

One would expect that easy discharge was always available for the hill drains; but where the watershed is wide, misdirected discharge from higher levels may escape aside into shallow pockets between the foothills where, the incline being less steep, the clearance is slower. The diagram can only give a very elementary idea of this mountainous subject, but even a slight insight into the principle of hill waterworks should add interest to a hill walk, and make it possible for the holidaymaker to pick out the artificial drain lines upon a hillside, and wonder at the ancient skill thereof.

OLD LAND DRAINS AND CONDUITS

The principle of conducting rather than coercing water accounts for the continued efficiency of many complicated conduits serving antique establishments. Such communal buildings, being of necessity placed near running water, took in their water supply from above and discharged it below, the water thus running a slightly diverted, rather than strongly enforced course.

Also, the architects (being less separated from their plumbers) adopted their conduit systems more sympathetically to the flow of the water. Lead pipes of thick sheet lead, secured into lengths, and frequently bulging like an accommodating sausage roll, took the water under, or through. Strong stone tunnels (*see* Land drains) ran it in freedom under roads or heavy buildings. Wood and earthenware pipes took it through marshy or dry ground, and most joins were bedded in resilient clay.

Also, many early water supplies ran freely and continuously, so that there were few taps to give or check the flow, suddenly altering pressure. Therefore, in time, the continuously running water supply, scoured out its own bed, silting up some accidental dip, forcing a constricting passage, rubbing out some sharp bend, and relieving alternating pressures by bulging out the clay of some soft join. (Rather as a vein in damaged human tissue adapts its growth to new tensions.)

Many small runnels of water around old ruins now appear to be completely natural, but were originally cunningly devised, and springs of water now rising in unexpected parts of a ruin are quite probably a centuries-old burst pipe.

LAND DRAINS AND COTTAGES

Hundreds of old cottages were condemned because there was no damp course when, in fact, they had excellent damp courses which had been destroyed out of ignorance that they existed. Most old cottages of 1600 to 1750 were built by men who intended to live in them and, knowing all about keeping out the damp, intended them to be dry and warm.

Their land drain was set at least four feet down, exactly under the drip of the roof (diagram). The base of the land drain was well below the foundation level of the cottage walls, and was set so that it encircled the building, and discharged at the lowest point well beyond it—frequently into a well, if one was conveniently placed. The land drain was filled with loose rounded stones; sea or river pebbles were carried some distance if obtainable,[1] the smaller ones making the cobbled surface close to the wall, the larger stones being placed in the drain. Broken stone was used in default of rounded stone, but rounded were preferred, as they did not pack together, and the object was to keep the drain base as open and loose as possible. Sometimes, cross stones were wedged across, making a culvert over the loose drain stones, but the work would be done (preferably) before autumn rains, and once the flow through started, the water-way would be kept washed clear by every storm. The drain was then filled in to the surface with large gravel, and the surface levelled with a tilt away from the building. It has been subsequent generations, people who had become industrialized and lost their knowledge of the land who, out of sheer stupidity, destroyed all that made those cottages warm and dry (*see* diagram).

The old thatch usually stood out more than a foot beyond the wall plate, so that every straw or reed on the surface of that thatch dropped its water a foot clear of the house wall. The wide eaves sheltered the top portion of the walls almost down to first floor level. Below that, the base of the walls sloped slightly outwards and, where the walls were plastered, the plaster was "run out" over the solid foundation of stones or doubled-walled brick. Beyond this, from the base of the wall, a close packed cobble paving carried the dry ground out, as far as the edge of the deep land drain.

[1] "Budleigh pebbles" in Devon and the "Pitching pebbles" of Northants are good examples, as also the "cobble" paths of Yorkshire and elsewhere.

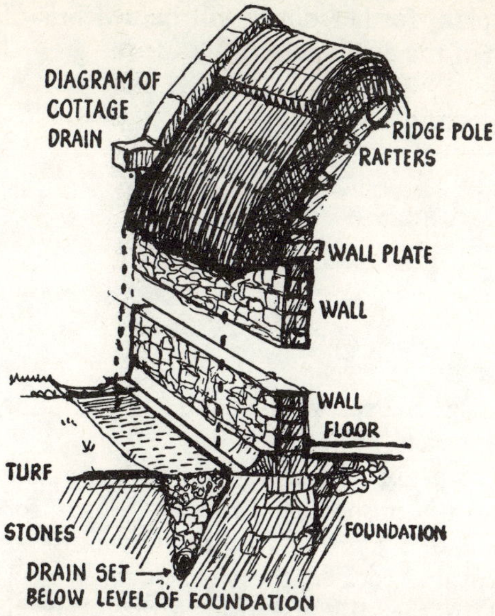

Within the house the floor level was kept much above the outer ground level, and the tiled floor was laid direct onto this dry level. (The old floor tiles were porous, not glazed.) There was no possible underfloor draught; there was no underfloor space, only a level of dry sand or dry ash over an underlay of gravel, so that both ventilation and insulation were well arranged (*see* diagram).

Now see the destruction of all these good plans.

The dry stone border around the house is dug up and filled with rich soil and manure, and well banked up against the walls so as to get the plants to carry the wet as high as possible. The draining course is trodden solid, so as to make a barrier to hold *in* the water around the walls. The top of the drain that had so carefully been left open and of loose gravel surface, is cemented over into a path, and even rounded, so that the curve throws the surface water inwards where it can accumulate and do most damage!

Within the house the driven-in-water soaks up into the sand and gravel and ash, under the porous tiles, which soon show damp mould, so they are taken up and a floor laid on joists, which of course soon rot! If successive generations had thought out how best to destroy those old cottages they could not have planned better!

I guarantee that if many of these genuine old buildings were intelligently excavated they would disclose traces of this good old land drain system. If they remove the earth under those inappropriately-placed flower borders, far below will be found the broken cobbles. If they pickaxe away the hard path, further down will be a debris of stones that were once the bottom of the damp course.

SITE DRAINAGE ON HILLS

The small diagram explains the old hillside building—very common in mountain districts.

Undercutting action makes excavation comparatively light work. The fallen earth is pushed outwards and down, forming the raised platform. As a rule a primitive soak-away pit is arranged early by collecting excavated rock as the work progresses, and a stream arranged to run past the gable end, if not actively piped into the building. In old and neglected buildings the surface soil alone frequently filled in the space behind the house, which caused a damp back wall. Better workers removed this soil and spread it below the platform, to make the deep soil of a vegetable garden over which the house water could soak down freely.

WATER PIPES (OF WOOD)

"Water trunks pitched and fixed, per foot 8*d*." *Builder's List*, 1780. These would be the hollow tree trunks used as water pipes. They were frequently charred within (by thrusting through a truss of burning straw) and pitching would be outside and probably around the inserted joints.

Water Gutters

"Gutters 6*d*. foot. 7*d*. if pitched." From the context we believe these were the iron roof gutters—the yard gutter was usually of stone or brick.

DRAIN PIPES

Drain pipes hold crowds spellbound. When a thoroughfare is taken up to expose the entrails of a city, people hang over the holes entranced.

They see the coloured electric nerves, grouped as for an anatomical demonstration—the rounded, brown, and black intestines that curve past complicated joints. And when, metaphorically speaking, an appendix operation is progressing, excited speculation disregards all boundaries of rope or red-eyed lanterns! Everyone is drain-minded, if given the opportunity, and the more deeply you study drains the more enthralling they become.

The earliest pipes, of wood or clay, used to be set end to end, or wedged together. This caused either a leak or a ridge at the join, and though the ridge was arranged for a drop (*see* diagram) so that the current ran over, not against, the obstruction, it was a potential trouble. Modern pipes are made to set with joints that leave the interior pipe smooth. This construction complicates design, so that the many hundreds of different pipes require technical understanding, but a simple classification of the most ordinary is interesting.[1]

The ordinary, earthenware drain pipe can be either round or oval in section. The oval pipe, by concentrating the contents, ensures a narrower and more forceful flow, and so has its uses where the current is weak or variable, etc. The ordinary circular pipe can be of 3, 4, 5, 6, 7, 8, 9, 10, 12, 15, 18-inch diameter (or larger) and, in all sizes, there are two ends. One end is in-socket, and one insert and, all being straight, they can be set right or left. But if repairs require the conjunction settings from different directions there must be a butt pipe capable of two insets, or a double socket pipe.

Now, if it's required for a smaller pipe to discharge into a larger one (more usual than the reverse process) a taper pipe is required, again socketed either end, and all these pipes must be made to fit in varied stock sizes.

To carry the straight pipe lines left or right requires another complete set of pipe bends (available in every diameter as in ordinary pipes). According to the situation, and with consideration of the content and flow, you must obtain a quarter bend, medium bend, or small bend; and again, in case of change bore, there must be a corresponding number of taper bends to fit. Note that nearly all these pipes are also made in half sections, sometimes for use as surface channel pipes, sometimes for repair, and sometimes to form an inspection length (*see* diagram). All these are simple bends, being set in one plane, but with a change of level you require bends that can be set upwards. A rest bend (and these must also be slow and

[1]All water passing through pipes is retarded by friction. The shape of the pipe is involved, but always the smoother the pipe, the easier the passage. In economic periods old workers among the hills used to level the flow by setting rough unglazed pipes down a steep slope, and using glazed pipes to "help her along the flats". Wherefore, today, new rural water boards believe they have unearthed two distinct systems laid down at different dates, whereas it was only the pipes that changed, not the period of position.

quarter bends) may be of different lengths. There is also the knuckle bend, and the swan and elbow bends. The elbow bend can be right-angled or rounded.

Junction pipes are complicated by having variously placed entering sockets, and the square, oblique and curved junction has to be catered for in all sizes.

There is the Y pipe, and the oblique spaced pipe, and many, many others among the "plain" drain pipes that encircle us.

There are, among these circumstantial pipes, certain ones inviting inspection, sometimes called "access" pipes. (For a channel pipe is not officially classed as an open access or an inspection unit. It is considered more as a "state of emergency".) Because stoppages usually occur on curves, or at junctions, inspection pipes are frequently set there, and you get the double inspection junction pipe, again in assorted sizes, and made right- or left-handed.

The trap or lock pipes are known to most householders—the simple bend below the sink that forms a water lock and prevents air from the far side re-entering the house. This lock type is used in lavatory fitments, and these pipes require the statutory air pipe that must be carried above roof level. The earlier lavatory locks were most complicated experiments, working on basin principles and curious funnel shapes.

The simple downspout trap and the gutter trap are known to most householders and all gardeners. The gutter trap is often square, as grids are now of iron, but round grids of pierced stoneware fitted the old round sockets, which were used for gullies around many old buildings. Curiously, these old-fashioned "pot tops" are now used in some modern chemical works.

The common-or-garden gully, under a downspout at the end of a path, is made on the "dib hole" principle, and includes a water lock. The diagram shows how the stoppage occurs when the dib hole has filled up, higher than the lock, and it explains the straight-edged slot (which is a

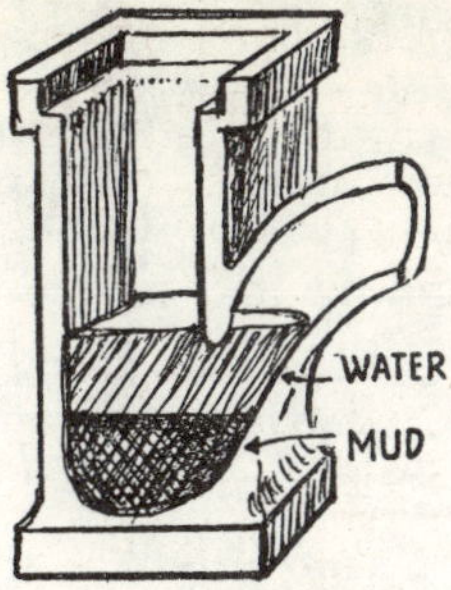

chord of the same diameter as the circle of the outpipe). Some gullies have lift-out fitments (as for example the grease-trap gully, for a kitchen sink[1]), but for the garden gully, an old iron ladle, or trowel, will clear the accumulated silt easily. These gully traps represent a whole range of sizes and uses. The old farm gully usually had a long concave grid, to

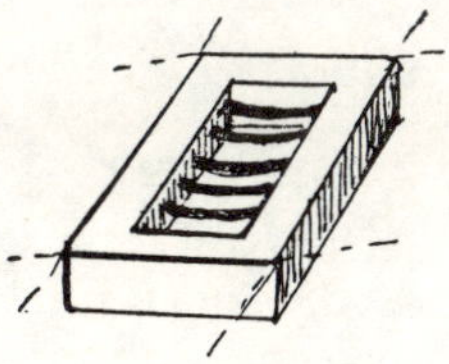

avoid breaking by cartwheel, and also as a straw resistant. Roadways have special grids that may change according to the county boundary, and the maker's name is usually incorporated with the county's. These road gullies are large and heavy and usually the grid is hinged on. If, however, you have ever dropped some valuable down a municipal grating, you will find, after the municipal road man has lifted it up, that most arrangements of the great city gullies are similar to the little one in your own garden. And, though the silt is now sucked out through flabby suction tubes into vast containers on a municipal lorry, the roadman still has an old long-handled mud scoop held in reserve for emergency use, and retrieves your loss in exactly the same way as you would clear out your own gully under your own rainwater spout.

The principle of the gutter and gully being appreciated, their adaptations have increased interest. When a surface current crosses a wide space a long channel gully covers the distance, or where an open drain dives down steeply, an extra iron baffle, set at a nicely calculated angle, prevents the downswept debris from choking the pipe.

Discharge pipes often have traps, or baffles, for protection and, in the

[1]Grease-trap gullies work on the principle that fat and grease float on the surface, so that the flow must wash the surface water aside into a trap where it can accumulate and be removed, and space left unblocked for the water to flow past and under.

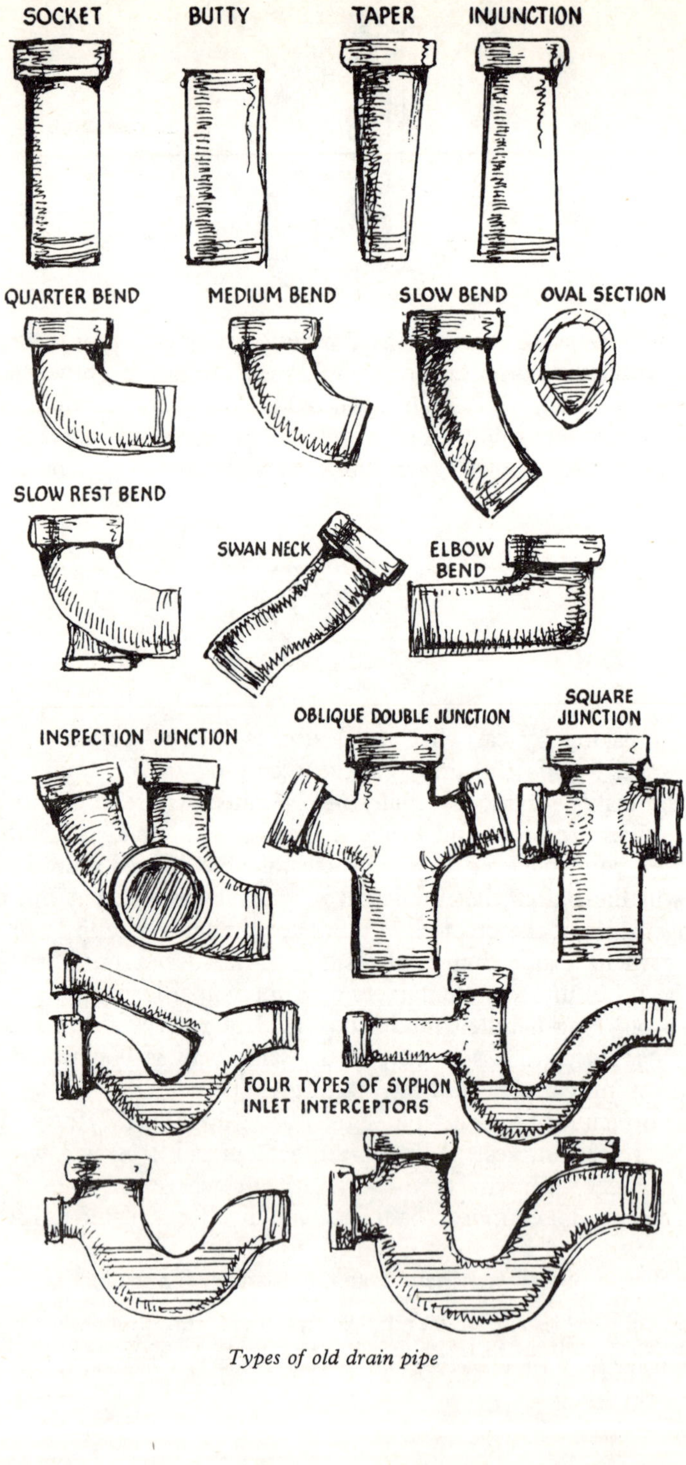

Types of old drain pipe

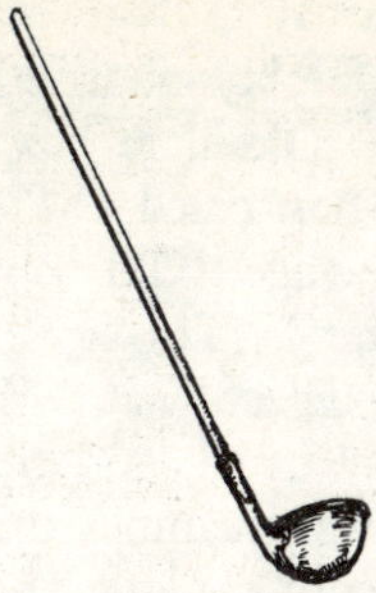

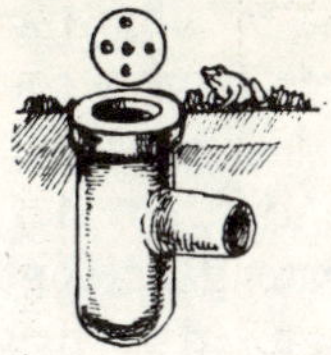

case of sewage disposal in tidal waters, automatic traps are fitted that open only under a certain depth of water.

To a builder these various pipes are an A.B.C. that he takes for granted. Few people appreciate the enormous fund of specialized knowledge carried so competently in the head of a workman.

Drain Pipes and Bracken

It is interesting that the transport of these heavy drain pipes and stone ware is closely connected with the increase of bracken on grazing lands. This coarse bracken, so long used for bedding, fuel, packing, etc., was kept in bounds by regular cutting and carting. Then pneumatic tyres made transport possible without the fern packing, and different threshing methods left straw useless for thatch so more straw was used in the steading. But it was the new lorry tyres that made it possible to transport slate, earthenware and pottery, almost unpacked, and so led to the present overgrowth of bracken.

DISCHARGES

The simple screw release at the base of a bath or basin trap is known to everyone who has ever unstopped a washbasin. The small discharge caught in a bucket below demonstrates the much greater flood that follows the unstopping of some main waterway. Some dry and apparently unused water courses are simply outlet courses specially made at strategic points for exactly the same emergency.

Canals and mill dams and reservoirs of many types are fitted with these. In the case of the commercial canals they are sometimes extraordinarily long, as the water must run for some length of time, and be lowered into the nearest available river. The stop taps for canals, being planks (*see* diagram, p. 138), drop into cross slots. Mill "shuts" are variously arranged (*see* Water Mills), but once you let your mind run to waterways you unearth a lot of interest. The point to realize is that the waters on the wild hillside, and the waters in the household drain, *run in the same way*; it is the pipe and drain that have to alter, to suit the water.

WATER AND SLATE

Slate has a layered texture and when freshly quarried can be split along these folia to almost paper thinness. Old slate knappers say it is divided by water films when fresh, but when dried the slate solidifies and may even develop a bent or warp cleavage. Old workers call such slate "dead" and say it has "lost its water". This quality of holding water makes slate dangerous to use over direct heat. Mantelpieces of slate (often disguised as marble) were very usual, and being dried and far from direct heat, were safe, but an unwary camper using a flat slate for a bakestone, is likely to have it suddenly explode and fly in pieces by reason of the imprisoned steam.

Along the layer, slate is waterproof, and troughs and runnels of slate can replace stoneware, and do so in many old buildings. In slate districts quite long water courses are conducted in slate grooves. Some of these actually conduct the water through the house, forming excellent cold storage for the larder, and milk coolers for the dairy.

THE LEADING OF THE WATER IN THE LOWLANDS

WATER MEADOWS

The low earth and stone dykes of these ancient *leasons* or *water leas* can be seen in most agricultural districts by a river. Their construction ties up with the early shortage of winter fodder and grazing lands, and shows the survey skill of the ancient landowners. The entrance from the river was arranged upstream, but against a suitable breakwater curve, as sudden flooding would have swept away dykes and caused damage. The autumn overflow slid quietly in and flooded the lands that had been levelled in making the dyke walls. A stop-gap allowed the flood to flow on into the adjoining leas and, after passing slowly over all available grassland the water poured back into the river lower downstream, leaving a deposit

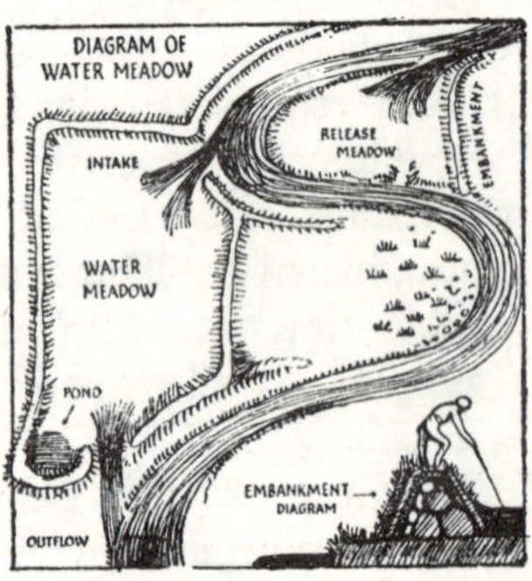

of fine silt over the roots of the grass. By its subsidence and residue it tended each season to make each enclosure more level, so that even today some water meadows are flat as bowling greens.

The dyke top was usually flattened to make a narrow causeway to get around the fields, as no man or beast could walk across the softened surface without poaching it. Sometimes you can locate the use of old fields by their old names, for field names commemorate history kindly. Near churches there is often a bell field, still hollow from an old casting pit. Martyrbones field on the Stour estuary remained unexplained till the new tractor unearthed the old bones of a monastic cemetery. Long acres, and Short acres, are common. Bucken fields were probably whitesters or washing grounds, and the water meadow has left two names—Flutter field (*la fluer terre*) and Basket field (*là-bas sec*).

THE ANTIQUITY OF THIS WATER CONTROL

The antiquity of this stream leading and diversion is proved by a traditional miracle attributed to St. Bridget. An entire community was at work, digging a new route for a water course, when one of the families appealed to St. Bridget to let them change places to easier ground. St. Bridget told them she would see to it, and next morning the old stream bed was dry, and the water was already running in the new channel.

One wonders how many ox-bow lakes are entirely natural, or owe their formation to ancient help, of which all traces have long since gone.

THE LEADING OF WATER OVER THE HILLS

The smaller rivers and larger streams provided power as valuable as the main rivers, for they provided inland transport, and were cleared and dredged and used for the towing, or floating down, of goods. Paths were cleared on either bank for horse, donkey, or man towing, so that when the canals came, the idea of towed transport was not new to the countryman. Streams were harnessed to mills, tilt hammers, and all manner of engines, either directly, in their natural course, or the water was dammed up or conveyed to position.

The antique architectural aqueducts of the continent have no counterpart in England. In England we conveyed water great distances and diverted, or rearranged, our streams, but it was always done in a quiet sort of way, with very little fuss.

Drake's *leet*, which he conducted to bring fresh water to his ships at Plymouth, has its catchment high up among the bogs of central Dartmoor, and winds its levels cunningly for miles across the moors. It is an aqueduct, in that it conducts the water, but it is the individual effort of a sailor, not an engineer, and today the clear moorland stream runs so peacefully that few realize it was formed by naval enterprise.

Sometimes a waterway was the result of one farm's need, and was carried out slowly by that farm, year by year. Sometimes it was the combined effort of the farm above, and the mill owner below; especially on hill farms where woollen mills might spare labour in a slack time to help the hill farmer drain his sheep walks (which drainage would increase the stream).

The amount of old workings that can be traced across the hilltops show how the mountain population has shrunk, and how much engineering skill has been lost with the closing of the smaller woollen mills.

Sometimes the waterworks used only one stream, but more often hill draining work gathered many streams into one channel, and often these channels were sunk in *cuts* like canals, or carried on stone and wood

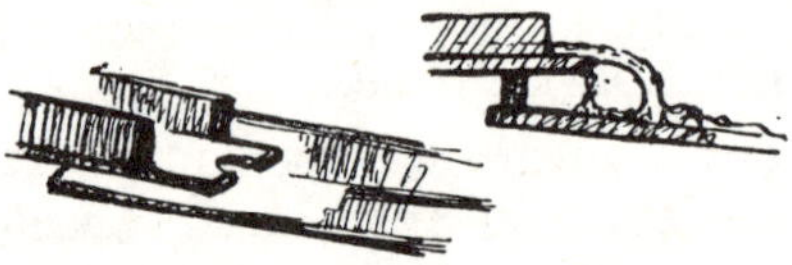

aqueducts across valleys. There are thousands of these small waterworks, small channels and the remains of old wooden and stone waterways all over England. I have traced many when walking across the mountains. One could follow the lines of the natural stream and find it blocked, and diverted, and joined up again further on. Between the two beds would be a swampy place where the wooden water troughs had fallen and perished, and piles of carried stones that had once built the pillars that upheld the troughs.

To realize the importance of a running water supply on the hill tops in a dry summer you must understand the economics of early English farming. Up to the eighteenth century, the difficulty of feeding livestock through the winter resulted in great herds of beasts being driven across the country to the great seasonal autumn markets, and the slaughter and salting down of winter stores.

All winter the precious fodder hay was supplemented with the high cut corn straws and, in spring, as soon as the few debilitated beasts were fit to travel, the lower main farms closed their meadow lands and sent all the livestock up to graze on the hills. There the breeding was done, and there all summer the dairy work was carried on, butter churned and cheese made, and all the animals fed and watered.

For the summer months the hill farm had to support all the work that *most needed* a good water supply.

Wood fuel was scarce so peat was used, and as the transport of large heavy cauldrons for boiling water was almost impossible, tubs, churns and cheese vats were scalded by filling with cold water, and throwing in red-hot stones from the fire. (Fire-cracked stones are one clue to the position of some old mountain dwellings.)

The hill-top waterworks for the summer farms were not made in one year nor one century. So long as the hill farm remained in use, the old men, shepherds and cowherds, and boys too young for the harvest fields, lived up there through the long summer months. The dairy work required water, while the cattle grazed quietly. So all the long daylight hours were spent by the men and boys in improving their waterworks, by leading in an extra stream, deepening a level length, or building a small weir to check an overflow down a steep drop. What man or boy can resist playing with running water on a long hot summer's day? The water runs were built of necessity, but built with the cunning of love.

The wooden aqueducts of these hill farms have perished, the stone supports have fallen, and the abandoned summer farm is derelict. What has survived is the imperishable knowledge that came not from books on engineering, but from working experience, a skill with water transmitted from father to son for generations. So that, when a later industrialized England drove those agricultural workers overseas, they took with them their instinctive feeling for the ways of water to help many a thirsty and dry land.

The derelict aqueduct on the hills

ONE EXAMPLE OF A COMMERCIAL AQUEDUCT

We give this example of water conducted in triumph across a valley by Mr. Telford and his chosen workmen, because it happens to be near our home and well known to us.

The first bare and impressive aspect of the structure is now masked by trees and flowery verges, so that the massive embankments pass unnoticed as natural contours. "It was designed and executed by, and under the inspection of, that British Archimedes, Mr. Thomas Telford, to carry a stream of water for the supply of the Ellesmere Canal; to the proprietors of which, in the year 1804, Sir W. W. Wynn, Bart.,[1] in the most liberal manner made an important donation of the waters of Bala pool, as far as they were wanted.

[1] Sir W. W. Wynn, Bart., was indeed a Baron and his family continued the privileges and responsibilities of the feudal system till the end of the nineteenth century.

This aqueduct, the most extraordinary structure of its kind in the world, was begun on the twenty-fifth day of July, 1795, and was finished on the twenty-sixth day of November, 1805, having been ten years and five months in building. It is one thousand and seven feet in length, and one hundred and twenty-six feet eight inches in height, from the surface of the flat rock on the south side of the River Dee, to the top of the iron sideplates of the water way. There are nineteen arches of forty-five feet span each. The piers, eighteen in number, are constructed of square masonry, and the arches and water way are composed of cast-iron.

At the south end of the aqueduct is an embankment of earth, fifteen hundred feet in length, and seventy-five feet high. The water way is eleven feet ten inches broad, and five feet three inches deep. There is a broad towing-path on the east side, guarded by a strong iron palisade running the whole length of the aqueduct. From the north end the canal is continued for a distance of about three hundred yards, and there terminates in an extensive basin, which affords a double wharfage with iron railways.

On the twenty-sixth day of November, 1805, the canal was opened in the following manner. The procession of boats advanced towards the noble structure now commencing its public utility. The complete sense of security in which they floated one hundred and twenty-six feet above the River Dee was a just acknowledgment to Mr. Telford. . . ."

"The procession of boats was as follows: in the first and second boats, the committee; in the third, the band of the Shropshire Volunteers in full uniform; the fourth was occupied by the engineers, the owners of mines and foundries, etc. with their families; the fifth and sixth boats closed the procession, gaily ornamented with flags, and loaded with coal, the first commercial product that had ever passed over the valley on this noble bridge of union.

The evening was calm, and the favourite tunes of 'God Save the King' and 'Rule Britannia' floated in the air, amongst the echoes of the vale. Many people (probably more than eight thousand) were stationed all around us, from the tops of the mountains to the banks of the Dee, and were cheering and exulting, with intervals of silent astonishment. All within sight or hearing were expressing their sense of the general happiness."

This description gives the authentic atmosphere of cheerful enterprise, typical of the period.[1] The poverty and misery of industrial centres are well studied and quoted, but history now neglects the best spirit, the transformed ghost of the lost feudal system that survived within this type of self-contained enterprise.

[1] The village that supplied the firewood for smelting is still called Coed Poeth (hot wood).

His workmen adored Telford—all knew him by sight and felt free to consult him, as he frequently consulted them. Even the casual labourers he recruited locally felt proud of *their* part in the achievement, and the best stayed on and worked with him on other jobs. Telford's enterprises were large, but never became so large as to become impersonal. The work provided not only good or better wages, it was something that all felt worth doing.

This new "cut" transported stone, lime, tiles, bricks and coal to and from the Black Country, and the prosperity of the district depended upon it. It was also the excuse for water parties, after the old Elizabethan tradition, with laughter and music, which carried on in Wales far longer than in England. Not only the barge horses, bright as their barges with painted "roller" beads on their harness, and strings of dusty donkeys crossed the aqueduct. Riding ponies galloped over, taking friends across on social visits; a terrifying idea, when the riders rode high above the iron rail, and a slip entailed swimming the horse the entire length of the bridge.

The stone and iron structure is still sound, though the neglected tow-path is badly worn, and all the handsome quay has been taken over and destroyed by a new chemical works. If the praiseworthy efforts of Inland Waterways can preserve this thousand-foot-long playground, it will be the effort of those who rebel against the enforced noise of present popular amusements, and seek peace where it may be found.

THE WATER ROAD OR CANAL

The old watermen called all canals "cuts" as, to their sight, the water travelled along a trench "cut out for it". Sometimes it was "cut" into the side of a hill, sometimes "cut" through a hill, but even when on top of an embankment the actual "cut" in the bank was hollowed out and clay lined and banked so that, in effect, a canal is a continuous long tank with an intake and discharge, though the "tank" may be miles in length. Countrymen had always "led" water about, but not until the canal

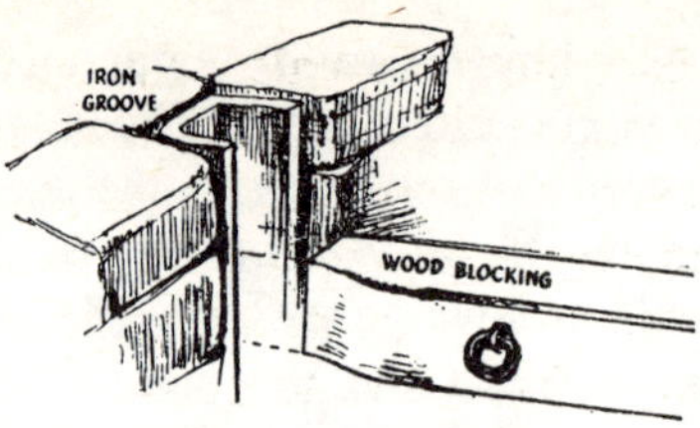

"Shuts" on a canal are lengths of planking, slid into iron grooves, the planks are stored alongside the towpath when not in use

period, when Telford and his contemporaries built aqueducts for industry, was there any impressive architecture to show, or any great credit given, to the designers of waterways.

The canals were for transport and had only localized effects on domestic water problems. In places where the canal ran soft rain water through a hard-water district, all the cottages beside the cut soon had their own private standing stone, from which they "dipped up enough soft water to fill the boiler", but unless this was done on a scale large enough to attract attention the water stealers usually got by unrebuked. This was not the case where a linesman in his tied canal cottage, or a lock gatehouse, kept guard on stealing canal waters.

I remember when one of our garden walls adjoining the Ellesmere Canal needed repair, the workmen seriously consulted the local linesman as to procedure before lifting out a pail of water to mix the mortar.

After "Closing Time" the difficulty had been amicably resolved. My mother, as owner of the wall, paid half-a-crown to the "Port of Ellesmere Authority" for permission to draw accommodation water for a period not exceeding six weeks—and the linesman lent us the bucket!

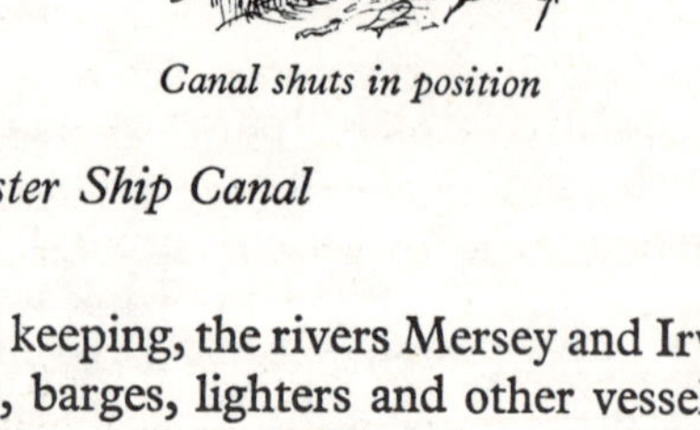

Canal shuts in position

Preamble to Manchester Ship Canal

REPORT 1840

"the making, and keeping, the rivers Mersey and Irwell navigable and passable for boats, barges, lighters and other vessels from Liverpool to a place called Hunts Bank in Manchester, will be very beneficial to trade. Advantageous to the poor, and convenient for the carriage of coals, cannel, stone, timber and other goods to and from the Towns and parts ajacent. It will very much tend to the employing and increase of watermen, seamen and *be a means to preserve the highways.*

"The Railway was constructed ostensibly as an addition to the means of conveyance, to reduce its cost, and to obtain a degree of punctuality etc., etc., . . . Without entering upon discussion, I may advert to the remarkable fact that the success of the Railway is attributed to the conveyance of passengers! at this time regarded as unimportant.

"They (the rivers) are to a great extent controlable by art and rendered applicable to purposes suggested by circumstances which are consequent upon the process of civilization."

SOME PROBLEMS OF PURE WATER SUPPLY FROM RESERVOIRS

"*Potable Water* refers to water which is drinkable as a result of being free of pathogens, toxic materials, tastes, odours, colours and other undesirable physical, chemical and biological characteristics.

Raw Water refers to water which is available as a supply for use, but which has not yet been treated or purified.

Recovery Zone. The area of a stream in which active, primarily aerobic, decomposition of the pollutant is occurring.

Stabilization. Biological transformation of organic wastes into more durable metabolic products."

Glossary. U.S. DEPT. OF HEALTH EDUCATION & WELFARE

Firms of Water Engineers, Biological Institutes, and many Research Laboratories all work full time on reservoir water. The subject is far beyond the comprehension of the ordinary householder. But even a short description will show its varied interest.

Most reservoirs are set high among the hills, it is mechanically easier to dam across a narrow valley; the intake of water is likely to be pure; and the height insures a good force of flow for the distribution system. (Hill folk call it "a good lift".) The rain and melting snow water that fill the innumerable hillside rills is about the purest water on earth. (Lower water that has passed through layers of earth and rock may acquire mineral properties.) These rills, cascading down over bare rock, are aerated by pure hill winds and have little time to acquire any form of life—animal or vegetable.

Later, when several rills have combined to form gylls and swift brooks, small pools may allow some water plants and animals to collect, but the natural balance of minute water snails and water fleas, scavenging their microscopic foods, keeps the water clear, and the movement keeps it fresh.

At quite high altitudes, peat and soil erosion, etc., may affect the water, and some rocks give grip to growths of algae, but unless a sheep has died, centrally and recently, you do not find colloidal and fatty pollutions in mountain streams.

The problems arise when "running water" reaches the reservoir and becomes "lake water" (or even static pond water).

In large lake-like reservoirs, water currents and wind stir the water, aeration is usually adequate, and fish and plants usually establish a balanced purification. (Though we believe that where the reservoir fills over long established farm lands, local trouble may arise for some time, and modern engineering tends to prepare the area more thoroughly before the filling up proceeds.)

Problems become more urgent when the water enters the distribution system, as smaller impounded supplies approximate to static conditions, which allow the rapid development of vegetable and fungoid growths. Even smooth tanks and pipes allow these forms of life to develop. Some of these clog the flow, others actually destroy the retaining surfaces, and all need expert treatment. Mechanical cleaners are used, but most of these necessitate complicated alternative distribution of the water while the clearing work is being carried out. Control by chemical means (chlorine and copper sulphate are common usage) may sometimes increase the difficulty, because, if any one growth proves resistant, the destruction of all rival growths gives it unpredictable advantage, and the treatment may starve out the animal organisms which had previously controlled its spread. This childishly simple description of their extremely complicated science brings up the old problem of how much understanding can exist during *any* given period, between the householder and the expert. Even today the average householder knows little of the bacterial studies used by the experts on behalf of her water supply. The householder today is only likely to meet with "objectionable deposits" at the discharge end of her Municipal Water Supply. Pipe moss and the long strands of grey filliant that may invade even the down-spouts from the roofs, or choke surface runways. Mats of debris, embedded in slime, may accumulate in waste traps; strange fungoid forms appear like magic around defective joints in the plumbing; these are the only tokens the householder knows.

Many domestic bleaches, being based on chloride, clear algae from their surface holds, and housewives have learnt to use it to clear the green surface growth that makes her brick paths slippery: Though some bleaches and disinfectants may disrupt the working of the septic tank.

A municipal sewerage disposal plant can, in the care of an enthusiastic, active chemist and gardener, vie with a municipal park, and deserve a band-stand, to set amidst its well-manured flowery gardens! Others are less ornamental, and in most of them the disposal of the surplus "sludge" is still controversial.

As a gardener (not an expert scholar) this residual "sludge" seems to be most usable for dry corn products, or for legumes, where the seed only is eaten and the lush watery haulm is composted. For brassicas, saladings and most soft fruit, the sludge can be objectionable, though good for encouraging old long planted orchards, or reclaiming barren stony lands for replanting. But the findings of the "peasant's" experience are often cheerfully rebuked (if not successfully debunked) by the scholar, and the subject of potable water is interesting from the beginning to the end of the entire system.

WATER COMPELLED

PUMPS, SCREWS AND RAMS

The design of any pump varies so much, according to the depth of the water and volume to be raised, that we can only list a few basic types—a tall long-handled pump giving leverage for a heavy lift, a short-handled pump suitable for cistern work, a garden pump, etc. The outward appearance varies even more than the mechanism. The village pump may be encased in wood, packed against a post, and set under a canopy of thatch—or, in the north it may be of monumental stone. In London Aldgate Pump and many others still stand firm; and the print on Plate 11 shows Tottenham old pump being used to fill water carts. One small item you will find on nearly all pumps—a knob, just on top of the spout, on which to hang the bucket!

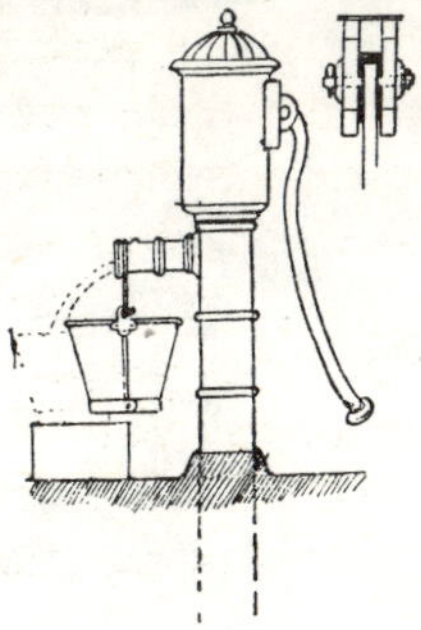

A stand, often the drain grid, to position the pail before pumping

There are also rotary pumps, and other rotating handles which turn an Archimedean screw. This screw has had many adaptations since its inventor leapt from his bath shouting "Eureka!" It can be operated by hand or treadmill and there is a pinioned screw that turns, like a mill, by the force of the running water, and all these pumps and screws can be operated mechanically. The ram still supplies many country houses. This was a new idea in my grandfather's time, and in the stillness of a Sunday evening, when the queer, mechanical heart-beat could be heard, the local chapels denounced those backsliding males who sneaked off to sit, mesmerized, in the leafy wood, adoring an "idolatrous ram".

ARCHIMEDEAN SCREW

There was a development of the screw by which the stream supplying the screw with water also supplied the power to turn the screw and so raise the water.

A light paddle wheel was fixed on to the shaft of the screw, and this paddle wheel, being turned by the force of the running water, turned the shaft. If the stream had sufficient force it worked, but the ratio between the weight *on* the paddles and the weight *in* the screw had to be delicately adjusted.

Hand driven screw

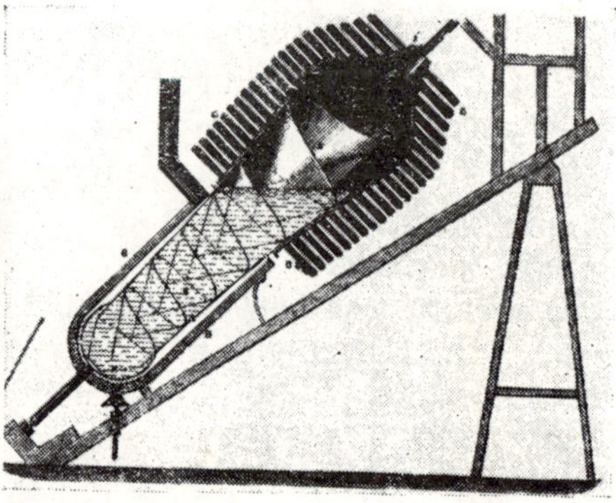

A Danside type of screw

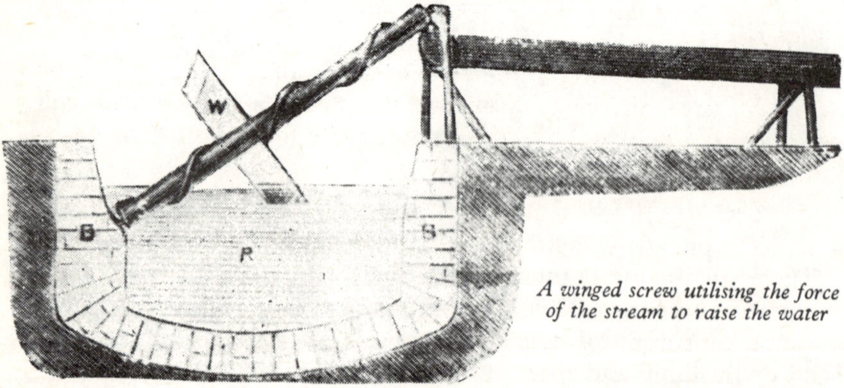

A winged screw utilising the force of the stream to raise the water

THE TUBE WELL AND PUMP

"This kind of pump (and well) was used by the English soldiers during the Abyssinian war . . . You drive the tube through to water-bearing strata and you can pump up the water in due proportion to the moisture of the said strata at the blast holes—and by continual pumping the vacuum produced by the suction will cause the water to flow towards the blast holes. Such is the construction of the tube wells which we have heard so much about these last years, but you must not at all times expect such wells to yield that plentiful supply which can be obtained from a properly constructed well. Nor can you expect these pumps will work with the same ease, because in the tube pump you are depending upon the interrupted pressure of the atmosphere, which is hindered by the air having to get down to the lower strata before it can reach the blast holes." (I.e. it is like drawing water from a *closed* vessel—unless you can let the air in you can't draw the water out. Thus, such early tube wells would "draw" for a period and then, unless the lower strata was very loosely knit, air would have to be sucked down the tube before the water could come up.)

Notes taken from a periodical of 1883

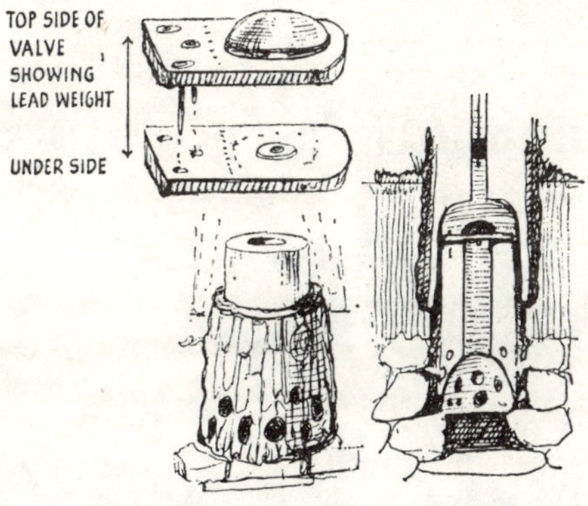

CLACK VALVES

It is the two clack valves, one in the bucket of the plunger and one over the base of the shaft below, that makes the suction lock and (incidentally) makes it the *second* stroke of the pump handle that delivers the gush of water raised by the *first* stroke.

The diagram explains this:

1. The plunger goes down and sucks the water up from below and lifts it half way up the tube.

2. The plunger goes down again *through* this water (valve opens) and sucks up a second supply—at the same time lifting the first supply level with the pump spout.

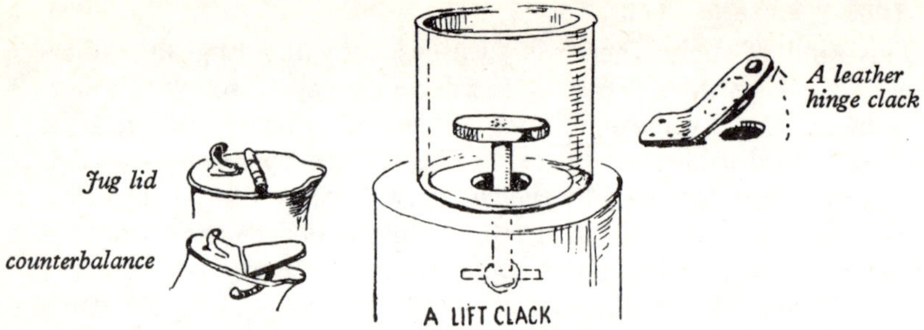

If the pump stands idle for so long that the lifted water leaks down and the parts shrink in drying, water may have to be poured down from above to fill the tube above the plunger and several strokes may be needed before suction is again established.

The length of the lift, i.e. the weight of water raised by the plunger, depends on the bore, and the depth of the water, and somewhat on the weight of the plunger and leverage of the handle.

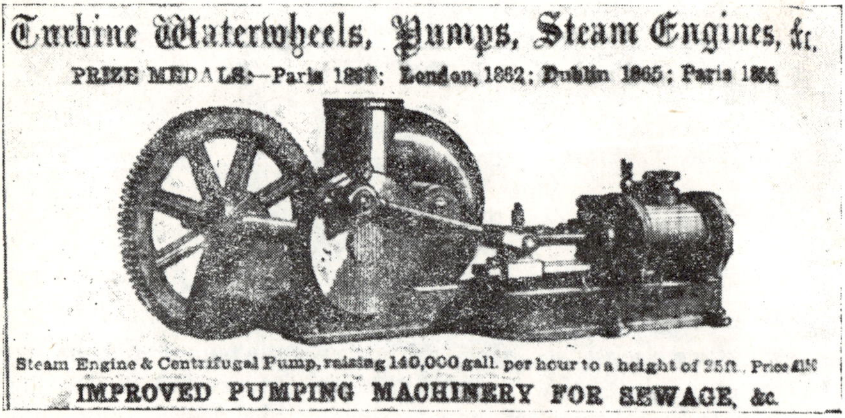

The little oil engine arrives. The Bath and West Show of 1869 *showed a small centrifugal pump worked by a little oil engine that solved the problem of "laid on" water for many rural establishments. These small oil engines only ran for some hours daily—just long enough to fill the overhead cisterns. Their strong little iron bodies, mummified in dried oil and dust, still clutter hundreds of rural outhouses, and the adequate cisterns they filled have long since perished (or remain to puzzle the modern householder). The people who did appreciate the size of these cisterns were the old firemen, for in the days of slow horse-drawn fire engines an adequate supply of water* in *the house was the only hope of saving it.*

HYDRAULIC OR WATER RAM IN A BRISTOL HOSPITAL

"This useful self-acting apparatus is the invention (or at least so first recorded) of Mr. Whitehurst of Derby, during 1772; afterwards improved upon by Montgolfier and subsequently by his son. A very short time after this latter improvement the invention was re-invented by a plumber at Bristol, and it has since that date been many times re-invented.... The story goes that a Bristol plumber was engaged at a hospital in Bristol to fix some piping which descended a long length down from above. The tap was the ordinary ground-in plug-cock pattern which turned very easily, so the act of turning it off arrested the water quickly, and by reason of the momentum produced by the weight of water, combined with its velocity, caused the lower end of the pipe to burst. We are told that in this case this phenomenon occurred nearly every time the tap was turned off. After several attempts to remedy this exasperating evil, without avail, the plumber soldered on another small pipe just behind the tap, and every time the tap was used, the 'cut off' water rushed back with violence, up this escape pipe. It occurred to the plumber to carry the pipe to a higher level; still the water rushed up, and he, being determined to investigate the matter, and to find out how high the water would rise, carried the pipe to the top of the building, where another cistern was provided, and supplied with water without trouble or expense."

From the 'English Mechanic', 1883.

We do not vouch for it being true, but it's the sort of thing that might easily happen.

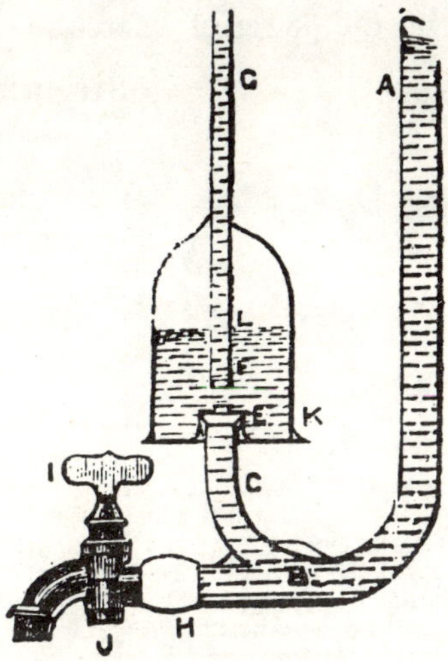

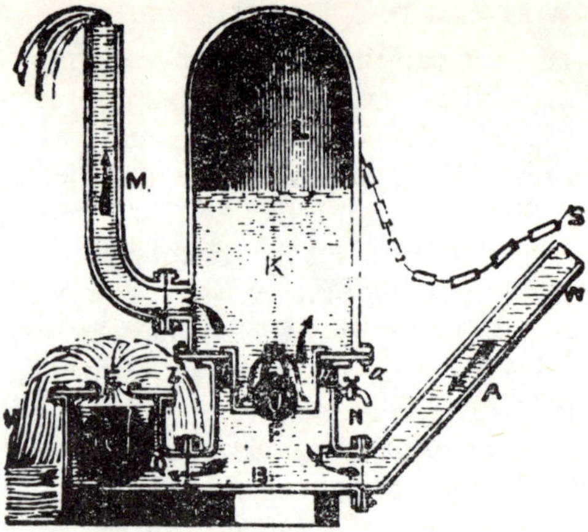

THE RAM ON THE 19TH-CENTURY SCOTTISH FARM.

"A ram may be described as a sloping pipe in which the stream runs, having a valve at its lower end, to be shut at intervals, and a small tube rising near the end towards a reservoir above where it receives a portion of the water at each interruption of the stream. Water allowed to run for one second in a pipe ten yards long by two inches wide and sloping six feet, acquires momentum enough to drive about half a pint, on the shutting of the cock, into a tube leading to a reservoir forty feet high. Such an apparatus, therefore, with the valve shutting every second, raises about sixty half pints (i.e. four gallons) a minute. The valve ingeniously combined is called a sniffling valve. This ram could supply water from a riverlet to a cistern in the farmhouse standing at a height beyond the power of a force pump."

STEPHENS, *Book of the Farm*

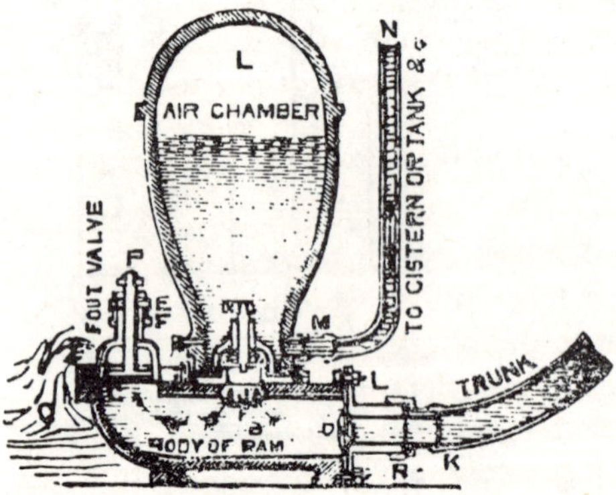

FOUNTAINS

WATER FOR THE GARDEN

"Gardens must alwaies be, so they be easily watered, if not with some running stream, some use to be made of mill, or such like, as may serve the turn and a natural streame. Columella would have you make your search for water when the summer is on the late part of ——, which is in September, before the entrance of winter, for then you may understand the strength and goodness of the springs, when, after the great burning heat of the summer, the ground hath long while continued without rain. If you cannot thus have water; you must make some standing pond, at the upper part of the ground."

He carries on to say that if completely destitute of water, "the ground must be delve, three or four foot deepe, when it will well be able to abide what so ever drought do happe".

The English garden fountain played down the centuries, though never to the extent and delicacy of the French fountains, or with the volume of water in many continental ones.

The best fountain period was probably that of the formal architectural garden of the late 1600's. By the 1700's the jets had become stronger and risen higher, and there were more of the flowing type of fountains that often served a bathing pool. The dripping well type developed best at the fern craze period of the 1800's. About the 1850's ferns were a fashionable study, not too difficult for the amateur, and giving scope for one of the pleasant rural pursuits of the period. Fern cases that stood in the window were popular, and whole conservatories were given over to fern culture. The purchaser of a Victorian villa near Llangollen was puzzled by a small glass-roofed room or conservatory. It had a garden door and was about six feet square and reaching to the level of the upper windows. The floor was laid with the usual Victorian cream-and-blue tile patterns, but the walls were a honeycomb of cement pockets, roughly shaped like swallows' nests, and varied in size from little crevices barely two inches across, to deep pockets a foot wide and a foot deep. An old lead pipe jutting from the centre of the floor had provided an ornamental spray and there had been room for hundreds of ferns of every description. It was a Victorian fern house and the green stained cement was still as hard as the rock it was supposed to represent.

This period of fern-fountain enthusiasm depleted the misty hills of many rare varieties of fern, and developed a type of fountain called a "mist spray", wherefrom the water dripped down through fern-embowered grottoes to a moss-grown pool, completed by a clump of six-foot Royal Osmunda fern and low pond weed and lilies.

Most of the Victorian fountains depended on a natural water pressure, or used their own reservoir built high on a water tower in the kitchen garden. (The trick fountain that could be turned on suddenly and drench the unsuspecting guests was mercifully reserved for the few eccentrics.)

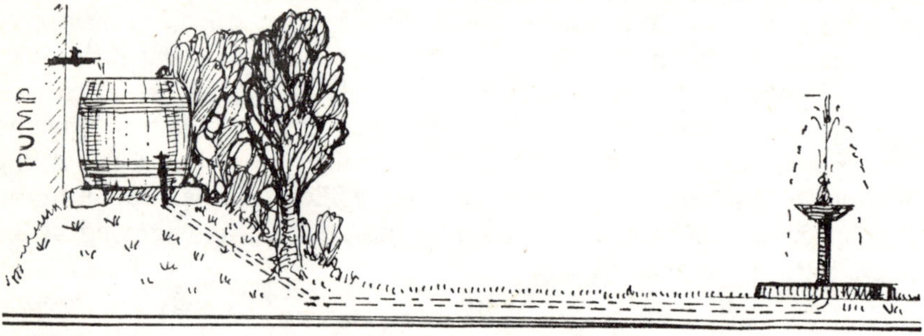

The very simple construction of many Victorian fountains. The tank is concealed behind the shrubbery

Instructions for a Garden Fountain, Date 1868

"Get a water barrel to hold about 150 gallons and place it at an elevation of 20 ft. or more anywhere out of sight. Connect an inch pipe to the bottom of the barrel and lay it along (under ground is understood) to where the fountain is to be placed. Narrow the aperture of the fountain end of the pipe and drill a few holes about 3 inches from the top" (to form the spray).

The author finds this simple "garden note" interesting as the fountain in their garden was built at this date and to these instructions. The barrel, a 6 ft. high tar tun, is now giving way, but the ½-inch lead pipes hold on, and as the garden is on a hillside the fountain plays a good 16 ft. high. The only addition is a ball tap to the supply barrel to turn off the water automatically.

THE INDOOR FOUNTAIN

The table fountain developed with the elaborate dinner parties of the 1890's. Flower and fruit arrangements had become so wonderfully ornate that it was difficult to invent anything new, and the carved ice blocks that melted slowly through the long courses were replaced by little fountains that played down over the central flower arrangements.

Later, after the first Japanese exhibition at the White City in Shepherd's Bush, the fountains were adapted to run little streams through the Japanese table gardens that grew hundred-year-old trees less than a foot high, and set out tiny porcelain figures, mossy banks and wooden bridges.

The table fountain was never more than a toy, but it did stimulate invention, and may have inspired some plumber to a more useful study.

The ice-block fountain, with goldfish, in the old Queen's Hall, its green fern-hidden rim surrounded by red plush upholstery, was probably the last, most typical, and best loved of all Victorian indoor fountains.

WATER DOMICILED

Household Water

"He the which wyll dwell at pleasure, and for proffyte, and helth of his body, he must dwell at elbowe-rome. Having water and woode anexed to his howse, fir yf he be destytuted of any of the pryncypalles —that is to say, fyrst *Water*, for to wasshe and to wrynge and to bake and to brewe—and for parrell [peril] whych might fall by fyre, it were a great dyscommodyous thynge. Better it were to lacke woode than to lack water."

A. BOORDE (12th century)

"The constant supply of hot water has now become almost a necessary in all well-regulated famillies whose wants in this respect (baths) demand a daily and liberal allowance."

WALSH, FRCS. 1859

Hot shaving water was usually rain water from the side boiler of the stove, and no woman washed her hair, or her face with anything else but "soft" water. Most hotels supplied rain water to bedrooms. Little hotels in Devon and Cornwall brought it up in thick red earthenware mugs, and the hot brownish water smelt of moorlands and baked clay. Grand hotels used covered brass or enamel cans (and mankind said it wouldn't lather, if it wasn't rain water). River water was used for washing clothes if the well water was hard.

THE WATER SYSTEM (*See Reservoir, plate 16*)

After the "wild water" is collected from the catchment area it runs into the main reservoir, usually held back behind dams up in the mountains. From here the water passes by pipes to the local supply reservoir (usually covered tanks nearer the town) and from these it runs to the service pipes. Through these it reaches the residential district, and from the service pipe a connecting pipe takes it to the grounds of the house. All this is controlled by the water board or local water company. Therefore a stop tap (under the control of the company) is placed just outside the entrance to the grounds, and usually a second (under the control of the householder) just within the grounds—so that either side can call off the water supply independently. Beyond the boundary, the actual pipes and plumbing are the property of the householder, but he remains responsible to the water company and pays water rates for his supply of the water (and his right to complain if it is not satisfactory). This can only be a very general explanation, as local conditions and local councils vary as much as the water.

The length of the owner's pipe, between the service pipe and his house, depends upon the layout of the grounds. In large gardens it may be complicated and varied, with extra stop taps for fountains or garages. On a large estate, the whole arrangement of main pipes to a private estate reservoir, and supply pipes from it to the house, may reproduce the whole lay-out in miniature and be a system within itself. But, on the whole, the *dividing point between the water board and the householder is the stop tap at the boundary of his land.*

Having brought the supply pipe underground to the walls of the house it must enter, preferably underground, and modern builders usually leave an open drain pipe through the walls for the water pipe to pass through. Where water is being introduced for the first time into old houses, the builder has a rabbity job, and where old houses are stone built the methods of mediæval sappers undermining a fortress are reproduced! Many Victorian rockeries resulted from "what they got out, before they got in". Sometimes, where the old successive foundations have thinned out to wall thickness, the pipe has to be got through high above ground level.

Once inside the house, the main stop tap is placed. Even if there is another just outside this is advisable, as this is the tap which enables the whole house to be drained dry if shut up through winter's frost, or for any other reason.

Now comes an historical point that dates the arrival of sanitary arrangements.

When plumbing was still primitive and refinements ignored, the special drinking water was still fetched from some outside spring or well, because, as grandmother said, "Water that has been so *harassed* about in pipes cannot be wholesome"[1]. Therefore to avoid any possible pollution the first tap for drinking water was placed where the water first entered the house, frequently in the kitchen. Today, where any water supply is dubious, or an old suspect water supply has been supplemented at a later date, you get a special set of direct supply pipes serving taps marked "drinking water".

Apart from this possible complication all the water goes to the top of the house, fills the house cistern up in the roof space, and from there is carried down to the hot-water system and where it is required.

The round copper drum (a cylinder) is where the circulatory system is

[1] From this period (in England about 1800 onwards) are the carafes with covering glasses that once stood on every bedroom washstand—but are now found only on the "Speaker's" table at board meetings, or to indicate which is "the Lecturer".

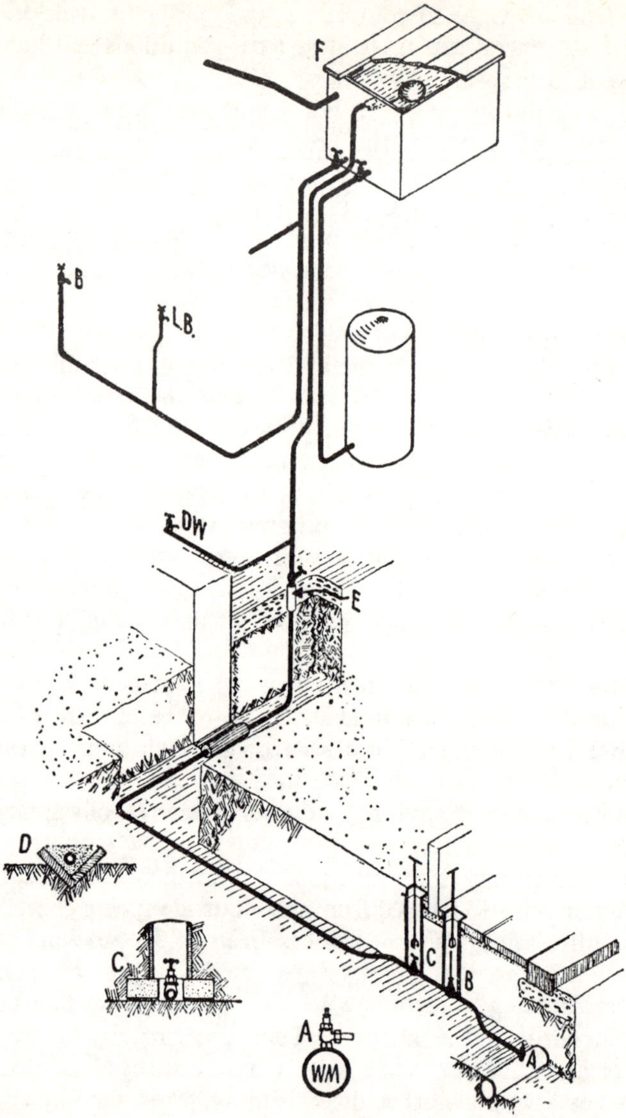

Water systems diagram by permission of G. J. Nash., F.R.S.H., F.I.P.H.E., R.P.

joined to the saddle boiler, behind the kitchen fire, or to the separate water heating system. The round copper drum is the store for the hot water, and is pleasantly familiar in our airing cupboards.

Thus the wild white water of the hills, caught by the engineers, doctored by the chemists, and controlled by boards and companies, becomes domiciled and domesticated.

THE BOILER

THE CAULDRON BOILER

> "By Saxon law, if the man put the heavy cauldron of water on to the fire and it boiled over (or it was upset?) and scalded the baby lying by the fire, the woman was held to blame, for leaving her helplessly swaddled baby in such a dangerous position."
>
> *From the Penitentials of Archbishop Theodore, translated by T. Wright, E.E.T.S.*

Few people nowadays realize how completely separate were the water heating and cooking processes in the centuries of open hearth fires.

Roasting was done before the fire, the fat dripping down into the dripping-pan below. Baking, if not arranged under an iron pot on the hearth, was done in a beehive oven, often in another room. Boiling was done in iron or brass pans, balanced on legs over, or suspended above, the fire. Another form of boiling, more like cooking in a double saucepan, was done by standing separate covered pots upright inside one large cauldron of boiling water that was almost constantly on the fire, and was the first real boiler. This boiler usually had a wooden stand inside that was held down by the pots and goods balanced on it, and some items might be cooked under this slatted stand. For dyeing cloth, the dye material was packed below and the cloth swum loosely above it.

There were, in large establishments, extra boilers[1] built outside, or in sheds, to supply water for baths or washing-up, and the boiler was one of the first items to be placed away from the main hearth and be built in over a separate fire. In Saxon MSS the oven is shown as an independent unit, sometimes outside the house. Later, it moved in alongside the main fire, for though still heated separately, the logs direct from the fire could be used, and the hot ash raked out back onto the fire again. The gradual enclosing of the open fire, and the use of iron fireplaces, finally gathered all three fires under one chimney, where they were all arranged side-by-side in a row, thus becoming the kitchen range (*see Food in England*).

The side-boiler of this early period still continued in use in some cottages. It was easily filled from well or tap, and being constantly by the side of the fire, supplied hot water without using any extra fuel. For ordinary purposes, it was supplemented by the kettle, but for clothes washing the wash boiler soon evolved as a large separate heater (*see* Laundry).

[1] Caernarvon Castle shows the stone foundations of a row of these extra water boilers, and they are shown also over fires, outside taverns and hospices, in many MSS up to the fifteenth century.

The outside boiler in the yard continues in use in old farm steadings to the present day, providing an independent supply of hot water for farmyard needs. These can vary from scalding the bristles off the pig, to a hurried shave in the harness-room!

DETAIL LEARNED FROM THE OLD OPEN BOILER

A structural detail, often unnoticed, is the expansion curve allowed for on old hand-made pot stands.

If the top surface were made absolutely flat, the pan would wobble on the raised centre as soon as it became hot.

The spokes that distributed the heat towards the outer edge of the boiling pan were as few as compatible with rigidity, and were designed to take the legs of the stand, which were riveted on from below, so that the top rim of the stand remained smooth.

If you examine old experienced brass pans, you will often see a small central spot about the size of a penny where the central boss of the iron stand had risen till it contacted the brass.

TO THE CIRCULATING BOILER

Boiler Burst at Claremont

"We went through the large dark Kitchen with its immense fire and admirable hot plate dresser. In the back kitchen the boiler had just burst."

KILVERT, 1870

With cold water let in at the top and hot water let out at the bottom begins the long and honourable line of circulating boilers: the boot boiler, side boiler, saddle boiler, back, and top boilers, etc., and all the hot water systems which are heated from under, behind, above or below the kitchen stove. Curiously, it was sea-captain Parry, of the North West Passage, who first installed a boiler that used the heat, otherwise wasted, up the chimney.

Captain Parry described how the snow is introduced down one opening and the water drawn off through a brass tap (exactly the same as the early type of side boiler, where cold water is poured in at the top and drawn off below).

THE NAVY LEADS THE WAY

"Some material alterations were made in the interior arrangements of the ships which experience suggested as necessary, and I must not here omit to notice a simple, ingenious and effectual contrivance, now first adopted, for melting snow for our consumption as water, without any additional expense of fuel.

The smoke issuing from the galley fire, and indeed its heat generally, does little or no service beyond the ordinary purposes of cooking. It occurred to Messrs. Lambe & Nicholson to occupy a portion of the aperture through which the smoke ascends, by a metallic vessel or tank of considerable capacity, allowing the smoke to pass freely up on each side of it and thus to communicate a constant heat to the vessel. This apparatus, which was so little in the way that it could not even be seen, produced, without any increase of fuel, and with the temperature of the external atmosphere nearly at zero, sixty-five gallons of pure water from morning till night, so conducive to health and comfort."

Captain Parry's second voyage in search of the North West Passage

With the coming of the circulating boiler (that is, water heated and stored in excess of the boiler's direct capacity) back and saddle boilers were fitted, so that the central fire draught could be made to draw the heat of the fire under, and through to the back of the boiler which, as the water heated, caused it to rise up and fill the reserve tank above. The cold water sank down to keep the boiler constantly full. (This is a very brief outline, as the simple mechanics of the ordinary kitchen boiler are known to everyone.) The complicated modern thermostatically-controlled gas and electric immersion heaters are beyond the scope of this volume, though some of the earlier designs, as adopted for bath water, will be described under Baths.

NEW WINE IN OLD BOTTLES

From 1850 the average country house continued to depend on its coal boiler for hot water, and as this was usually part of the cooking range it was frequently a choice of dinner or baths, according to which damper was drawn out. Sometimes the water boiler had a separate existence outside, and was stoked with coke, morning and evening (frequently by the gardener, who sometimes had a side pipe to the greenhouse, though this was usually a separate system).

In many cases these old heating systems, that had carried on for fifty years or more (with recurrent repairs and replacements) gave out from sheer overwork. Sometimes, the old furred-up pipes trickled more and more slowly till, in old age, they ran too slowly to fill a bath before it grew cold. Sometimes they choked up, and there was a violent explosion, often in the midst of preparations for a dinner party. This was because the extra heat of the cooking range, and the rapid drawing off of bath water, left the boiler behind the fire almost empty, and full of compressed steam. This then blew up, throwing chunks of cast iron about the kitchen, amidst clouds of steam and hot soup! Sometimes the end just came quietly, lack of domestic help caused families in "reduced circumstances" to give up the bedroom washstand with its ewer and basin, and "go to wash in the new bathroom to save trouble". This used more running water, especially if the bedroom toilet supply had been carried separately from some soft-water pump. This change to the bathroom finished by furring up the old system completely, the old lead pipes perished in their plaster, so that the time came when a *new system had to be installed.*

This meant the complete upheaval of the whole house, including redistribution of bedrooms (to turn some into new bathrooms) and the blocking of passages and insertion of tanks and cylinders in most unlikely places. In old hotels this rearrangement often accounts for huge bathrooms whose uneven floors tilt down to balconied windows. In castles, curious slits within the thick walls show where old "wardrobes" and "places of easement" have been chiselled out to insert a bath. This is possible because the walls in old castles were constructed as a stone sandwich, the hollow filled with cement and rubble. So, by removing the inner wall and scraping out the mortar, shoring up the ceiling and laying down a floor, you got a cave about four foot deep—which would take a bath and the bather if not too fat. (A plastic waste pipe could be taken out through a suitable gargoyle.)

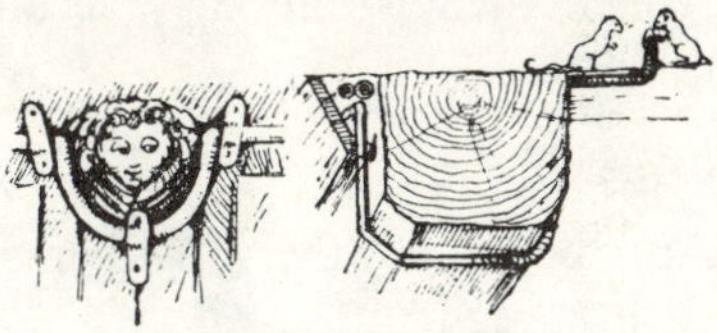

Today, even in the best conversions, the new water system leads a detached existence. Its roots may be cement set in some erstwhile dungeon, or wine cellar, or stand isolated and aloof within the huge old open fireplace (looking like a small inadequate idol in a cathedral). From this new boiler, the new copper pipes disperse all over the house, pervading it with gurgles and whistlings, but they never combine *with* the house. The pipes go up the walls; upheld by little copper tentacles, they lie gleaming, high up along the cornice; they disappear suddenly through the ceilings, and pop up out of mouseholes in the floors above. Sometimes they pass along, encased in plaster board, or they slink across a room, like ivy along one of the oak beams. In bedrooms they rise hollow white pedestals, like porcelain lilies, supporting hygienic washhand basins, all set about with suitable tiles, but always, and for ever, they are an "installation". The water system that is *born in the house* belongs to the house, as one of the family. But an "installation" stays apart, like a visiting aunt; someone one is very glad to have, but one can't help wondering how soon she'll go.

DRIPS OF WATER FROM CONDENSATION

> "Beneath thy leaden tubes, to fix a vase, and catch the falling dew-drops; which supply soft water; salubrious, and far the best to soak thy hops and brew thy generous beer."
>
> DECKER

The condensation on cold pipes was an early problem and is still unsolved. Cold pipes crossing a hot room cause much trouble. In old houses enclosing the pipe does not always cure the damp, and if it conceals it and it accumulates, the result may be worse than the cure.

Hammering

This is the name given to the extraordinary sound made by water when sealed up in a pipe or closed tank from which all air has been driven out, as in the case of some hot pipes where a vacuum is caused on cooling. There being no air resistance, the water falls in a solid body with a bang, not a splash. It is not a very common phenomenon, but may account for some ghostly knockings and spirit rappings.

DRINKING WATER. ANCIENT AND MODERN

> "At Carlton in Leicestershire, owing to the water, the inhabitants have a strange uncouth wharbling in their speech."
>
> CAMDEN BRIT

Today, on the whole, we do not worry about our water supply, unless we have not got one, or it is chlorinated, or turned off, or very hard. Once we are "on the main" we accept tap water as it comes. But thirty years ago many small country places lacked piped water and so collected their different supplies of water for different purposes. Thus, old household books always gave definite instructions as to the *variety* of water to be used for various purposes. Ale was to be made with well water, washing done with rain water, and many cooking recipes insisted on freshly drawn spring water or water that has stood overnight, etc. In our own house (originally seventeenth-century and altered every twenty years since, like most ordinary country houses in England) we had tap water laid in by 1890 (some of the small bore lead pipes still exist), but till 1918 someone always took the big can and walked about a quarter of a mile to fetch the drinking water. This flowed out from the mossy bank, in a strong curve like a scimitar, bright as diamonds, with silver lights flashing through it. It was carried back in a wooden pail balanced on the head, or in tin buckets slung from a wooden shoulder yoke. The big ewers on the bedroom washstands were always filled with tap water, but the glass water bottles with their drinking glass covers were carried downstairs and filled with fresh drinking water.

Travel on foot and horseback made people more knowledgeable about drinking water. When going over the hills one did not drink till near the top, where water ran swiftly or waterfalls crashed down, white, onto the rocks (that was water worth drinking). Over the flat tops of the hills, the slower undecided streams of the "divide" tasted of peat, and some were so brackish they wrinkled your mouth like old walnuts. Snow water was never drunk, it was considered dangerous, producing goitre.

Drinking water for saddle and transport horses had to be considered by travellers. Many old routes followed rivers for guidance (*see* plate 17), but also because they provided water for the animals. That is why when posting and coach travel developed the new hard roadways had to be punctuated by stone water troughs every few miles. These troughs were not for the earlier drovers or pack horse trains. They had to rely on longer stretches of river, or streams, or fair-sized lakes on their routes. For, to let fifty or so thirsty mules, or a herd of young bullocks, fight their way to one small trough would have been dangerous. The long wooden troughs, like those still used to water long ox teams, were probably fairly common, and old engravings show such wooden troughs lying by some old pumps, but the cattle troughs would soon decay, after falling into disuse. "Watering the horses" was a definite consideration when gigs, coaches, and all manner of traps went trotting up and down the country. It was during that same period that people also were going up and down, taking the spa waters, and dipping, drinking, gargling, and discovering new mineral springs, and really *taking an interest* in drinking water.

In the 1700's and 1800's people spent holidays taking the waters, and the intelligentsia talked spa waters as today they talk wines. Frequently it was the excess of the wine-drinking that made them so knowledgeable about the waters.

DRINKING WATER IN SPECIAL ESTABLISHMENTS

Clean drinking water in good supply was urgent for all religious settlements. In an old record, giving a close study of pioneer monks searching for a suitable building site, the running water supply is stressed firmly. Static water would not serve, and the romantically beautiful placing of old abbeys, had originally more practical than aesthetic value.

A town or village settlement might develop unpredictably, a castle or camp be sited of necessity; but a religious housing scheme usually had some constructive intelligence as guide, and was a (comparatively) finite design for a definite purpose. Therefore, their water usually came in at the top, and went out at the bottom, and they usually arranged for an independent supply for use by outsiders. In almost any old religious housing you will find the abbey water supply is independent of the outside, public or road-side well. Much the same precaution is found at inns, where the household supply is kept apart from that free to travellers (*see* Tavern spring).

Even a slight note on the early reformed Cistercian rules shows the importance of clean water. (We choose Cistercian as they did field work and sheep farming, and were as likely to need water as any other labourers.) They rose at 2 a.m. and prayed till dawn, *when they went to wash.* The timetable depended on daylight, and so varied between summer and winter. When light was come they met in chapter, *washed and clean*, and after that they worked till 11.30, when they *washed hands* and came to their breakfast (bread, vegetables, wine and water or metheglyns). Afterwards they went to the dormitory to sleep till 2.30. On rising they were *bid to wash* and *have a drink of water*. At 5.30 vespers, and the second meal of the day (fruits and salads and breads in summer, hot vegetable broths in winter). This wash before meals and after coming in from work, and drinking freely between meals, sounds positively hydropathic compared with the contemporary reports from cities and towns (*see* also page 138).

DRINKING WATER IN THE COUNTRY

Springs, rivers and wells supplied us direct for centuries. We carried our water, and raised it in various ways, and constrained it to run where and how we wanted, and used its power as it flowed past us. As the little hill streams were held back in mill dams for small homesteads so, later, huge lakes were pent up in the mountains to supply water to towns and cities. In places where the only available water supply was below the town, the old local wells and the storage cisterns changed to pumping stations and raised water towers, and only some private house water supplies and the village spring continued in use. The dangers of the larger communal water supplies (that had been a growing problem since the sixteenth century) became rapidly worse with the growth of the cities and towns. The division between drinking water and washing water that, in the country, had been only a matter of convenience and taste, became serious. The problem began earliest in localities that depended upon wells. It was *less urgent on the hill sites*, for springs were less easily contaminated and cleansed themselves. The early plagues and epidemics all spread in the low-lying localities, or at the bottom of valleys. The instinct to fly to the hills to escape infection was taught by hard experience; few connected it with the cleaner water supply. The lowlands were said to breed "mysts" and "infected aires", and "certain fevers" and "agues". *Always, from the earliest mediæval periods, those who sensed the dangers, and fought for the good of the community, had to fight the inertia and obstruction of the very people they wanted to help, and the difficulty of supplying people with clean water was always far less than the difficulty of making the people keep it clean.* The whole subject of town water supply is far beyond this simple book, so we have selected examples, not from the great achievements, but those behind which can be seen the pattern of trial and error.

First we give an example . . .

DRINKING WATER IN TOWNS

In April 1859 there was a meeting to form an "Association to erect Drinking Fountains in the Metropolis". The Earl of Carlisle spoke from the chair—"Referring to their statistics it would be seen that if the poor people of London were as thirsty and as fond of a drink of clear

15. The Elan reservoir. A Welsh valley in the high hills, flooded behind a stone dam, now appears as lake water.

16. Early construction work on an urban reservoir. The work is done by man and horse power; note the circular horse-mill on left and tar-spreading on right.

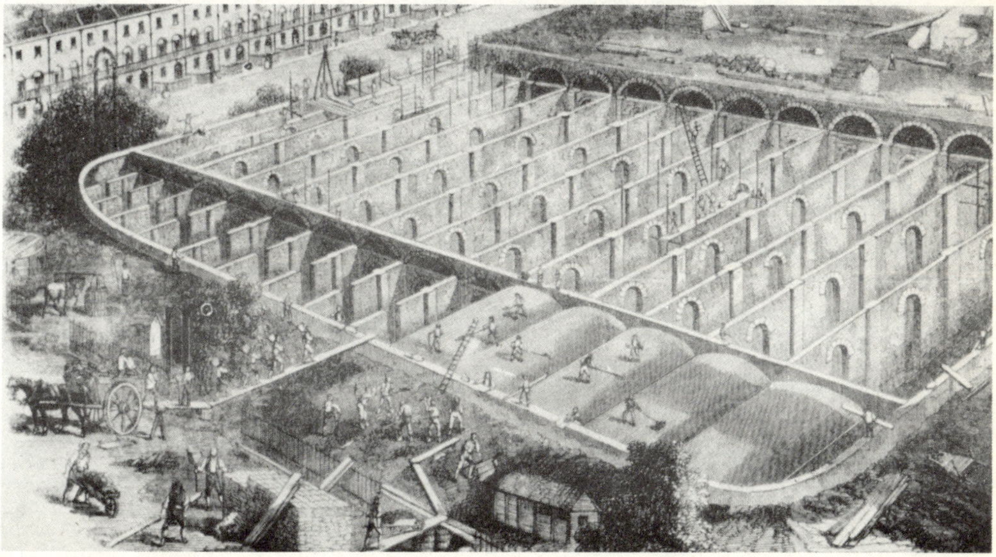

17. The rivers give continuous guidance. Bridges (or fords) mark mileage, and serve as landmarks. Long distance steerage is towards (or between) the mountain peaks (characteristically portrayed). *Example,* to reach the town in distance on left: face the highest peak ahead, walk on the right bank of the river, past two bridges; after a sharp bend in the river, follow the tributary on the left, and the town will appear on the opposite bank; take ferry across.

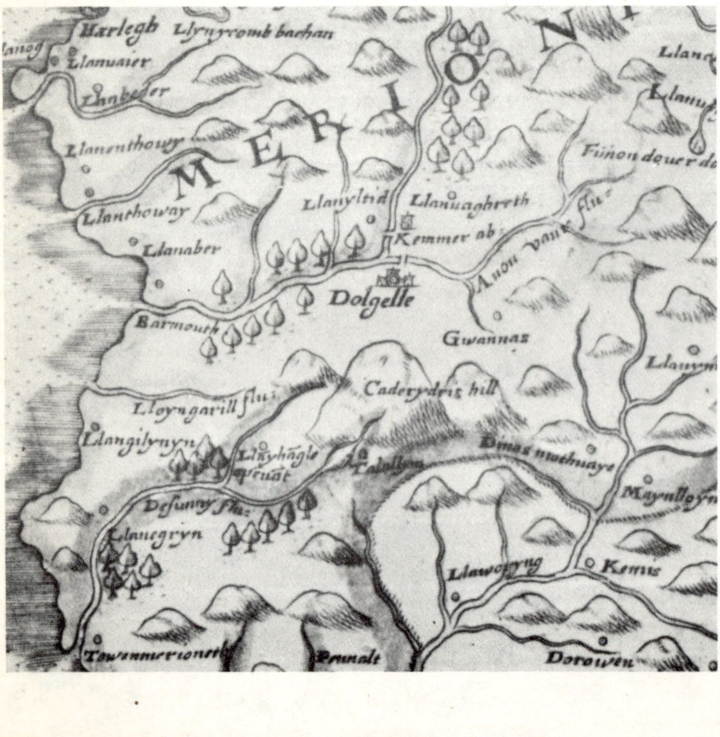

18. By studying the Italian "sketch" map, the Welsh "plan" map is easily understood. Rivers lead to passes over mountains, or through wooded glens. The line of coast towns suggests a connecting coast route, and ferry service and hostel would be expected between Barmouth, Llanaber, Llanenthowys, etc. From Towennierionet one would go up river behind the two hills, passing back to the coast road at Llanegryn.

cool water as the people of Liverpool, it would follow that no less than 132,000,000 draughts of water could be taken in London annually from these fountains. He (Lord Carlisle) was sure the meeting would agree with him that gin palaces and beerhouses, and the habits of intemperance and drunkenness, which were amongst the most besetting sins of their poorer brethren, would soon show a diminution . . ." etc.

Lord Shaftesbury affirmed: "Hundreds were driven into public houses merely from the difficulty of getting a drink of anything but intoxicating liquors," etc.

The estimated costs of erection of a fountain varied from £10 to £30 (and there was some discussion on this). The matter came before the Charity Commissioners and subscription forms "for the convenience of charitably disposed persons" were printed and distributed.

Here it is interesting to note that, in the issued Will Forms of that date for the "charitably disposed persons", their executors are to stipulate that the endowed fountain is provided with a proper filter.

The Vestry of Islington decided to "erect five drinking fountains, at a cost not exceeding £15 each", and a Mr. Gurney promised them "Something additional in order to make them ornamental".

The New River Company agreed to "supply water by meter, at *6d.* per thousand gallons, where delivered under 60 ft. from Trinity High Water Mark, with a slight increase beyond that height".

A student will find it of interest that most of London's solid pumps date from before the eighteenth century. The well in Cornhill was "discovered" in the 1700's, but drinking fountains of great diversity rise thick as mushrooms from 1800 onwards.

THE LENS

> "The world of the invisible; a world shut to our ancestors, was first entered about 100 years ago. It breeds monsters of unheard of form and manner of life. It abounds in miracles, as much as do the remote Indies; but is explored with lesser peril, for it lies everywhere at our very feet and is not sought out for gold. . . .
>
> The lens, which images alike the solar spots and the infusoria. In this interval, what indeed is great and what small? Man; for he thinks and suffers."
>
> OTHO FREDERIC MULLER, 1786

THE VICTORIAN AND MEDIÆVAL REACTIONS TO THE LENS

Although the lens had been known much earlier, and used in the seventeenth century, the microscope was not available for public interest in England before the late eighteenth century. An ardent minister, quoted in a Victorian novel, uses almost the same words as Johann Eichhorn, who was also a pastor: "I have devoted myself to this invisible world . . . and spent my leisure moments on it, so far as my professional duties would permit in order to know God in His smallest and invisible works, and I have found Him very great therein . . . not those vastly heavenly bodies . . . not these alone declare the Glory of the Almighty . . . the smallest also show, just as distinctly, the perfections of their Creator." Eichhorn's small *Natural History of the Smallest Aquatic Animals* was published in 1781. The author may have seen this quoted in Hudson and Grosses' two volumes of 1889. Later, the pious Victorian minister is given a microscope, "a brass instrument by one of the best London makers" (plate 26 shows one of these of that date).[1]

The use of the microscope became a popular hobby during the late 1800's; it was a period when the leisured classes enjoyed study, and fine lenses for microscope, telescope, or wet plate photography, were a new and delightful acquisition (in the days when a Zeiss lens was treasured, and camera cuss was spelt with a K). Gifted Victorian amateurs spent happy hours grinding and silvering mirrors for reflecting telescopes or, with what we should now consider hopelessly inadequate apparatus, cutting and manipulating lenses, and listing and classifying the diverse microscopic water creatures, all of which were at first called collectively "Infusoria".

Historically, this early optical period is specially interesting, because it suddenly justified beliefs that the earlier mediæval scholars held which had been suppressed by the church. In the nineteenth century, the structure of society somewhat approximated to the earlier mediæval feudal system. The earlier "feudal despot" was likely to have been a "military man" and the later "manufacturer despot" was likely to be a "self-educated technical scientist"—but both knew their job, they had good service from their workers. On the workers' level the mediæval peasant could see the magnifying effect of a raindrop, or adjust his round bottle of water to throw concentrated light upon his fine work—but their thoughts had to wait four centuries for the lens to justify their surmise.

The seventeenth-century "raree show" had given way to the late eighteenth-century "majic lanthorn", and by the nineteenth century, enlargements and diagrams could make discoveries visible to the Victorian peasant, and the Victorian "lectures on natural science" had a parallel with the mediæval "public discorses". The thirst for "something new" is eternal. The avidity with which the newly "educated-and-so-able-to-read-for-themselves" Victorian workers soaked up information, is proved in every child's primer, or domestic servant's guide, every volume of which devotes a chapter to "Natural Phenomena", or "Scientific

[1] *The Old Helmet* by Elizabeth Wetheral. A novel that successfully recruited Methodist missionaries for the South Seas, and gives an excellent description of early settlement in Australia.

Expounding of the Universe" (both terrestial and celestial) and the strong religious bias that sought to find pious explanations for everything is also mediæval. Another point is the "conversational ability" of both periods. People of both periods enjoyed exchanging information—the Victorian "conversatisione" was curiously reminiscent of the "gathering in hall" which greeted returned adventurers, or visiting scholars. People "got together to hear something new", and all who heard carried the information away, and so it spread abroad. This "penetration of information" is the very tide water of history—and the contemporary jests are the flotsam and jetsam left at high water mark. Thus the rise of the "Temperance Movement" produced the contemporary jest of the reformer who showed his audience the teeming microscopic life in one drop of water—and then dramatically killed all by alcohol; therefrom he got the reasonable response: "Sir! we will never touch another drop of water *without* alcohol!" Historically it is impossible to over-estimate the effects of the microscope; it revolutionized medical studies, enforced boiled and sterilising methods, induced new and better water supplies and made a small fortune for the manufacturers of patent filters.

Time ceases to exist under a lens and the user of a microscope enters a timeless world, in which monsters move and pass, and whole dynasties rise and fall, between the least joint of a decayed mosquito.

A DIGRESSION ON THE INFLUENCE OF THE STUDY OF WATER BY THE USE OF THE MICROSCOPE

To appreciate the mental effect of the discovery of "Infusoria" (as the Victorians call the microscopic life in water) we must estimate what could be understood by the unlettered (but not inarticulate) peasant of much earlier centuries. The mathematically-minded St. Augustine, following many earlier thinkers, set man's material existence amid the all-pervading "essences" in which man's mind was free to rove, which "mind" was itself "of that essence" (so it was able to do so).

The fact that man's mind was thus free of "eternal verities" was congruent with early Christianity, it explained the necessity for an eternal god to be born a man. Therefore, the early church firmly refused a soul to all "lower animals" (to the confusion of many minds, and the complication of mediæval magicians). For example, Geraldus Cambrensis in the eleventh century was confronted by the problem of a monk requested to administer the Last Sacrament to a dying woman, bewitched as a wolf *till death*. (It was, as Giraldus said to the Bishop, "a very debatable point".)

Till the lens came, mankind, as a whole, seemed to have felt himself comfortably static, complacently placed in the "eligible central situation" of *his universe*.

Now the lens jettisoned him into a precarious position upon a sliding scale, alternatively estimating further in either direction. (The position in which he still remains.) When man's interest extended heavenwards, medicine men cultivated the influence of the planets and worked out horoscopes for the good of mankind. When he, by aid of the material lens, cultivated the infinitely small, he produced "cultures" for the good of mankind.

This short note can only be a crude outline of long centuries of struggle, in which men of wisdom and understanding died: holding the visions granted to their human minds.

FILTER WATER

Water Filtration and Purification

> "... Perhaps one of the greatest difficulties a conscientious filter-maker has to contend with is the want of knowledge upon the subject among the general public, who are apt to think that as long as a filter delivers clear water they have obtained all that is required; and, carrying out the same idea, judge whether a filter is required at all by the same rule. Now no test is more fallacious, as we often find the brightest and coolest waters (generally pump water, or that drawn from wells) to be the most unsafe, and frequently the very properties for which it is most highly prized only indicate its highly injurious contamination ...
>
> 'Self-cleaning' is another very favourite term which, although a

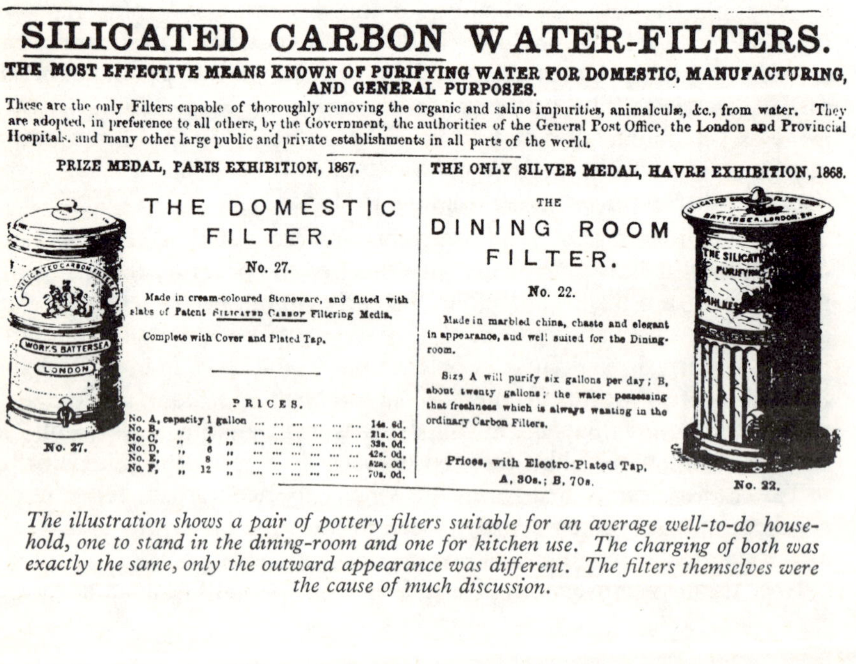

The illustration shows a pair of pottery filters suitable for an average well-to-do household, one to stand in the dining-room and one for kitchen use. The charging of both was exactly the same, only the outward appearance was different. The filters themselves were the cause of much discussion.

complete misnomer, has its weight with the public, who appear to think some inscrutable power is present utterly destroying the impurities. Again, how commonly do we find filters advertised as 'warranted to remove lime from water'. On this point the exercise of a little common sense leads to the enquiry of what becomes of it, as it cannot be oxidized like organic contamination, but must be removed bodily. Now London water contains about 14 grains of lime to the gallon, which is a very large amount, and would soon stop up any filter removing it; but whoever found any perceptive quantity of lime in any filter that had been working for even a number of years? . . . The great difficulty with the general public is having no standard by which to judge of the value of a filter. . . ."

Advertisement, 1877

The Filter

When laid on, water became general in towns, and the ancient wells and springs had become so polluted by drains that drinking water was a serious problem; the water filter was in general use in almost every home.

The washstand ewer could be filled from the tap, but for a long time the drinking water in the bedroom water bottle was filled from the filter. All cooking was supposed to be done with filtered water, though as it was usually boiled this was not insisted upon. The households who could rely on a trained staff, usually left it to them to attend to the table water. (It was considered a point of good service to pour that water into the table jug from a great height, or throw it briskly back and forth between two jugs to aerate it, and remove the flatness caused by filtration.) Also makers of domestic filters used to construct a certain number of ornamental filters (Doulton's, being a London firm, rather specialized in these) suitable to stand in the dining-room, so that the water could be used direct, even if it was "flat" (*see* Gasogene).

When fresh drinking water was unobtainable, and the piped supply not to be depended upon, then filters were provided, large and utilitarian for the kitchen, and more ornamental for use in the dining-room. The enormous number of these great pottery filters which still survive, though few are in use, testify to the undependability of our early piped drinking water.

There were special filters also supplied to public houses for the water served with brandy or spirits. (These may still be found behind some old country bars though they are no longer in use.)

Charcoal was the basic charge for most pottery filters, and required frequent renewal or recharging.

Country doctors advised cottagers who used doubtful wells to construct their own filters with a leaking bucket and burnt wood from their fires, and careful mothers learnt to use the steam water (distilled) from the inside of the family kettle lid to give to babies.

Men working near streams learnt the traveller's trick of digging a shallow well about a yard from the stream on the lower side. This small well soon fills and after scooping empty a few times usually runs clear enough for ordinary usage.

THE MEDIAEVAL EXPERT

Andrew Boorde is sound upon drinking water. He does not altogether recommend it neat (what good ancestral butler would do so?), but water "when converted into good bere, meade, or metheglyn is holesome".

Boorde says the best is "rayne water so be it clene and purely taken" next "roungyn water", and all best water runs swiftly from the east to the west over stones or pebbles. "Ryver or brooke water if clere is to be praysed", and "standynge waters which be refreshed with a fresshe spryng is commendable". Boorde sensibly warns against wells that are "still and not running" (in this we believe he means sunk wells, not sluggish springs), and warns everyone to "be ware of all waters which be standynge and putyfyed with froth, duckemet [duck meat?] and mudde", as "if you dress meat with it, it shall engender many infermities".

Boorde the expert also advises filters of linen cloth, and that drinking water be diluted with wine (*see* page 334) and fruit drinks, raspberry or strawberry, etc., be well boiled and let grow cold again before use.

THE ASSAY CUP

This was a regular custom at tables in the households of all important personages. The cups were most ostentatiously washed at the table and Boorde makes a ceremony of the holding of the drying "towel end" by the "cheefe dignitie", and later the cups to be washed "in basons prepared". The whole affair was to avoid poison being introduced into the table drinks, and at some tables the eatables were also tested by an official who stood by.

The idea is less absurd when you realize the remote position of the outside kitchen, and long procession, often down ill-lit passages, before the prepared dishes were laid upon the table. Supervision outside was impossible, a mediæval kitchen was far too complicated and the staff too diverse.

Anti-poison cups were popular. Those made of unicorn horn were considered the best, as the unicorn, when he stopped to drink, perforce dipped his horn into the water before him, and so never drank poison.

As the demand for unicorn horns outran supply, dishonest eastern dealers used to sell norwhale horns as "real unicorn". These substitutes did not work, so all such horns should be tested before purchase. The simplest way was to put poisoned water into the cup, and give it to a pigeon to drink (the customary columbarium on the premises made this bird an easy catch). If the pigeon died, the horn was spurious. The extremely long, elaborately mounted, "whole horns", still surviving in some cathedrals, may have been well-testing horns. We submit this theory with diffidence; but have never yet had any other satisfactory explanation for these curious reliques. They usually belonged to bishops or church officials, and their extreme length and position (in both time and place) suggest this use.

The usual horn drinking vessel was made from the wide end of a cow's horn, sawn level, and the bottom piece that formed the base was pressed

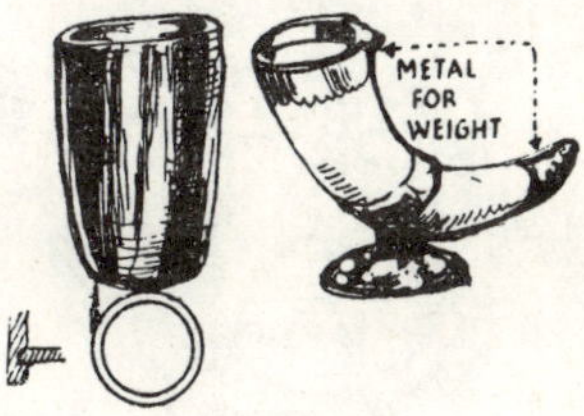

down inside till it wedged tightly at the narrower end. Sometimes these base rounds were a piece of flat horn, cut to fit and spring in. Sometimes they were of wood. Horn was best, as wood, swelling up, tended to split the horn. Crystal and glass bases were used, and the horns' rims bound with silver.

ICE (AND ICE HOUSES)

This is classed with drinking water, as its main use was for the table though also considered as a medical supply.

Some of the curious small buildings of early centuries, classified as small underground passages, possibly drains, may have stored ice, but we can find no direct evidence much before the 1600's. After that, every homestead had its ice-house, well designed, and carefully stocked.

Architecture varied and the drawing shows a general type. The ice, cut in blocks, was hauled over the frozen ground, the way being made easy by a snowplough, and water flung down to make a nice "slide". A bed of crossed wood planks covered with straw was raised over a drain to let the water escape, and more straw was added around the pile. Insulation was well studied. The ice house was opened with care, and supplies lasted all summer.

On an estate, the ice-house was usually tucked away in the wooded barrier that grew beyond the grounds proper. It might be as much as half a mile from the house, depending on the position of the lake and slope of the land. Each ice-house varied individually. I have reconstructed one remembered from a Yorkshire estate. It was a rounded stone, igloo shaped, over a deep stone-lined pit, the floor of which was rounded pine boles. Within the stone structure was an oak timbered inner structure —very reminiscent of a coal mine—because built by old colliers. A smooth oak board (half a split trunk) was shifted to slide the ice in, or slide it out; and an overhead pulley took the weight till level with the entrance. Then it was swung onto a small mine's truck for transport by

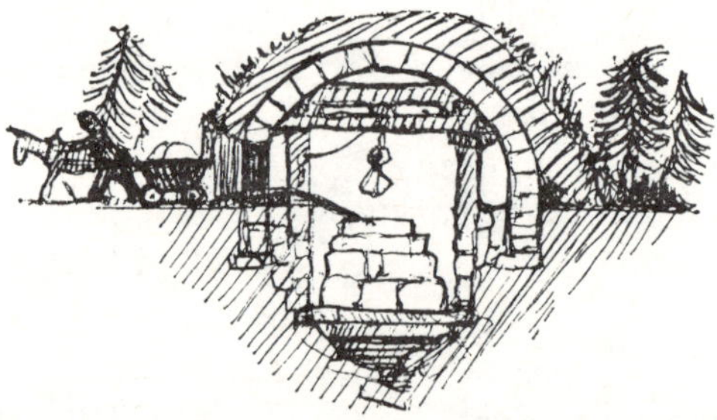

an ex-pit pony. Layers of straw were laid between the blocks, to make subsequent splitting easier, and the ice had to be built in pyramid form or it froze to the side walls, immovable as it "settled".

When I knew this place, it was derelict, and grass and shrubs had so buried and blurred the outline (covering the original earthen and turfed cover) that it looked like an unexpected natural mound; the door had fallen in, and down below the rotted pine boles cold water dripped into the colder black pool below—for the old drain had long since become blocked by tree roots.

Long before the refrigerator came into use ice was considered indispensable for the elaborate jellies and creams of the late eighteenth and nineteenth centuries which could hardly have been prepared without it.

A block of ice was set on a ballroom supper table and the ice carvings that have intrigued passengers on the great modern liners have a long tradition. Some of us remember the ice block in the old Queens Hall.

The Ice Box

This was complementary to the ice house. In large establishments blocks of ice were carried up from the ice house and put into the ice box. Smaller houses bought their ice from some local dealer (usually the fishmonger.) The ice water was drawn off to fill the glass bowls in which the butter floated. It was also used to set jellies and creams and chill the puff pastry, etc.

On hot summer nights the finger bowls on the dining-table would be filled with ice water, and lumps of ice would clink in the crystal water jug. Crushed ice filled the wine-bottle-pail below the sideboard, but though ice pudding was served frequently, ice in drinking water was never as usual in England as in the States.

> "A neat form of refrigerator or cooler, herewith illustrated, is designed by Mr. A. M. Lasley of New York and the following description is given by the *American Artizan*: The construction, and the convenience resulting therefrom, are apparent at a glance. . . . The design will afford a hint for the construction of an ice safe which may be ornamental as well as useful, and if the space between the outer and inner vessels is filled with non-conducting material, one charge of ice would last for a considerable time. . . ."
>
> *Advertisement*, 1871

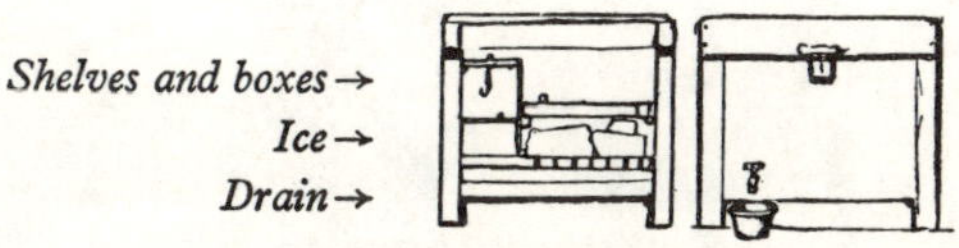

Zinc-lined wooden chest

The ice box still continues in use in many old houses, and some modern ones, so needs no explanation. It used to be of thick wood, lined with lead, with compartments for storage, and drain holes below the ice container that allowed ice water to be drawn off through a tap.

The water—the important part of ice storage—was taken after frost had cleared the lake, so that it was reasonably clean, and might even be made in tanks by some spring on the estate. For the ice box, the smaller householder usually relied on the local butcher or fishmonger to supply it. In any case, it was not usual to drink ice water; it was used for cooling creams and jellies, or some wines.

During the French wars there was a suggested tax for one year on "the silver in tankards of taverns". It was argued as useless, as the victuallers would only conceal their tankards for a year. (One wonders if some of the tankards dug up, or found concealed in old premises were hidden as a precautionary measure? Many seem to be about the right date.)

AERATED WATER

"'As useless as a gasogene!'

"'A what? . . .'

"'Well, as useless as any elaborate thing evolved for a specific purpose which no longer exists.'"

MARGERY ALLINGHAM

The gasogene provided soda water for the Victorian household long before bottled table waters were in general supply. There were several patent designs—the later "sparklet", which worked by gas discharged from small bulb containers, and other types, some of which continue in use today, but the large, wire-covered, double bubble "gasogene" was very usual upon Victorian sideboards.

The powders (bicarbonate of soda and tartaric acid) were supplied by the gross and packed in alternate blue and white folders.

The directions sound complicated, but the gasogene only took a few minutes to charge and the soda water was ready for use immediately.

THE GASOGENE OF 1874

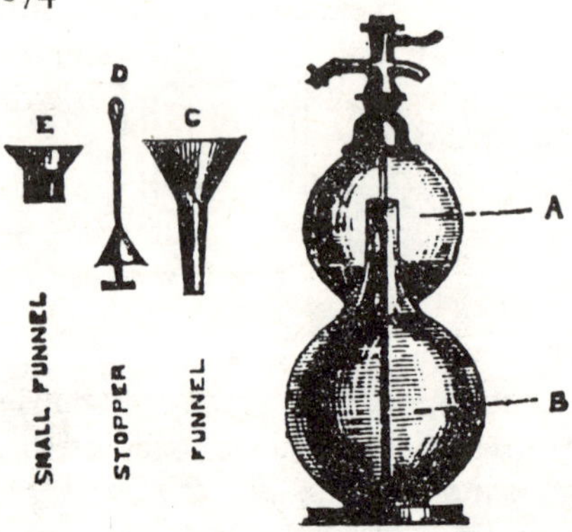

Directions for use: First, nearly fill the lower globe with filtered water by means of the long funnel. Take special care that no water passes into the small globe. Take out the funnel and put the stopper in the neck of the lower globe. Second, place the short funnel above the stopper (which should be quite dry) and pass into the small globe a charge of acid and soda. Remove the stopper and funnel. Immediately place the top on the bottle and screw it down tight. Fourth, incline the bottle and so pour water into the small globe until it is about a quarter full; shake the apparatus from time to time with a circular movement, keeping it always upright. To prevent explosion draw a wine-glass full of water from the machine after being five minutes in charge.

THE HYPROCRAS METHOD IS THE REASON FOR INCLUDING IT IN WATER DRINK

The water drinks from the seventeenth century onwards are usually "laced" with spirits or wine. The old "taes" and "infusions" of simpler use, that were made of herbs, grains or roots (ex. salop), continue in favour and some use spice flavours. Hyprocras, a very early spiced wine, that dates from at least the thirteenth century, is interesting because of the method used in its preparation. The ingredients were as varied as those used for the later "punch" brews (for which everyone had their own special recipes). This elaborately spiced drink was made by pouring the wine slowly through pockets of spices in the ends of long bags or "sleeves". It took its name from the shaped sleeves of Hyprocras' gown. Though it is always misleading to suggest an equivalent, this strong spiced wine was served somewhat in the fashion of a modern cocktail, before, or after, the long official meal in hall, or at small intimate bedroom parties.

This pouring the wine through the spices was just a simple way of controlling the exact flavour. Wine absorbs flavour so rapidly (specially if warm) that it was easier to put the wine through the spice, than dip the spice into the wine. For example, if on the first "run through" the flavour of cloves was found too strong the clove bag was omitted, or if the cinnamon was not strong enough, you ran it twice through the cinnamon bag. By this method the valuable spices were preserved for continuous use (till worn out) and for centuries instructions for making drinks say "pour over" the spice, or lemon peel, or whatever flavouring is used, rather than "put in" the flavouring.

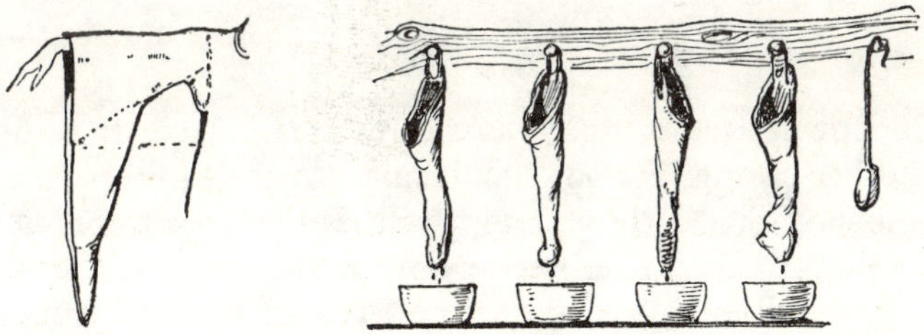

TEETOTALLERS, WATER DRINKERS

One would expect the teetotal temperance movement to have produced a crop of soft-drink suggestions, but though America specialized in them and New England novels stressed the excellence of coffee, there are no special recipes in English cookery books of the period. The intolerance of the early twentieth century for teetotallers, abstainers, vegetarians and "food faddists" in general, can hardly be understood by young people of today. The first vegetarian restaurant in London was thought very eccentric and one was taken to dine there in an enterprising spirit of adventure. Most of the dishes were foreign, many Indian, which aroused interest as there were few foreign restaurants open in London at that time. In private households a "teetotaller" was treated as a rather tiresome invalid! I remember my mother's exasperation: "Why did he not let us know before he came! so that we could have brewed the poor man some barley water." A "vegetarian" was a plain nuisance! "Tiresome creatures, wanting Brazil nuts and salads, and drinking orange juice!"

About the only time people were supposed to want soft drinks was after sets of tennis, or at children's parties, when lemonade was provided. Cyclists and other slightly undignified pioneers were addicted to cold tea, and they had to carry it with them, as inns and pubs did not even supply mineral waters, though fizzy ginger beer and a colourless lemonade in glass bottles with glass marble stoppers were sold in village shops.

The bottled, condensed, and tinned fruit juices that are the basis of most of our present-day soft drinks are all comparatively modern.

BATHS

> "Look on the Bath as a very admirable and propitious work of Divine Providence."
>
> BISHOP KEN, 1711

> "Unaccommodated man is no more but such a poor bare forked animal as thou art."
>
> *King Lear*

Why Christianity vetoed nudity is controversial. Excesses at the Roman baths and other excuses are not convincing. In the earliest acute stage of religious modesty St. Marie of Egypt refuses the consolations of religion till she had flung[2] a cloak over her shadow on the sand!

Yet squires and knights of the earliest crusader period are instructed to bathe in streams and rivers, and bathing in holy wells was public and commendable. The twelfth-century monk stripped for his bath in the open air, as cheerfully as Bunyan's seventeenth-century Christians (and note both undress on the spot). Mediæval people shared tubs with gusto, and it was the gossip and time wasted in the eighteenth century "stews" that was objected to, the nudity was accepted as cheerfully as in a modern turkish bath! Kilvert, a country clergyman, was indignant at being obliged to wear trunks on Bognor beach in the 19th century, and yet in the twentieth century Margate invents a water tent "to preserve complete privacy"!

A MONK WHO DID BATHE FREQUENTLY

This "Bath" is taken from a sermon, proving the efficiency of the Mass in releasing souls from purgatory.

"There was a Monk, Felix his name,
Of whom is told this Ghoste tale,
Besides his home there was a path
Where hot springs fell into a bath,
And this monk often did there wende
To bathe himself, as he had need.
And there—all ready, ever found,
A man, who served him, foot and hand.
He dragged his hose off, and his shoon,
And afterwards did help them don.
(And everytime that there he cam
Was waiting for him—this good man.)
The priest, he came there so oft,
And the man served him so softe
(But never asked him why? wherefore
He waited on him ever more?)
Only; each time the priest was ready,
The man he came and served him ably,
The priest said, 'He serves me this way
His travail I'll requite some day.'
So, on a day—when his bath he sought,
He two bread loaves with him brought.
Into the bath the priest he got
To wash himself, as well he ought,
And the man came unto him again,
And helped him; with might and main.
So, the priest when he would homeward go
Gave to the man, the loaves two,
And thanked him for his service
(More could he not do otherwise!)
But—the man answered the priest again
'This bread thou broughtest me in vain!
For never more shall I eat bread
For I am dead.
And a man, who is dead
Never more shall he eat bread.'
The priest then asked, 'In what mannere
Is it that thou waitest here?'
And the ghost answered him and said,

'I was a man ere I was dead.
And this service I am in
Is the payment for my sin,
So now, I pray for charite,
Offer on the altar? Thy love for me,
And I beseech thee, for this thing,
That you six masses for me sing
For were six sung, I might me wende
Unto the bliss withouten ende.'
The priest all that weeke long
For his ghost he prayed and sung
And when the Masses were all done
He came back—and Found him gone!
So knew that priest that he was brought
To BLISS, for that he found him not."

AND THE ABBESS WHO DID NOT BATH FREQUENTLY

"The Abbess Ebba, King Egfried's aunt, received the veil and clothing of a nun from the hands of Bishop Wilfred . . . she built a convent and became the Virgin Mother of many virgins vowed to God. She displayed the pattern of Heavenly Life in word and deed.

It is said that, from the time of her entry she never wore linen, but only woollen garments, and that she washed in hot water only before the Greater Festivals, such as Eastern and Pentecost and the Epiphany, and then only after she and her assistants had helped the other servants of Christ to wash."

BEDE, A.D. 660

THE MEDIÆVAL INDOOR BATH

The mediæval bath was a tub, wooden, solid and well used. Recent historians emphasise the dirt of mediæval people, their own contemporaries testify to their cleanliness.

Mediæval artists and writers describe very definite arrangements for tubbing. Probably it varied socially, occupationally and climatically, as much as today. The elaborate private baths and swimming pools, pithead baths for miners, and total lack of baths in agricultural workers' cottages, would confuse a modern historian. The mediæval mobile tub could be taken into the bedroom (in Victorian manner), but the static tub was set in a separate room, arranged under a hook in the ceiling from which hung a tent-like canopy. That kept off the draught and kept in the steam, and provided privacy (if wanted). Boiling water was carried in from the iron cauldrons that boiled outside, cold water was set handy, soap floated in a wooden bowl, and towels were adequate (and probably warmed by being wrapped around the hot-water can—in Victorian manner).

Where a proper bathroom, complete with hook and drain, was missing, a pole could be used to uphold the canopy. For smaller soaks, or simpler folk, the canopy was draped around the bather's own neck and hung over the edge of the tub, and might, on a campaign or journey, be the traveller's own cloak. Some bathers, dispensing with mediæval conventions, just wallowed openly and companionably, but the open-air communal bath houses, with fun and games and gossips, were popular on the continent long before they reached England. Such summertime frolics were probably as seasonal in use as the modern open-air baths are today, but the bathroom did exist, and its position was, even then, dependent upon the proximity of the "boiler" (though the "boiler" in mediæval days was a static iron cauldron). We have seen in MS. drawings, curious wooden ducts that seem to be water chutes leading direct to and from the boiler cauldrons, and there are holes pierced through stone walls, too high for drains, but set exactly right to take the water baled out from an iron cauldron (*see* page 176). Big metal water jugs are shown in MSS. being lugged upstairs; household labour was abundant, but "the nearer the boiler the hotter the bath" was already good sense in mediæval times.

The bath tubs were usually oval in shape (mankind being six feet long and folding in the middle) and this shape remained the standard one for tubs for many centuries. The mediæval bath tub remained as the "under buck" tub that long continued in use for washing, brewing and salting. Such oval tubs are easier to lift than round tubs, easier to reach across and they take a side of bacon very comfortably!

Large round tubs were more suitable for communal bathing. In some the bathers were arranged like sleepers in an army bell tent, feet to centre, but there were far more private oval household tubs. Later, the large public bath houses became completely public and the love-making and gossip that went on there was scandalous! Several contemporary authors comment upon it.

In these large bathing establishments, back scrubbers and music and refreshment were supplied. Even in the smaller more frivolous households, a hot bath session was a pleasurable event, and was conducted in much the same way as a mixed party swimming today. They had lutes, and recorders, and marzipan, instead of wireless and ice-cream, and perhaps rather more mediæval gusto.

A NOTE ON MEDIÆVAL BATH WATER

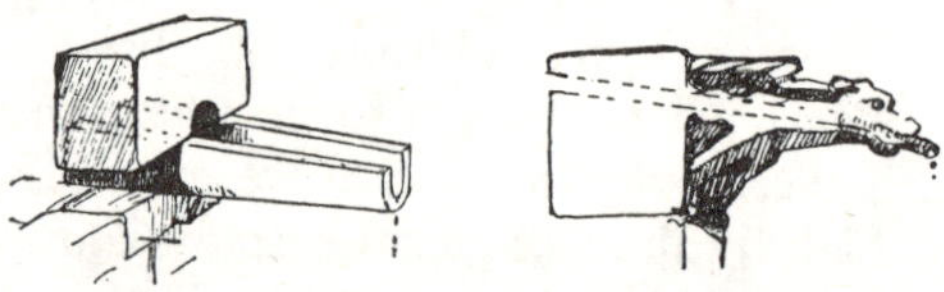

Roof spouts to throw clear of walls

The curiously-placed slot holes found in some buildings suggests their use as conduits for bath water.

The slots are placed too high for urinals or drains, but are exactly placed for baling water from a cauldron—and their position does definitely suggest the filling of tubs set in the adjoining apartment (or in some cases outside the walls, possibly into a small shed or bath enclosure).[1]

The pipe through the wall, if not of stone, would be the usual wooden pipe, with a stoup attached at the baling end.

By using a light movable conduit at the delivery end several tubs could be filled in a row, by simply altering the angle of the conduit (a serious consideration, as a large wooden tub full of bath water was heavy to move). Also one could have more water added on demand, though, if boiling it would be advisable to get out of the tub while it poured in! The tubs were easily emptied through a spigot hole.

WATER BATHS

"This par-boiled young dispenser employed by a thirteenth-century surgeon, is stirring medical ointment in a water bath. These shallow

[1] *A New England Farm* describes an exactly similar conduit through the wall of the dairy down which the skimmed milk was poured to fill tubs arranged outside, and the historian, Ford Maddox Heuffer, gives a description of such a "courtyard tub" in his novel *Ladies Whose Bright Eyes*.

19. The "lead" or aqueduct for London's "New River Water" was a trough of wood caulked and braced with timber posts, on a brick and earth embankment.

20. Telford's aqueduct for a canal across the Vale of Llangollen was a trough of iron supported on 120-ft.-high stone pillars, beyond a long earth embankment that terraced the hillside for some distance.

21. Water-power forge on a swift mountain river. The chute and mill duct begin on right of the weir. The wheel may have worked a trip-hammer for breaking ore.

22. The strong stone foundations remain today supporting a footbridge.

23. Filthy Fleet river. Note the sewer outlets and lowered buckets.

From MS. Lib. Trin. Coll. Camb.

metal water pans, raised on iron stands above open fires were a form of bain-marie, most necessary when stiff and sticky mixtures needed cooking. Note his clothes tucked up to prevent them flapping up the ashes from the fire, or catching alight from the open flames."

OUTDOOR BATHS A.D. 1600

"But the Interpreter would have them tarry awhile, 'for,' said he, 'you must orderly go from hence . . . take them, and have them into the garden to the Bath, and there wash them clean from the soil which they have gathered by travelling . . . and they came out of the Bath, not only sweet and clean, but also much enlivened and strengthened in their joints'."

Pilgrim's Progress

The out-of-doors bath house would be taken for granted by Bunyan's readers. All the larger country houses built them, and though the eighteenth century frequently converted them into garden ponds, their original use was as a bath. In towns, the bath houses had become public meeting places for women folk, almost the equivalent of the coffee house enjoyed by the menfolk. Mrs. Pepys, typically urban, had spasms of cleanliness, during which she attended the bath house and made a show of keeping up the good habit, though, as her husband said, "it won't last".

One out-door bath well known to me adjoins a very old path between a Cistercian monastery and its grange and was probably used by the monks. In the sixteenth century a lower pool was made that may have doubled duty with a mill pool. This lower bath was used both for pleasant summer splashing and for medical treatment by all the local folk. About 1640 the houseowners covered in their outside bath house, rebuilding the walls and mending the broken floor of the bath. Fashion passed, and in the nineteenth century, baths and plumbing were inserted into the Georgian mansion. The old outside bath, with the water drained off, became an outhouse, and finally a nettleful ruin. The lower bath has silted up, and the spring is now taken for the local waterworks.

I have illustrated these outside baths rather fully because few people realize how much the old English garden owes to them. The outside bath was the original cause of many ornamental garden pools and later of some sunk gardens.

OUTDOOR BATHS 1854

"I have the pleasure of announcing to the Ladies and Gentlemen of Fairmeadow and its vicinity, that my Bath House is now completed and ready for the reception of those who are disposed to regale themselves in a luxury peculiar to the once polished Greek and noble Roman.

To the Ladies, Tuesday of each week will be appropriated to their exclusive benefit; the white flag will be the signal; and I assure the Ladies, that due respect shall be scrupulously observed, and that they shall be guarded from each vagrant foot and each licentious eye."

LONGFELLOW, "The Fair Meadow Advertiser", *Kavanagh*, 1854

A FARM-HOUSE TUB BY THE FIRE, SEVENTEENTH CENTURY

St. Distaff's Day, 1637

"Partly work and partly play
You must on St. Distaff's Day
From the plough soon free your team[1]
Then come home and fodder them
If the maides a spinning goe
Burn their flax and fire their tow!
Scorch their plackets;[2] but beware
That ye singe no maiden haire.
Bring in pails of water then
Let the maids bewash the men
Give St. Distaff all the right
Then give Christmas spirit good night
And next morning, everyone,
To his own vocation."

This bath night rhyme tells of some of the fun and games possible on farms that kept a dozen or so men and women workers all living together. St. Distaff's seems to have been the girl's equivalent of the boy's Plough Monday.

[1] The plough boys finished at first yoking (about noon) to get ready for their plough boy supper.

[2] The voluminous skirts of this period fastened behind with an open placket. "Keep thy foot out of brothels, thy hand out of plackets." *King Lear*.

"Plough Monday, the first after Twelfe night be past
Biddeth out with the plow.
The worst husband is last."

TUSSER

Plough Monday remained a definite half-holiday in our Nottinghamshire village till late in the 1920's.

Then ploughs were mainly horse-drawn, and each ploughman had his apprentice boy with him in the furrows to lead the team, or do other odd field work, while he "learnt the hull of the job" under the expert's eye. On Plough Monday all the lads from local farms clubbed together for a feast, the materials for which had been gathered up for months! If a maid wanted water fetching, or wood chopping, she'd promise him "a cake come Plough Monday" or overtime on the farm would be remembered on Plough Day, so that by the previous Saturday the lads would have a banking account in good will, promises and hard cash! As soon as dark fell, they'd go around collecting, all with blackened faces and strange disguises (since reprisals were to be avoided). They went to each farm collecting the goods and subscriptions, and they *pulled an old ploughshare along with them*. If the farm paid up handsomely they'd just scratch the ground by the gate (to show they'd been) but if the farmer's wife was mean, and the pie or bacon, etc., that had been promised, was not forthcoming, they would drag that plough too and fro before the door, raising up enough mud and muck to tread into the house and keep the women-folk cleaning and mopping for weeks!

When all the food was collected, it was handed over to some trusted inn-keeper with instructions to make them a real good supper come Monday. The cash and the inn-keeper supplied the beer and no farm boy was expected to be home before midnight (or up early next morning).

On the farm the women-folk, set free of cooking the boys' supper, and the girls, lacking their playfellows, would also want a night off! The older men got a cold supper (a certain red cabbage pickle was called "ploughboy" and served with the cold meat), and, with their young rivals away, they got their chance with the girls. The bath tubs of Saturday night were set down by the kitchen fire. On this night there were no boys to carry the water and "make their selves useful", so the men had to help themselves, but churlish must have been the old chap who couldn't persuade some lass to scrub his back for him, and hand down the clean shirt!

Work on those seventeenth-century farms was desperately hard, but the food, though simple, was good and plentiful, and when young people are strong and healthy and well fed, the heaviest work does not prevent fun and games and courting! The distaff was constant employment, but required less concentration than modern knitting, and the tools, spoons, and toys carved by the men show enjoyment of leisure. Nor are the songs lacking in laughter. One gets tired of the constant harping on the drudgery of housework in the olden days, and the heavy labour and misery of wash days and having to carry great pails of water and so on. The work was hard, but we put in this example to prove it could also be fun![1]

THE COLLIER'S BATH BY THE FIRE, NINETEENTH CENTURY

The collier's bath is now laid on at the pithead, but in the bad old times when the collier was overworked and underpaid, and knew all the evils that followed, the collier's bath was in a wash tub and his wife, or daughter, scoured the black off before the kitchen fire.

The miner and quarryman always had special characters. They were loyal, courageous, tough of mind and sinew, and usually had an inborn love of music. This was born perhaps of the strange echoes among which they worked in caves and galleries. Voices circling, repeating, altering, delaying, and sounding back wrought a curious fugue, disturbed by the ringing of metal on stone, or the thunder of a blast, and always there were the small whispering sounds of air, and seeping water, for which they listened instinctively.

The birds and pet mice the men carried in caps and pockets were to sense firedamp. So the collier came to be a skilled breeder of song birds, and racing pigeons, and fancy mice. Long ago, miners were a race apart from other workers, they had their own separate laws, as only a fellow miner could judge another's crime. For example, if a man was convicted of stealing coal from another seam, only those "down pit" could judge if it was of intent or by accident. The penalty was for the offender's hand to be nailed to his windlass. If it was accidental, the nail passed between the fingers and he had no worse than a slight scar to remind him to be more careful. But if he was known to be a deliberate thief, the hand would be so smashed that it could never again grasp a pick.

Such individual people developed very individual households, and the bath was also very individual.

By the 1900's, when I knew the Wigan pits, the miners were hard working, tough, good-natured chaps, whose skins, though pitted with black specks of embedded carbon, were fine-textured as a child. They were well-built men, deep of chest and muscular. They wore thick wood and leather clogs which, though looking clumsy, fitted extraordinarily well, and their feet, when they kicked off the clogs, were well shaped and strong.

The rows of small two-storey houses in which they lived all had good square wash houses, with a separate entrance from the back yard. (The

[1] It was in London, and two centuries later, that Dickens portrayed the "slavey" as a poor downtrodden soul. The farmer's wife would be as ill advised to neglect the health of her dairymaid as the farmer to neglect the health of his cows.

sanitary conditions were, in contrast, scandalously bad, the disgusting night soil cart still creaked and slopped around at night time, pulling out the tubs of ordure from behind the foul privies. The stink was horrible. *See* page 232.)

The streets of the towns were noisy with rough stone *sets* and the sound of hundreds of iron-bound clogs, rocking along stone pavements, marked the times of shift change, as did the long windy wails of the various pit hooters. (Twenty or more hooters at a time could be heard rising and falling and overlapping, a distinctive hooter from each pit. The sound carried for miles on a still day.)

My own brother worked "down pit" and I remember his return, coal black, only eyes and mouth visible, and his pit clothes so saturated with sludge that they dried absolutely solid. Like all miners, he always kicked off his boots, sat on a newspaper, and drank a cup of tea before tub and supper. One night, the boiler having gone wrong, every cooking saucepan and kettle was filled and set on the kitchen stove to provide his hot bath water, and, being a helpful chap, he carried up the pans himself. A moment later a howl brought us running to the bathroom, where, from out of a cloud of steam, came a voice: "O Lord, *I've got in with the cauliflower!*" (A foolish scrap of laughter to remember. Perhaps all laughter was more easily evoked before we became sated by synthetic amusement over the air?)

Now for the ritual of the collier's tub.

Shifts varied; about an hour before the men returned the woman lit the boiler fire in the wash house and set the tub, and pail of cold water by it, on the floor. Clean shirts and towels hung ready on the airing rail in the kitchen, and the coat, trousers, clean neck-cloth, socks and slippers (or, if it was an early shift when he'd be going out again, the light clogs), would be "set on chair". The men entered the wash house by the yard door, shedding their heavy clay-coated clogs and hanging their pit clothes up by the boiler to dry overnight. They then baled the boiling water into the tub, and "got theirselves clean", using solid bars of soap, a scrubbing brush, and swilling off by standing up and sluicing down. They then "hollered" and "the missus" handed out a clean shirt, and they finished dressing in the kitchen, before sitting down to a "reet hot supper". It was a ritual to have supper in comfort, in shirt sleeves and stockinged feet, with a pipe and paper by the warm kitchen fire, and afterwards to put on his coat and go down to the local.

Some of the later brick-built houses had hot and cold laid on to bathrooms upstairs, but unless the women and children used them, the bathrooms became extra bedrooms, or store rooms, or pigeon lofts! The miner stuck to his downstairs wash house, as he saw no sense in "traipsing coal dust through the house to get upstairs to change in a bloody cold bedroom".

On getting up next morning the process was reversed, the men getting into their pit clothes in the wash house and picking up their "snappins" and dinner pails as they went out.

Usually the men, in the morning tipped out their last night's bath water and filled up the boiler "ready for the missus to light the fire again".

On Mondays, after the household washing was done, the water in the boiler was used to give kitchen and wash house a good scour and swill; but, with the wash house having a separate door in from the yard, *the worst of the pit dirt was shed in the wash house and very little was carried through into the spotless kitchen.*

There were some badly-managed households where the menfolk were slovenly and inconsiderate, or the women-folk inadequate, but the average of personal cleanliness was extraordinarily high and more bath water was used with less fuss by miners than most folk. Some of the old hands refused pithead baths when they were first installed, being horrified at the idea of going out into the cold after washing!

Compared with the shirt handed out warm, and the hot supper by the kitchen fire, an iron locker and a shower seemed spartan, and likely to lead to pneumonia. (There was a sudden outcrop of red-flannel chest protectors during the first few months of the new pithead baths.)

VICTORIAN BATHS

The Moon or Splash Bath

The old round baths, called variously "moons" or "splash baths" or "bedroom baths", were in use well into the 1900's, and a few may be found in country houses today. One did not sit in them, as in the "Oxford hip"; one stood upright, and they were not nearly so uncomfortable as generally supposed. The "moon" was round and shallow, about three feet in diameter, with a sloping rim about a foot wide. These baths were usually painted white inside, and brown outside. There was a spout or lip, arranged in one place, and an oval wire handle directly opposite. All the best bedrooms had one, usually on a stand rather like a towel rail, set against the bedroom wall. In households where there were several young ladies the bath often stood outside on the landing, and in old-fashioned hotels, or "family" establishments, the baths hung by their handles on a peg in the housemaid's pantry. The procedure then was to ask for the bath (and tip extra), but in the ordinary way a moon bath appeared each morning as a matter of course.

This was the methodical routine for a Victorian moon bath: enter the maid, with a large folded flannel sheet, herring-boned around, and about a foot larger than the bath. This square was laid down before the wash-hand stand, and the bath laid down on it, close under the edge of the washstand (the lip to the left, the handle to the right). A bath mat was then laid down just beyond the flannel, to the right, and the maid vanished downstairs to fetch the hot water. (If there was a man servant, and the maiden was comely, you often heard a male step on the stairs, and the clank of the water can being set down on the landing outside your door.) The maid then carried it in, and set it on the floor by the bath, draped it cosily with your bath towel, peered into your ewer to see you had sufficient cold water available and left you to it.

How you arose depended on the weather. If there was a fire in your room you sprang up, bundled your curls into a cap, flung off your enveloping nightdress, and took up position at the washstand. But whatever the weather, you first tipped a little of the hot water into the bath, to take the chill off the cold tin from your feet. Then, standing in the middle, like a pink lighthouse, you poured half the hot water into the wash basin and washed face and neck, and rinsed and dried them. Then, taking flannel in hand, you soaped vigorously from top to toe, redipping and flannelling, till you were foam-flecked as Venus, and had used up all the first half of the hot water. Then you filled up the wash basin with the remainder of the hot water, seized the sponge, and sluiced down. This was where skill was required, that your sluicing swished down you, and into the bath, not off you and onto the floor! It was surprising how the soap clung; one never seemed to have left enough rinsing water. (How fat folk managed I can't think; the overhang must have been so difficult.) If you were naturally brave, or the doctor said you needed bracing, you dipped your sponge into the *cold* water ewer for the last rinse and trickled it down your shuddering spine. Then you leapt out onto the bath mat, and towelled yourself with a right good will, finishing (if young) sitting down flat on the floor drying between your toes. Bath salts were not used, except medical "sea salts", nor was talcum powder, but toilet waters were enjoyed and were usually homemade.

After that you dressed, and while you were at breakfast the maid returned, tilted up the bath by the wire handle (you see why it had to be set down to the right), poured away the water over the lip into the pail, gave a wipe around to dry the tin, and replaced it on its stand. She then took up the floor flannel and bath mat, and carried them away. With luck, there was a rack downstairs on which towel and flannel mats were hung to dry. It sounds an awfully long procedure, but you only got *one* can of hot water, and "no lady should take longer than ten minutes over her bath".

The Oxford Hip-Bath

Though contemporary with the round "moon" bath, the hip-bath stayed in use much longer. A few still exist in hunting districts, for it was mankind's special choice for saddle stiffness after hunting and, later,

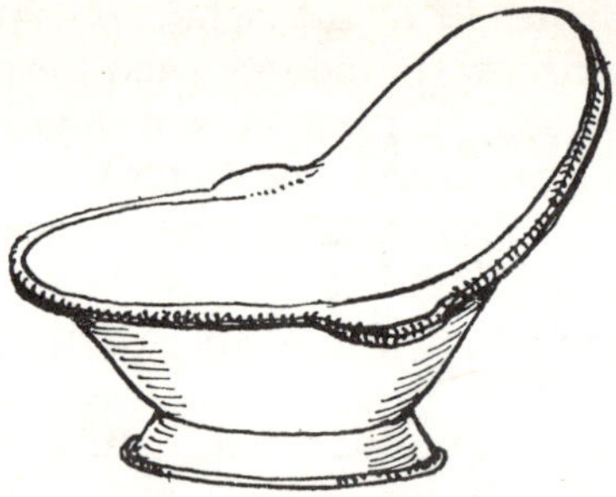

for the same cause, enjoyed by those who adopted the new, and slightly infra dig. sport of bicycling.

The armchair shape of the bath and its rounded base made it very comfortable to sit in. The water reached well up to the waist and one could leave one's legs, knees bent, hanging over the front edge, or take them in with one, sitting chin on knees and soaking luxuriously. For a prolonged wallow, one kept a can of extra-hot water alongside and draped a bath sheet around one, bath and all, leaning back in steamy content.

Many thoughtful Victorian women adopted the hip-bath, as it had advantages over the "moon". The shape used rather less water, and kept it hotter, and it was less draughty. One of its advantages was that if you were "taking a hot bath to ward off a chill", you could put your feet over the rim into hot mustard and water at the same time.

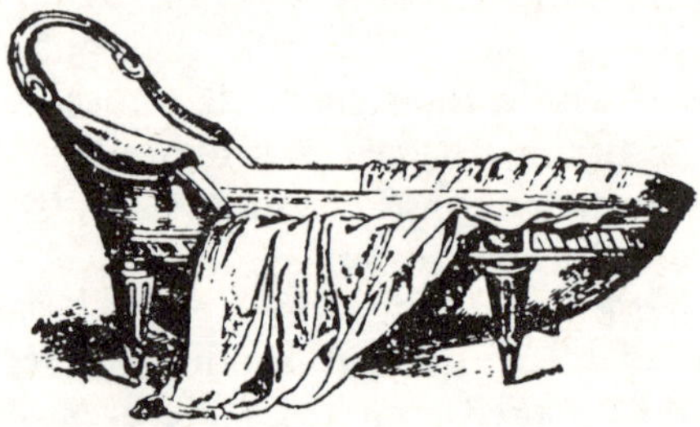

Victorian Baths—as Furniture

The bath tub (assorted shapes and sizes) carried into the bedroom continued long in use in large country houses and the best hotels, but the number of smaller town houses was increasing rapidly, and their inhabitants, frequently off-shoots of the county estates who had gone into trade, wanted the same bedroom baths, but lacked space. Whereby came (not only in baths) the period of discreet disguise. Commodes were built to represent small chests of drawers, or disguised as a pile of imposing volumes of books, and hip-baths were hidden under voluminous drapery.

English workmen were far behind the French in designing any type of tactful furniture. They did make good solid armchair "commodes" for the elderly, and little "pot chairs" for babies, but on the whole the Englishman called a spade a spade and a tub a tub and left it to the Victorian spinster to screen off the washstand and disguise her bath.

THE COLD BATH

> "It was an intense frost. I sat down in my bath upon a sheet of thick ice, which broke in the middle into large pieces whilst sharp points and jagged edges stuck all round the sides of the tub like chevaux de frise. Not particularly comforting to the naked thighs and loins, I had to collect the floating pieces of ice and pile them on a chair before I could use the sponge, and then I had to thaw the sponge with my hands for it was a mass of ice."
>
> KILVERT, 1870

The Victorian novelists and poets enjoyed medical drama. More people "sank into a rapid decline and faded away like flowers" than could be accounted for by specified complaints, and the villain was always struck dead at the convenient moment, without apparent cause (or coroner's inquest).

Doctors were usually "hastily summoned" and frequently arrived "when all was over". Brandy "forced through the pallid lips of the unconscious heroine" never drowned her (it seldom even choked her) and the things done to those "rescued from a watery grave" only killed off characters "better dead".

It was probably this dramatic instinct which accounted for the (apparently) prevalent use of the ice bath to reduce fevers. The idea had always cropped up in various forms, and was the kill or cure method resorted to when "life was despaired of". The delirious patient was lifted from the bed, and immersed in a bath of ice-cold water, or wrapped in sheets wrung out in ice water, and broken ice enclosed in a rubber bag was placed over the affected part.

How closely this cold-bath treatment approximated to modern deep-freeze usage we cannot know, but this "ice bath in fevers" was definitely popular with Victorian authors. It should not be confused with the simple cold-water treatment used to promote sweat.

The cold bath was considered bracing and insisted upon every morning in most Victorian households, and boys' schools. Where young ladies evaded this, a cold sponge down was enforced. All doctors advised it and Victorian doctors were deeply respected.

The cold-water treatment went to America, and is admirably described by Mark Twain in Aunt Polly's cure of Tom Sawyer's depression.

"The water treatment was new then, and Tom's low condition was a windfall to her. She had him out by daylight, every morning, and stood him up in the woodshed and drowned him with a deluge of cold water; then she scrubbed him down with a towel like a file, and so brought him to; then she rolled him up in a wet sheet, and put him away under blankets, till she sweated his soul clean; and 'the yellow stains came through his pores' as Tom said . . ."

Tom Sawyer

Cold-water Cures at Home

Hydropathy became popular rather later than spas. It may have been reaction to the dirt of previous centuries. Also new plumbing had put bathrooms into the new middle-class small "villa" houses and these bathrooms marked a rise in the social status, akin to the aerials in the early days of TV. Old-fashioned country families continued imperturbably to use the old tin hip or moon baths, filled from brass canisters.

Unless you kept your own coach, travel to spas was expensive, and if you lodged at the fashionable spas, such as Bath or Tunbridge Wells, the extravagance of social snobbery made difficulties for the inexperienced.

This last perhaps had more influence than is realized, for the new artisan class was just achieving a sturdy independence of opinion and, in the male line, a tendency to prefer solid personal comfort to social aspirations. This class had the money, so all these considerations are subtly reflected in the advertisements of Dr. T. Nichol's water cure: "There is no reason why people should not take the water cure at home if desirable. *All our best houses are furnished with baths*, and it will not be long before no house will be considered tenantable without one. Even in the country, it will take little experience to fit up a water-cure apparatus —a tub, which any carpenter can make, will answer for the plunge bath, two pails will form a pouring bath. A 'douch' is simply a stream of water falling from the height of a few feet, a 'sitting bath' is a half-filled wash tub (the old under-buck tub?). Wherever there is pure cold water I would engage to give the water cure."

The doctor panders to that increasing number of "clerks in lodgings": "A sheet, a sponge and towel and a small bath can be taken *anywhere*, with them and a wet sheet, a blanket pack can be carried out. Vapour baths are good, but dry blanket packs for sweating, and wet sheet packs, are as good for home treatment." The complete treatments, that the doctor himself gives, include "alternating heating and cooling compresses, rectal injections, water emetics, and water rubfacients".

A Simple Shower Bath

"Screw a strong iron pulley (b) into one of the rafters of the ceiling (a); put a stout rope over the pulley and attach to the end of it a large

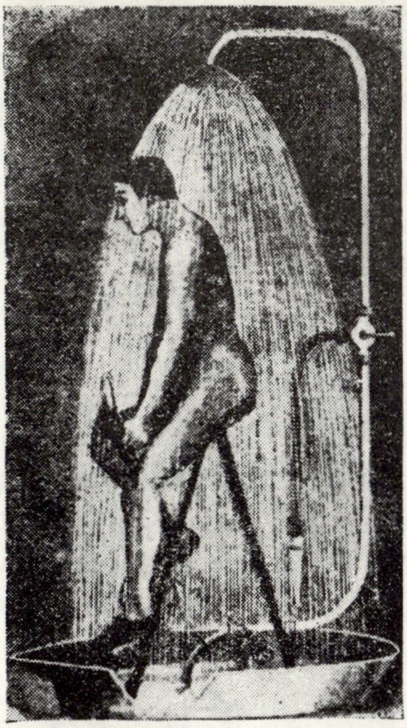

A Velocipede shower bath

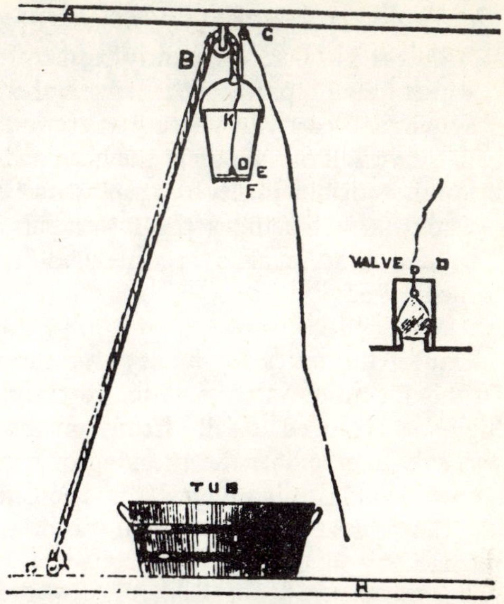

A simple shower bath

galvanized pail. Bore 50 or 60 holes one-eighth-inch diameter in the bottom of it; then solder a false bottom (e) into the pail about 1 inch above the perforated bottom. In this bottom put the valve (d) (which can be got at any brass founder's). Attach to it the cord (k) and carry the cord over the small pulley (c). Fill the pail, hoist it to the required height, then fasten the rope in ring (g) in the floor (h). Put your largest tub under the pail, get in and pull the string (k). Some sort of curtain will be required to prevent splashing of the water off the bather. '*Showerbath*' will easily devise the hanging of a curtain to prevent this."

A complicated one of about 1890

A Velocipede Shower Bath

"The 'velo-douche' is an eminently practical device for combining exercise and morning ablutions.

The device consists of a shallow tub into which is secured a framework carrying a bicycle saddle, a handle-bar, pedals, sprocket-wheels and chain. . . .

When the rider has exercised sufficiently, he can reach backward and turn the cock so as to let the water pass upward and out of the sprinkler. The harder he pedals, the larger the stream. . . ."

A strenuous idea of 1897, *when cycling was a new and popular sport*

The Douche for Lunatics (*Medical Thesis of* 1870)

"*Shower baths* are constantly used to relieve congestion of the brain, which they do partly by causing a shock to the whole of the nervous system and partly by causing a reaction and increased supply of blood to the vessels of the skin of the head and face by which the brain inside is relieved, but in severe cases it is better to put the feet into hot water, and sometimes the lower part of the body. It is, however, seldom that invalids are justified in using these means without medical advice."

One of the cures for lunacy was the use of the douche bath (1870). In this form the water was used forcibly. A column of water twelve feet high was arranged to fall directly on the head of the patient. Its weight was said to resemble the breaking of a column of ice, and the feeling of stupefaction lasted an hour. It was considered a specific against delusions, and the "threat of the treatment was often sufficient to control the wildest maniac".

Douche Baths (*Disapproval of*) *Ten Years Later*, 1881

"A navvy, or other muscular machine, with a torpid brain, may probably take cold showers on the head with advantage; but where the brain is working up to strain point, anything promoting an additional blood supply in that direction is undesirable, as tending to apoplexy."

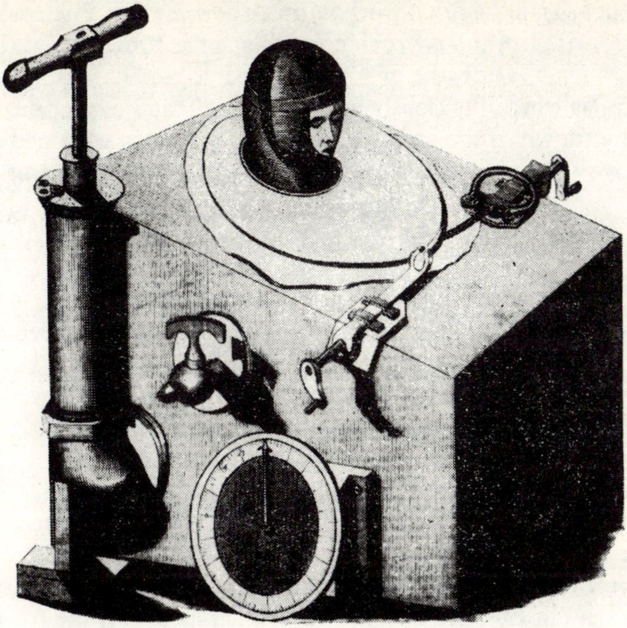

THE VACUUM BATH

"A patent was granted on the 8th of July 1867 to Mr. William Edward Newton of 66 Chancery Lane, London, for an improved pneumatic apparatus for the treatment of diseases in an attenuated atmosphere. This was the result of a communication from abroad. In explaining the invention Mr. Newton states that many beneficial results may be derived from it in the treatment of certain disorders, by exhaustion of air over the surface of the skin of the patient; a scientific and safe method long since recognized by the medical profession.

The principal feature of the invention is a light portable apparatus, easily put together and taken apart, which may be used for treating diseases in an attenuated atmosphere. Fig. 1 is a view of the entire apparatus in use. The large receiver is intended to accommodate the entire body of the patient. This receiver is composed of several parts and sections. The base is made of wood or metal. It is oval and has a rim about four inches high raised above and around it, in which is cut a small groove into the bottom (with an airtight joint). In it is inserted the pipe E, the base being raised on a block to permit this pipe to pass under it, or it may be inserted in the side. On this base sets the conical case, which is made in two parts. As shown it has a base set upon and a rim fitting within the base F. The framework is covered with tin, and is provided with a collar fitting round the neck of the patient. Over the whole is fitted a rubber cloak, with an elastic collar which fits closely around the chin and face of the patient and comes down to the base. It is bound close by a cord tied around the groove F.1 thus rendering the entire receiver perfectly air tight."

Extract from Mechanical and Scientific Journal *of* 1867

This grim contraption is a serious medical treatment. It was an extreme development of the simple "cupping" treatment that had been in use for centuries.

If you make a cup or small basin hot and press it closely over the flesh, the vacuum formed as the cup cools, sucks flesh up, and holds it, raised, so long as the cup holds an airtight position on the flesh.

This draws blood to the spot. This treatment by suction, when combined with hot fomentations, could be applied over a wide area, or to give relief over some joint. In some cases, it could be used to draw up and extract foreign bodies, or matter, from a wound. It was more used on the Continent than in England and was developed as one of the treatments of mental disorders. Long continuous immersion in hot water was found to reduce the pressure on the brain. So the idea of combining the hot water treatment of the bath with the vacuum treatment came into use.

THE STEAM OR TURKISH BATH (BOX TYPE)

The steam bath had a slow development. It was also used for mental defects.

The treatment may have relieved pressure on the brain, if the stricture around the neck did not cause strangulation (*see* illustration).

Long coffin-shaped baths were more comfortable (*see* illustration), and there was also a tin tank, in which you were set to boil, carefully enclosed. Most of these seem to have had an explosive end (but history does not report if the bodies were recovered).

Comfort and security came with the wooden cabinet model which was inexpensive and became popular. Methylated spirit stoves set under

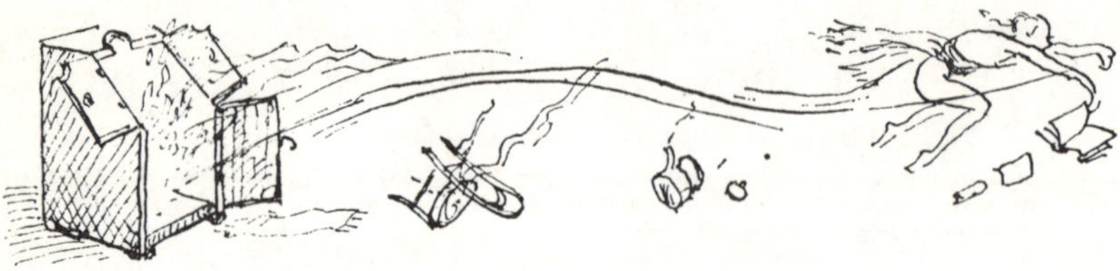

Bookworms and Turkish bath

steam kettles were used in all early models; the later type had a trap door, which allowed for the insertion of a gas ring, and the replenishment of the kettle, but these were only for houses in which gas was available.

These wooden cabinet baths were (in our memory) made of pitch pine, and arrived packed in eight sections, with long brass butterfly screws and bolts for putting the parts together. There was a floor (on four pottery casters), two sides, and a back, a low front door, two side flaps that folded inwards like hansom-cab doors, and a top piece, with a scooped-out neck hole, that shut down over your shoulders and wedged onto the side flaps. Outside, the cabinet was very handsomely varnished. Inside, there was a narrow wooden seat, upon which you perched precariously over the boiling kettle, and tried to keep your dangling legs out of line of the direct steam jet!

As these cabinets had interior latches it *was* possible to burst forth if the kettle did boil over, but once the floor was flooded there was no space to put your feet down. The agile had to leap upwards, and outwards over the front half-door (which landed them warmly damp on to the cold slippery bathroom oilcloth, causing severe abrasions).

(Later models had hand holes in the side flaps, and a book rest, but in our scholarly household this was a source of error as, once immersed in a book, the reader let the kettle boil dry, and not till the wooden seat caught fire beneath him did he wake up par-baked!)

We treasured our ancestral Turkish cabinet through three moves till, in the timber rationing of the 1940's, the local carpenter had to use the wood to make an airing cupboard for the evacuees' napkins. (I still regard the charred seat piece with regretful interest when I go to replace the winter blankets.)

The canvas Turkish bath, advertised as "the collapsible", lived up to its name. It was a floppy affair on struts, and never found much favour with the sturdy British customer who rightly pointed out that one could do quite as well with an army blanket and a kitchen chair.

Thus returning full circle to the mediæval method! (*see* illustration).

The term "baggage" dates probably from the middle of the eighteenth century when the Bagnios, Turkish-styled bath houses were a cheerfully accepted fashion. The places were warm, dimly lit, and the bathers were well supplied with wine and food and "well-trained ladies" so that the night passed pleasantly. These professional ladies of the bath were extremely clever and very charming and entirely accepted as a fashionable necessity.

PORTABLE TURKISH BATH

"The latest novelty in the way of baths is the patent portable Turkish bath, by means of which it is possible to have a very good substitute for the regulation bath in one's bedroom.

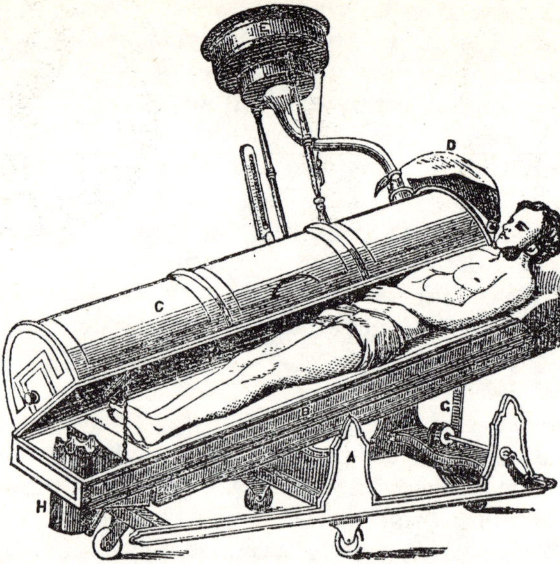

"A portable Turkish bath that secures absolute privacy. An ordinary domestic servant can adjust it in a few minutes. It can be taken to the bedside of the invalid, and brought to the level of the bed by a rack and pinion. A shower bath is attached."—B.M.J. 1873.

"The heat can be raised in less than ten minutes to 180°F. and to the full temperature of 220°F. in fifteen minutes. The heat is obtained from gas, spirit or other suitable means. It is under perfect control and can be maintained at any degree up to 220°F. that might be required. There is every facility for shampooing, the arrangements in this respect leaving nothing to be desired (?). A shower bath is attached, by means of which a copious discharge of tepid or cold water can be obtained suddenly or gradually, at the pleasure of the bather or attendant.

"One of the great advantages of the patent Turkish bath is its portability. It can be turned round completely in a space of a little more than its own length. It can be taken to the bedside of an invalid and brought to a level of the bed, by means of a rack and pinion, so as to cause the least possible amount of inconvenience to the invalid. An ordinary domestic servant can take it to pieces, and readjust it in a few minutes."

Rampu Chudder Shawls. The fine, closely-woven woollen shawls that came from East India had a great reputation among the Victorians about 1880. The cloth became popular through the new Turkish baths, for it was of a light silky texture which made it ideal for a bathing wrap.

The shawls were incredibly light and warm, and withstood the changes of temperature and continuous washing without shrinking or thickening.

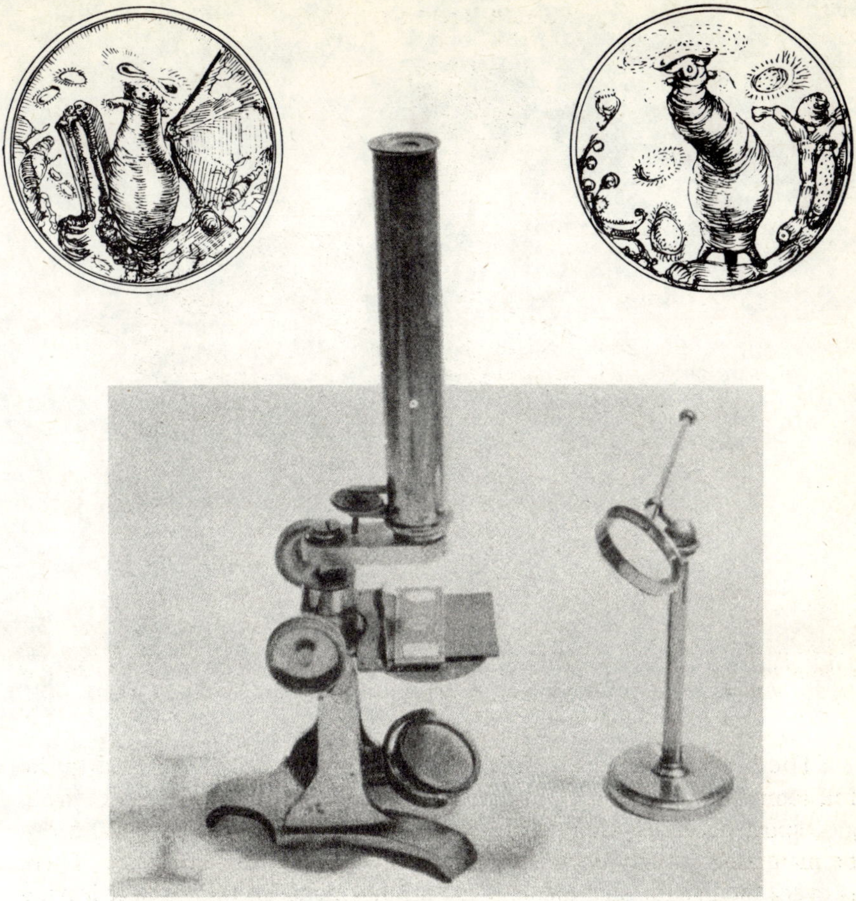

24–26. The rotifer in the joint of a defunct midge was drawn through the old low-powered lens of this 1850 brass microscope. The lens was small and the field restricted, but this type was popular for the new study of "Infusoria". The stand on the right condensed the light on to the reflector below the slide.

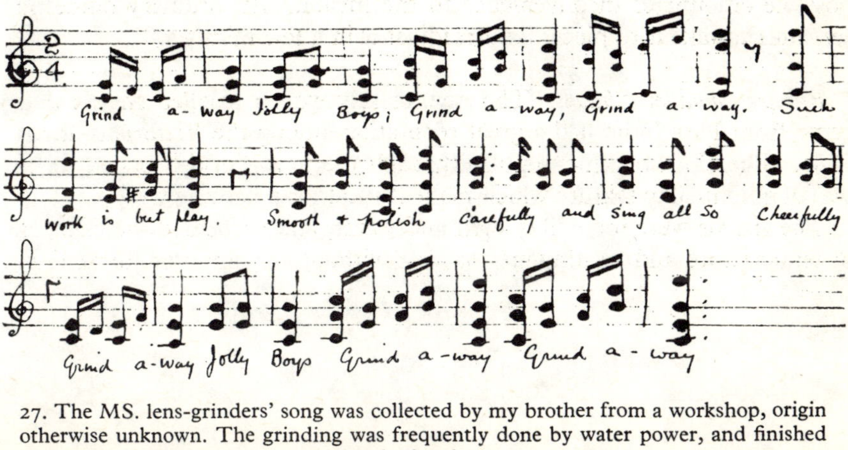

27. The MS. lens-grinders' song was collected by my brother from a workshop, origin otherwise unknown. The grinding was frequently done by water power, and finished by hand.

28. The beach chapel at Rhos-on-Sea probably originated as the cell of the guardian of the adjacent fishing grounds. The domestic water supply (in the cell) later became "holy". The chapel is situated on the old coast route from which an inland route deviated at this point.

29. The Holywell bathing pool, supplied from St. Winefred's copious spring, rising behind the central archway.

30. The lovely facade of the Spa that failed at Ashby-de-la-Zouch. The water was brought to the baths from a spring deep in a local coal mine.

THE IMMERSION HEATER FOR THE BATH

The immersion heater preceded the boiler for the self-contained bath. Self-contained as distinct from the can-filled and scooped empty tub. The static bath was filled with cold water, and the heater set down into it. A lamp, charcoal or oil stove circulated the water, till till it was hot enough to use (or the lamp went out!).

There were numerous designs for this. This one, by a Mr. Havell, was published in 1869.

> "The difficulty of heating sufficient water for filling a bath in a house not supplied with boilers adapted for the purpose, indicates a want which many inventors have in vain attempted to supply. Mr. Havell, the patentee of the stoves which Messrs. Groggon and Co. are now manufacturing, has surmounted the difficulty in a very striking manner. If the mountain will not come to Mahomet, Mahomet must go to the mountain. In like manner, Mr. Havell, finding that the bath could not be conveniently brought to the fire, has wisely concluded that the fire ought to be brought to the bath. Instead of placing cold water over a stove to warm it for the bath, he places the stove in the cold water with which the bath is filled. Supposing the bath is filled overnight, the intending bather on getting up in the morning has simply to plunge the stove in the water and in less than half an hour his warm bath is ready for him."

ANOTHER FORM OF IMMERSION HEATER FOR THE BATH

To Use the Spirit Stove

Spirit

Gas

"For a full-sized bath, pour a pint of crystal oil down the airshaft (in winter it might require a little more), then drop a piece of paper down the chimney, and light with a taper, as for gas. When the water is hot enough shut the lid of the airshaft to extinguish the flame, and do not remove the stove till it is quite out. If removed before the fire is out the boiler may be deranged."

The stoves were "well constructed and were not liable to get out of order."

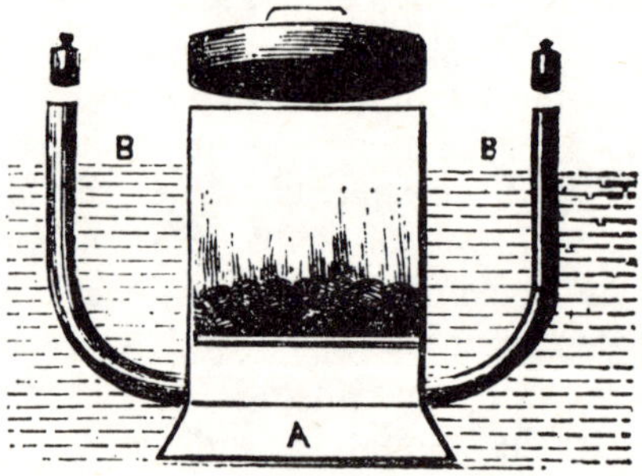

This apparatus produced a competitive design which was considered much simpler.

The apparatus, of which a diagram is here given, has been in use in France to my knowledge for at least eighty years, and I think it is as effective and much cheaper than Havell's. It is a cylinder of sheet iron, containing the fire, usually made with charcoal or coke. The two side pipes allow a current of air to pass down to the fire. The foot of the stove is filled with any heavy material—stones and cement will do—and the covers are forced down when the fire is extinguished. Two pieces of iron strengthen the end of the pipes, and prevent their being broken when raising the apparatus. I think any mechanic could make one at a very trifling cost. The difficulty with these, and other designs, was that the water cooled almost as fast as it was heated.

Judging by results, the older method, of throwing red-hot stones from the fire into a wooden tub of water, heated more water more quickly, but that necessitated a large fire and many stones. The former had to be kept in, and the latter taken out.

THE SMALL ATTACHED BOILER. EARLY MODEL FOR THE BATH

This followed the immersion heater, and was rather like it, but attached outside the end of the bath. The stoves were usually stoked with wood or coal, and short pipes circulated the water between bath and stove. The chief difficulty was the ratio between the amount of the water and the size of the stove, as the water in the bath cooled about as fast as the small stove could heat it, and there was no reserve. Once the stove was burnt out, one could add cold but not hot.

Another problem was that the very short pipes furred up so rapidly (as the spout of a kettle furs up disproportionately to the larger space in the kettle).

This fixed-on heater was practically an attached kettle, but the principle of the circulating boiler developed from it.

The use of gas for heating bath water

"It is asserted by Mr. Defries of 145 Regent St., that he can raise 45 gallons of water in a bath from 50 to 95 degrees Fahrenheit in 6 minutes! with a consumption of less than 30 units of gas costing 2*d*.

"If *this is true*, it is superior to all other methods, as the ordinary gas bath takes about 25 minutes to heat."

1857

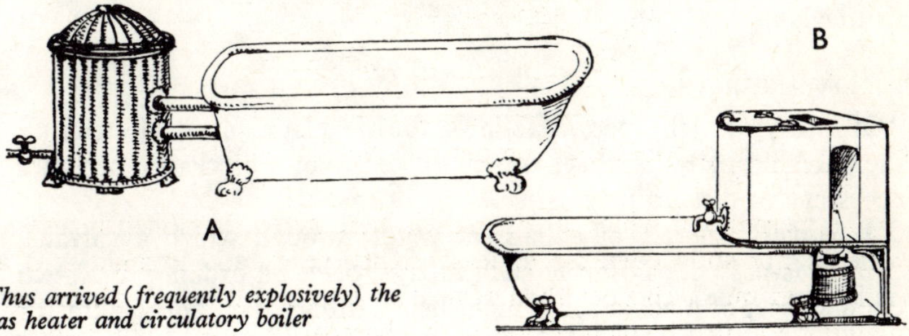

Thus arrived (frequently explosively) the gas heater and circulatory boiler

Diagram A shows the heater adapted for use with a gas ring, which after lighting, swings in under the boiler like some of the early geyser designs. But this was in *no* sense a geyser, as it only boiled the water already in the container; there was no continuous flow. Some stoves used oil instead of gas, or even worked on small coal fires. The only advance was the circulating of the water in and out of the boiler, not round and round it, as in the immersion heater. Diagram B boiler used an oil lamp to heat the water and allowed the bather to regulate the flow while *in* the bath. By supplementing the supply of cold water by bucket or can, it was just possible to obtain two hot baths running.

A Bath in Leprosy

"Rec Fumariae Lapathi acuti, scabrosae camomillae meliloti, slaphidisagriae finipas, piperis logi, nucis mufcatae sulphuris nitre aloe sauripigmenti ana, q.f. Boyle them in water and vinegar sufficient."

Emollient Baths

These have been used down the centuries. Here are some recipes of about 1850.

A Beauty Bath. To 30 gallons water:
6 lb. bran
1 lb. potato flour
2 lb. gelatine
1 lb. linseed meal
4 lb. marshmallow roots

and any other herbs to scent. The whole to be boiled and bottled.

An Alkaline Bath. 6 oz. carbonate of soda and additional potash and borax.

An Acid Bath. 1 oz. mureatic nitric to 30 gallons of water.

Iodine and Bromide added to the water makes it soothing to the nerves.

Domestic mustard added to the bath water is one of the most powerful *stimulants.*

THE GALVANIC BATH

"Of late years [the period follows the development of electricity], the galvanic bath has been much talked about, so that it becomes necessary to discuss its merits.

It consists merely of a bath of water through which a galvanic current is passed. To make such a bath, place an ordinary bath tub upon a sheet of mackintosh which, being rubber, is a non-conductor of electricity and so has the effect of 'insulating' (as it is called) the bath. Fill the bath to a convenient depth with water, and to the water add a handful of salt and a wineglass full of vinegar, to increase its conducting power.

Next, get a galvanic battery (one having 30 or 40 Leclanché elements is sufficient) and place it beside the bath.

To each of the poles of the battery, affix a suitable length (3 or 4 yards) of insulated telegraph wire, having its extremities freed from the gutta percha or other insulating material.

Place a length of stout broom handle across the bath, resting on its two edges, and round the middle of this twine the bright metal end of the positive end of the wire, covering it with a piece of flannel.

The bather then gets into the bath and the end of the negative wire is placed in the bath itself. As soon as the bather holds the broom handle he will feel the shock of the current. The current travels from the positive pole of the battery, through the wire on the broom handle and down the bather's arms, and through his body to the negative pole in the water. The author states that the bath is a very powerful stimulant to the skin but beyond that he knows nothing of its curative powers.

It was said that the electric current could extract metallic bodies and substances from within the body, but the electricians say there is so far no evidence of this, though some quackish establishments point to discoloration on the sides of the bath as evidence of having withdrawn mineral elements that were lurking on the patient's body."

Extract from the English Mechanic *of the period* 1887

THE GALVANO-ELECTRIC BATH. POTIN'S SYSTEM, 1875

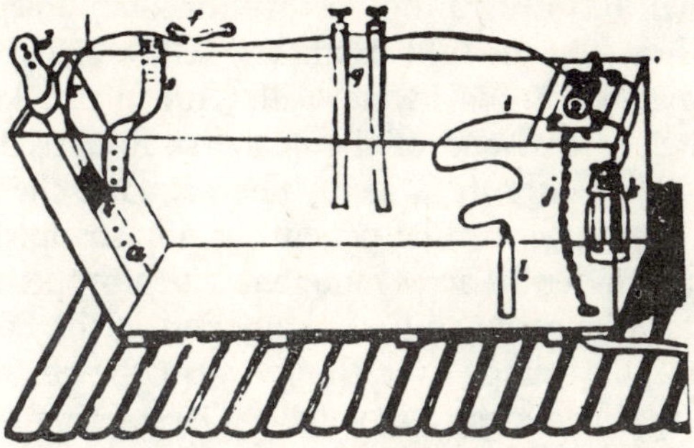

"A drawing reproduced from *The English Mechanic and World of Science*, 1875.

"The bath is of blue slate, grooved and bedded in with red lead, and cramped up with iron cramps. It should stand on a wooden cradle and the floor below should be tiled.

"A zinc plate at the head end, where a webbing head rest is provided across the bath, is connected by copper wire to the coil on a board at the foot. This coil is set above the carbon and the acid and zinc cylinder (which could be accommodated outside the bath if necessary).

"The hot and cold taps are fitted with rubber hose piping."

ELECTRIC BATH

A "Do it Yourself" Treatment of 1887

". . . It may not be generally known that sea water is the best excitant for dipping the Pulvermacher's chain, and also for the bath itself. I was once on board a large steamer when I heard a paralytic passenger complaining that he had forgotten a supply of acid and could not use his chain. I got a fishing line, and let down Pulvermacher into the ocean, and very much gratified the invalid by an unexpected shock. Get the half of a very sound beer hogshead, scald it, and let it dry. Get a piece of sheet copper about 2 in. square, $\frac{1}{4}$ in. thick, drill a hole in the centre and tap it with a screw. Take a piece of stout copper wire 3 in. long, tap one end with a screw to fit the hole in the above plate. At the other end of the wire make an eye or ring. With copper tacks fasten the plate on the inner side of the cask, about a foot from the bottom. With a gimlet bore a hole straight from the outside to the screw hole in the copper sheet, then pass the end of the wire through the wood and screw it in very tight. Put up a wooden peg in the wall of the bathroom at such height as a 60, or maybe a 120 element Pulvermacher can hang at full length, so as just to meet the eye of the wire. Draw the tub to within 6 in. of the wall and hook on to it with a small bit of wire the Positive (or zinc) pole. Pour water till the tub is three-fourths full. Hang the yellow or negative pole by a piece of string to the peg in the wall. Attach two long insulated conducting wires to that end of the chain, sufficiently long to allow 2 ft. of the same to enter the water. The points of the wires should have electrical conductors. The patient, having stripped, should put on an elastic tape under his arms mounted with a copper hook and eye buckle, which can be easily shifted to any part of the body requiring galvanic treatment. I made everything except the chain myself, but all such small appliances can be bought. On entering the water, the bather will take one wire in either hand and fasten the other wire to buckle. Though in perfect health, I always enjoyed these baths; but it is possible they might be injurious in some cases of organic disease. For torpid liver, piles, rheumatic affections, defective circulation, paralytic symptoms, and disorders of debility, they are undoubtedly beneficial . . ."

Magnetic Night Caps

A curious sideline that developed from the electric bath was the magnetic night cap. At that time, most folks wore night caps. Men wore woollen ones, like a wide short stocking, with a tassel at the end and strings under the chin.[1] The ladies wore shaped cotton caps, with frills, and a bow under the chin.

The magnetic cap was more sternly designed. Red flannel was recommended, double, with magnetised strips of metal sandwiched between the layers. Some makers favoured a light watch spring, others used strips cut from "crinoline steel", the more mechanical considered old telephone magnets suitable. Whatever metal was used, the caps had to be recharged frequently.

THE SAND BATH

"Faire in the sond, to bathe her merily lyth Pertelote,[2]
and alle hir sustres by,
Agayn the sonne; and chauntecleer so free
Song merier than the mermayde in the sea." CHAUCER

[1] If you remember, the unfortunate Mr. Pickwick got his chin strings knotted and was unable to uncover to the distressed lady upon whom he had accidentally intruded.

[2] One has no need to apologise for letting Pertelote fly into the chapter on Baths, she was such a perfect little lady.

Sand was a natural product, but like peat and mud wallows it had to be artificially arranged for use. The sands around Woburn were most used. These varied-coloured sands used to be packed down in fancy patterns in sealed glass containers and sold to visitors as paper weights and ornamental souvenirs. Tall round paper weights full of this coloured sand can still be found in old junk shops, though time has blurred the sharp edges of the patterns. (The sand's other domestic use was to fill egg-timers.)

For bathing, the sand was baked hot and then packed loosely around the stiff joint or paralysed limb. The slight surface friction on the skin and comforting penetrating warmth does seem to have been of use. One old man described to me the treatment on his hand and arm. The hand had been rough cut across the palm on a dirty scythe. "The doctor he washed it out, and bandaged it up, and said as soon as the skin was healed I was to keep working the fingers, but the guides (tendons) were stuck fast in their runs, on account of the inflammation, and I could get no manner of movement out of her. So I got an old tin trunk and filled her full of sand and baked her hot as I could bear, and sat by the fire with my arm in her to the elbow. After a while I could shift my thumb a bit and I'd keep groping around in the hot sand and byen' bye it got so I could grasp it, and one night it seemed to work lose all of a sudden."

Apparently sand was also used where movement had to be avoided. The limb, or the whole body, was laid on the hot sand and more hot sand poured over and around it without disturbance. (There would be no alteration in the weight of the limb as there would be in a water bath.) Afterwards the sand was drained away from below. This treatment, they explained, was for broken bones "after they had set, but when the blood was not running free again".

One would expect the treatment to have been used for rickets in children, as it would provide amusing exercise without weight on the legs, but I did not hear of the sand baths being used for anything but rheumatism, stiff joints, paralysis and palsy. The sand bath has a special interest as it seems to have been entirely a rural speciality. It may have originated among the sand-casting metal workers. Who can tell?

The cure remains today in the old-fashioned sandbags. These were made of firm calico (old bed ticking was popular) and had loose removable covers of flannel.

The bag had to be large and loosely filled so that it was pliant, and could be hollowed out to make a trough in which the painful joint could sink to rest. A second bag would be laid on top, the sand taking the weight and the finger or foot being thus enclosed in a casing of hot dry warmth. These sandbags were hotted up in the kitchen oven, being turned and shaken up while heating, so that they became evenly hot right through. When scorching hot they were withdrawn, slipped at once into their flannel covers, and rushed to the sick room. Sandbags for mumps, toothache, earache, etc., were sometimes allowed the refinement of a linen cover. They had one advantage over the bread poultice—the patient could not eat them!

WALLOWS

Mud and Peat Baths

The mud and peat baths reached England from the continental spas. They were definitely medical.

The peat baths were considered great beautifiers and soothing to the nerves. The Irish aristocracy (resident in England) praised them, but did not use them. The tannic acid probably had some effect upon the skins of the bathers. The mud baths depended for effect upon their mineral content and consistency. Neither of these baths was found in England as natural baths, but was artificially arranged and very little used.

BATHS FOR BABIES

"Always they cry jangle and jabe
that unneth they be still, unless they be asleep.
And when they be cleansed, anon
They defile themselves again.
And when one washeth and combeth them, they kick
and sprawl and put (push) with feet and hands
and withstand with all their might."

BART. ANGLICUS

Christmas carols and reproductions of Della Robbia plaques have given the impression that, from the Dark Ages to the end of the mediæval period, all babies were at all times trussed up in swaddling clothes and that it was a very cruel practice. Yet no one condemns the Indian squaw for packing her baby down on birchback, and the Esquimau babies are remarkably happy and healthy, though packed up like parcels for convenient transport. (Mediæval, Indian or Esquimau babies might suffer less discomfort than some modern babies, bumped along in springless pushchairs, with a strap around their middle and a pile of knobbly parcels shoved behind them.)

It is wrong, therefore, to generalize over babies. Bart. Anglicus's baby, "putting and sprawling", sounds active enough, and the later description of the old nurse is sheer love and beauty. Bartholomew explains this problem of the swaddling clothes. The nurse is to play with the child and encourage its activity, feed it and comfort it if it falls down and sing to it "low and crooningly" when she would have it sleep. She will "gently draw down its legs and arms and bind them softly so that they grow straight", *because* (this is the point) mediæval diet, especially in winter, was deficient, light and sunshine were deficient, especially in castles and large fortified houses, so rickets was prevalent, less from any need, than from not understanding the cause. The peasant or slave (if well used by a fair master) had a far better bone-forming diet, with the wild fruits, plants and roots of the woodlands to eat, than some house-bound noble babies.

If you study the hundreds of well-known mediæval paintings of the Madonna and Child, the greatest number of Holy Infants who are obviously bad cases of malnutrition are usually those whose Holy Mothers wear the most elaborately styled gown and richest jewels. Some of the later Flemish painters working for affluent merchant patrons show this, whereas Raphael and Angelo and painters who found their models among the sun-browned country mothers, show babies full of health, naked as God made them, and as clean as love and washing could enforce!

There were just the same contrasts everywhere, contrasts caused by poverty and wealth, care and neglect. Mortality was high and medical care varied, but mother love remained unchanged, and the swaddling clothes and flat wooden lath were accepted by the mediæval mother as a precaution against bent legs and curved spines, so she used the best precaution she knew.

> "He neither shall be washed in milk or in wine,
> But in the pure spring water, that flows from Bethene."
>
> *Old Carol*

The use of wine for washing was probably against fleas, and it was a mild disinfectant.

Much instruction that seems strange to us now had sensible causes when the instructions were issued. Mediæval babies were washed in warm water, or perhaps oiled clean in quite a modern manner. In winter they probably were not tubbed so frequently as today. Breast feeding was the rule, and wet nurses were tried out till one was found whose milk suited.

Bones were given to chew and suck, and lumps of coral were popular for teething babies.

The only item of toilet I cannot find used on the mediæval baby was talcum powder! They used goosegrease and fine lard and soft wax to prevent chafing. On the whole, mediæval babies were bathed and dried in a perfectly normal manner, and "when they be cleansed, anon they defile themselves again".

Notes on the Use of Cold Water for Children by G. John Wesley and his Opinion of "Swaddling"

Few know this medical book. It is a curious pamphlet, published in Bristol about 1755. Strange to find Wesley advising "powder of dried toad". Some of his cures are reasonable—"Camphine is safer than Opium" (for some complaints). "Apple water and lemonade are cooling drinks." His "hot compress of Comfrey roots" had been standard use for strained tendons for many centuries. Wesley states sensibly that "no child should ever be swathed tightly" as such early restrictions "lay the foundation for many diseases". He advises that all children should be dipped into cold water every morning. He does advise the taking of "a few hot baths before starting the course of ice-cold ones" and completes his advice by the covering insurance that "every man who applies to the Physician should choose one who fears God". (After some of his "cures" we feel he had better do so.)

Babies' Baths

One small ingenuity (it was not a disguise) was to make the babies' bath with strap handles and fitted lid so that it could be used as a small trunk for travel packing.

NIPPLE WATER

"Jean's paps wi salt and water washen clean."

A. Ross, 1778

Dairy maids used to rinse their hands in cold salted water before handling the butter. In hot weather the salt would make the water colder and the salt act as scouring agent, so the use of water and salt to toughen the nipples of nursing mothers seems reasonable.

SEA-WATER BATHS FOR CHILDREN

In 1858 the Royal Sea Bathing Infirmary at Margate (a hospital for scrofulous patients) wanted £5,000 "on account of the increased demand for more sea bath treatment".

They wanted two extra wards able to take in one hundred children (though they'd start work on one ward of fifty beds if necessary). Accounts show the costs for seven months:

	£	s.	d.
Food	1,693	14	0
Nurses and ward servants	378	0	0
Other (office?) salaries	265	0	0
Pumping the water for bathing the children	53	0	0
Rates	10	0	0
Laundry	38	0	0

The scale of costs reflects this worst period of malnutrition in the London slums and the private efforts by reformers. If one contrasts this food bill with bills from similar institutions in the previous century, one judges that the food and fresh air had quite as much effect as the salt water.

SEA BATHS

Sea-bathing with Caution, 1850

"All are agreed that bathing is a healthful practice, first because it is cleanly, and second because it is a precautionary measure against the risk of life by drowning. 'We are fully prepared,' says the *Lancet*, 'to endorse the proposition that boys should be allowed to bathe as often and as freely as may be practicable. It is, however, necessary to raise a protest against the recklessness which too commonly attends the recourse to bathing as an exceptional, or at most, a *seasonable exercise* by those who are, though eager perhaps, not always physically fit to bathe. There is, practically, less danger in bathing all the year round than in doing so only at certain periods.'

When to begin bathing, in what weather to bathe and under what conditions of the bodily state are *questions of considerable importance*. The general rules which should guide the judgment are, doubtless, in the main physiological—that is to say, they relate chiefly to the functions of life and their healthy performance. Obviously, it is not right to dare the dangers of a chill, either when undressing or by immersion in cold water . . . because it is from congestion of the nervous centres we get cramp so often in bathing. The fact of the *reaction* does not, of course, constitute the whole phenomena of bathing, but it is so important and comprehensive that we may take this as the point on which everything turns. Conditions under which a vigorous return of blood to the surface cannot be confidently counted upon are not favourable to bathing. If, therefore, the weather be chilly, or there be a cold wind, so that the body may be rapidly cooled at the surface while undressing it is not safe to bathe. . . .

In short, the aim must be to avoid *two* chills. First, from the air, and second, from the water; and to make sure that the body is in such a condition as to secure a quick reaction on emerging from the water, without relying too much on the possible effect of friction by rubbing. Thinking these brief hints out, it will be obvious that both weather and wind must be carefully considered before bathing."

Medical Tract of 1850

Water for Pleasure

The sea water around England, for centuries our bulwark, was not connected with much public pleasure before the Prince Regent developed

Sea Water Bathing.

MR. LLOYD

RESPECTFULLY informs the Public, the above Vessel (of Forty Tons Burthen, so constructed as to fill herself in the Sea) is constantly kept going to and from the Ocean, to Black-Friar's Bridge; from whence the Water is conveyed to his Baths, in *Bagnio Court, Newgate Street,* and deposited in Reservoirs under Ground.

TERMS OF BATHING.

SEA WATER.	L.	S.	D.	SPRING WATER.	L.	S.	D.
Cold Bath, per Month	1	1	0	Cold Bath, per Year	1	1	0
Ditto, Single Time	0	3	0	Ditto, per Month	0	10	6
Warm Bath, each Time	0	7	6	Ditto, single Time	0	2	0
Or Six Times for	2	2	0	Warm Bath, each Time	0	4	0
N. B. Children dipt at	0	1	0	Or Six for	1	1	0
Sea Water sold at per Gallon	0	0	6	Vapour Bath, each	0	5	0

Ladies and Gentlemen Cupped at the Baths, or waited on in Town or Country
BY EXPERIENCED CUPPERS OF BOTH SEXES

Bright Town, and so brought about the seaside resort. Till then the sea had always belonged to sailors, dreamers and adventurers, and was used with trepidation by landlubbers who could not get across any other way. There had always been a great deal of coasting trade. Farmers on the coast used the sea for transport and long ferry services carried goods and passengers to river ports. Rivers were used far more than today. Any study of early and mediæval industry shows the importance of downstream water transport, and tidal rivers were much used for their two-way traffic. River waterways were used for summer pleasure, with music and friends. Most rich Londoners kept their own stately barges, but sea water was not popular. The only people who got into sea water (and that unwillingly) were vagrants and exiled criminals. For them it was the cold wet ultimatum, into which the law enforced them to wade, crying "Passage for the love of God", in hope that some boatmen would "get them away from that place". (Where they landed again was nobody's business and probably a great number were simply dumped back into England on the next convenient "hard".) It is surprising the number of "pilgrim" boats that plied across to the Continent. The word "pilgrim" was elastic. The gathering up of pilgrims was, during the Crusade period especially, under the management of the Knights Templars and Hospitallers, who arranged huge camps at strategic points behind ports of embarkation. To these embarkation points the passengers were shepherded and, having been fed, confessed and blessed, they were shipped away most competently. We have traced one such route from the camp at Temple (the name persists) on Bodmin Moor, past the remains of a large hospice (now a private residence) down to the beach-side chapel (now a café) at Exmouth. (Other routes led to Plymouth). These pilgrimages were the early English equivalent of the tours organized today. Tours to Rome or Oberammergau, etc., and, as today, many went with mixed motives. The genuine pilgrim, the sightseer and the commercial traveller, automatically segregated themselves into groups and, in case of pirates or shipwreck, hoped there were enough of the devout aboard to cover their fire insurance!

The rounded bow-breasting wooden craft certainly lacked stabilisers, and the packing was incredibly close, truly "men may leave all games that sailen to St. James". Considering the discomfort, the number of these boats was extraordinary. Interesting research awaits, in the early east coast shipping, where hundreds of small "pilgrim" boats became derelict after the Reformation, and were bought up by the fishing fleet. This in turn became a very useful Naval Reserve for Drake (who knew those waters well from his boyhood days).

There was also privately-owned shipping, belonging to important people. Such a fleet regularly carried ore from Cornwall to Bewdley, to supply the Boult's smelting forges in the Wye forest (an industry that lasted till the destruction of the forges during the civil war). Or it carried the china clay for Coalport, or supplied the specialised "copper boats" of Red Wharfe Bay in Anglesey. These working fleets apparently kept one cabin boat for the owners' travel, but the pilgrim boat was the ordinary water omnibus for centuries but, with few exceptions, *the sea-water holiday* for pleasure *dates only from the last century.*

The south coast towns developed first.

And after Queen Victoria took her family to Scotland the Welsh coast resorts became popular, mountains became "picturesque" and sea water "invigorating" (though Rhyl, one of the earliest resorts, was flat as a pancake and there was more sand than sea). "Good posting" in the 1800's was the equivalent of "convenient by rail or coach" today. The political situation that, in 1800, brought a hundred Irishmen to Westminster and

---

The advertisements are selected from guide books of 1870 onwards.

Llandudno.

Prospectuses, with Terms and other Information, on Application.

LLANDUDNO HYDROPATHIC

ESTABLISHMENT AND WINTER RESIDENCE FOR PATIENTS AND VISITORS.

RESIDENT PROPRIETOR AND MEDICAL SUPERINTENDENT—

H. THOMAS, M.D.

This Establishment is situated on the Parade, and commands a full view of the Bay, with its surrounding magnificent scenery; and is conducted so as to afford all who visit it seeking health the comforts and cheerfulness of home.

"The house itself is admirably adapted for the purposes to which it is applied. Larger than many of our Liverpool hotels, it contains abundant accommodation, the rooms, corridors, staircases, &c., being spacious and well arranged. It is thoroughly warmed and ventilated throughout, an advantage which invalids must in winter keenly appreciate; and the domestic arrangements are carried out by the housekeeper in such a way as to ensure the comfort of every visitor. . . . . . The system and punctuality observed throughout the whole of the domestic arrangements, and the civility and attention displayed by all the subordinates, really ensure what Dr. Thomas so much desires, the cheerfulness, comfort, and happiness of his visitors.

"Now comes a very natural query. What does all this cost? All I can say is that I was satisfied, and with me economy was not to be lost sight of. *Those who wish to ascertain the exact charges can write to Dr. Thomas for a tariff.* They will find it *pro rata.* If they want private rooms, instead of using the general drawing and dining rooms, they can have them, though not for nothing. But those who cast their lot among the general company, and take their meals at the table d'hote, will find, as I did, that they get first-class hotel living and accommodation at much less than first-class hotel rates."—*Liverpool Mercury*,—February 26, 1874.

Visitors to Llandudno not residing in the Establishment can have the following BATHS between the hours of 7 a.m. and 6 p.m.:—

Hot and Cold Salt and Fresh Water Baths, Turkish Baths, Seaweed Baths.

The Bath Rooms are part of the Establishment, and contain, in addition to the ordinary Hydropathic appliances, *four Russian Vapour and two commodious and well-appointed Turkish Baths.*

A notable feature of this Establishment is the profusion of salt water employed. It is pumped in direct from the Bay.

a whole covey of New Irish Peers into the House of Lords, helped (since it became necessary to get these Irish from London back to Dublin as quickly as possible). No one wanted the sea-coast route, with the difficulty of having the coach taken to pieces and carried over Penmaenmaur. Always there had been too much sea water along that passage to Bangor (even Giraldus the Welshman had complained about it in 1199).

Therefore Telford's new road from London to Holyhead, without a gradient needing a trace horse, was a triumph of road and bridge building and opened up the west at a propitious period. The industrial north and the Potteries were accessible, Welsh prices were low, and provisions good. The boom in spa water was over, but enough "wells" remained, and most seaside resorts offered bathing establishments and homeopathic treatments for those who enjoyed the sea *air* but were not brave enough to use sea *water*.

There were hotels (the new railway hotels were enjoyed by the modern-minded), and apartment houses and many small houses in the principality let "rooms with attendance".

In many ways the seaside resort remained unchanged till fifty years ago. The small cottage we rented was primitive in the extreme; all water was carried in pails, clothes washing was done in a stream and the privy was at the end of the garden (and supplied with dry sand). The beach was furnished with half a dozen rickety wooden vans on wheels, which an old carthorse clattered over the shingle, and drew out to the edge of the sea. There would be a rattle of trace chain, a bang on the van, "Hold tight", and away one bumped, the clothes inside swinging wildly from a rusty nail and the water splashing up through the floorboards. The swaying door frequently flung open, to the embarrassment of the half-stripped bathers (the horse wore blinkers) and then, after the bathe, the suspense; suppose the tide should rise before rescue? for shoes were left in a trustful row above high water line.

To wet the head (to prevent apoplexy), to take a hot drink on coming out, to be scrubbed dry till one howled for mercy, and never to stay in longer than half an hour—such was sea-water bathing fifty years ago.

Margate apparently pioneered sea bathing "for ladies whose moderate means, and delicate susceptibilities precluded the fashionable expense of Brighton. Special sloops of 80-ton burden leave London for Margate on Wednesday, Thursday and return for Margate on Fridays and Saturdays. These 'Hoys' carry 60–70 passengers and the fare is *2s. 6d.* It takes 8 hours with a good wind (but might take 3 days if the wind is against them). However, the Masters are careful decent men, and allow of no Impropriety. They transact incredible business."

A tent-like arrangement that folded down onto the water from the

The bathing wain

van and completely hid the bather from view, was the invention of one Benjamin Beale, a Quaker, and was, we believe, first used in Margate.

The hooped tent hinged above the door of the van over steps that led down into the water. The ladies disrobed in the van, and bathed within the seclusion of the extended canvas. It must have become very hot inside the small tent under a hot sun, but in cold weather it must have kept out the draughts! It was said that "by the aid of this contrivance ladies who have been excluded from the benefits of bathing in most parts of England, may now enjoy all the pleasures of bathing in so private a manner as to be consistent with the most strict delicacy!"

LACK OF BATHS AND ULTIMATE PARLIAMENTARY ACTION

"The Flea is a little beast that grieveth men, and is of wonder lightness, and scapeth peril with leaping not running . . . and doth let (hinder) them that would sleep with sharp biting and spareth not Kings."

BART. ANGLICUS

Crime and dirt were unenviable products of the industrial revolution. Previously mediæval dirt was, perhaps, more a matter of choice than necessity, for the mediæval standard of cleanliness varied enormously, socially, politically and religiously. The mediæval hermit was considered rather more spiritually-minded if he disregarded the comforts of cleanliness. Yet no confraternity of villains would consider it disloyal to wash. The beauty of purity and freshness was considered desirable if not always attained (*see* Chaucer's *Lovers*). With the crowding of erstwhile country people into unnatural and horrible housing conditions in cities, dirt became unavoidable. So there arose a brotherhood of dirt that was something new. Since cleanliness was possible only to the ruling classes, any attempt by a fellow worker to make himself conspicuous by cleanliness was considered an attempt to "leave his own tribe" (a move resented

31. An outside spring house and adjoining open-air bath, such as was popular in many 17th- and 18th-century gardens.

32. Mediæval indoor hot-water tubs. The cosy draught curtains did not exclude amicable intercourse.

33. A late-Victorian tin bath tub (that would be filled from a covered hot-water can). The wash-hand-stand is white-marble-topped and the china toilet set is embellished with gold and mauve violets. (Loofah and bath sponge should have been replaced in their appropriate containers.)

34. The Box mangle. The "box" was filled with stones and lead, etc., and wound backwards and forwards over loose rollers which pressed the linen laid below. It could be used to extract water, and later, with dry rollers inserted, to press folded linen smooth.

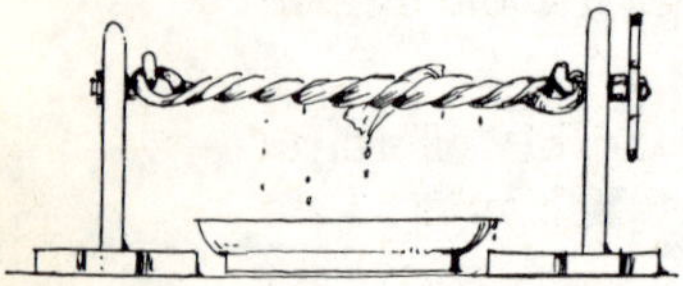

Aston's wringing machine.

Method of folding sheets, etc.

Chain net for small articles.

35. The early "wringers" were used by Irish linen manufacturers, and copied as a domestic convenience. Large sheets, etc., could be slung direct between fixed hook and twisting wheel, and smaller articles were encased in chain mesh. The earlier forms of mangle were for years called "wringers".

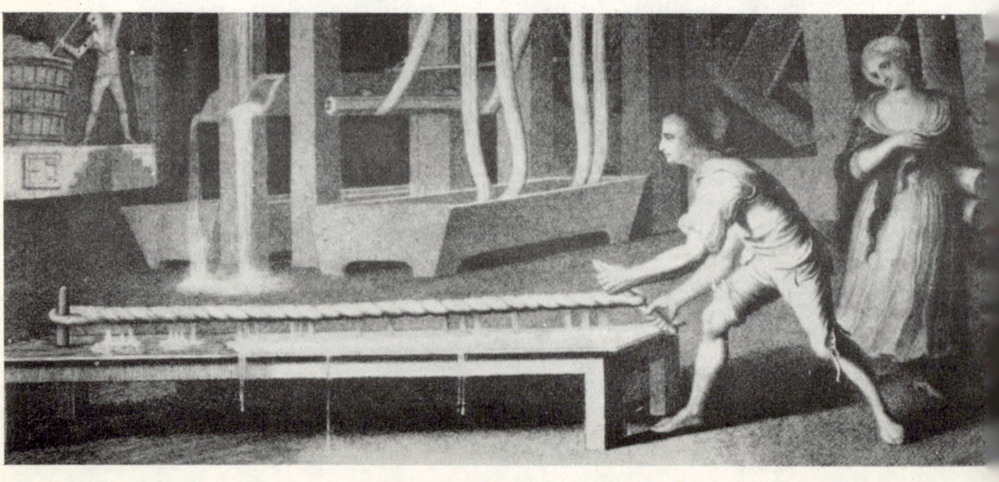

by any herd) and the greatest evil of the huge factories, and crowded cities, was this driving individuals into herds. Living conditions literally "herded them together".

Sieving historical data from the tracts and novels of the period, you are aware of this. The early "ragged schools" used to provide soap and water and towels for their pupils, and "he's washed his face" was the accepted sign that a pupil had begun a mental rebellion against the herd, and was sufficiently brave to face the jeers and taunts of his fellows.

Admittedly the "virtuously clean cottager" and the "spotless apron" of the "deserving poor" are overdone in the reforming pamphlets of the period, but the cleaning of crime, by the cleaning of dirt, was an accepted working principle.

The speech by the Bishop of London at a public meeting in the Mansion House in 1844 now sounds patronizing and sanctimonious, but the job was done and the ribald broadsheet of the great unwashed that commented upon it, showed appreciation as well as laughter. Compare this speech at the Mansion House with the broadsheet sung in the streets.

The Speech

BATH AND WASH HOUSES FOR LABOURING CLASSES
Public Meeting in Mansion House—1844. Speech by the Bishop of London.

"We have seen of late the commencement of laudable efforts to better the conditions of the poor by improving their habitatus. I am afraid a long time must elapse before the exertion of benevolent individuals can be crowned with complete success.

If we can't at once place our labouring poor in such comfortable dwellings as we would desire . . . may we not do something to alleviate the evils which press upon them by promoting the formation of Public Baths and Wash Houses?

I will not, in the presence of members of the medical profession, enlarge upon the benefits which must result from the frequent use of baths (as frequent ablution is extremely conducive to health). I lately inspected the Public Baths and Wash Houses which have been established (in Liverpool) for about two years. As many as two hundred and twenty labourers have bathed there on one Saturday though there be only eight separate baths and one vapour bath. The Superintendent, a very intelligent and benevolent man, told me one labourer remarked to another, 'Why, I feel as if I could do another week's work now I have been in the bath!'"

The worthy bishop then points out that, being clean, they will be more disposed to observe the Lord's Day.

The question of modesty and pride is then considered at length and large common baths are shown to be unpopular, "as so many would feel difficulty and delicacy about going into a public bath who would be exceedingly glad of a private bath for a small sum, and the advantage (highly estimated at Liverpool) of having as much cold and warm water as pleased and which he may turn on for himself".

The speaker then pointed out that not only labourers, but clerks and apprentices, and others, used the baths, and were willing to pay a slightly higher price.

The speech then turned to washhouses. ". . . Many now listening are not unacquainted with the fearful state of the streets and alleys of the vast metropolis—take for instance the case of the parish of St. Giles . . . densely crowded and miserable. Many thousands of the poorest have been displaced from their hovels of filth and crime, but what has been the result? These parts of London which before were crowded are now overcrowded—there are houses in which every room is occupied by two or three families." He then speaks surprisingly of the parish of St. George's, Hanover Square, where nearly a thousand families had only one room each, and of his own parish of St. Botolph's, where "one comparatively small house with sixteen rooms had sixteen families and sixty-four people in it", and he quotes a sanitary report of unhealthy people and children all sharing one bed.

After that, the speech gets down to the washing which "is put off as long as possible and in many cases done in water already dirty, and the using of a substitute for soap "all too horrible to mention". (In fairness, these substances were traditionally used in "bucking" linen by clean county laundries!)

Next he speaks of the distance and difficulty of fetching clean water. The sanitary reports are then brought out again, and an interesting side-line is the discontinuing of "bleeding" as "medical men now hardly ever venture upon bleeding, because the constitution requires stimulants rather than depleting processes".

This point leads to a discussion on the use of liquor as a palliative and the increase of drunkenness and disorder.

There is one objectioner who questions the advisability of "herding families together to wash", but the superintendent of the Liverpool washhouse reported that he had "never observed any evil for twenty or thirty all washing their clothes together and if they did talk over their grievances I know no great harm and care of that!" *So washhouses arrived.*

And there is the characteristic cockney song that commented upon that serious meeting at the Mansion House, the ribald broadsheet upon the speech:

Baths for the Million—1845

"A song of Praise at present times
Is my design to chant sir,
And if You'll listen to my rhymes
The reason you will grant sir!
We've Railroad schemes, on every hand,
But, sure the chaps no silly 'un
Who to Cleanliness, a railroad planned
A WASHHOUSE for the MILLION!
    Ri tooral looral looral loo
    Ri tooral looral LI Do.
Sure! purity outside and in
Should be a People pride'o;
Now Dirty Dick, and Dirty Bob,
Coal heavers and flue fakers
From Saffron Hill and sweet St. Giles
Will turn out Clean as Quakers!
Lord Mayors, and Bishops, patronize;
And quack the Grand specific;
Though some do say ''tis but a gag'
A National Soap-ore-ipic!"

THE SLIPPER BATH (L.C.C.) (OR THE PUBLIC BATH HOUSE CONTINUED!)

The only part of the slipper bath that remained in use in England was its name. It was the "Sabot" bath of France, boot-shaped (the name may have carried on to the boot-boiler, which heated the water for baths).

That the name was transferred to the ordinary long white baths when vitreous enamel had given them their glossy polish, was the very plausible explanation given to me by an attendant at the public bathhouse that used to stand in a square behind Warren Street Station. (A square now blitzed flat, and used as a car park, but still showing the rough nostalgic tracks of ancient plumbing.)

These baths were a late Victorian attempt to provide facilities for the mass of small houses and tenements that crowded that now rapidly altering district.

The bath section was a long corridor of cubicles with built-in slipper baths, their wooden surrounds scoured white. A slatted wooden seat across the far end and several hooks for clothes comprised the furnishing. The tap was one enormous affair nearly a foot wide, and there was a notice warning the bather not to be *in* the bath when the water was turned on. This was wise, for the supply was controlled by the attendant from outside in the corridor. There would be a cry of "hereyar" and a cranking sound, and a cascade of boiling water crashed down into the bath. The steam rose in billows! Then another cranking sound and the cold crashed in, followed by the cry "Howsat?" "More cold, please" (another crashing waterfall). "Too cold now!" Crank, crash and "Howsat now?" "Oh! Oh! scalding, cold again please." "Well, make your mind up, lidy."

One finally succumbed to the heavenly agony of being par-boiled rather than waste more time, for twenty minutes was the official time allowed for 6*d.* Using two tickets wangled you in for forty minutes, but we were hard-up students (no grants in those days). If it was a slack time, one might soak placidly for an hour undisturbed. A small cake of yellow soap, and two clean towels of huckaback texture and board-like hardness were included for the 6*d.*

On your way out, you cast these towels, damp and *slightly* bent, into a bin below the watchful eye of the box-office attendant who sold tickets at the door. The scraps of soap used to be collected into an old pillow case by the bath attendant who, when you'd finished, went in and slung it, foaming, round and round the bath, to remove the scum, afterwards brushing out the bath with boiling water and drying off the rim before the next customer.

I'd like to register gratitude and commendation to those bath house women. They worked hard for long hours and were a cheery, friendly lot. Customers who brought reports from other less-well-run establishments were well heard. They kept *their* baths spotlessly clean and polished till they were indeed "proper slippery".

On busy nights the "two women" "and the door" kept good-natured order. On slack afternoons all three sat and drank tea, and gossiped hospitably. They taught me a lot about London. It was one of them who gave me the explanation of the name. "They *are* slippers, dearie! You being young are all right, but some of the heavy sort, their feet fly from under them and they comes down on their backside (slap!). Proper dangerous it can be! And I tells them to lay one of their towels on the bottoms before they gets in. The bottoms of the bath I mean, dearie."

PUBLIC SWIMMING BATHS. WAVE BATHS

The swimming bath is medically recommended from about 1879. Four "well-qualified doctors" agree that "little or no salt, or water, is absorbed by the skin", and the good effects of sea-bathing are obtained by alternating heat and cold and exercise.

So they suggest the "wave bath", in which the water is kept moving, and shortly after this date several municipal baths had an arrangement by which the water was kept in motion.

The doctors' "Health Primer" stressed that the best of all baths was the swimming bath in which the bather could "indulge in the free exercise of his limbs". Now that physiotherapy makes much use of buoyant water for treatment of paralysis and stiffened joints, it is interesting to realize it was recommended in 1879.

WASHING THE FEET

Barefoot or shod depends more on custom than ground conditions. For centuries country workers all walked barefoot, picking their way over the rough hills on small grassy patches between the rocks. They put on shoes only for church, or visits of ceremony.[1] Mediæval MSS. show that

1400

the stockings left off at the foot, with a strap under the instep, and socks and shoes slid off easily to dry the feet before the fire. Under these conditions to wash the feet was as simple as to wash the hands, and on long walking journeys very necessary. The "dirty stinking feet of the common people" are not much remarked upon before the sixteenth century, and by the eighteenth century the division between shod or barefoot seems to mark the growing split between the agricultural and the urban people. Because, by the nineteenth century, it became a sign of poverty to go barefoot, as most country people still made their own shoes. Thus, those agricultural folk who survived the enclosures and remained on the land are shown wearing good home-knit stockings and sturdy leather boots, but the urban victims of the industrial revolution go ragged and barefoot in the streets. Later, the tracts of the period bewail the shame of not having any shoes to go to school and puts scorn upon the truant who "takes off his shoes to run away barefoot".

TRAVELLERS' FOOTBATHS

> "So much does hospitality here rejoice, that it is neither offered, nor requested by travellers, who, on entering any house, deliver up their arms when water is offered to them. If they suffer their feet to be washed, they are received as guests, for the offer of water to wash the feet is, with this nation, an hospitable invitation. But if they refuse the proffered service, they only wish for (daytime) refreshment not lodging (for the night).
>
> GERALDUS CAMBRENSIS, *Description of Wales*, 1199

[1] Longbow men sometimes seemed to have worn one leather shoe, as a footguard, to brace the end of the bow when stringing it.

These went out when motor cars came in. Till that date all inns, post houses, hostels and every private house provided footbaths in bedrooms as a matter of course. When you kicked off your walking shoes, or struggled out of your riding boots (with the help of the boot jack also provided) you expected the servants to fill the foot tub, as you expected the Boots to clean the footwear. It was part of a routine service.

Perhaps only in youth hostels or sports resorts is the footbath and its subsequent "slipperd ease" appreciated today. But the carpet slipper, lovingly embroidered in cross-stitch, was the complement of the footbath, and was worn *on* carpets, till late Victorian days.

FOOTBATHS, MEDICAL

1800

These were of hot mustard and water for chills, or strong soda and water for rheumatism, or alternately boiling hot or icy cold, to "draw down the pressure for headache or apoplexy".

RELIGIOUS AND FOOT WASHING CEREMONIES

Many religious communities of monks and nuns, and certain bishops and clergy, carried out a devotional foot-washing yearly, in memory of Christ's washing the feet of his disciples. An example known to me was the very simple service that was carried out in the laundry of a convent. It was a private devotion between the members of the community. I saw it, accidentally, framed in the dark doorway of the outhouse, and the beauty of the picture stays clearly in my memory. The work sisters were sitting on a wooden bench in the stone-flagged laundry room, their black gowns and white coifs patterned in shadow on the blue-white walls, the scrubbed wooden tubs of water and rough brown towels catching the sunlight on the dark stone floor.

The simplicity of this devotion was probably usual in all religious countries, and remained unchanged for centuries, but with the rich and devout this religious exercise became most handsome. The early ceremony in Westminster Abbey, where the kings and queens, with their priests, knelt and washed the feet of beggars (in number the same as the years of the sovereign, so that, in effect, he grew more humble the longer he lived), ceased with James II, and the distribution in gifts of goods and clothing was of more importance than the washing. Thus, in the Maundy[1] Thursday ceremony the ruling King or Queen of England now gives purses of special coins, in lieu of the traditional food and clothing, and there is no foot washing at all. The original foods given varied from the dishes of eels, baked to a jelly with barley, and thick cakes of bread enriched with chopped dates, to whole joints of beef and measures of ale.

This description, condensed from the *Gentleman's Magazine*, gives a fair picture of the ceremony, as conducted in the Banqueting House in Whitehall in 1731, when "48 poor men, and 48 poor women (the king's age being 48) were *served* for dinner with boiled beef and shoulders of mutton, and small bowls of ale. After dinner came the *distribution* of food. For this was provided one large wooden platter of fish (raw) and a pile of bread loaves; one large dried cod, red herring (smoked and salted), and white herrings (pickled). Each person had one platter full of these, and afterwards, shoes, stockings, linen, and woollen cloth were distributed. Also to each, a leather bag holding one penny, two penny, three penny, and four penny pieces of silver, and shillings of value about £4 to each person". Afterwards "in the Royal Chapel, Whitehall, His Grace the Lord Archbishop of York, Lord High Almona, performed the annual foot washing as *formerly done by the kings themselves*".

Today, different purses, all donated separately, approximate to the value of the complete alms, and the privilege of being one of the "Maundy beggars" is eagerly sought after.

HAIR WASHING

"This is that very Mab
that plats the manes of horses in the night,
and makes the elflocks in foul sluttish hairs."

SHAKESPEARE

The curious knots found in the windblown manes of horses are still called elf-knots, sometimes witch-knots. Indeed they are so intricately knit it seems they must be the work of fairy fingers, but when a mother found such knots in her daughter's hair (and the daughter was not a changeling) she suspected the maiden had allowed her "neat head wimple to be pluckt off and she'd gone a-dancing with kilted skirt and flying hair" (exercising a witchcraft the mother too had used!).

[1] The word Maundy is thought, by some, to have derived from the French Mendiant—a beggar.

Hair was washed with soft water and some of the soap-worts and herbs that are still popular today. Infusions of rosemary, maidenhair fern, and camomile, have been used for centuries. We can find no early record of hair brushes, but combs were used, as Borde says, "Comb the head with an ivory comb, nothing refreshes the memory more".

"*Combes*—Wood combes be made of light and close wood as blackthorne.
Box Combes be made of Box tree.
Horn Combes be made of ox and cows horns.
Ivory combes be made of elephants teeth.
Bone Combes be made of the shank bone of horses.
Tortoise combes be made of sea or land tortoise chell and the counterfeit of this sort are horn stained with tortoise colours.
Crocus combes be made of crocus wood.
Lead combes be used by such as have red hair and to make it of another colour."

17th cent. list

HAIR WASHING 1870

"Being tub night, Polly, with great celerity stripped herself naked to her drawers before me, and was very anxious to take off her drawers too for my benefit, but her grandmother would not allow her. As it happened, the drawers were so inadequately constructed that it made uncomingly little difference whether they were off or on, and there was a most interesting view from the rear. Her grandmother washed her head with soft soap and hot water in a tub, the little image kneeling down in her drawers on the cold stone floor with her head in the tub close to the open door into the road."

KILVERT, 1870

BARBER'S SHOP

The word "brasiere" was used to denote a barber's shop, for there were kept small charcoal fires to heat the curling irons, provide hot water, and for drying towels, etc.

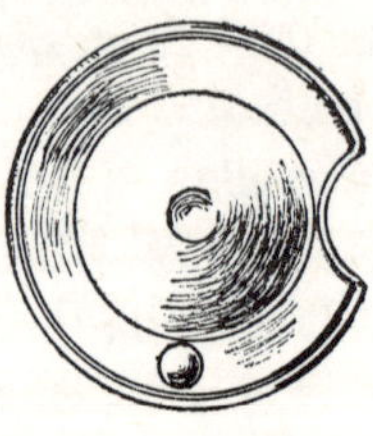

SHAVING WATER

The cut-throat razor, which in different forms had been in use for centuries, is now almost obsolete, so that the many shapes of shaving water jugs and mugs are not needed. In Victorian hotels the shaving water jug was delivered separately from the usual hot-water can, and in private houses the beards of gentlemen guests were unobtrusively studied, and adequately provided for, by the resident "gentleman's gentleman".

The cold tub did not extend to beard removal. An authoritative guide (date about 1850) states that "hot water seems an indispensable desideratum" and it is "desirable to dip the razor into really hot water before using (temp. 160°F.). Lathering cannot be laid on too thickly as the chief point in preparing the beard is to render it as soft as possible, it is much easier to cut a soaked bristle than a dry one.

All hotels and gentlemen's rooms were provided with a strong hook for the strop leather, and there was a patent form that hooked over the top of the door, for use when travelling. Strop pastes varied. Crocus martis and hogs lard, jeweller's rouge and melted suet, finest emery and spermaceti ointment, blacklead, diamond dust, red ochre, and chalk were used, also the powder from puff balls, and a smooth "strop fungus" that grows on old birch trees.

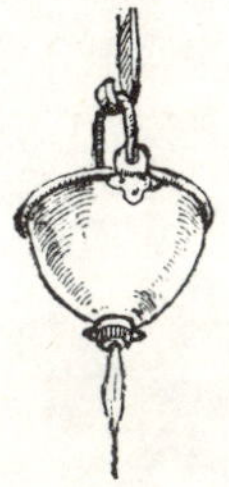

The Barber's bowl

The pendant cistern with tap release continued even after water was laid on, as the supply was more reliable, and more easily controlled

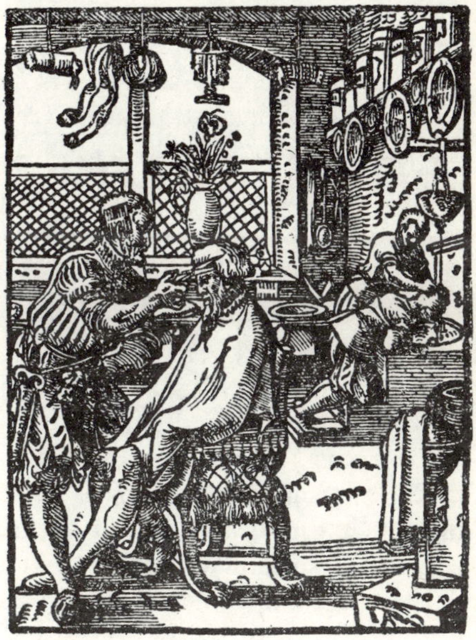

There was also a razor paper invented, one side of which was "coated with impalpable powder compounded of calcined sesquioxide of vion and fine emery". This paper, used to wipe the razor after use, "preserved the edge and prevented the frequent use of the strop".

Water supplied for the gentlemen's shaving was almost invariably rain water. I remember a landlady in a hard-water district being most distressed because the supply had run out, and her lodger stood out with a mug in a heavy shower, in order to obtain sufficient. It took some time after prolonged drought for the storage tanks and rain-water barrels to fill up, and then the water had need to settle before it was clear enough for use.

Beards

"As long as any berdes be worne
Mockynge shall not be forborne;
With berdy'd men we will not drynke
Because it doth in theyr berdes synke.

Some berdes (he sayth) doth grow a pace
To hyde an evyll colory'd face.

Of berdes (he sayth) there comes no gaynes
And berdes quycknyth not the braynes."

Old rhyme

WASH AND BRUSH UP

"On rising, after you have evacuated your body and trussed your poyntes, and combed your head, wasshe your hands and wrestes and your face and eyes and your tethe in colde water."

BOORDE

THIS WASH-AND-BRUSH-UP WAS GENERAL USAGE

Old people will remember in cottages the little wooden washstand, with jug and soap dish of white pottery, to which you carried up a pannikin of boiling water for a clean-up after work was done: a homely and comfortable wash, out of date after bathrooms and running hot water arrived.

The spontaneous washing of hands and face on waking was not confined to the richer classes, it has always belonged to every woman in nearly every century. Here is a vivid little picture among the miracles attributed to the sainted King Oswald.

"A rider on horseback, crossing near the place where the King had died; his horse, which had for some time showed signs of great distress, stopped and, after the rider had removed the saddle, the horse immediately went aside and rolled on a certain spot, and at once recovered. The rider, being a devout and observant man, at once guessed that the spot chosen by the horse was specially blessed, and marked the spot with care. Riding on, and arriving at his inn, he told of the horse's cure, and as the niece of the landlord had long been paralysed they at once put the girl into a cart and took her to the spot, where they laid her down and she had a good sleep—and awaked completely recovered!"

Then, "she had them bring to her water, to wash her face and put her hair and wimple into neat order before she walked back to the inn with great joy".

THE WASHHAND STAND

The washhand stand's place varied with the customs of the users more than the period of use. The early lavatory, where water ran continuously in a stone trough, was common usage outside the refectory of most monastic and communal establishments. Gloucester Cathedral has a good example. Probably estate workmen had a similar wooden trough near their entrance to the great hall; some place where they could wash their hands and "clean up a bit" before coming in to meals. At this period the high table used basin and ewer during the meal, so quite likely the work people made some simpler arrangement for themselves.

Finger licking was all very well, and done at high and low tables alike, but the historian's emphasis on uncouthness below the salt seems overdone, if the labourer was to have cracked chilblains and salt broth—then surely he would howl for a bowl of warm water! Why not? The scullion was probably a fellow sufferer even if the head cook was one of the upper servants!

The use of the washhand basin is very human and enlightening. The fourteenth to sixteenth centuries show all manner of fixed basins, with little filled cisterns hung above them. Small washhand stands are shown in most varied positions, upstairs and downstairs and in my lady's chamber, as well as at the barber's shop.

Washhand and toilet stands always accord with their usage even more than their period. (The ablutions shed of a modern army camp is curiously mediæval in its communal arrangements.) And the small metal tank of mediæval times looks curiously like a small individual Ascot heater! (Both ran faster than early tap water.)

The idea of the small individual unit using *carried water* lasted to Victorian times, the Georgian version of the washhand stand being extremely small and the Victorian version excessively large—and sometimes very ornate.

A definite change came about 1900, when the long flat toothbrush tray was replaced by the Edwardian upright vase. The last period of the heavy cut-glass bedroom set was the worst word in fashionable unsuitability, though these sets, flashing and sparkling in icy brilliance on wide white slabs of glistening marble, were terribly impressive!

The simple plain jug and basin sets of the same period, often of enamel ware, suitable for maids' bedrooms, were often of good sensible design, and rested on plain wooden stands with holes cut in them to prevent the basin from tipping up.

There was also the iron pedestal washstand, sometimes with a central plug that spilt the used water down into a vast tin container below, and little metal soap dishes that swung in and out around the basin like homing pigeons. The concealed washstand was used in the bedrooms of invalids, early bed-sitters and old-fashioned offices.

The Factory Acts insisted upon fixed washhand basins for workers and at first caused complications with the water supplies. In one hurriedly equipped munition factory during the First World War some hundreds of us had been given the temporary solace of a dozen enamel basins, set on a bench by a water tap. With mediæval precedent we heated pokers in the adjacent smithy fire to warm the water. Unfortunately an inspector turned up! So the law took its course. A workman was sent hurriedly to fix each basin to the bench; which he did by driving a large nail through the bottom. Instantly all twelve basins leaked! And not one could be lifted from the bench to refill. We became even more mediæval!

But, on the whole, every century has found fixed basins with running water sensible for community use, and the small individual wash usually relied on carried water and a more mobile arrangement.

THE WASHHAND BASIN

The "washhand" basin continues an ancestral name, for it derives direct from the basin and ewer carried to guests before and during dinner (*see* illustration).

That most perfect of marshals, Andrew Boorde, describes its use: "Half an oure, before thy Lorde go to mete, the Marshall shall commande the panter to make redy the ewer and cover. Then shall the sewer, go to the ewer, and take a towell uppon his shulder, and when it lyketh the Lord to axe water, than shall the Marshall and sewer goo by and brynge the Lordis basyn and ewyn, and shall delyver the towell to the worthyeste that beth aboute hym (that is the best server at hand). But the Marshall himself shall uncover the basyn yf it be coveryd and holde it in his handes unto (until) the Lord have wesshe, and then take it to the squyre who brought it and he is to bere it to the ewy and anone commande water for all them that shall sythe at the borde."

Note the etiquette of the marshal himself, holding the basin for the lords, washing and handing it back to the squire to return to the ewy (i.e. the washhand *standing* place)[1].

Most monastic communities made excellent provision for hand washing before and after meals.

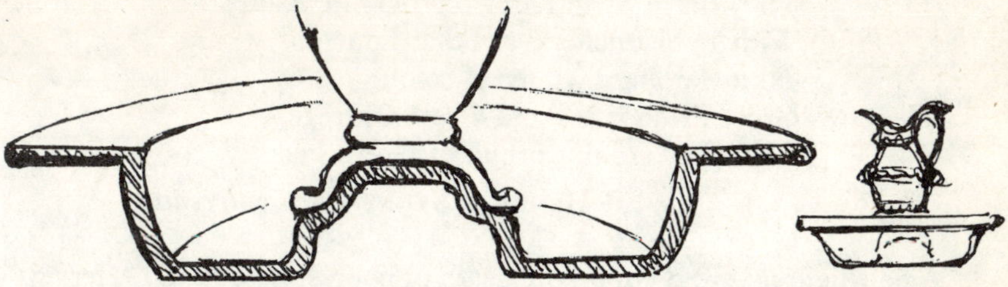

The ewer and basin, now in bedrooms, was originally the washhand basin and ewer of richly ornamented gold or silver on the sideboard in the dining-room. The sideboard was aside from the main board, and from it, the washhand basin and water were carried to each guest, as required, during the meal. When two pages carried the basin and ewer, it was easy, but it was a skill to hold the basin on one hand and pour the water with the other. The boss in the basin made the job easier, and raised the ornate base of the ewer above the used water.

The Victorian washhand basin and ewer were ancestrally the washhand basin and ewer of the mediæval dining-table, where one page held the basin while another poured water over the fingers. It might be done ceremoniously with scented water for etiquette, or efficiently with warm water to remove the gravy.

That jug and basin matched was important in both periods and in both periods fashions and shapes changed. Victorian basins grew larger or oval, mediæval basins became more shallow, or wide of rim, etc. One form of mediæval basin had a raised central boss that fitted into the hollow base of the jug. This looked handsome, and the jug wobbled about less when carried, also it needed less water and was easier to use if the attendant was single-handed. He could balance the shaped basin on one hand and trickle water from the ewer with the other.

A RULE OF THE POOR CLARES

"At mele and at the soper in all times thy shall soone (sound) the small belle, and after, till the Sustren (sisters) have wasschin there hondis and assembled to gyders."

[1] We wonder if, in those tactful days, this little ceremonious custom was not arranged to give the Lord and his trusted marshal, the opportunity for a moment's unobtrusive contact? One can well imagine the hurried "My lord, I *had* to place the bishop next to so-and-so, both demanded it", or a quick, kindly, "Good man, Boorde! See if your cooks can fling up a milk dish for Lady X, who I hath a belly acke", or even the civil query, "Is all well, m'lord?" That small civility between the lord and his trusted butler, held behind discreet by-play with the clean towel, was too opportune not to have been carefully preserved by both, for centuries!

THE "BEAUTE THAT COMETH NOT OF KINDE"

Of proud wommen I should tell
O they are so proud and fell,
For those that are foul and fade
They make them fairer than God e made,
With O blaunchers, or other flour
To make them whiter of colour
Great Pride it is—and Great Outrage,
That they are not proud of God's image."

HANDLYN SYNNE, *thirteenth century*

"A new light is thrown upon the death of poor Sophie P. Dr. Hervey of Tooting, who attended her the day before she expired, is of opinion that she killed herself by quackery, that is, by cosmetics, and preparations of lead or mercury, taken for her complexion, which indeed, was most unnaturally white.. He thinks therefore, that this pernicious stuff got into her veins and poisoned her. Peggy P., nearly as white as her sister, is suspected strongly of using the same beautifying methods of destroying herself, but as Mrs. Thrale has hinted this suspicion to her, . . . we hope she will be frightened and warned to her safety."

FANNY BURNEY'S *Diary*, 1779

DEW WATER

"O it's dabbling in the dew that makes the Milkmaids faire."

Old Song

The dance of the milkmaids through the London streets on May Day continued into the nineteenth century. In 1721 it was still a notable event and visitors commented upon the pretty sight. (Cows were kept in London at that date, indeed a few cows existed in a stable behind the Hampstead Road till 1926. They were behind Osnaburgh Street and near an old bakehouse that continued to bake the Sunday joints for the district, till the whole building was destroyed by the Blitz.) On May Day the milkmaids washed and polished their round cream pans till they shone like silver, and added any other bright trimming they could get to a green-garlanded pole, which they carried around with them and used as a Maypole for dancing around in open squares.

This dance of the milkmaids seems to have been accepted by authority at least as early as 1677, for a statute of the date forbade any citizen to carry "a bent bow, or arrows in his belt, a sword out of its scabbard, or any hand gun with powder and matches", exception being made for "all the usual May Day games".

Dew was a difficult beautifier to collect, and figured more as an inducement to early rising than a cosmetic. Rain water, however, was insisted upon for toilet purposes in Victorian times.

DISPOSALS

"Now I am terrified at the Earth, it is that calm and patient
It grows such sweet things out of such corruptions.

. . . .

It gives such divine materials to men and accepts such leavings from them at last."

WALT WHITMAN

PRIMITIVE SANITATION

"My passion for latrines used to be unbridled. It still is, where the people are sufficiently progressive to appreciate them. The African pulls down his village and makes a new one, a few hundred yards away, every four or five years. Occasionally he moves several miles, because all the fertile soil in the neighbourhood has been exhausted. Usually, however, he moves simply because his old village has begun to smell, and to be infested with vermin.

The village has become insanitary largely through the fouling of the surrounding bush."

K. BRADBY, 1943, *District Officer, Africa*

This is exactly what would happen in Saxon England, when most of the land was covered with indigenous forest and clusters of mud huts were built near the water supply. Air survey shows how constant was the movement. Settlements were abandoned and rebuilt a little distance away, for no apparent cause, and terraces of small fields, easily levelled by pulling down the sliding earth of the hillside, are shown from the air, though lost to ordinary sight.

Within a generation the wild crept back; wind, rain and the patient worms flattened down the fallen mud walls into rough rounded humps, and another generation moved back, and rebuilt on the old site, frequently without knowing of its existence.

The speed with which a mud hut can be removed is surprising. The doorposts, often the only timber in the structure and notched with the census tally of the family, were dug up and transplanted. The new site would supply light stakes from the yet uncleared wood; and the water (for the new position must still be near a stream) provided willow and rush for walls and thatch.

It is interesting to note that the hair incorporated in the final plastering often preserves the colour of a breed of cattle (or goat) long perished. The moss (sphagnum), also used for this early form of fibrous plaster, usually perished. Also connected with sanitation, and as an example of the cheapness of the huts, was the burial of lepers. The lepers, who existed sometimes on the outskirts of villages from the twelfth century onwards, were buried in and under their own huts. If the leper showed no sign of life, the thatch was fired and the earthen walls of his hut thrown down over him for his burial, and the remote place would soon be forgotten.[1] One wonders how many of the single skeletons found, together with a few household utensils, under remote earth mounds are from these hut burials. Some of the "waters" (sulphur, etc.) and ointments supplied for use in leprosy would (like the tannin of the leather worker) act as preservatives.

THE MEDIÆVAL PRIVY — 1400–1500

> "Beware of draughty privys and of pyssynge in draughts, and permyt no common pyssyng place about the house—and let the common house of easement to be over *some water* or else elongated from the house.
>
> Beware of emptyng pysse pottes, and pyssing in chymnes."
>
> BOORDE

This did not mean *down* "chymnes" (there were few available at this date), but pissing into the back of the fireplace, onto the accumulated wood ash.

The mediæval privy, garde robe, place of easement, etc. (they had as many tactful names for it as we have today), also conformed to modern building requirements in that it was set against an outside wall. There were a few complicated contrivances, to accommodate exceptional circumstances, but a direct drop outside was the regular arrangement. As late as 1570 Tusser forbids "pissing in chimneys", but some of the small closets, set into the wide stone chimneys (the sort of holes that get labelled "priests' holes", "bacon smokers", or just "chimney sweeping holes"), look suspiciously like emergency privies, especially when they occur high up, on bedroom floors. With high piled wood ashes smouldering day and night in deep open fireplaces, an up-draught was continuous, but against this, the collecting of urine for bucking was general usage. Many old fireplaces had direct drops down to a cellar where the accumulated wood ash could be stored till used for soap-making or collected by the ash carrier.

[1] Some words from the excommunicating service said over a leper "The prayers of the devout are yours and the fellowship of the saints and love of God . . . Henceforth eat and drink with none save lepers. Die in your own hut . . . The Lord be with thee.":."

The placing of the castle privy, set out from the wall like a swallow's nest, made it most unsafe to use during a siege, as the besiegers could shoot upwards—so when the grating was not well defended on the outside, or cunningly concealed behind masonry, it was set inwards over a short steep slope. Washing down the slope from above may have been the first suggestion of a water closet, though some early hut privies were built over a running brook, and some bridge houses utilized the rivers below.

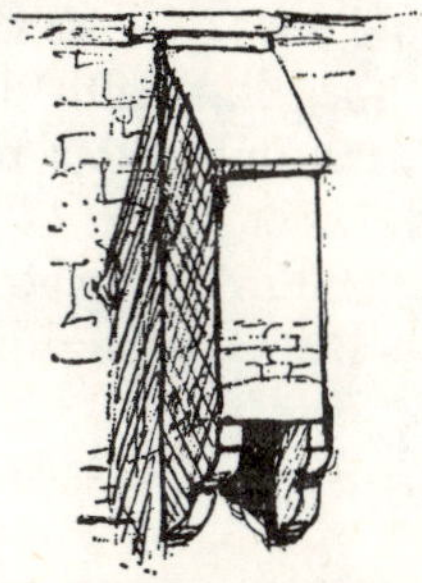

Drain direct to moat. Beaumaris Castle

A Privy Miracle

This direct-drop mediæval privy figures in a most incredible Miracle of the Virgin.

A certain monk fell so deeply in love with a painting of the Queen of Heaven that he stole it. The loss being discovered and the picture traced to his cell, the sinner, in desperation, fled down the corridor and flung it down through the privy grating. This caused considerable discomfort to the community, as every time anyone entered the privy, the Lady materialized, hovering above it. This ultimately led to the contrition of the thief and the restoration of the picture, and lest it be thought I lie, the whole story waits for all to read in a MS. of the British Museum.

THE EARTH CLOSET THAT PRECEDED THE WATER CLOSET

As an example of unchronological development, Newnham College still had dry earth closets well into the twentieth century. At that time, in a flat district, they were preferable to water closets. They were on the bedroom floors adjoining bathrooms. A similar earth closet remained in an Oxfordshire house till 1936. It was on a top landing and furnished exactly like any Victorian water closet. It had a yard-wide mahogany seat with hinged cover, cork lino on the floor, and a Bradshaw on the wall. There was no pottery pan, instead a wooden shutter sloped forward from the back. This shutter dropped down, when the side handle was pulled up. The lever simultaneously released an avalanche of earth that crashed down across the shutter sweeping all before it. The wooden chute below continued down the outside wall of the house, to end behind the garden potting-shed.

The importance of privy earth being finely riddled and so dry that it "poured" like water, necessitated it being baked for days. Small houses frequently pushed a tin of fine ash into the cooling bread oven, together with the logs and sticks set there to lie and dry out for the next firemaking. In this Oxfordshire privy the tin of earth dried out on top of the green-house heater—and there were always words between the housemaid and the gardener because he would sneak the sterilized earth for his seedling boxes. The dust-dry earth was filled into the hopper that formed the sloping ceiling of the closet, through a trap door in the attic. This trap door was kept firmly bolted "as it would be very possible for an active burglar to climb up the chute and so obtain access to the attic". A curious echo of the idea that for so long complicated the designs of mediæval privies.

A NEW DRY-ASH COMMODE—1873

(This Victorian example had many earlier forms.) "To feed the commode raise the lid A of the ash box and throw in the refuse just collected from under the firegrate. Fasten down the lid tightly, and when you wish to use the commode, raise the cover, the mere doing of which causes a certain quantity of ashes to pass over the screen, the finer portions dropping through the screen fall upon a shovel, or distributor, and the cinders roll over the screen down the sloping board and onto the drawer, to await removal for reburning. After using the commode, pull down the cover when the shovel, before at the horizontal, now falls to the sloping position, and throws the fine

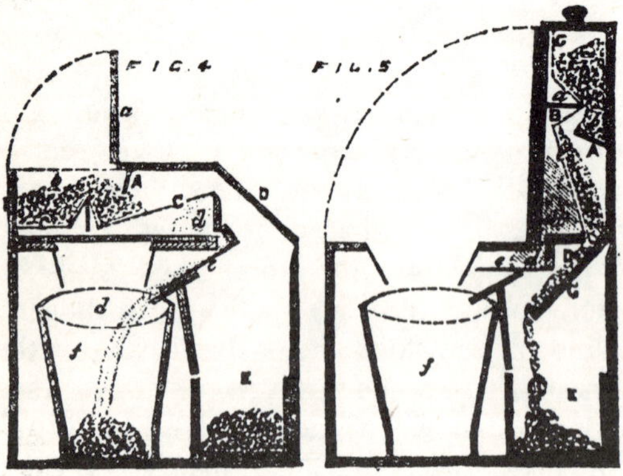

The simple bucket is replaced by a removable drawer in a later model

OXFORDSHIRE EARTH CLOSET, 1930

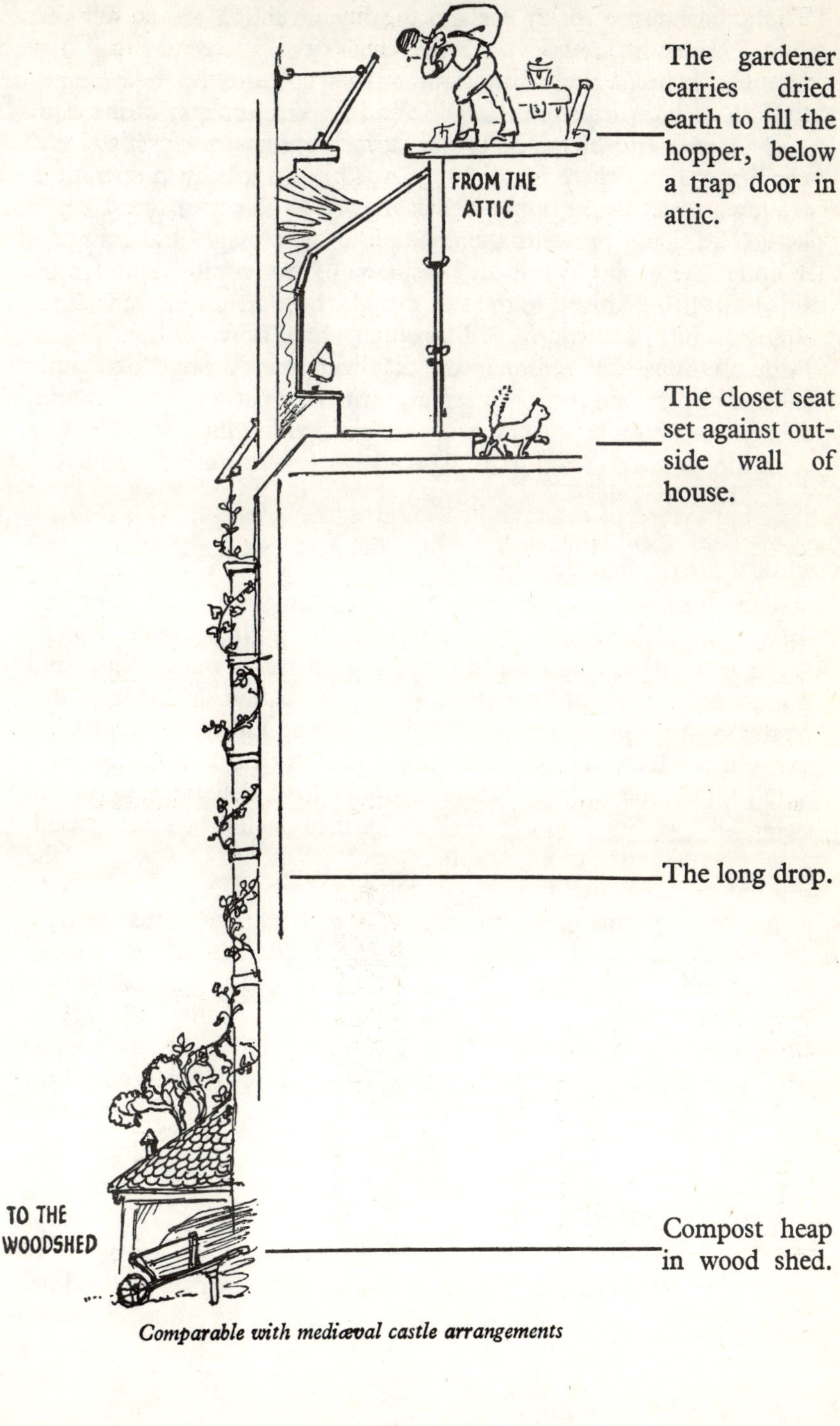

Comparable with mediæval castle arrangements

ash over the soil in the receptacle. The wooden stage serves to measure the ashes that pass over the screen after each use.

The advantages which I claim for my invention are as follows: First, novelty in method whereby certain work, screening and distributing, is performed in one-fourth the space used by the ordinary dry ash screens. Second, simplicity in arrangements, absence of mechanism in the shape of cranks, levers, springs, pulleys, swivels, weights, chains, etc., yet is self-acting. Third, efficiency in operation, as only a small quantity of ashes is allowed to pass over the screener at each use; this prevents the choking up of passage, and insures a thorough screening. Fourth, easiness of application, the entire apparatus being hinged to the seat, may be fixed in any closet without alteration of brickwork, or additional covering, as with other closets. Fifth, cleanliness, by reason of the dust being kept confined, and only allowed to pass into the soil receptacle when the cover is down. Sixth, cheapness of cost, as the entire apparatus is within the closet and free from the weather. Seventh, design, a very desirable one which ought to render it popular."

PORTABLE EARTH CLOSETS

The Earth Closet Company, in advertising their excellent dry earth closet system, refers disparagingly to portable water closets. "The faint depressing odours common to portable water closets and night stools are one of the greatest miseries of human life, and one of the most frequent means of communicating infection." The advertisement then described the preferable dry earth closet in great detail. The one they recommend would have delighted Kermode, being an "adequate four-holer" to be constructed of sound wood. For private houses there is a more "refined model", of which "the reservoir is calculated to hold enough for 25 times".

Ash for the same, must be dry, and was, by an ingenious arrangement, chucked forward when the side handle was shaken. "The ashes of anthracite coal are recommended, but the ashes of bitumenous coal must be sifted and wood ash must not be used." This cinder refuse used to be carried down the Thames in barges and used to fire the bricks in the Kentish brick yards. In simple country privies coal ash was never popular, they preferred dry earth or sawdust, as that could later be buried to the advantage of the garden.

W.C.'S VICTORIAN

"'That's the Best W.C.,' said Mrs. Scott. It had white glazed paper with a lot of blue in it, a blue and white basin, a frosted window, surrounded by panes of red glass, and mahogany furniture. There was a scent of Pears soap. 'It's a nice one,' said Rose, 'solid.' "

SIR RONALD FRASER, *Rose Anstey*

They remained "solid" for a century, being built in the strong Gothic tradition. They stayed solid, in old country houses, for years and years. Their great character was that they were solid and "roomy". Usually there was an enclosed, wood panelled, washhand basin, with a grey marble slab surrounding a circular white basin, complete with chained plug and solid taps. A towel rail stood separately. A looking-glass was sometimes set upon a small dressing-table, with a tray; or sometimes the glass hung on the wall flanked by a pendant clothes brush. Also, there would be a cupboard and a strong chair.

The W.C. itself was built up against the wall with boxed-in sides, and a lid a yard wide, that closed down over a decorated china pan, with a sunk pull-up handle on one side, and a sunk box to hold paper on the other side. (If there was a lamp in the room, this box also held the box of matches.)

The floor was covered with well-polished lino, and rugs were placed before the throne and door.

The window recess usually had a few books and "an old Bradshaw in case of emergency". The window, of patterned glass, might be leaded and probably had a curtain to draw after dark. The inside bolt was of polished brass, the outside key was always turned at night, as a W.C.

Kirkwood's Tubular Water Closet.

Fifty of these Closets were fixed and in use at the Exhibition Building, and obtained a flattering testimonial from the Contractors, Messrs. Fox and HENDERSON, and a Prize Medal. They have been ordered for the new Building at Sydenham, and fixed in several Public and Private Establishments, with the most complete success. This closet is clean, protected from the escape of effluvium, simple in construction, and efficient in action; dispensing with all cranks, levers, and weights, and requiring no special cistern or service-box. It is not liable to get out of repair, and is, moreover, cheaper than any *complete* Closet offered to the public.

The prices of this Closet vary according to style of fitting up, from £3 15s. to £12 12s. All are the same in the essentials of the Water Closet.

The free-standing type

window was considered a likely burglar entrance. "Once inside he had only to flush the water and no one would suspect him" (and judging by the row those cisterns raised no one would have heard him).

If the ground floor W.C. belonged to a house of "great gardeners" it might contain gloves, trowels, seed catalogues and weed killer, but it would be tedious to recount all the strange extras placed in old W.C.s. The most disconcerting was in a Bedford suburb, where my aunt kept a bust of Shakespeare just inside the door, so that if the door was accidentally left ajar, no one would know it was a W.C. (I used to find the Bard's speculative gaze slightly embarrassing.)

THE SANITARY DISINFECTING COVER (GREENBURY'S PATENT)

For Slop Pails, Commodes, &c.

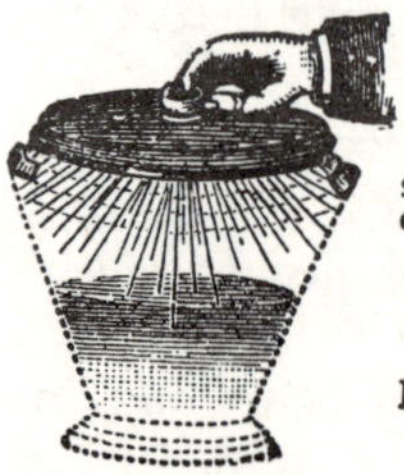

This Cover has a Chamber, which can be filled with Condy's Fluid or other disinfectant. By pressing the Ball in handle a spray is injected sufficient to disinfect or deodorise the contents.

Sizes 7¾, 8½, 8¾, 9¼, 9¾ inches.
Price 6s. 6d. post free.
10, 10½, 10¾ inches, 7s. each.

MILNE, SONS, & MACFIE,
2, King Edward Street,
London, E.C.

MAY BE HAD FROM ANY IRONMONGER OR CHEMIST.

SEWAGE DISPOSAL. THE DUNG CART AND CESS PIT

The river chart (page 60) shows how many mediæval waste trade products were used up before they reached the river and ultimately became fish food.

The removal of household ordure was mainly a question of private enterprise. While the average household, even on the city fringe, remained agriculturally-minded and kept a cow or pigs, the manure, human and animal, combined, as in remote farms today, and all reached the land as manure. But inside cities the conditions were horrible, with open sewers and accumulated filth. The large establishments, schools, or earlier monastic buildings, arranged for drainage to cess pits (and the arrangements for swift hand-washing by the privy are often surprisingly adequate).

The situation grew worse through the sixteenth and seventeenth centuries and the description of the lime-pit burials after the great plague, and the conditions of the ditches surrounding St. Bartholomew's Hospital and the Eastside marshes, have a desperation of filth.

The student can find records of industrial London in the 1800's, but

G. HARDY,

Chimney Sweeper & Nightman

No. 1, HARLEY-MEWS,

WIGMORE-STREET, Cavendish-Square,

Begs Leave most respectfully to inform his Friends and the Public in general, that he continues to sweep Chimnies of all Descriptions, cleans Smoke Jacks, Smokey Coppers, and extinguishes Chimnies when on Fire, with the greatest Care, and Safety.

G. H. anxious to obtain a continuance of those numerous Favours, which he has already received, assures those Ladies and Gentlemen who may favour him with their Commands, they will be executed in the most decent Manner, as he superintends the Business himself.

SMOKEY CHIMNIES CURED.

Drains and Sesspools cleaned on the Shortest Notice.

CHIMNIES SWEPT BY THE YEAR.

To prevent Mistakes, please to take Care of this Bill.

Printed by W. GLINDON, Rupert-Street, Haymarket.

few realize how recent are these horrors in some provincial towns. I can remember the dung cart collecting tubs from the outside privies down the back streets of Ashton-in-Makerfield 1900. They did not always come by night. The carts, which were nothing but great open tanks drawn by a carthorse, had to move slowly to prevent rocking and slopping the liquid. The tubs were hauled out with iron tongs, through wooden shutters set in the privy wall below the wooden seat. One man stood on the cart and hauled up, one stood below and heaved. There was a slobbering splash, followed by a thump, as the dripping tub was dropped down and shoved back and the horse paced on to the next privy. The stench was indescribably foul and the horrid sounds lasted a full hour. If the cart men were delayed, the tank overfilled and splashed onto the road, to lie another week matted-over with ashes thrown out by the inhabitants.

The process was still completely mediæval in its horror. Probably the open sewers of the mediæval city stank less, being open, and there could be some earth burial. In later years, a water cart charged with carbolic was sent around to sluice the gutters after the cart, and lime was thrown down on the spilt muck.[1]

At this period most country houses had their own cesspits, either dug alongside an outside earth privy, or connected to it by a private drainpipe from the house (down which the bath water was emptied daily). At intervals, cash and a tot of spirits were left on the kitchen table for the night-soil men, who either cleared the cesspit, or (if it was an outside wooden privy) they would just earth-over the used site, and dig a new one. Many small orchards are thus accounted for (the job being a winter one and the time right for planting).

SEWAGE GAS. A NOTE OF 1866

> "At a certain declination sewage, of a given consistency, will run downhill, but the gas generated by the mass only flows upwards. When the sewage flowed into the Thames this gas had the advantage of a large open surface of water through which to bubble and escape. Now this sewage is confined in sundry brick buildings underground, there to ferment and exhale pestiferous gasses; and thus, as the filthy mixture flows down from the high grounds to these receptacles, up flows the gas to Upper Clapton, Hampstead, Highgate, etc., through elevated districts acting as a chimney for the gas . . ."

[1] "The owner of every house already built, to which no sufficient privy or ashpit is attached is to provide those conveniences, and to fit them with such proper door and covering to the privy as the Health Committee shall consider requisite. Two or more privies or ashpits may, with the approbation of the Committee, be used in common by the inmates of two or more houses."

Council Bye-laws
LIVERPOOL, 1842

SEWAGE INTO CEMENT

Note on sewage disposal from a science magazine of 1872:

"The new method of disposing of sewage by making it into cement has been practically and successfully tested during the last six months at Ealing, a village to the West of London . . . the principle of the process consists in mixing with the sewage quantities of lime and clay; the former combining with the carbonic acid of the fecal matters forms carbonate of lime, which is precipitated. The lime and clay are thrown into the main drains high up, to ensure complete incorporation and to destroy the slimy glutinous character of the 'sludge' . . . the success of the process depends on the fact that the precipitated matter supplies, to a considerable extent, the fuel necessary for the burning operation.

After the water is drawn off from the settling tanks it is dried on tiles, and the heated gas that passes below the tiles is obtained from the refuse of organic matter deposited below the precipitate. The quantity of carbon is small but the hydrogen given off gives intense heat."

The long report for the Society of Arts was read by Major-General Scott and finishes by reporting that the "liquid drawn off can be used as fertilizer, and his expert, Dr. Lethaby, estimates "that 10,000 persons can produce a ton of cement a day".

THE COMPLICATION OF CORPSES—AND A NOTE ON HAMLET'S GRAVEDIGGERS

London was a conglomeration of villages, each having its own church, and each villager expected to be buried in his own churchyard. As the small churchyards filled up, an inaccurate rota and increased population made each new interment a gruesome resurrection. Bodies in Elizabeth I's time, had, by law, to be buried in wool shrouds (alive or dead you had to support the wool trade). It was some centuries before coffins became usual, so there was no warning, and Hamlet's gravediggers were only doing the usual thing when they unearthed the comparatively recent Yorick. The situation, so fantastic to us, would not seem unusual to an Elizabethan gravedigger. In some graveyards bodies were piled one on top of the other, till the top corpse was barely below the surface, and the flat slab gravestones of the late sixteenth and seventeenth centuries served to keep off scavenging animals as much as body snatchers! As most churches had been built on rising ground the rain from the churchyard drained down into the local wells and polluted the water. As late as 1874 Battersea had an outbreak of sickness that was believed to be caused by corpse-contaminated drinking water.

One extract from the Chadwick report (1866) is sufficient:

> "I have no doubt whatever that the burial grounds are a continual source of pestilence . . . they are undermining the stamina of thousands, the graveyards of London are the plague spots of its population. The putrid drainings from these pollute its wells, seethe beneath its dwellings, and poison its atmosphere. Some parts are still honeycombed with deposits of the putrescent remains of millions of its citizens (and with cesspools and other abominations). The vaults of many churches are little better than charnel houses!"

THE MANURIAL VALUE OF A FAIR

Market Management

The ground staff of agricultural shows would be interested in the arrangement made by their forerunners who laid out the huge temporary mediæval markets.

Such markets were a valued asset to the local community, and improved the land on which they were held. Water was laid on. Not at one small tap, but lavishly, down wooden ducts, and at special points men sold drinking water, if wanted. But ale was brewed locally, and had to pass the test for strength before issue!

The whole market was run as a complete township—having its own customs and its own catering, and its own court of law (the "court of dusty feet"). It had its own lime pits and dug latrines. The problem must have been far larger than any modern gathering for, lacking swift transport, people came and stayed for the whole week, and the disposal had to include the blood, and offal, of the meat carcases from the cook shops, and the droppings of hundreds of horses and cattle and pigs.

One advantage—the mediæval ground staff could use quantities of fern (bracken), in itself a deodorant and the reeds, that replaced the cinders and duck-boards of a modern wet day, would be far more easily burnt. "Bone fires" would be kept going day and night, and the smoke would keep down flies, so, while condemning the awful mediæval stenches, we should give credit to the way they tackled some problems.

AN EARLY URBAN ATTEMPT AT WHITSTABLE

Having now given a cross-section of insanitary conditions it is fair to give an example of the way an average small town *tried* to tackle the job.

A Fair Example of Arranging Water Works for a Small Town in the Nineteenth Century

The drainage of any town, in relation to its water supply, varied according to its position, so that it is difficult to choose an average example. We have selected these extracts from "A Preliminary enquiry into the sewage, drainage, and supply of Water, and the Sanitary conditions of the inhabitants of the Town of Whitstable" by the Superintending Inspector, Mr. Thomas Webster Rammell, because they give such a convincing picture. The date is 1849 and the district is close to the old large brick and tile works of north Kent. This would make the conditions good for obtaining materials, but the flatness of the land, and comparatively small water catchment, would make the work more difficult. So this could be a fair assessment of early town water works any time between 1700 and 1900.

The town had approximately 3,000 inhabitants. The old water supply was unchanged for centuries. Whitstable had formerly no other supply of water for domestic purposes (with the exception of the stagnant water in the ditches and, of course, sea water) but that derived from some springs which issue from the southern side of the hills, about a mile and a half distant, and which were private property.

This supply was far from abundant, the water was brought into the town in carts and sold to the inhabitants at the rate of ½ and ¾ farthings per pailful. (This cartage was rather uncommon—villages were usually built on or near a fresh-water supply; in this case the fishing industry built the village near the shore.)

First Attempts at a New Supply

About fifty years ago, a Mr. Nutt projected a scheme for conveying the water of a spring, situated upon the bend of Clapham Hill, into the town by means of wooden and earthenware pipes. Earthenware pipes were used to convey the water across the higher land, and wooden pipes were laid in the lower levels, where the column of water could create a considerable pressure.

The earthenware pipes, manufactured at Hythe, cost sixpence each, measured one foot in length and two inches in diameter. The water was pumped from the spring by manual labour to a height of about twenty feet to a cistern, communicating with the line of pipe to the town. (In the town it was distributed by cart and pail.) The water was clear and good, but the scheme failed in consequence of the spring becoming exhausted.

Second Attempt

Shortly after, a stratum of water was discovered immediately under the bed of clay on which Whitstable stands, at a depth of 60–70 feet. On being tapped, the water rose in the bore upon the principle of the artesian well, and since the discovery the town has been supplied from this source.

The Wells

The inspector then describes how the wells were sunk, "about 4 ft. diameter and 10 ft. deep in the surface clay, to serve as a reservoir, and a hole 2½ inches is bored with an auger through the base of this surface well, into the stratum below. The top well is usually well lined with brick work, and the bore with a wooden tube. But often this bore hole is left quite unprotected." (The rising water would tend to scour it clear.)

As the wells were so easily and cheaply sunk "a large proportion of houses possess their own separate wells, though sometimes several houses use the same well" (exactly the same case as London.)

Now the Sanitary Aspect

"The greater number of the wells are kept in a most slovenly manner, very commonly without a cover, and with a pool of filthy house water stagnating near and at times dripping into them."

The local schoolmaster states that the school well is at all times affected by bad land drainage and surface water. House water conveyed (i.e. running in an open gutter) to a point near the well falls through a grating there into an underground drain; the overflow from the well also falls into this grating, and when the grating stops up, flows back down into the well. The schoolmaster "thinks that house water percolating through the earth also affects the wells.

"This surface drainage and the open gutters in the streets are extremely defective. In many cases the gutter is almost flat, so that water easily lies stagnant in it," and the writer goes on to say that often in wet weather he has been "obliged to cross Harbour Street on stepping stones, placed by some individual in a disinterested spirit for the good of the public".

So much for the small town's water supply by wells.

The refuse is received in vaults sunk under the privies, or by tubs, or by being at once deposited on the banks of the marsh ditches, by the privies being constructed over the ditches.

A few houses have drains communicating with the sewers. These drains were originally only constructed for surface drainage. These sewers discharge into the harbour. The vaults are emptied (at intervals). The tubs adopted chiefly by the seafaring people near the shore are usually discharged into the sea, or one of the ditches or pools on the beach.

The privy over the ditch is preferred, and is in most cases a slight wooden erection, often without a door, with its base on the ditch side, often visible."

The churchyard is reported by James Wood, sexton, as very full. "Graves are 5 ft. deep, and when we had cholera about 60 people were buried in 3 months and I could smell the bodies. The ground was very dry at the time. I have buried a few inside the church (one in lead) have heard no complaints there." So much for the conditions of the town. *One can trace the growth of the problem, increasing with the growth of the town.* For a village of less than one hundred fisherfolk, living on the same spot, the springs (and sea water) would have been adequate and the refuse, open to the air and scavenging gulls, no more than a high tide or heavy thunderstorm would sweep away.

Mr. Rammell "recapitulates his conclusions" that the state of Whitstable is such as to warrant the application of the provisions of the Public Health Act, and the additional special powers to effect the drainage of the flat suburban district. He then works out the rates to cover a completely revised water supply, and a sewage works for the removal of refuse, which at last he "hopes may become a source of revenue". These short extracts from a long report can only give an outline of the situation that was arising all over England, but they do give a fair picture of the many thousands of small town waterworks problems and the work they did before the Public Health Act.

WATER DOMESTICATED

SOAP AND WATER

"Though thou wash thee with nitre and make thee much soap."

JEREMIAH

"Soap too is very useful. . . . It is an invention of the Gauls. This substance is prepared from tallow and ashes; the best ashes being of beech and elm. Soap is of two kinds, hard and soft, both are much used by the people of Germany . . . the men more than the women."

From PLINY, A.D. 23

PLANTS AND METHODS USED.

The many soap-worts still haunt household sites. Sometimes the plants found in woods or lanes seem completely undomesticated but a search usually finds the ruined hut, or the dim outline of farm lands which have been overgrown, or submerged under factory buildings. Soap-worts and dairy-worts are two of the many plants by which researchers track down routes and centuries-old habitations. Because, centuries ago, far more plants were known to country people, many were known to have "soapy" virtues, and could be used in different ways for different purposes. Thus, the unripe nuts of the horse chestnuts chopped up and macerated in water could be used for cleaning wool. The Ragged Robin also made a cleansing juice. The water in which broom blossom had been steeped was used to wash sheep, but this was probably more for its curative properties, as "broom salve" had been the regular shepherd's ointment before being superseded by tar dressing ("To spoil a good sheep for a hap'orth o' tar" was a shepherd's saying.).

SOAP WORT—*saponaria officinalis*

The term "officinal" seems to have come into general use about 1693. The store-room of monasteries, where the medical herbs were kept and medicines prepared, was called the officina, as distinct from the food storerooms, or cellar stores. The officina was what we should now call the dispensary or, if in a secular mansion, the first-aid room.

Probably after the Reformation the apothecary stock became the "officinal" and the term came to serve as the official name for all plants of recognized utility. (A very necessary label, where so many names were given to different plants in different districts.) Today the country name of soapwort is given to many plants which contain the soapy principle (saponine) and also to some that have little value for soap, but have other cleansing uses. Sorrel, or rhubarb juice, cleaned the brass skillet. Marestail scoured the pewter, etc.

Gerard states that the official soap-wort was used in baths as a water softener to "beautify and cleanse the skin". Fuller's herb is one of the many names given to Saponaria officinalis. The concentration of the saponine principle in any plant was of interest to the chemist, but to the housewife it was more urgent that it should be available in convenient form.

The making of both leys and soaps for different purposes was a household craft and it is still rather hard to understand *how* some of the plants were used.

For example, bran could be rubbed on dry and hot to clean furs, but a *ley* of bran was used to wash glazed chintz. Yet to "clean with bran" would cover both processes.

For the washing process a ley was made by steeping bran in water and then boiling it and straining it off. (The result looked like thick barley water.) As the chintz hangings from beds and curtains would be dusty but not greasy (that is, the dirt would be lying loose *upon* the highly-glazed surface of the chintz, not deeply incorporated in the texture of the fabric) the bran water, ley, levered off the dirty surface starch by the mechanical process of swelling up the cotton fibre below. This forced the starch "skin" above to float off loose, when it was "held" and "carried" by the thicker solution of the bran water above and the old starch glaze, tallow polish and dirt floated off in clouds.

"Lifting the dirt" was the accurate description of the washer-woman, who on this account liked to immerse her chintz in as wide a bath as possible, and so would not use the tall bucking tub, but the flat shallow under buck.

After the first dirt had been "floated up" the ley was poured off and the fabric immersed in fresh and hotter bran water. Dirty portions were given a good shake and the process repeated till the last water ran clear. Then the chintz was rinsed, dried, restarched and polished (*see* Irons).

Bran was not the only "dry" material used to make ley. Holland and unbleached linen were bucked with the sawdust from fir trees. The brownish colour was preserved, and a faint turpentine aroma clung to the holland. This was one of the reasons why "holland bags" were recommended for storing blankets and wool.

There were also leys for soaking. A ley for embedded grease would be a strong soda solution, possibly following a rubbing with lard or oil. (As the mechanic's wife of today soaks her husband's working overalls in paraffin before boiling.)

Leys for stains might be made of some strong acid plant. The usual household ley for sheets, etc., would be made from wood ash and urine. Some households found that the ashes of certain plants increased the strength of the ley. Any gardener who cares to analyse the ash of his autumn bonfire will be surprised at the variation in content caused by the differences in the predominant type of weed.

The basis of household soap was a ley made from wood ash, and such a ley could be purposely made from certain woods and plants and used to boil the soap mixture. So, though the soap did not entirely depend upon the plant, the plant helped in the formation of the soap.

Even the plants laid across the drain holes in the sieve to prevent the fine ash from washing away too quickly could be specially chosen for their job.

All this detail was understood by the householders and the knowledge was carried by their sons and daughters who emigrated to find new plants, in New Worlds.

And how long this tradition lasted! One of the causes was expense, as the drop in price that followed Mr. Gladstone's budget was not felt until the middle of the nineteenth century. It was in the 1800's that one of my old aunts told me that when she was in Africa "our soap gave out, and I asked the boys if they had not a soap-wort such as we used at home? And they found me one."

Therefore in 1931 in the Low Veldt I asked an old Dutch farmer if he knew of this soap root? His face, the colour of dried grass, slowly wrinkled into a smile. "You ask me for what I have not remembered since I was a little boy, and played with the little Zulu boys, for always little boys must wash before they dare go home!" And so Du Plessis led me out and dug up for me a thick "crocus" corm. He knelt down by the water and the root[1] lathered for me, as it had done for my family in the same place a century before.

SIMPLE INSTRUCTION FOR HOUSEHOLD SOAP

"Stir a large bushel basket full of clean wood ash into two gallons of rainwater and leave it overnight, then strain it off and boil it down with clean fat till the water has all been evaporated or absorbed into the fat, which is now turned to soap."

Various ingredients could be introduced at different stages in this one basic recipe. The two gallons of water could be an infusion of some plant. In straining off the ashes, the plant may have been laid in the wooden tray, so that salts and scents of the plant were taken up by the

[1] Mr. Werner, of the Kirstenbosh, S. Africa, very kindly reported this plant as the *Helinus ovata*. The bush *Notlea* and the wort *Vaccarie vulgaris* are also native soap plants. The common soap aloe, *Aloe vulgaris*, also contains saponine.

hot water as it poured along through the leaves. This was done, as otherwise the large holes in the wooden draining trays would not retain firewood ashes. Or the plant may have been macerated in the warm fat, a method still used to extract flower scents and essences.

Scented soap could be made this way and certain plant oils could be stirred into the soap mixture while it was still soft.

Other worts (for example, glass-wort) would supply salts and would have a definite influence on the texture of the soap.

SOAP MAKING WITHOUT MUCH BOILING

"Make a ley of 1 part quicklime, 20 parts of water, well slaked. Add 2 parts (by weight) of common carbonate of soda. Boil the mixture and strain through a cloth.

To make the ley into a soap, concentrate it by boiling down, then mix 1 part of the strong ley with 2 parts of olive oil and keep it well-stirred till in the course of 7 or 8 days it becomes thick and white, and the excess water separates out and gives a white firm soap."

The sort of fat used, the addition of beeswax, or a tallow, would vary the type of soap produced. In the days when soap was made at home it is safe to believe there were as many different types of soap as there were households.

THE MAKING OF TRADE SOAP

"Some can, with a pound of sope,
Get them a kyrtelle or a cope."

Political songs ED. VI.

Soap was always a lucrative by-product.

The "trade" soap-boilers worked downstream below the slaughterhouses, where they also collected the fat from the lime vats, the clearing of the horn and hoof workers, and shared stinks with the tallow chandlers, glue boilers (and all the water-polluting trades that must, by law, be carried on *below the city*). Here too came the refuse for burning on the potash hearths, and some of the less pleasant sources of ammonia—and up the river came the kelp and marsh salt.

The soap-boiling industry was governed by the position and trade of the river and the produce of the country around. Most cities had their soap-boilers, but naturally those sited by the huge autumn cattle markets, such as Bristol, London or Hull, had the greatest seasonal supply of animal fats. Most of the English trades used animal fat as basic material, whereas the continental olive-growing districts used olive oil. The linen and flax industries supplied their local soap boilers with linen seed oil (but palm and coconut and most vegetable oils did not come into use

"Two years ago I used your soap, since when I have used no other."

—*Punch*, April 26th, 1884.

until much later). The sodas and salts varied, but on the whole were more constant than the fats, which is a reason why people still made their own soap long after the ordinary trade soap was in supply, and why toilet soap, Castile and French soaps are so often mentioned, and the word "refined" is laboured upon all early trade cards. "Extra refined", "only the best materials used", had far more urgency in the early primitive soap trade. By providence, the greatest supply of fats came in the cold days of early winter slaughter, but the vats, large enough to cope with the seasonal supply, had to wait through hot summer weeks to fill sufficiently.

Basic Proportions for Trade Soaps

"And soap makers and their sons are knights for silver's sake
And lords sons be their labourers, and have most gaged their rents
and to support this realm, have ridden against our foes
To comfort the Commons, and honour the king."

Piers Plowman

The trade proportions varied considerably, as did the constituents, but for centuries the average basic proportions were 10–14 parts of soda and 15–20 of potash to every 100 parts of fat.

The older soap-boilers frequently put the whole of the dry kelp, larilla, or rough "hearth" potash into the vat with a sprinkling of quicklime and added sufficient water to slake the lime, which produced violent heated action through the mass.[1]

After this had "worked" the vat was filled up with water and left to stand, stirred at intervals, till the soluble salts had been dissolved into the water and the solid debris "settled" or "floated" in the vat. This water (by now a strong *ley*) was then drawn off; the tap being set in above the sediment level, as in a wine jar (*see* illustration, page 328). This vat tap was also plugged with a truss of straw which filtered out any smaller particles and prevented stoppage of the tap. The vat was then refilled with water, possibly three times, and the leys *of different strengths* were set aside to be used as needed during boiling.

The experienced workman usually judged the strength of the ley by smell and touch, though other indications, such as the floating of a straw, or the appearance of the surface as it cooled, were also studied.

This type of skilled estimate was the old bond between workman and householder. The woman, when testing the strength of brine, tried "if it floated an egg"; or "she cooled the brew water till she could see her face reflected on the surface". (These were the small treasured instructions by which knowledge was transmitted between experts.) After the ley was prepared the fat was put into the boiler, over a gentle heat, till just melted, and the soap-maker ladled in the ley gradually, while stirring the fat. As the translucent fat became opaque and milky, with the alkali of the ley, he added more ley, sometimes from the strong ley and sometimes from the weak ley, the skill being to keep the mixture smooth and well blended, so that it thickened evenly. (Any cook who has made white sauce will recognize the technique.)

[1] *Transport* was the key to this method. As soap boiling was done by the riverside below the city, the kelp, etc., was easily landed, and as the slaughter houses (for fat) were also downstream the materials were ready to hand; but inland or for private manufacture the kelp, etc., was burnt "at the stone" (or hearth) and the rough alkaline salt used direct.

The cooking of the soap mixture continued from 24–48 hours, depending on the skill of the worker, the heat of the boiler and the type of materials used. At the right moment, the soap-maker added a sufficient quantity of common salt, which separated the residue of spare water from the soap, the fire was instantly withdrawn from below the vat, and the whole left to cool.

The lighter fatty soap mixture floated on top of the salted water, which was later drawn off from below, and the soap was again melted and mixed. Usually this remelting entailed the addition of a measure of fresh soft water (this makes for *bulk* of soap, but the soap then shrinks excessively on drying out). It was at this final stage that scent and essences or colouring matter, etc., were usually blended in. The soap was then ready to be poured out into moulds.

This basic method of soap-boiling was capable of as many variations as there were materials and soap-boilers in the household or in the trade.

In the trade it was subject to stringent laws. Some countries forbade the use of whale oil, others specialized in olive oils or linen seed oils. Much depended on the waste product available from some other local manufacture. While slaughter houses downstream from mediæval cities supplied animal fat—oil was not much used in England. In private households, long after the making of soap had been discontinued, householders used to purchase cheap basic soap and remelt it, scenting it and adding their own ingredients to make their own special soaps.

AN EXAMPLE TO SHOW THE EARLY WORK OF THE SOAP-TRADERS

"Apud Bristollum nemo est qui non sit vel fuerit saponarius."

RICHARD OF DEVIZES, A.D. 1200

The records of the Bristol soap-makers go back beyond 1562 and it is a sign of the domestic origin of the trade that the early companies included women. The women were unable to read or write and could only make their mark when signing the registers, but they were considered worthy members and probably their hard-won knowledge of the ways of soap was the companies' most valuable asset.

The earliest records noted the glut of fat that came each autumn, after the slaughter of the droves of cattle sold at the huge West Country cattle fairs. There would be fish oils even at that date, but the early local source of supply would be animal fat. In 1610 the expanding trade with the New World was bringing commerce across to the West of England, and at Bristol the soap-makers began to "build a new hall".

Little is known of this hall, but it was apparently a comfortable meeting place, with cushioned seats, a table and a "standish" for inscribing notes and signing records (the "presentation office inkstand" or "standish" has a long and honourable ancestry). They had an "hower glass" (to curtail the speeches?), a fine "fireplace and fire irons and bellows" (to sit warm while they listened to them?), a "money bag" (to pay for drinks?) and "a silver cup to hold the master's drinks".

It all sounds very clean and comfortable, and they also had enough regalia to make a good show in civic processions.

After this date, records show the increased complications that were the result of trade expansion. The controversy arose between the users of fats and tallows and the users of the imported oils. Olive oil was conveniently imported from Spain to the Bristol quays, so was whale oil and the fish oils from the Cornish pilchard presses (also the Irish thornback oil). Legal rules forbade the use of these oils, but they were imported, and they raised a stink that could be smelt as far as the Customs House. They were known as "trane oils".

A ballot was taken among the soap-makers, and it was agreed that only clean olive oil was to be used, but the opposition seems to have let the oils include "knutt oyles" and "nepe oil" and gradually the stink of trane oil returned until the exasperated legal outburst ran:

"*NO* trane, herring oil, *or any grece or unholsome licour* was to be even kept in the house of ANY Soapboiler."

For years, Bristol soap had been sold by the vat, and called "Black sope", for in the deep vat the transparent mass looked black and contrasted with the solidified bars and cakes of white and yellow soaps. (It was the soft soap of our young days; the dark greenish jelly that came in round tins and was easier to spread upon the scrubbing brush, than the hard yellow soap of the laundry.)

The wood ash of burnt thatch, that had been worked with water and quick lime to provide the ley for the soap-boilers, accumulated around the soap works in greyish tips and dumps. (The Bristol glass-makers used this waste product to great advantage.) Just as the housewife used the scraps of waste fat, the end of her tallow dips, and ashes from her burnt-out fire (the waste products of her housekeeping) to boil into soap, so the trade *used waste products also*—the finest olive oil was not used for soap, only the dregs of the crushing mills; the fats and tallows were not the edible fats, but the refuse discharged from the tan pits.

The ash used in the trade was obtained from household ash pits, and the burnt refuse of thatch and barnyard which was collected from the boilers by special scavengers. This use of refuse meant that soap boiling was a lucrative trade, based mainly on waste trade products and therefore always taxed to the uttermost.[1] This kept up the price of soap and caused

[1] Their long competitive war against taxation went on for years. At one time, no less than twelve British soap-makers were in Fleet Prison for refusing to pay the soap import.

economical country householders to boil their own mixtures long after new riches, or extreme poverty, inclined the urban population to buy their soap, or go without! This is only a small point, but it dovetails with the cause of the extreme dirt of the industrial areas, *and the fact that emigrant families, usually from the depopulated rural areas, knew how to do it and cheerfully made their own soap, by their old remembered recipes* (though these had to be modified for the new materials available in new countries).

> 1619. Patent for the Manufacture of Soap in Scotland, granted to Nathaniel Udwart.
>
> Because "the soap previously used in Scotland had been imported and compoised of such pestiferous and filthie ingredients as no civile Kingdome, yea the verry rude barbarianis, will nocht allow—yeir . . . trye the sufficiencie of the soap . . . as unawares, when the privat gayne to the honnour, credite and reputation of thair native country. Strangers hanting and frequenting this Kingdome, may not abide the stinking smell of the naiprie and bynning clothes waschin with this filthie soap."
>
> 1621. "The council (trade) haveing found Uduarts greene soape to be als goode and sufficient as the soape of that kynd broght frome Flanderis, they find it expedient for the better tryeing of the said soape . . . that the provost and baillies of Edinbrugh be thame selffs (or some otheris to be nominat be thame) sall troyse a thrise everier yeir . . . trye the sufficiencie of the soap . . . as unawares, when the soape is boylled and sall couper the same with Flemies soape, and yf thay sall find ony defect in the fynnes, thay sall acquent his majesties counsell thairwith."

COMPETITION

As, to a certain extent, each city was automatically provided with its own waste products, soaps varied locally, and this was a cause of trouble. In 1633, the London Soap Masters (always keen competitors) "claymed Power to Assye Soape under the great Seale of England" and this caused a considerable lather down at Bristol! The "Assyers" rode down in state solemnity and collected samples of Bristol soaps to try out against the "Accredited Brands of London". It must have been fun!

Certain linen napkins were collected and brought before the field. Bristol opened their side with two redoubtable women laundresses, Sara Willys of the Rose Tavern and Elizabeth Delhay of the Dolphin. These two women washed the said napkins with great gusto in the presence of the London assyers, and proved that napkins washed with the soap of Bristol were as *white* washed and as *sweet*—"in good faith Rathere Sweter" than those washed with the assye soap. "Yett;—was not soe much soape expended of the Bristol Soape as of the other"—and "so it appeared to all present"! Victory! (Free drinks all round at the "Dolphin" and the "Rose"!)

KELP BURNING FOR SOAP

The best Scottish kelp was £20 a ton in 1876. "The weed is burnt in hearths about fourteen feet long and rather narrow across, to ensure a draught. It is part dried, and the fire started with dry fuel, for which old thatch and drift wood are collected. The fire burns slowly about eight hours, then it is encouraged to burn more swiftly, till the ash fuses down to a 'floor'. More weed is then added and this is continued till the floor of ash is thick and solid. Then it is splashed with cold sea water, crackt and sold by the pannier full. The residue ash is a good phosphate manure."

Trade report, 1876

VARIETIES OF SOAP FOR DIFFERENT WATERS AND USES

Several makes of soap were on the market as early as 1750. "Marseilles" soap was made from olive oil and soda and "Castile", one of the earliest and most expensive, was also an olive oil soap, supposed to be made with the purest oil. A contemporary English make was a "honey soap"—said to have beeswax in it. It was scented with citron oil.

By the eighteenth century Brown Windsor is mentioned, and later in the century, coal tar and carbolic soaps were advertised. "Green soaps", made of vegetable oils, were considered good for common use as a toilet soap. For scrubbing and household use there was a curious mottled soap, streaked with blue like a Danish cheese! The effect was obtained by using a solution of sulphate of iron in the boiling water. The idea was that any surplus alkaline in the soap was decomposed by the sulphate, and showed up as bluish streaks. This decomposing of the "free" alkaline was designed to make the soap more mild. Whether it made much difference was questionable, but it was a very popular soap.

This and other common yellow bar soaps (*see* Trade Soap Making) were bought by weight and stored in dry cupboards till evaporation had somewhat hardened them. One custom (by careful housekeepers) was to slice the bars while new and "trim them to the hand". That is, they cut off the corners and sharp edges, making neat tablet pieces, and the trimmings were dissolved down in boiling water to make soap jelly for laundry work. A favourite jelly for washing woollens had a measure of turpentine stirred into it, as the oil loosened the dirt and the slight aroma discouraged moth. ("Soft Soap" is described in the trade section.)

Floating Soap

The exceedingly light "floating" toilet soaps were produced by special treatment of the soap mixture in a water bath.

> "The apparatus employed for making these soaps is a copper pan, heated by a water bath. In the bottom of the pan there is a step (a pivot?) to receive the lower end of a vertical shaft to which arms, or paddles, are attached, for producing constant agitation."
>
> URE, *Dic. of Arts*, 1842

These floating soaps, "Swan", "Lilly White", etc., remained popular till the 1930's. Now they seem to have gone completely off the market.

Scented Soap

> "The commodities that we brought home were pepper and Elephants' teeth, oyle of palme . . . etc. . . .
>
> There are great store of palme trees, out of the which they gather great store of wine . . . and . . . they have good store of sope and it smelleth like beaten violets."
>
> J. WALSH, MASTER, *Voyage to Benin beyond Guinea*, 1588

Soap Soluble in Sea Water

The following is given as a soap soluble in sea water. Oil or fat 40 parts, resin 10, fish glue 40, soda or potash 1, oxalate of potash 1. The oil and resin are saponified as usual, but with an excess of alkali, the glue, previously rendered gelatinous by solutions in oxalate of potash, is then added and the whole heated with constant stirring to 50 deg. or 60 degs.

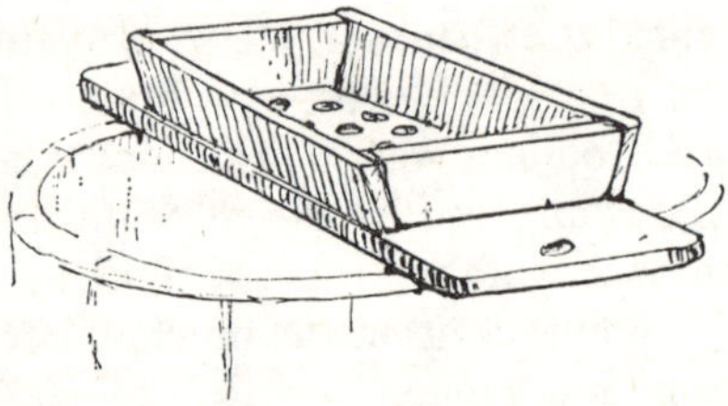

Wooden tray to hold soap worts and ash, etc., through which water was poured into the buck tub

A TAX ON SOAP

> "That in England and Wales and Berwick, from a survey made in the year 1690, the number of Houses are 1,300,000, besides Colleges, Hospitals and Cottages. Then, allowing that each house uses 1 lb. of soap a week (few using less and many more) that makes 52 lb. a year to each house.
>
> The tax at 2*s.* the hundredweight will (therefore) produce yearly £60,357."
>
> *A Parliamentary Suggestion*

THE AXENCARER OR ASHEN CARRIER

Among the guild laws of the soap-boilers was one that prohibited the taking away of another firm's "axencarer".

The word is queried as an "ash riddle", but a small item would not figure in legislation and a large trade item owned by each firm for its own use would be difficult to steal. Also, the context indicates a pronoun.

In my own research on mediæval waste products (for a reprint of Tusser), I have found an individual called an "ash carrier". He was a person who went around the countryside buying up old thatch or waste household ashes, or any debris that could be burnt to make ley for the soap-boilers. He also supplied the potash-makers. He was in fact a scavenger, a pre-corporation-dustbin-collector, who specialized in burnable rubbish, and worked his special district as systematically as the modern collector of old iron. These men worked for special soap makers and were paid on delivery. Some districts were more "ashful" or some collectors more acquisitive than others, so to intercept another man's Axencarer and acquire his load, or services, was the equivalent of stealing or seducing the firm's travelling representative!

THE USE OF FERMENTS IN CLEANING

I have not been able to obtain historic proof of the old usage of ferments for cleaning cloth, etc. Yet anyone using yeasts must have seen how their "working" action loosens dirt and clears any substance with which they come in contact? Years ago, when every household baked its own bread and brewed its own drink, yeasts of many types were in constant use. Ferment spores infected the wood bucks and tubs that held milks, meads, and ales, and other liquids, and as the wooden tubs and casks had to be kept damp (to prevent shrinkage) many of them, standing filled with water in a warm place, may have provided leys of considerable use in laundry work. The brew house of old was not the modern sanitary place of measured chemical process, but nearly always a fungoid-infected shed, or warm bakehouse.

Other fungus growths had many uses, from staunching blood to sharpening razors and subduing bees, and I will stake my reputation as a washerwoman that many mediæval ancestors used spreads of yeast and other liquids for bleaching their laundry—but I cannot prove it yet.

THE WASH

Go wash well, saith Summer, with sun I shall dry;
Go wring well, saith Winter, with wind so shall I.

To trust without heed is to venture a joint,
Give tale and take count is a huswifely point.

Where many be packing,
Are many things lacking.

TUSSER

LAUNDRY

A note from "instructions to the Laundry Maid" dated 1815:

"Do not wash with any sort of water, unless it has stood two or three days, for when newly taken in it is always thick and muddy; if it is from a stream where there is a muddy bottom, it will be better to let it stand for four days."

The greatest change in Britain is in the uniformity of water. There are still a few country places where they do the washing at a spring, or in the river, and as late as the nineteenth century, "laid on" water was not in general and copious supply. So where "the wash" was not carried down to the water, the selected water was carried up to the washhouse, often overnight, to get an early start. In some hard water districts tubs were filled directly after one wash and a piece of quicklime or lump of soda put into the tub so that the water could stand for a week to soften. Choice of water was always most important for any laundry work. In other ways washing in general changed less down the centuries than the subsequent "getting up" of the goods, for this last process depended more on changing fashion.

The long crinkled robes, at one time fashionable with the Saxon ladies, were apparently dried into their folds and pleats; the effect would be obtained by washing the fine linen and pleating it over narrow rods. Smocking and sewing up the pleats would soon follow this folding. The crisp white veils that float from the steeple head dresses in the fourteenth century would be dipped in gum water and "tented" (i.e. dried taut on hooks). Heavy woollen goods would be "trodden clean" under water. Colloidal solutions, made from hides and horns, lather well and cleanse excellently. In fact, "size" competes with "bran water" for the washing of chintz and fine woollens right into the 1800's. So does ox-gall, and though today we prefer our ammonia out of a bottle, the effect is similar to that which they obtained from the household chamber pots.

The earlier "leys" used for "leying bucks" were liquids, and for centuries the soaps made by the household seem to have been what we today call "a soap jelly".

It was the nineteenth-century washerwoman who used *hard* soap (and seems to have rubbed it into woollens to turn them into felts). In cities her lack of rinsing water did not help her. Perhaps it was some uncomfortably "felted" socks worn by some Member of Parliament that induced the "Washhouse for the Million" (*see* page 209) movement, for it was the restricting of water, newly laid on through the small inadequate pipes, that made rinsing impossible. Before that, the rinsing was done in the running water of river or spring, as is shown in hundreds of pictures and MSS. down the centuries.

One item in the following brief survey requires note. Salt in any fabric causes it to become damp with the slightest humidity in the air (*see* page 327). So when Bede, in his sensible account of the brother who had a stroke when washing the blankets from the monastic guest house, makes him go down to the shore, we may, sensibly, remember that it was a tidal estuary (*see* page 73). The good Brother Bodudegn would not have remained hospitaller for all those years if he had not understood how to wash blankets!

The influx of American washing machines, the instructions for washing ostrich feathers, poke bonnets and lace, all give the "history of the period". Even the wringing machine, from the Irish linen factories, and the rescue of the shipwrecked bales off Penmaenmawr are sidelights on history, making rainbows in the soap suds for any student of history.

THE EARLY ENGLISH HOUSEHOLD WASH WAS EXTENSIVE AND FUNDAMENTAL

What we call "THE wash" and consider as one process was originally several different ones. When much of the household cloth was made in the household, much of the specialized washing or "dressing", now done by the cloth makers, was done at home. For, though every "spinster"[1] in a community had to be continually spinning in order to make enough thread to keep the looms busy, weaving was going on continuously, and the resultant blanket, sheet, or bolt of fine household linen would be dressed and finished in the household.

Even when the weaver took over the thread and did the weaving in his own shed, on a barter-exchange basis, it was quite likely that he would return the cloth direct, straight as it came from the loom, and leave the final washing and dressing, or dyeing, or bleaching and tenting, to be completed by the owners.

Therefore, for centuries home washing might also include the walking (i.e. pounding under water) of wool cloth, the making of dyes, and the bleaching of linen. All the "process work" that we now buy ready done by the manufacturers. Therefore, one has to consider all early laundry work as definite processes for definite materials.

SHEEP WASHING (WOOL)

> "Wash sheep, for the better, where water doth run,
> And let him go cleanly, and dry in the sun:
> Then shear him, and spare not, at two days an end,
> The sooner the better his corps will amend."
>
> TUSSER

[1] In 1730 a London Mercer still advertised "Ladies own spinning woven into poplins".

"*Washing the Woollens*" began by washing the sheep's wool.

It is impossible to generalize on the texture of the earliest English wool. It is thought that the Normans brought finer cloth, but the Saxon's sheep had the better wool. When every sheep walk had its own hirsel[1] the type of wool probably varied as much as the grazing units. Historians have never decided on the exact quality of the early mediæval fleece. Some thirteenth-century scraps of cloth show coarse hairs and rough texture, but carved drapery and illuminated MSS. display the gracious folds of very finely woven woollen goods, with a smooth nap. Other samples of cloth used as a box lining, etc, may have been intentionally of coarse, hard-wearing type.

From the thirteenth century the Cistercians carried on a good trade in wool and improved both yield and quality. By the sixteenth century, under Elizabeth I, the wool trade was pushed forward so as to alter the whole pattern of English farming. Now, sheep were bred for the quality of the wool, rather than their value as mutton.

In those days, English wool was renowned for its fine texture, but the finishing and dyes for cloth were bad. All recorded instructions to Elizabethan sailors admonish them to "study the dyes of foreign countries" for "*we have the best wool in the world, but for lack of good dyes our cloth trade suffers*". By the seventeenth century English wool was probably as good, if not better, than the best wool we have today.

This rapid survey of the "wool sack" is needed for two points of interest. During all these centuries, the wool had always been washed on the sheep's back, thoroughly *washed* (not just dipped) and rinsed in running water, and the sheep were not shorn until after the wool was perfectly dry and the "yolk" had returned down the full length of the staple. This "yolk" was the natural waterproof dressing which penetrated inside and outside the fibres. Old breeds of hill sheep, with long straight wool, provided so much of this greasy waterproofing, that if (as the shepherds would say), "you grease their mouths with good meat" they could shed off heavy mountain rain like an oilskin.[2] (It is the lack of this yolk in the fleece of new-born lambs that makes them vulnerable to rain. They can

[1] "Hirsel". The complete population of sheep living on one sheep walk, a flock of sheep, may be a collection of lambs, or ewes, or a mixed lot going to market or to the mountain, but the hirsel is the complete natural herd; rams, ewes and their lambs all running together. The leaders, rams and ewes, know the whole mountain, can lead their lambs to the best grazing places as the fodder comes into growth, know their way to the sheltered places in storms and do not often perish on rocks or fall down ravines. They also know the watering places, and have worked out their sheltered sleeping crevices. It is still, in some places, illegal to sell off a complete hirsel, as, unless the experienced native sheep are there to lead the way, the new hirsel would starve, or at best, exist very poorly for some years.

[2] I.e. If well fed on good grazing. It was well said that the "best grease for a sheep was to grease his mouth with good food".

stand a healthy frost, but wet soaks them down to the skin, and a cold wet rain storm will kill lambs almost instantly.)

The early rural washerwoman who "took her wool from the sheep's back", knew all about this yolk, treasured it in her spinning and preserved it in her washing. Today most sheep are not washed, only dipped against maggots and infection and the sheep's skin lacks the stimulus of the cold swim and time to bring back the yolk before shearing.

Washing-pool and sheep washing.

A second point was the *time of shearing*. Correctly, it should be done exactly when the old wool is about to be "shed". The scanty winter fodder thins the hairs, so that a weak length comes near the skin, and the weight of the old fleece, the summer heat and the seasonal growth of the animal, make the old fleece slowly drop off. This natural "shedding" can be seen on old ewes as, if they lamb early, the shepherd does not remove the ewes' wool, for fear of cold. So by August, the old ewes trail around the lambing pastures, with disreputable clots of wool dropping off them. This dropped wool used to be the valued perquisite of the spinster. (Now it is neglected, and shows the lack of the old shepherd's pride in the appearance of his ewes.)

The spinster valued this wool, for though thin it was *tapered at both ends*, like the Shetland wool, which used to be roo'ed or plucked off, and so had qualities that made it excellent for fine spinning, the thread being more even than that of cut wool.

These two points, the yolk and the taper, are qualities in wool texture that have to be understood before the washing methods can be appreciated.

"SPOILING A GOOD SHEEP FOR ½D. OF TAR"

Washing sheep's wool, to ensure a good growth of fleece, was important in old farming economy. The idea of a special shampoo dressing was to kill lice and clean the skin of any eruptions that would cause the sheep to rub and scratch and tear the wool. Every old shepherd had his own timing for the various processes, and most had their own recipes. The earliest mixture was a decoction of broom and gorse flowers with some soap worts. A solution of tar was, we believe, favoured from the twelfth century; by the eighteenth century sulphur replaced the broom blossom and tobacco juice was added to the tar and soft soap mixtures.

The sheep was dropped legs down on a slatted stool and the mixture poured down the parted fleece direct onto the skin. Properly, from a long spouted tin jug made for the purpose, but very often from the spout of an old teapot! (This accounts for finding old pewter teapots in remote field corners or on stone walls.)

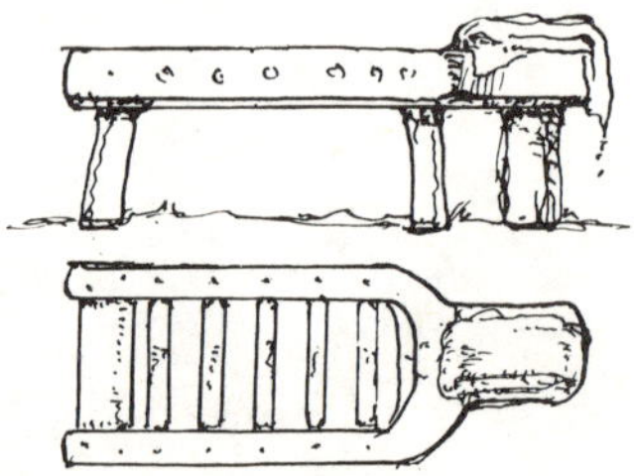

N.B. The shape of the stool varied with the size of the sheep and the shepherd. We show a large stand, suitable for the fat sheep of an opulent Midland farmer; it could be scaled down to a small stool, as used by a Welsh shepherd to fit his little mountain sheep.

Note to Washing Wool

This wool oil was secreted most thickly around the udders of the milking ewe, where it served to prevent chafing of the teats. From this natural lanoline, the mediæval people prepared their ointments and wound dressings. Also they used the wool for padding to prevent chafing under armour or saddles, etc. Pads of it, lightly oiled, polished metal surfaces against damp. Herdsmen all over the earth discover this animal-wool oil and use it as a natural lubricant dressing.

WASHING WOOLLEN CLOTH

When, in the smallest rural household, the housewife expected her husband to keep a few sheep to supply the family with blankets and clothing, the washing of the fleece (though it usually reached her clean from the shearing) had to be undertaken, and the "lifted" and gleaned and gathered wool had always to be washed before use. This preliminary wool washing was carried out in cold running water and the loose dirt got out by mechanical action in beating and rinsing, so that the natural oil was left in the wool. (Bleaching was not done to wool for ordinary usage.)

If the wool cloth was to be dyed and made into a smooth cloth, then heavy pounding and stamping was used, and ley made of potash and ammonia was soaked into it. Urine provided a cheap form of ammonia. It was called chamber ley, or piss-pot ley, and some of the old privies had long seats with many holes, not only to accommodate many work people at once during a crowded dinner hour, but also to set aside a few holes over tubs for those who could "oblige", and so collect the urine separately.

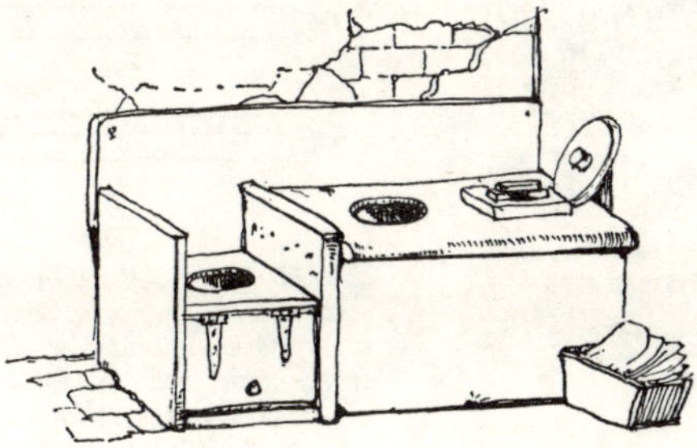

An adequate privy with urine collector

As a comment upon this coarse and homely method, we are told that a Roman Emperor industrialized the idea. He fitted commodious cisterns of suitable commercial size into the streets of Florence, to induce the general public to contribute to the reputation of Florentine cloth by supplying its fullers with ley for their vats.

WASHING WOOLLEN BEDDING

Wool bedding was usually made of discarded wool—that is, the loose wool "discarded" after the two carding files had combed the wool for the spinster's distaff. This wool would have been washed, and they would also wash any "gleaned" wool (the loose pieces caught on thorn bushes or shed by ewes). All such wool bedding would be washed like feather bedding, but the ley for wool would be different, as for feathers a lime ley was usual.

This clean wool might also be used to make quilts, sandwiched between a linen top and blanket underlayer. Then it would be washed as any ordinary blanket (but not wrung or pressed). Some wool was washed and used for stable work; horse collars were more often straw filled, as being cooler and lighter, but wool was used to stuff carriage pads and saddles. For wool drying, wind was better than sun.

WASHED WOOL SHIVERS

St. Blaise[1] was the patron saint of the woolcombers and their guilds' procession on 3rd February must have thrilled every spinster. The big red jars, that still mark some of the small oilshops in London were comber's jars where they kept warm the oil combs, and the description of their guild procession carries on the mediæval tradition.

An old red oil jar (sign of wool comber)

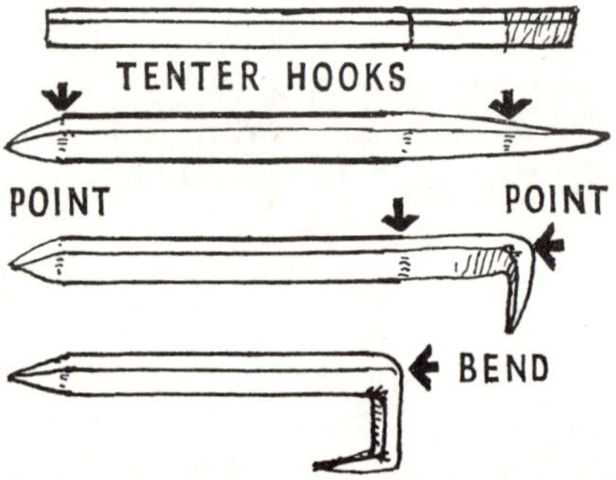

The hand-wrought nails were pointed at each end—the hook end being drawn out and bent twice after pointing sharply. They averaged one hook to the inch, and the tenter lines could cover a field of several acres. The measurement 2¼ ins.=one nail possibly came from these hooks

First came the masters on fine horses, with silver white shivers. The masters' sons rode behind them, also on good horses, bearing their colours. The apprentices followed, also mounted, and wearing their uniforms. Then came the music, then representatives, acting for the King and Queen and Court, with attendants. Then Jason and his fleece (a set piece, probably on a cart). Next came bishops and chaplains with their attendants, and then the long rabble of shepherds and shepherders walking two by two, and the wool sorters, all wearing fancy caps and woollen wigs, and waving variously-coloured shivers. Glossy with oil, glinting in the spring sunlight and floating in the wind, the long silky shivers must have made a beautiful show between the cold grey stone houses of the north country. (The description comes from Yorkshire in 1814.)

BEING ON TENTERHOOKS

Woollen cloth, after fulling and cleaning, was dried under tension, being hung upon tenterhooks.

It was impossible to bleach wool with lime or other dressing as this destroyed its texture. The whiteness of wool depended only on the cleanliness and fineness of the fleece. Wool has, when newly-shorn, a pearly sheen and billows like a cumulus cloud.

[1] See page 80.

It is pleasant to note among the properties ordered for a mediæval mystery play:

"2 fleece for the angels to stand on and one large new fleece for God Almighty's cloud".

In the process of "waulking", the cloth from the looms was beaten and felted together by the bare feet of the walkers, who stamped it in the water. Afterwards the wet tumbled cloth was stretched out to its statute width, on tenterhooks. The small holes in the selvedges of good Welsh flannel are the marks of these tenterhooks.

The tenter poles stretched in long lines far across the open fields near the mills. Both the top and lower poles were set with rows of small hooks and the cloth shrank to its even width in tension between the rows.

This technique was (and is) used for some types of drying washing to obtain special results. The pointed vandykes that border a fine Shetland shawl are the result of drying on "tenter frames". All forms of fine Honiton, and other looped laces, were dried, pinned, or hooked out to shape.[1]

PASSING THE BUCK

All washing could be called "bucking", but all washing was not done by bucking.

"Leying bucks" was a type of washing used for certain purposes. For example, when the linen came clean from the loom it was finished at home and only grass bleached. When that linen had become a dirty sheet, then it was "bucked".

Both processes might, and often did, overlap. The home weaver did not go on weaving indefinitely, but would weave a calculated length of sheet to suit herself. For tablecloths especially, the household weaver would do a special weave for a special household, or for a dowry.

The housewife would *know* her own linen by its weave, and would bleach it herself, flat on the grass, through the April showers and sunlight.

LEYING BUCKS

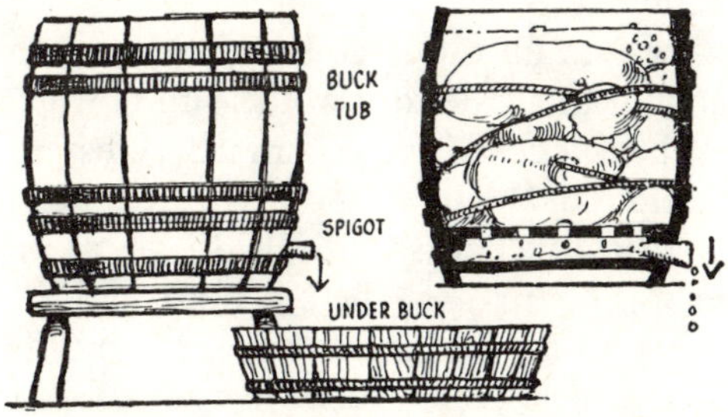

[1] Parchment is dried in much the same way.

> *The Buck Tub* was like a deep round half-barrel with a tap set in an inch or so above the bottom. It stood upon a strong stand that raised it quite a foot from the ground, so that the tap could discharge into a more shallow tub, called an *under buck*, set close below (*see* illustration). These shallow wooden tubs were used for many purposes, from brewing beer to raising dough, or pickling hams, but the name "under buck" stuck to them for centuries.

Leying bucks were the larger part of household laundry. Large items, sheets, covers, tablecloths, etc., were "bucked" rather than washed. Bucking *was* washing, but the terms seem to have been used interchangeably, much as we today speak of "doing the laundry" or "doing the washing".

Before you condemn mediæval phraseology as indeterminate, consider your own. "I'm doing the washing" indicates a household job. "I'm doing the washing for the laundry" indicates counting clothes and packing them into the laundry basket, which brings us to Falstaff's buck basket.

The Buck Basket was the common name for a basket of many uses. Falstaff's basket would be almost four feet deep, up to four feet in diameter, rounded, and carried slung on a pole between two men. The same buck basket that carried the washing down to the river, might well be used to carry the floor rushes up from the river. In the delightful old English poem of "Floris and Blanchflower" the boy lover gets himself carried up to his lady's bower under the rushes in such a basket. When Floris springs out, Blanchflower gives a startled cry and her maidens rush in, but Floris has swiftly crouched back into the basket, and Blanchflower disarms suspicion by explaining "It was an otter that sprang against my breast! An otter came up from the river in the wet rushes".

The same type of basket was used to carry the corn for threshing. It had a dozen mediæval uses, but if anyone asked for a buck basket they'd know what they meant, as today we might speak of a "clothes basket full of apples".

Cobbett speaks of "a small underbuck", but gradually the "under" drops out, and by 1880, in store catalogues, the shallow *under*buck is called a "bucktub" or simply a "buck".

To "lay bucks" was to fill the large bucking tub with linen in such a way that water, poured in at the top, would run down *through* the folds. For this purpose "buck sticks" were jammed across the tub, here and there, to take the weight of the linen and leave space for the water. (This was skilled work.) When the bucks were "laid", they were "ley'd". That is, the "ley" water was poured into the buck tub, and left to soak a while. Then the tap (or plug) at the bottom was opened, and the dirty ley water run off into the underbuck, from which it was scooped up and poured through, again and again, sometimes using stronger ley, sometimes fresh clean ley, and sometimes a *hot* ley. The linen was turned and rearranged on the buck sticks so that all parts were done evenly. The problem was to avoid pockets and pools of washed-out dirt soaking into folds. For this reason the clean things were laid at the top, and the dirtiest at the bottom of the tub.

After the dirt was all disolved or loosened, the linen was well rinsed in running water, if necessary laid out flat and bleached by sun and wind and repeated soakings of water thrown over it. The beating, rubbing and scrubbing which sometimes followed bucking (for an obstinately dirty patch) was part of washing. Just as today the laundress will attend to some dirty patch especially, before giving it a boil. The "clothes boiler" and "dolly tub" were the next development that superseded the static bucking.

THE DOLLY TUB AND PEG REVOLUTION

The hand tool always precedes the machine, and the old lumbering, clumsy, dolly tub and peg, that made an epoch in the laundry, still influences the delicately adjusted, toss, tumble and spin washing machines of today.

Previously in bucking and most steeping processes, the water was made to run through the fabric; the dolly tub and peg drove the fabric through the water. The turning peg, wheeling outwards, spun the work outwards against the walls of the tub, and when, later, for structural strength, the galvanized tubs with corrugated sides replaced the smooth wooden tubs, the corrugations added a rubbing action and slight cross-current to the general "spin".

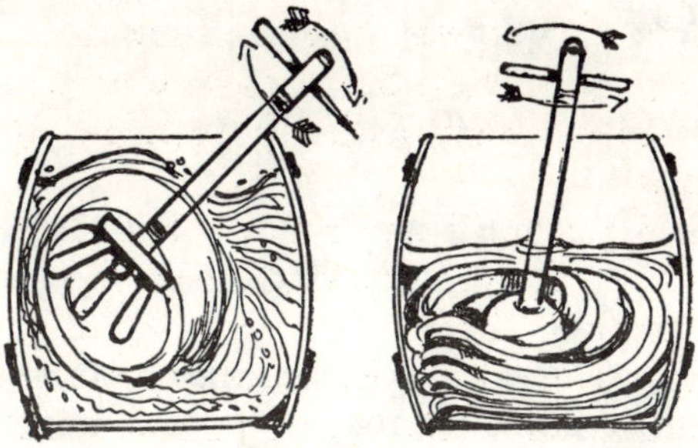

The metal tubs had to have reinforced thick rims, to take the roll of the peg, and these rims usually have small holes at intervals to allow for complete drainage when the tub is overturned to empty.

The spinning action lifted the linen up and flung it outwards, and the abrupt turn and change of direction forced the linen *against* the current set up by the previous turn. The heavy dirt tended to accumulate in the "back water" below the strong main to-and-fro current made by the wheeling peg.

The "pegging" was strenuous, but not heavy work. The peg, being of wood, was upheld by the water, and an expert used the trick of rolling the shaft of the peg, to and fro, upon the side of the tub, so that the effort came only in the change of direction that swished the cloth through the changed current of the water; this was a skilled knack like that of "trundling" a mop to spin it dry.

The fault in usage came of having too little water in the tub to float the linen, and too heavy a weight of linen on the peg. To spin one sheet in deep water was a light twisting action, but to *lift* four sheets, in insufficient water to float them, was simply to give a slow heavy stir that degenerated into a pounding action.

Significantly, the heavy solid peg head that fostered this technical error developed in the crowded industrial districts where water was poorly supplied or had to be carried. (The drawing was made outside Wigan.) The diagrams show all this more clearly than words can describe it.

Long immersion in hot water, with intermittent drying periods, made construction of these wooden tools difficult. Nails and screws cannot be used. Wedge work and dowel pins alone hold the 7 or 10 parts firmly together through their strenuous usage.

Some details of the wedging of the lower "pegs" and the base of the central shaft are shown, and three evolvements of the crossbar handle.

The peg

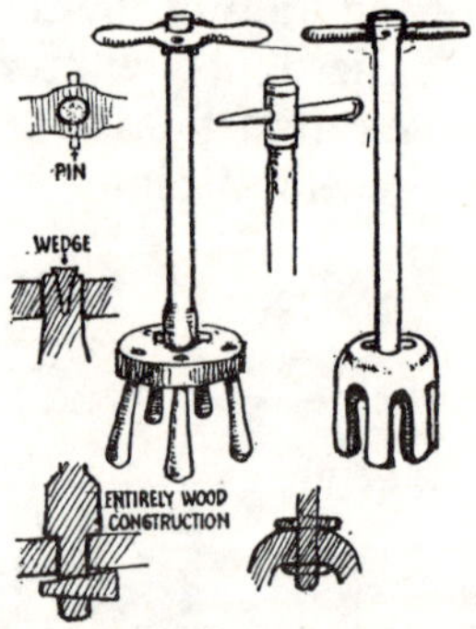

The "dropped over" (which weakened the crossbar so that it broke in the centre), the "pushed through" (which weakened the head of the central stave), and, finally, the simple direct design, which used the crossbar as its own wedge. This proved most successful, as no extra dowel pin was required, and the working action only drove the bar more firmly into the head. Also, the crossbar could be withdrawn and used as a "boiler stick" (to stir the boiler), a nice piece of structural design. The spinning action lifted the linen up and flung it outwards, and the abrupt turn and change of direction forced the linen *against* the current set up by the previous turn. The heavy dirt tended to accumulate in the "back water" below the strong, main to and fro current made by the wheeling peg.

The posser, presser, or squasher

The copper-bottomed substitute for the peg was not turned but lifted up and down, with the action of the old plunge churn, and it pumped and sucked the water through the linen. Later the copper base was adapted to stand at the bottom of the boiler and circulate the water up through the linen like a fountain (*see* below).

THE WASHBOARD

This simple washing-board was a contemporary of the dolly tub and often used in connection with it. It was rather more than a foot wide and long enough to stand on the base of the tub. The top part was panelled with ridged wood or corrugated zinc, against which the clothes were rubbed up and down (to the rhythm of the "Irish Washerwoman"). The latest washboards were made of thick, smoothly-ridged glass.

The rubbing action was hard on the knuckles, which accounts for some early washing gadgets.

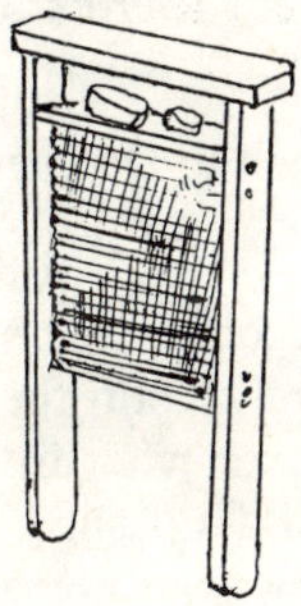

A washboard

The presser

LINEN NOTE

This fabric varied in weight and texture, according to use. "A hardened sark" was the ordinary working shirt of thick (not necessarily coarse) linen generally worn by all men, wool next to the skin being considered penitential! (This is one of the arguments used in the everlasting controversy as to the quality of old woollen cloths.) In a Cumberland church (Crossthwaite?) the minister's stipend included the right of grazing his geese on the common, also a whittle (vitual)-gait, which was the right to take his dinner at any table in the parish for seven days, and a "hardened sark". This would be hand spun and woven, but not necessarily bleached. The "Cutty Sark" was a short one.

The word "harden" is now applied to the rough brown scouring cloth or coarse apron material used by washerwomen.

BLEACHING

Q. What is bleaching?
A. The method of making linen white by exposing it to the sun and air; as when it comes from the weaver's hands it is the colour of flax, which is a light brown.
Q. How is the operation performed?
A. It is just steeped in bran and water, then well washed and spread on the grass to dry.
Q. What is next done?
A. Buckets full of water mixed with a strong ley made of wood ashes are constantly thrown over it, and the washing and spreading to dry must be often repeated.
Q. Was not linen formerly often steeped in buttermilk?
A. Yes, often it was well rinsed and frequently washed in soap and water until it became delicately white.
Q. Has not this tedious process been materially shortened?
A. Yes, by the substitution of chlorine or the fumes of sulphur for butter milk.

Child's Guide, a Victorian school book

"The Whitsters of Datchet Mead . . .
As it is whiting time, send him by your two men to Datchet Mead."

The Merry Wives of Windsor

Washing and bleaching were more seasonable occupations in Shakespeare's day, when the whole process relied entirely upon the weather.

Theoretically, a "whitster" was a linen bleacher who, in bright sunshine, spread the linen over the grassy meads and splashed water on to it to bleach it. (But, according to Falstaff he was transported in a buck basket under a pile of very dirty, greasy washing!)

Probably the words were used as loosely then, as the same terms are today, when bags for all manner of clothes, including wool and silk, are labelled "linen bags".

Bucking, washing and bleaching were different processes, but bucked sheets may well have gone on to be bleached after the dirt had been got out by washing. Anyone who washes white clothes knows this, and the whole process is confirmed in a Victorian instruction book, which states plainly that for all white goods there should be a "firsting" and a "seconding". "That is, a first wash to get out the dirt and grease, then a rinse, then a second wash to *get the white a good colour*." A quaint phrase, easily understood by any washerwoman!

Water Bleaching and Colouring

"1785—a chemistry of bleaching by acid was promulgated."

Early mediæval dye vats were of wood, containing boiling water which seems to have been drawn off, reboiled and poured through again in the manner of bucking, but by the seventeenth-century buck tubs for dye were made of metal and boiling could be done in them. Bleaching up to this date was done only by sunlight, water and sometimes lime.

By 1824 the bleaching was done with a boiling potash ley using the bucking method. The pan was set level with the buck tub and the mixture was drawn off constantly, boiled up and poured back. "The boiler being smaller than the buck tub the ebullition in the boiler must be", etc., etc. (and the authors take several pages to explain what their grandmothers must have recognized as "just bucking with boiling water"). For dyeing, they still used the old method of laying the material in water above open slats, from under which the dye rose and boiled through the material. Their great-great-grandmothers used an iron pot and dyed their wool by that same method. In fact the modern chemistry of the bleaching and dye vats continued to evolve on the simplest old-fashioned mechanical methods until about 1890, when aniline dyes revolutionized the industry.

GRASS BLEACHING AND MAYFLOWERS

The rebuilding of the *Mayflower* for its voyage to America caused controversy in the press because of the name.

Some correspondents contended that it was the May blossom, the sweet-scented foam on the hawthorn tree. But blossom is not a flower. Shakespeare, who loved wild flowers and knew their country names and uses, sings of Lime Flowers as "the blossom that hangs on the bough", but describes "Lady's smocks all silver white, that paint the meadows with delight".

Now, those are the Mayflowers "Cardamine pratensis" that Gerarde calls "the flower that blooms in Maie and Aprill, when the cuckoo sings without stammering", and "that country wenches call Lady Smocks". A drift of pale Mayflowers, wind-blown on a green meadow, does shine as silver-white as freshly lavendered ladies' smocks, laid out there to bleach in the spring sunlight.

Lime for Bleaching

Lime is mentioned for "bucking" linens far more after the late 1600's than before. It may have been used earlier. (It is difficult to imagine people who used lime for white-washing their cottages not seeing its bleaching effect upon the rush brushes and rags they worked with. Perhaps it was because they *did* see how lime will destroy woollen and linen fabrics, that they did *not* use it? Or it may have been the change from marle to lime in agricultural usage.) By 1700 most households used quicklime and soda to soften hard water.

The lime was "cast into a barrle of rain water" and left to stand overnight before drawing off the water for the first "bucking".

Lime as a Bleach

Chloride of lime was used to bleach linen white—exactly as such bottled bleaches are used today. It was not approved of by the trade who, in theory at any rate, relied on sunlight and splashing of water to bleach the grass-spread linen, but households used it to get badly washed linen back to a good colour. They used about half a pound of chloride of lime to two gallons of boiling water, set in a wooden tub. It was left (stirred at intervals) for two or three days and then bottled for use.

Sheets, etc., were bucked in the usual way, or at a later period boiled in soapy water, to remove grease and dirt, then rinsed absolutely clean before they were steeped in a bath of this bottled lime water. (One pint to two quarts of spring water.) "The linen is not to steep too long, must be moved about, and the bleach water washed out *very* thoroughly before drying." These instructions might be printed on any bottle of commercial bleach today, but they are at least 200 years old.

AMMONIA AS A "LEY" FOR LINEN

Ammonia was one of the first cleansing liquids to be packaged commercially and sold to the householder in "convenient containers" (at a vast profit to the retailer).

These bottles and containers were disparaged by the real chemists. In 1872 a trade paper stated that "the utility of Ammonia in domestic transactions is not unknown, nevertheless it is not so widely recognized as it might be, save when presented under some fancy name and sold at an exorbitant price! Whereas ammonia is nearly as useful in the household wash as soap, and its cheapness should bring it within reach of all". This is a curious sublimating of the disgusting urine tubs and putrefying hart's horns (which were most certainly "within reach of all").[1]

However, the eagerness with which an innovation is adopted is usually in proportion to the laboriousness of the process it supersedes, and the purchase of ammonia as a prepared chemical became swiftly popular, though the wording of the early 1890 advertisements contrasts bluntly with the anguished elegance of today. "Ammonia added to the foot bath absorbs the Noxious smells that arise from feet in warm weather." "The dirtiest hairbrushes will come clean in an ammonia bath" and "Ammonia in the water will remove the greasiness of an oily skin and remove dirt and dust and dandruff from the hair".

It is also recommended for removing grease spots, relieving heartburn and dyspepsia, and "it will clean paint and silver, and is good for rose trees". (One does hope the "convenient containers" had printed instructions on the outside!)

Soap Substitutes (*leys*)

"Put pearl ash into a jar covered for dust, and when it has become liquid dilute with double its quantity of soft water, and its equal quantity of slaked lime. Boil all half an hour, stirring and draining off the water, and adding more, till the liquid ceases to be acrid. Dissolve alum and chalk in bran water and use boiling hot."—(*Old MS.*)

SODA *v.* AMMONIA AS A LEY, AND BRADFORD ENTERPRISE

Though used in making soaps, the value of soda has always been controversial among experienced laundrywomen. A little soda softens some waters admirably, but too much soda ruins many fabrics. Some Belgian nuns, whose snowy white guimps shone through the smoke-laden air of the Black Country near Leeds, refused to use soda, saying it "set" the smoke and so made the linen a bad yellowish colour.

I remembered this when I found, in a Bradford washhouse, a very early Belgian recipe for washing linen. It was interesting as it was probably some traditional trade usage: "Soap suds, 2 lb. of soap to 3 gallons of water, 1 spoonful of turpentine to 3 spoonfuls of strong ammonia. Mix in a tub with a fitted cover, and *at once* put the linen to soak in this, and let it steep some hours—shaking the tub sometimes. Then wring out, wash and rinse in the usual way."

As the old recipe says that the mixture can be reheated and used several times, but fresh ammonia must be added each time *and the cover kept sealed down*, the whole idea seems to combine an old form of steeping and bucking with a very modern form of vapourizing detergent. The

[1] An old name for Ammonia, was Spirit of Harts Horn.

recipe ends with the assurance that "though the detersive action is great, the ammonia and turpentine have *no* injurious effect upon the linen".

(It was this district that later invented the method of teasing out (under chemical and mechanical action) the fibres of old woollen materials. These were combined with cotton to make the coarse felted fabric that was called "shoddy".)

INVOLVED USAGES OF HOUSEHOLDER AND TRADER

These notes on early washing gear are of interest as they show how trade and household usages became closely involved.

Some housewife would discover a new plant juice, and some tradesman would try it out, develop it and sell it back to her for household use. First a natural juice, then the synthetic equivalent in the same way. The pounding action of the churn, or spinning action of the brewing spider, and the dolly peg and rotary washer came into trade. To and fro down the centuries goes the passing of the buck!

THE COMING OF THE MACHINE

A mechanical substitute for the washboard

The servant shortage began to be felt and the "lady" unaccustomed to washing found it hard on the knuckles. So this small gadget was sold to the "lady of the house" rather than the professional washer-woman.

WASHING MACHINES. THE NEW AMERICAN INFLUENCE

"The washing and wringing machines of recent invention (1870) make household washing, where there is drying ground, both cheap and easy. In general, servants will not use machines, disliking the trouble of cleaning them. . . . Where these are possessed (with ground for drying) it is far better to wash at home. The family are safer from infection of all kinds and it is decidedly cheaper and pleasanter. . . ."

ROSS MURRAY, 1872

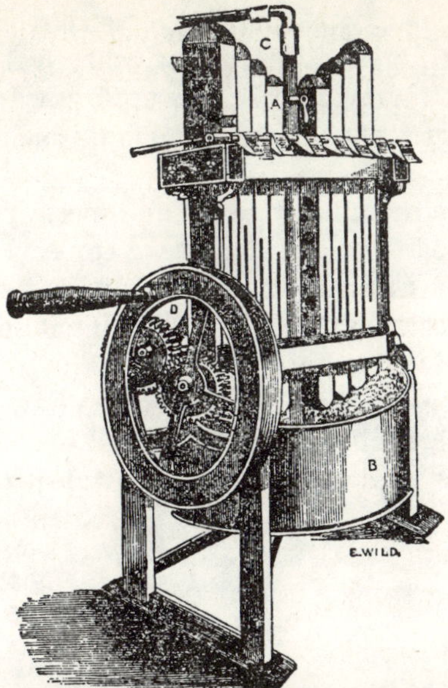

A.—Beaters. B.—Revolving Steam Vessel. C.—Steam Pipe.

An adaption of the common stamping mill

Macalpine's machine reproduced the old cam-shaft, used to crush ore-bearing stone by Cornish miners. The miners rotated the cam-shaft by the same water-power stream that washed the ore, as the lifting of the heavy stamps by hand power must have been heavy labour. It was not a mechanically sound invention.

The following "washing machines" both reached England from America. American inventions were popular imports of the period. It is interesting to the domestic historian that each model is based upon an earlier household usage.

One visualized the ancient "brake", used for hemp and flax, the old curd breaker, the butter hands and the ground and knobbly corn-crushers, all lying unused and dusty in a shed and himself "inventing something".

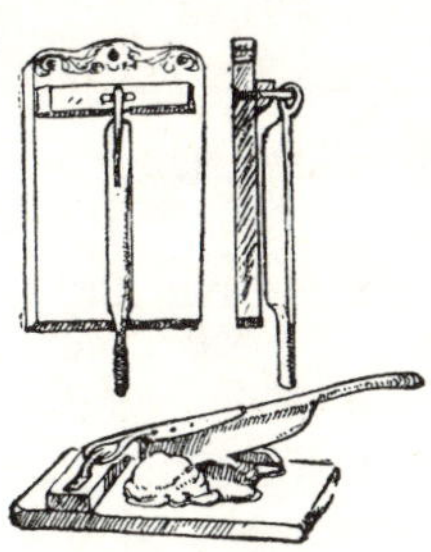

The common household brake

The heaviest brake, with a flat-hinged striker, broke hemp stems to release the flax fibres. The lightest brake was used for blending butter. The most common brake was used to work dough. The old bread recipes instruct you to put the dough through the brake and then knead it a little.

Some brakes are beautifully carved and most of them have pierced headings to the board, so that the brake could be hung on the wall when not in use. In this invention, the up-and-down action of the brake is adapted for use in the tub by hinging it on to a conical metal plunger or sucker.

A hand brake adapted as a washing machine

The brake action was not adopted, but the conical sucker carried on into later inventions and ultimately superseded the dolly peg.

BLUE

This was frowned upon by experts as liable to be used to conceal dirt by making the white grey (the common indigo blue being a dull shade). Ultramarine blue was the expensive bright blue and Reckitts were the earliest makers to introduce this blue direct into their starch.

TO RINSE

Rinsing was for centuries called the rench or the wrench, being less a verb than a noun. The larger washes and heavier fabrics of older times could not be lightly swished around. Old thick linen sheets were stiff, and so heavy that, when wet, it took two people to lift them! The thick quilts and covers and voluminous petticoats were bulky. Also the soap was less easily dispersed than lighter modern detergents. So the rench was quite a lengthy immersion, frequently twenty-four hours. Whenever possible it was in running water, or at least in water that could be changed frequently.

A tub set below a waterfall was an ideal rench and, using the same technique as in the old "bucking", the clothes were often lifted up on crossed sticks, supporting them in open formation, so that the water could run through freely.

If there was a clear shallow stream running swiftly over a clean pebble bed, sheets and blankets and "large pieces" would be spread out under the running water, held down at the top end only by large clean stones. The clothes would wave and ripple in the current and be clear very quickly. (In the 1920's I saw sheets done this way in the clear beck outside the little inn under Kilsey Craig in the limestone district of the dales.) Later, when tap water was available, the tubs would be set under a running tap, sometimes one below another.

The freshness of country washing was due to this thorough rinsing; the whiteness due to the bleaching of washing laid flat on the green under the sun and wind.

THE WRINGER

As always the first machines copied the hand methods, and the washerwoman, twisting the water out of the wet clothes, designed the first mechanical wringer. This name carried through to the earliest mangles, which were (and still are) called "wringers". Much depends on the requirements of the work, for after rinsing the washerwoman will say, "I put it through the wringer", but when the sheets are almost dry, she will say, "I mangle them smooth to save ironing". In both cases she will be using the same machine.

> The early wringer was made after the fashion of modern tennis net posts. Posts were set a suitable distance apart (for a six-foot sheet almost four feet). The heavy linen sheet was looped over two hooks on the posts or, in some cases, looped over one post and onto the hook at the other end. The short end of the loop was wrapped into the folds of the sheet. This allowed for considerable adjustment in length. Then the hook at one end of the wringer was turned round and round, giving a strong twist to the fabric and wringing out the water, which poured down on the laundry floor, or into a catch bag hung below the twist.

The constructive difficulty of this apparatus was to prevent the strong pull of the twist from dragging the posts together. It seems likely that at least one of the hooks was built into the laundry walls or driven into a beam in the ceiling, and the wash stick that had stirred the boiler and the two sturdy arms of the washerwoman continued to be used as wringers.

It is very possible that the single large hooks of wood that remain embedded in the beams of old washhouses may have been used for wringing. That this hook may also have been used to sling up the pig for disembowelling, or support the dripping cider sack or take the wool scales, would not preclude its use to the laundry woman. A "butcher hook" would be of iron and sharp pointed, but if the shed was primarily a washhouse it would more likely be of wood and thick and blunt.

THE PRESS AND MANGLE

The reconstruction of a press from a thirteenth-century MS. is an interesting piece of research because, though the tiny illuminations in the Bible Moralisee portray such mystical subjects as the wine press of the wrath of God, and Samson grinding corn, the objects in the drawings are material and contemporary.

Therefore this press (extremely like an old Devon cider press, but with the pumice wrapped after Monmouth fashion) proves the early use of the lever and screw and contains two forms of construction that make the slow evolvement of the laundry mangle interesting.

A thirteenth-century press

The supports for the screw must have been wedged under the ceiling beams (otherwise the screw itself would lift from the ground), but in this, as in most early agricultural implements, the exact balance and angle, etc., were arrived at by trial and error, and the calculations (if any) were worked out *from* the model.

The early box mangle relied for its weight on the heavy stones in the box above pressing down on the rollers.

The early upright mangle relied for its weight on the heavy weights slung on a bar below (pulling down) on the rollers. It was not till the twentieth century that *the screw*, pressing down on layered springs, replaced the basic idea of sheer weight. And these layered springs that worked the mangle were the layered springs that put the first motor-car bodies on the road. (For a mechanic's satisfaction, this twelfth-century press is included in this laundry section. Perhaps it was so used for pressing bales of wool or drying blankets? No housewife in any century, seeing what the men were doing, would miss such an opportunity!)

THE BOX MANGLE

"Cheer boys cheer!
My mother bought a mangle.
Cheer boys cheer!
She filled it full of stones.
Cheer boys cheer!
She makes me turn the handle.
Cheer boys cheer!
It nearly breaks my bones!"

"Mangling Done Here" was a common notice in cities during the late 1800's.

The large country houses all had their own laundry buildings (as also their brew house, bake house, game larders and ice houses). They employed laundry maids on their regular staff and sometimes employed extra help from a professional clear starcher. That is, a woman who specialized in all the intricate starching and ironing and getting up of fine linen and muslin. Frequently it would be the mother of the laundry maid, who had married someone on the estate, and so naturally came back each week to "take over the fine work". This expert would keep a corner of the laundry to herself, have her own polishing irons and spotless white blankets and take considerable pride in her profession.

Frequently she delivered the finished articles direct to the ladies' maid, or valet, or nurse, whereas the ordinary household washing went past the housekeeper's eye to the linen closet. These domestic details should be understood, because it is this change in this old domestic economy which was the cause of the notice "Mangling Done Here".

Country houses could spread out their laundries and drying grounds, but in the cities there simply was not room. Yet the new middle class (by tradition from above and below) always did their own washing and, as today, drying was the difficulty.

So there sprang up a race of retired laundry maids turned washerwomen who "went out" or "took in" family washing. Among this washerwoman class one would "invest in a mangle". At first it would be one of the large old box type, which would fill her cottage. It was probably "inherited" from some old country house, whose laundry ground had been built over by the new villa residences. To this mangle came the washerwomen with their baskets of wet clothes and, as most washing was done early in the week, the gathering of the clan around the mangle made the owner of a mangle a most important unofficial domestic agency.

(An early tract of the S.P.C.K. describes how an orphan girl is adopted by the "owner of a mangle" and, after religious instruction, is handed over to the care and encouragement of a "Most Respectable Laundry Maid" in good service in one of the "Best Houses", where she is introduced to the cook, rises through the ranks and ultimately marries the head gardener, washes his shirts and is, in the last chapter, preparing to wash nappies! These old period tracts give interesting side slants on social and industrial history.)

The box mangle (shown in plate 34) is a typical one. The size and mechanism varied. A side rachet wheel was perhaps more common than the chain, but the principle was the same: the heavy stone-filled box was drawn across a set of loose rolling pins which rolled out the linen below them. The "lower deck" of the mangle was smooth, with sunk water channels to the sides. Pressure could be adjusted by the weight of the stones *or* the number of rollers, as the whole weight of the box upon one roller gave more pressure than when the weight was distributed on four or five rollers.

This adjustment of rollers was important, as mangling was done for two distinct purposes by two different processes. The first process to wring out the water required several passages under heavy pressure. Between each passage the cloth would be refolded in a different form, so that the water was pressed out evenly. For this process a few *old* rollers served. For the second, the pressing process, the rollers were the smoothest, and so arranged to follow one after another that the cloth had all the wrinkles smoothed out and the folds "set" in. If skilfully done on evenly damp cloth, this roller mangling could take the place of hand ironing. It did not give the glossy finish of the hot iron, but for cotton sheets and "flat work" it was good enough.

(N.B. Napkins and table linen were later ironed and put in the screw press, but this process is described in the ironing section.)

Usually the owner of the mangle kept a few old blanket bits and clean sacking to run through the mangle and help to dry it out between wringing and pressing. Some would even have a couple of rollers padded with clean flannel for pressing fine stuff, crochet, lace, or embroidered "flats". There was considerable skill in using these cumbersome heavy box mangles, and, as the old song testifies, it was strenuous work.[1]

THE IRON UPRIGHT MANGLE

The iron mangle took up far less space than the old box mangle. It could fit into a small washhouse or scullery, so it gradually took the mangling back into the home laundry. In the country, where space was not considered, the large houses with their own laundry building kept the box mangle in use for another hundred years (the author saw one dismantled only a few years ago).

In towns the old women continued to do mangling for a time, using the new iron mangle and working for the women who took in washing. But soon these washerwomen bought their own mangles. Then households had the washerwomen "come in to do the wash once a week" rather than send it out. Thus the old notice, "Mangling Done Here", was only seen in the poorest and most crowded districts. In this way, from being considered "Quite a Respectable Position for a Widow with a Son to Turn for her", it became the last resource of the poor woman with a family to support. The domestic gatherings around the fire, the gossip over the cups of hot salop, all ended and box mangling died out.

This early form of upright mangle depended upon heavy weights, as did the previous box mangle. The two weights were slung down from the axle ends of the top roller and *pulled* it down. In theory, the weights could be changed to alter the pressure, but this was seldom done as the idea was to extract as much water as possible and the washerwoman frequently supplemented the weights by pressure with her foot on the cross bar.

THE SCREW AND SPRING

The next iron upright mangle worked entirely by screw pressure, not by weight. Early models had one screw set in the centre of overlapping

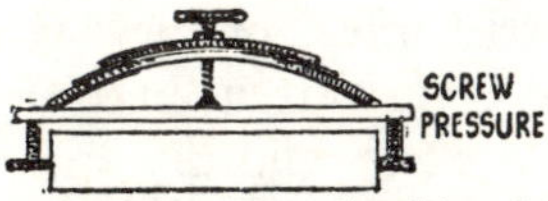

[1] During the last war, when the Blitz put plumbing lead at a premium, the bombs uncovered an old box mangle in a convent behind Euston station. In the box, supplementing the stones, were lumps and sheets of thick lead, guttering from an old church roof. It was the most valuable mangle of the year!

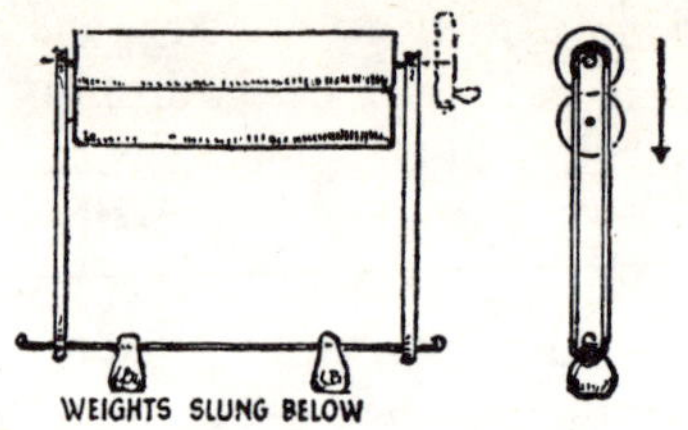

Suspended weights pull the rollers tightly together

lath springs and the two wooden rollers were turned on simple cogs by one large-handled wheel. A ledge on one side supported the wet washing as it went in, and another ledge caught it as it came out. The water ran down into a tub or "under-buck" below.

Development in all designs made the turning easier by gearing down the cog wheels that engaged the rollers, and by fitting equalizing wheels at the far end of the rollers to ensure even pressure. The iron frames of these mangles were imperishable, but the wooden rollers did wear out and village carpenters had a steady trade in re-turning or replacing mangle rollers. On account of its use (wet and dry and alternating pressures) any splicing or glueing was impossible. Each roller had to be turned from one clean flawless length of timber. This made repair too expensive and during the last war thousands of these iron mangles went for scrap.

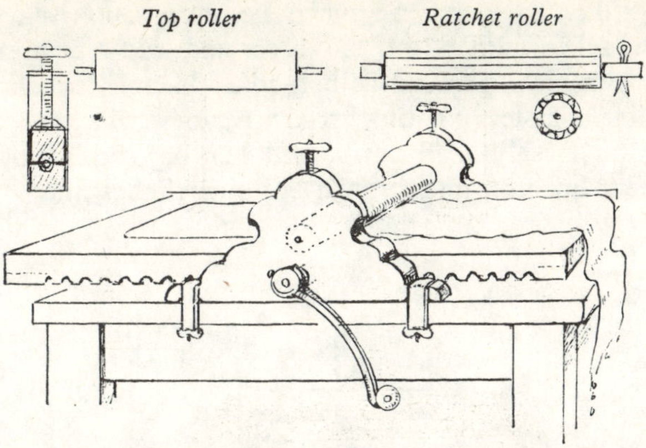

The ratchet engaged with handle to carry platform forward

An interesting and rare invention came between the old box mangle and the new upright one. KENT'S PATENT PORTABLE TABLE MANGLE combined the flat platform movement of the old box type, with the top roller, and a new screw pressure.

Two sturdy blocks were clamped down to the kitchen table; these supported the rollers. The lower ratchet roller drove the moveable platform through under the top wooden roller, which took the screw pressure.

"PORTABLE" was the astonishing word for an article noted for its old cumbersome weight. KENT PORTABLE was easily taken down, and assembled, and the parts packed into a shallow box when not in use.

It suggests adaptation from the early lithographic press, a process production popular at that time. Unfortunately, the drawing has had to be made from memory and some very worn cuts, but the principle is most ingenious.

A washing invention using alternating pressure and suction with rotation, thus inaugurating the spin dryer and dispensing with the mangle

TRANSPORT

At an early period the iron mangle was mounted on four strong iron casters, to enable it to be set back against the wall after use or trundled out into the yard on a fine day. So, when the repair shop was not far away it was quite usual to harness a horse direct and lead him in a slow and stately walk down the high road with Madam Mangle trundling behind, her four small iron casters rotating briskly, her new white rollers swaying and swirling on freshly-oiled gears, and her big turning handle tied, sash-wise, about her iron middle with her own clothes line.

LINEN PRESS

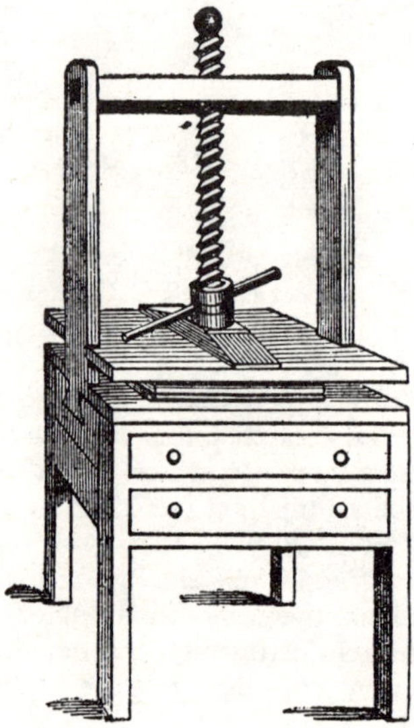

The linen press was never a water extractor. It belonged to the ironing and finishing part of the work. Some sheets and *un*ironed goods would rely on neat folding and pressure to give them a reasonably smart finish. Ironed and folded damask cloths and napkins were put into the press after ironing to ensure they lay flat and the folds were exact. A tablecloth had always to be laid with the pressed crease upwards and napkins, unless elaborately folded, had to be pressed flat as pancakes. Embroidered cloths had to be pressed over a blanket.

The drawers below held wrapping cloths and linen awaiting replacement in the linen cupboard, which, by its receiving the pressed linen, was often spoken of as "the press cupboard" or the "clothes press".

Artists buy up old linen presses of this type to take their paper store.

MANLOVE, ALLIOTT, & CO's

Patent Centrifugal Drying Machines.

These Machines form the most valuable and effective improvement in Drying Machinery yet introduced. As the water is thrown out by centrifugal force alone, all mischief to the goods that occurs in the ordinary operation of wringing is entirely obviated, and not the least disturbance of the texture of the materials being produced. The goods operated upon come out of the Machines very nearly dry, and a very great saving of time and fuel is thus obtained in the finishing process.

A very large number of these Machines are at work in different Asylums and Hospitals, Bath Wash Houses and Laundries, and in all cases with complete success.

The first spin dryer, later developed for separating cream on the farm before the Milk Marketing Board took over

DRYING CLOTHES

DIFFICULTIES ON THE N.W. PASSAGE. THE NAVY AGAIN LEADS THE WAY

"It was my intention to have caused the bedding of the ships' companies to be brought on deck for the purpose of airing, at least once a week but . . . whenever a blanket was brought on deck and suffered to remain there for a time, it acquired the temperature of the atmosphere . . . the immediate consequence on taking the blanket down again to the inhabited parts of the ship, the vapour condensed upon it, rendering it almost instantly so wet that it required, after all, to be dried by artificial heat. We were therefore under the necessity of hanging the bedding upon lines between decks as the only mode of airing it, and, what was to prove still more prejudicial, we were obliged to have recourse to the same unhealthy measure in drying washed clothes."

CAPTAIN PARRY, 1820

The search for the North-west Passage had great influence in developing heating and drying appliances. Captain Parry, most motherly of naval commanders, wrote five volumes describing his voyages towards the north-west polar region of the Atlantic. His reports dealt very sensibly with the problems of water heating, possible hot air transmission and the drying of clothes and bedding. (*See* Plumbing for his description of a new ship's boiler heated from the galley fire and the prototype of the household hot-water system.)

In the best tradition of the Navy, the Captain was able and willing to turn his hand to any job that circumstances required, diet and laundry-work included.

During the long arctic winter, while the ship was stowed under canvas covers, the men's quarters below deck were so cold that even their breath condensing on the ship's timbers coated the walls and bunks with a layer of ice, which on thawing out made the whole lower deck wet.

Not only the blankets and bedding, but the men's own clothes presented this problem of indoor drying in cold weather, and the first hot towel rail seems to have been an extension engineered from the chimney of the ship's galley, and used to dry clothes. London flat-dwellers and snow-bound country housewives alike, will sympathise with Captain Parry's note on the 23rd March (1820): "Being extremely anxious to get rid as early as possible of the drying of our washed clothes upon the lower deck, I had today a silk handkerchief washed and hung up outside under the stern, in order to try the effect of the sun's rays upon it. In four hours it became thoroughly dry. . . . This was the first article that had been dried without artificial heat for six months and it was yet another month before *flannel* could be dried in the open air."

It is pleasant to think of that brave Commander fingering his silk handkerchief and very seriously considering "the flannels".

The naval tradition of spotless cleanliness and trim appearance is truly well deserved.

DRYING CLOTHES OUT OF DOORS

"You will find linnen enough on every hedge!"

SHAKESPEARE

"By the way as they [Vagabonds] travayle through the country, where they chance to lie all night, the good wyfe hath spedde well if she fynde hyr sheets in the morning . . . a coverlet or curtains from the bed, or a carpet from the table, some bed clothes, or table napkins, . . . or some other things, Nothing comes amisse if it will serve to buy a drink."

REED, 1660

"At Cae Noyadd, the hedges covered white with drying linen. Mrs. Harley was washing, the floor littered with dry fern."

KILVERT'S *Diary*, 1870

THE MEDIÆVAL ROD, POLE OR PERCH WAS FOR HANGING UP CLOTHES (OR ACCOUTREMENTS) OR CHAIN MAIL (WET, OR DRY, OR OILED), ETC.

A well ventilated form of wardrode, or store (for clothes or hawks), seems to have been built into some rooms. This is not to be confused with the "garde robe" which was a polite way of saying "privy".

PROPS FOR CLOTHES-LINES

Clothes-props are essentially for the centre of a long clothes-line. They hold up the sagging heavy line and act as a boom to swing the line across with the changing winds.

These fourteen- to twenty-foot poles used to be sold by street vendors in Lancashire and Yorkshire. They were by-products from the shipping and timber yards. I remember, in Ashton-in-Makerfield, near Wigan, the "Props" man would walk along the streets sounding his long-drawn-out cry that began in the far distance as "Any Go'oad Clo-o o-o-s" and after a full minute end with his breath and an "O-O-Ops" that could have been heard a mile off. The props were slender lengths of pine or deal, with a careful subtle shape, sawn out at the top to take the line and with a shaped foot end to swivel in a "holey brick". In the country any long "bean pole" with a natural fork at the end served as a prop, and when the fork broke off the pole was just split down to grip the line.

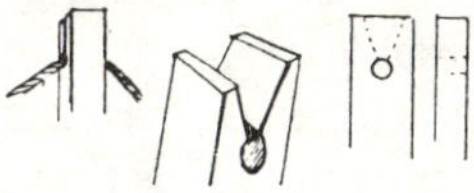

"A clothes-prop should have a shapely nose. Because two saw cuts meeting were likely to split the pole, and the wet line wedge tightly in the sharp groove, an auger hole was bored first, some inches from the end, and the saw cuts driven down to it. This gave a rounded groove in which the line could rub freely without friction. Where, in the country, a branched sapling was used, the natural crutch was sometimes corded across for the same reason."

"THE NAUTICAL" AND OTHER VARIETIES OF CLOTHES-LINE

All around our sea coasts one can often spot the home of a retired seaman in a suburban housing estate by his clothespost. The sailor raises a high mast-like post, lashes a dead eye to the top, and reeves the clothes-line through it. The sailor's wife pegs on her washing, in comfort, from deck level and then hauls it away higher than anyone else for miles!

The Wynds of the North use the same principle but horizontally, pushing out a long T-shaped clothes-post and winding out the clothes so that they flap far across the street. In the long rows of brick-built houses of the 1800's the passages that lead, like rabbit burrows, through to the back yards make capital drying grounds. They are covered in from the rain, and yet there is a terrific draught down them and, in some, a century of soapy flapping clothes have polished these side walls to a fine gloss.

CLOTHES-PEGS FOR CLOTHES-LINES

"The Maid was in the garden hanging out the clothes,
Down hopped a blackbird and pegged off her nose."

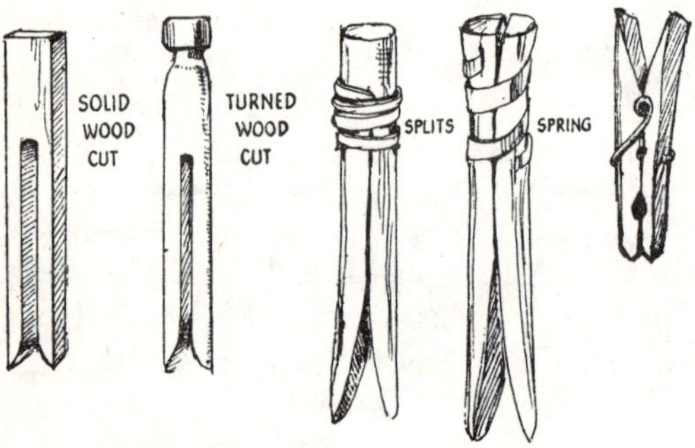

IMPROVED CLOTHES-PEG.

THE following description of an improved clothes-peg is given by the *American Artisan.* It consists of two jaws, each formed with a handle, and connected by a bent spring. Each of the jaws has a semi-cylindrical recess, as shown, and one has a rubber tooth D, which fits into a corresponding recess in the other jaw. The round hole fits over the clothes-line. The clothes are held by the rubber tooth D below the line, or the goods may be held by the grip of the pin itself upon the line. In either case, the cloth does not come in contact with the metal, and, therefore, is not soiled by such contact. The rubber tooth being flexible, it is claimed that the goods will not be torn.

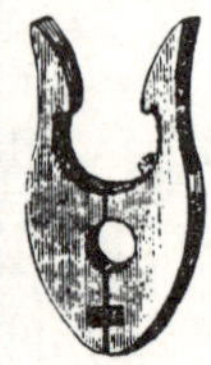

These used to be made by bodgers working in the woods and were sold wholesale by the long thousand to the retail shops, who retailed them by the dozen. Then, for a time, the gypsies had almost a monopoly of the trade, and used to make a very good split peg (i.e. split with the grain of the wood). These they sold in "lines" pegged onto two straight willow wands.

Unfortunately they have taken to making pegs whose unreliable heads are bound with scraps of tin. This tin soon rusts, and rust marks on linen are indelible. The modern spring peg, of plastic, is neat and efficient and will probably out-last the plastic clothes-line (if authors and office workers do not sneak them for paper clips).

"TIED" DRYING AND EARLY PLEATING

This probably accounts for the crepe effect of the eleventh-century ladies' gowns. The effect is shown by all MSS. illuminations of the period.

In some cases it looks like an elaborate smocking, yet in the few drawings of the garments when *not* worn it seems to be quite a plain fabric.

The early loosely-woven fine-linen fabric (or very thin wool) would lend itself to this treatment and it seems to be generally accepted by historians of costume that it was much used. The garment was twisted tightly while wet and the long damp "rope" was tied tightly in lines, closing or crossing, as the subsequent creased pattern was worked out.

Tied work

MEDIÆVAL PERMANENT PLEATS

In connection with this "tied" and "tent" drying many "permanent pleaters" were used in mediæval times. Resin, now used commercially, was not unknown then. Some was imported with the costlier spices and gums, so was not likely to be used by the household, but the gum that exudes from old pear and apple trees was used to set inks and "fine" wines, so it would most probably be tried out by the washerwoman and used to stiffen the fine gauzes and veils.

The conventional fold of these fine white draperies is shown clearly, on many manuscript illuminations and paintings. This transparent, knife-edged effect is quite different from the folds obtained by the use of thicker starch.

DRYING CLOTHES INDOORS

The open hearth and central chimney were not conducive to drying indoors. Hams could be hung by the smoke hole and take on a fine black anti-fly finish, but with the wide open fireplaces where the smoke rises direct, clothes can only be dried at spit level.

It is not until the closed range (or at least the partially enclosed fire) that airing racks across the ceiling became general.

Exceptions were the tall stone chimney faces with sloped cowls that were built first in castles and later in Elizabethan manors, but such grand living-rooms would not be so used. There is a charming picture showing a baby being bathed while auntie airs a towel and napkin before a log fire in the state bedroom—but for the small householder "Full sooty was her bower and eke her hall" and this drying difficulty was one reason for the accumulation of washing during the winter months.

CLOTHES RACKS

The engraving shown below, which appeared in the *Scientific American* in 1862 or 1863, represents a very useful American invention for hanging ironed clothes upon and also for hanging garments when not in use otherwise.

Improved clothes dryer and rack, 1862

PULLEY LINES

"Everybody knows (of course I am speaking now of the working classes) how annoying and dangerous to health it is to have to dry clothes on a washing-day in a house where children and grown-up people are alike exposed to the steamy atmosphere, and colds, coughs, etc., can scarcely be avoided where the old plan of drying clothes is adopted, viz., placing them on horses near the fire. The next better plan is to throw a line across the room, but even this is very inconvenient. . . ."

1872

The pulley clothes airer, that hung from the ceiling and could be pulled up and down, was *not* a very early invention. There must always have been clothes-racks overhead, just as there were always racks for drying out the sides of bacon, or hanging the laver bread up to stiffen. I have seen very old oak scantlings secured *between* the beams of old low cottage ceilings, but their strips of wood were fixtures, and polished with long usage. The pulley-cord arrangement, so popular in the north, needed the higher ceilings of the north. Also, it had perforce to await adequate chimneys to carry off the soot and smuts. Dried herrings could be smoked under the rafters of a thatch, but it was no place for clean linen.

The illustration here (*below*) shows a simple old cottage airer, such as was frequently constructed from a barrel top sawn across and pierced with holes to take the poles. The pulley wheels were mounted on long carriers which were thrust upwards through the kitchen ceiling

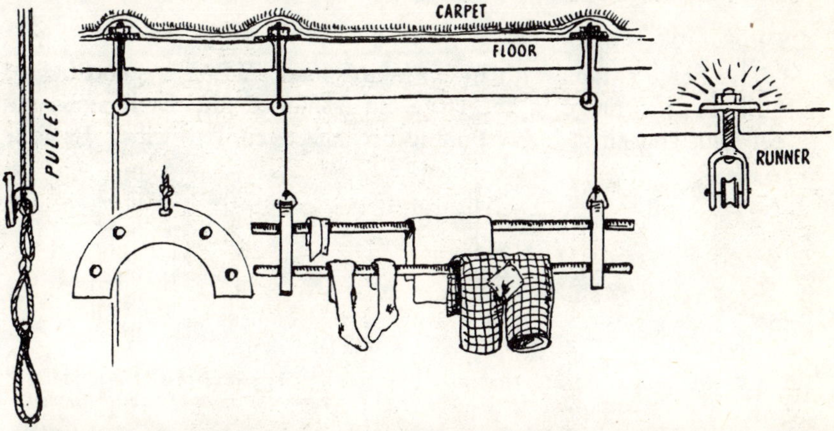

and secured by bolts upon the floor above, this arrangement causing strange sepulchral reevings and rattlings below the bed of the uninitiated sleeper.

The end mountings for these airers can now be bought at iron-mongers, usually complete with the three pulleys and a wall hook.

MEDIÆVAL CLOTHES RAILS

These long pulley hangers bring back to full circle the earliest mediæval arrangement of "rod, pole or perch". They were called "perches" (and when hawking was a fashionable sport were so used for the owner's special birds). These perches were held out, away from the wall, and over them hung the long clothing, cloaks, etc. (The chain-mail, caps, hoods and helmets went onto the ends.)

The enclosing of this perch-for-clothes by a wooden screen begins the ward-robe, or guard-robe (also one of the tactful names for the mediæval privy, or, as we would call it, "cloakroom"). In those days when shared bedrooms were usual, it may have sometimes been so used on cold and draughty nights!

THE HORSE OR MAIDEN

The horse shrank with its shrinking load. When it stood before the high iron range in the large old-fashioned kitchen it stood six feet high and aired heavy double bed sheets six feet wide. Its four

A homely cottage "Maiden" whose arms aired clothes

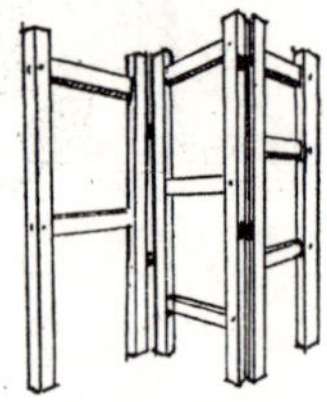

Six-foot clothes "Horse" to carry the sheets of an establishment

strong folds were usually double-hinged with oiled leather. Today a light little three-foot single-fold horse with metal hinges stands before the electric fire to hold "smalls" and recently there have been ingenious expanding horses that rise in overlapping tiers to cope with the "drip dry" situation.

FURNACE SLIDES FOR INDOOR DRYING

These were built into large private laundries or institutions. They were brick enclosures set above the furnace boilers and held long moveable rails on which the clothes were hung to dry and air. The great problem was to have the rails so large and smooth that they did not crease the drying clothes, and the sliding action so smooth that the clothes did not shake off as the slide rails were pushed in and out.

A net "floor", below the slides, caught clothes accidentally dropped off the rails, but if any small item fell right through into the furnace-room below, it was gone for ever! In my own recollection of our laundry slides, "Must ha' been lost off the slides, Ma'am!" was the regular excuse for odd socks. The entire brick enclosure was called the "*Airerer*".

SOCK AND BOOT DRIERS

The neat white socks and stockings of the 1780 to 1880 period were often dried on pottery moulds which could be filled with hot water for quick drying. A necessity when one's shoes were thin and low and one's ankles snowy white. It took months to knit a pair of ladies' stockings, with fancy patterns done in the finest cotton yarn.

The driers were sometimes made of white and sometimes of brown pottery. The characteristic narrow foot and square toe of Dickens' time distinguish them from the ornamental "bottle boots" (usually with corks) that can sometimes be found in old public houses.

Tin boot driers

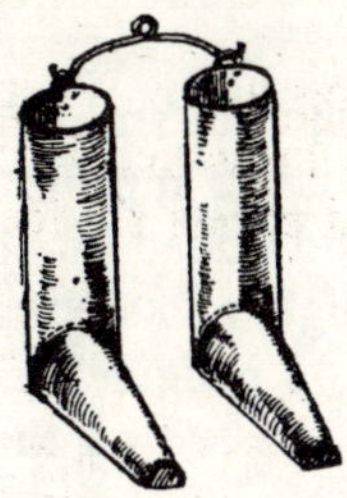

Pottery sock drier

STARCH

Arum maculatum

> "The most pure white starch is made from it (the root), but it is most hurtful to the hands of the laundress as it blistereth, and maketh the hands rugged and withall smarting."
>
> GERRARD

The Wild Arum, Lords and Ladies, Jack-in-Pulpit, Cuckoo Pint, Wake Robin, Starchwort, etc.

This plant has a long, interesting history (*see* page 366). It has been used in medicine for centuries, but somewhat dangerously, as the whole plant is poisonous. It was a cruel jest to trick a simpleton into biting the root, as the least touch of the sap gives an intense acid burning that lasts painfully for hours.

However, if crushed and washed in running water and then dried, the root produces a fine starch. Some Portland women specialized in this craft and sold the product as Portland sago (it is so listed in groceries of 1880). This was the basis of salop, a very fashionable beverage of the early 1700's, when it was enriched with eggs and cream. By the 1800's it had been replaced by tea and chocolate and became the standard drink of working men, when it was made of cheaper (and less dangerous) ingredients and was enriched with rum and sugar. With the end of salop and the arrival of the cheaper imported Indian arrowroot, Portland sago ceased to be made.

As a laundry starch, it dates from the sixteenth century, or possibly earlier. It was used to stiffen fine lace, especially the fine thread laces used for the edges of ruffs and cuffs. I have been unable to discover whether the term "a rose starcher" referred to the fine rose point laces, or to the redness of the hands of the laundress. Gerrard seems to suggest the latter, as the work was often done while the starch was boiling hot. This may have caused the rose red hands of the rose starcher. Poland starch was recommended in 1815 and all starches were to be very well boiled and strained before use.

It is interesting that lace, made with fine but strong linen threads, was washed more vigorously than the new Indian muslins of cotton thread. These were starched and then clapped and pulled into shape, not ironed. The starcher had to hold them up to the light and see that she had clapped every particle of starch out of the texture. I imagine that the embroidered Indian muslins, then so treasured, were pressed on the wrong side over a soft woollen cloth.

Starch and State

In the early days, most starch had a cereal basis. So, for a small commodity, starch caused a large amount of legislation. For example, in 1606 "Proclamation is made" that great mischief has resulted from the recall of the Monopoly granted by the Late Queen for the making of starch. Flour is consumed that could be used for food, and contagious diseases occasioned by the noxious smells from the making of starch. Therefore its Making in the Realm is to be utterly taken away." But in 1619 we find starch is again being made in the realm, and after a complication of disbursements and benefits, "which concern also the Customs of Ireland, or in default thereof the Customs of England", it is pointed out that "His Majesty had received *no* benefit either by importation or making". For the starch-makers "make such quantities that the Realm cannot well vent it".

The battles of the starch trades are always between the cost of living and the dictates of fashion. Large quantities of starch could be used freely by dyers, printers, hair powder and wig-makers, laundries and the trades using paste, till hard times and taxation raised the price of bread. Then there was an outcry against it. When starch was imported, duty made it expensive; when it was made in the realm it brought in no revenue.

Probably this continual see-saw of trouble caused the continuous research into materials for starch, and the laundry developed such a variety of stiffeners that almost every material and texture developed its own speciality. For the starches proper, all cereals were tried, including imported rice. Later, potatoes were used, chiefly in household laundries.

To make potato starch: Peel and grate several large raw potatoes into a basin of cold water and stir well. Let them steep, squeezing the pulp in your hands, then pour off the water and let it stand till the starch can be seen settled at the bottom. Pour off the water and dry out the starch.

Starch was sold loose for centuries, but during the Victorian period a special Glenfield starch was sold in packets and advertised as being "used in the Royal laundries". There was also a special starch recommended for furnishing fabrics (chintz?) as being made of white flour and specially good for gloss.

Stiffeners—other than Starch

Milk was used for lace, gum-arabic for nets and silks, and glue (size) for dark-coloured goods and woollens.

Parchment cuttings, bought cheaply from the law stationer, were stewed down till thick, strained through muslin and the resultant clear jelly was used to stiffen gauze and veils and fine clear muslins, etc. We believe this parchment size was used by the fourteenth-century ladies for the crisp veils that float from their steeple head-dresses.

STARCH YELLOW

"Villainous saffron."

All's Well That Ends Well

> "One Turner, a tirewoman and a Court Bawd, invented the use of yellow starch for ruffs. She was later hung for being concerned in the murder of Sir Thomas Overbury and went to the Scaffold wearing one of her yellow starched ruffs, which put them quite out of fashion."
>
> STUBBS, *Anatomie of Abuses*

This was an item of interest in one of the most dramatic and horrible executions of the eighteenth century.

A Mrs. Anne Turner, a pretty blonde widow, left by her husband to the protection of Sir Arthur Mainwaring (by whom she had children), was the product of that curious age of brilliance and vice, when the most coarse brutality underlay an exquisitely polished society.

On the shady fringe of this society Anne existed for the delight of many. She seems to have been trained as a dressmaker. (At this period the tradition of a resident dressmaker, or tailor, was arranged for by the month, the expert living and working in the household.) This job gave Anne the opportunity to visit many varied wealthy families, and so it was because of her trade that she invented a yellow starch, which tinted and stiffened the ruffles and laces of her clients. Because she made it exclusive and expensive, it became very fashionable, and a source of good income to Anne.

Later, Anne designed costumes for plays and masques and came to move amidst a society that was a strange mixture of intellectual attainment and light-hearted futility. Probably she did make and sell love philtres and provide questionable medicines, for in a period when abortion was a stage jest and paid adoption simple, such things were common. Poor Anne lacks the support of the kindly pen with which Defoe portrays Moll Flanders, and the disreputable side of her character lost nothing in its later publicity. She became invaluable in the clique that arranged for the poisoning of Sir Thomas Overbury. The trial, in which she was prosecuted, caused an enormous sensation, and the poor, pretty catspaw, who had been used by so many, for so much pleasure, was hanged, wearing her own gay yellow ruff.

THE FIREPROOFING OF FABRICS

This was a serious consideration in the crinoline period, when young ladies wore clouds of soft, inflammable muslin in rooms with open coal fires. The swaying motion of these huge circular skirts created a draught that fanned the flames. The instruction to "lie down and roll out the fire" was almost impossible and the size of the hearthrug hopelessly inadequate!

A preparation of zinc was sold by some firms, but the usual method was to dissolve alum in the starch water. Poorer folk were advised to use whitening instead of starch, or mixed with it, but there was *no* compulsory trade fire-proofing of materials. 'Rushlight cages" were made to safeguard the bedroom rushlights and the high nursery fireguard that hooked onto the mantelpiece was an invention of the crinoline period.

IRONING

"You want to see my Pa? I 'spose?
Wal no; I come . . . designin . . .
To see my Ma? shes sprinklin clo'es
Agin tomorrows irn'ing."

Biglow Papers

"'I don't know what is the matter with these clothes; I cannot make 'em look smooth.'

"'Why they're bone dry!' said Nancy, plunging her hand into the bucket. 'You haven't sprinkled 'em have you? . . . You just get me a bowl of water! and we'll have 'em done in no time.'"

E. WETHERED, *Wide Wide World*

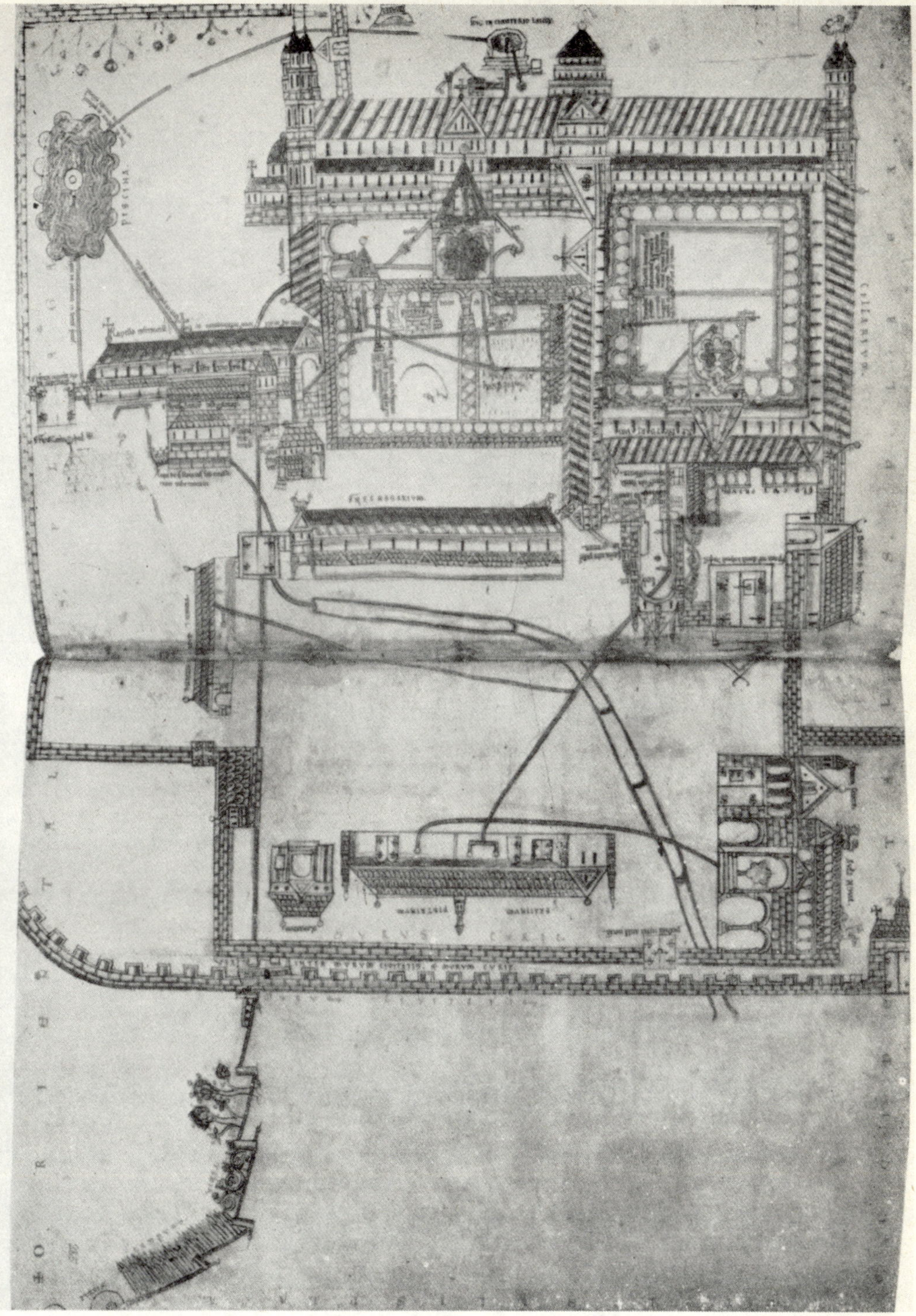

36. Early household water supplies usually ran continuously between source and outlet, thus avoiding alternating pressures by stop taps within the buildings. In "conducting" the water through the buildings, the "easiest flow" was taken, utilising natural declivities and avoiding abrupt turns.

37. *Washing hand-woven linen in the 14th century*

On the extreme left the "boiler" with handles; jugs alongside for dipping up the hot water and replenishing with cold.

Note: The linen is *not* being boiled.

Centre: A woman works at a "bucking bench" and several "under bucks" (shallow oval tubs) hold relays of linen "in process". The barrel on the right probably holds a washing fluid or "ley". Behind, two women using "bats" or "boles" beat the linen upon a sturdy bench.

On the right bank of the stream are three "whitesters": one bare-legged worker soaks the linen in the stream, another spreads it out flat on the grass and a man (far distance) throws water over the linen to help the process by keeping it wet and flat for the wind and sun to bleach it.

On the left bank, one woman hangs up the linen to dry, two others pull and stretch, and "taunt" the linen smooth and straight for folding, and another carries a basketful (on her head) back to the house.

38. View of London Waterworks and Westminster Bridge. Note the amount of river traffic plying between "stairs", i.e. landing places.

IRONING THE ELIZABETHAN RUFF

Autolycus, in his pedlar's pack, speaks of "Poking sticks of steel". These were used in getting up the starched ruffs. Previously, bone and wood sticks were used and the effect was obtained by letting the damp fabric dry over the sticks. "About the sixteenth year of Queen Elizabeth's reign" is given as the date when the making of steel poking sticks came into use. The steel sticks were much quicker to use, as they could be heated in the fire and then used to iron the creases into the ruffs.

The old-fashioned bone and wood arrangements continued in use for centuries, long before and after the specialized work on the fashion for ruffs. Pleated and folded effects were obtained for many caps and bonnets, especially in communities of nuns and sisterhoods, and for widows' caps, pillowcases, etc.

The illustration shows some of these arrangements.

The poking sticks are said to have provided the names: peck-a-diller, piccadillas, piccadilly. The street may have taken its name from the mansions of the rich merchants who wore these ruffs. It could be a pleasant position for a town house, on the hillside overlooking the Thames above the City of Westminster.

Ironing poking sticks

A form of box iron burnt charcoal, and a most handsome box iron of German make followed the sewing-machine into the heart of Africa! This had space for a brisk fire lit within it and air holes above and below. The proud owner swung it around his head to fan the flame, or waved it gently to restore the glow. The spent ash was emptied out through a neat damper at the end of the iron. This model carried its own stool to rest upon, had a bright red wooden handle, on a gilt mount of elaborately designed cast iron work, and was indeed a Jehovah among box irons.

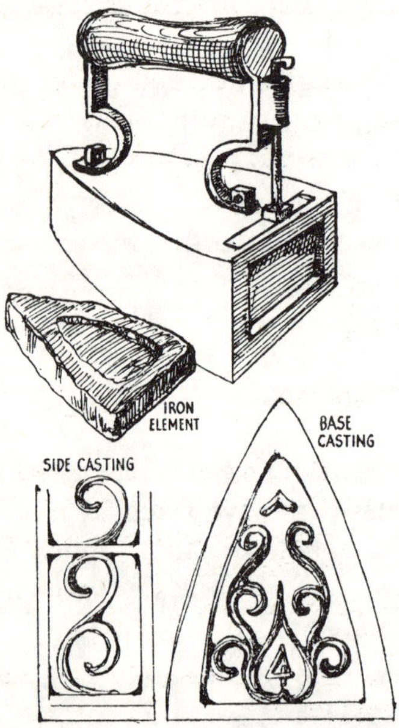

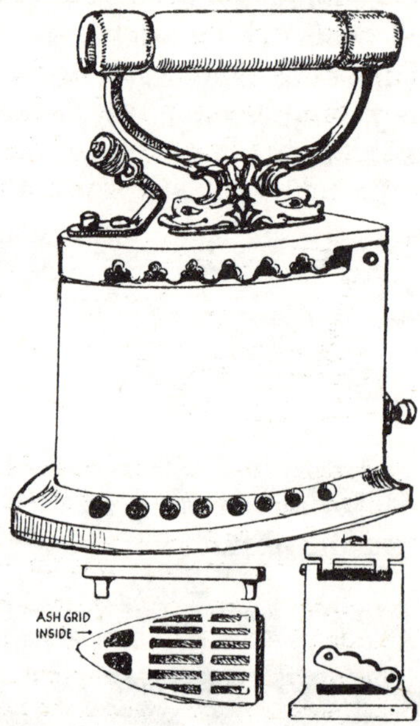

It was structurally necessary to raise the red-hot "element" from direct contact with the floor of the "box", but why such an elaborate design should have been cast *inside* the box, where it could only be seen by raising the door and peering within, is a problem. The figure 4 incorporated in the design was the official weight stamp (found on all irons).

Such a box iron was often kept in the nursery and borrowed by visiting maids to press guests' garments crumpled after a journey.

THE FLAT IRON

Surely this needs no description, though the electric and gas irons have replaced it in all but remote country places.

In their time the flat irons roosted like rooks in rows along the wash-house shelf, or clustered, an iron rookery, over the specially designed heating stones in all laundries. They were of various weights. The heavy for thick materials, the light for muslins. They never actually touched the coals or flames of the open fire, but were set to heat on the tops of kitchen ranges or later over a gas ring. The base was kept bright by rubbing it over fine emery paper while hot, and if necessary the surface was cleaned by passing it quickly over a wax candle and then rubbing it bright on some rags. A folded piece of clean brown paper, well waxed, was often used by laundry workers wishing to give a fine gloss to some starched linen. Miracles of crisp glazed firmness were produced on cuffs and bosoms of white shirts, with no more complicated tool than an ordinary flat iron off a small ironing stone.

The last of the old flat irons, roughed by neglect, carried on for years with a face-saving plated "shoe" clipped over its sole. This made it usable, but the fine action of the polished toe of the iron was lost. It was a makeshift that is just worth a mention.

(a)

(b)

(c)

(a) Each maker had his own way of securing the handle to the iron. The drawing shows a "one-piece strip of metal" folded to form the drip and "set" into the block. A more common design was in three pieces, a hollow rod and two "ends". The problem was the bolting down into the main block.

(b) A polishing iron—for glazing chintz, or collars and cuffs and "bosoms". The rounded base was kept bright and lightly waxed.

(c) The ironing stone, usually stood on a stone slab, was heated by coal and coke (and frequently had a tea kettle boiling on top)!

THE GLAZING IRON

The chintz, polishing or glossing iron was a form of the flat iron having a rounded base. This iron was used to give a high polish to the stiff, very specially starched surface of chintz or linen. The material was washed and starched in the ordinary way, but for glazing a bowl of thin starch was kept at the worker's left hand and sponged onto the surface of the material, directly in front of the polishing iron. Wax was used (a little) on the iron surface to prevent the damp starch from sticking and the rocking polishing action was carried on by the right hand while the left applied the damp glaze. Glazing chintz was very hard work and workers able to offer this craft could command very high wages. Sometimes a man came in to do this work, but ordinarily it was a specially-skilled member of the laundry team who was responsible for "bosoms" and glazed chintz.

THE ITALIAN IRON (*often miscalled a goffer iron*)

This belongs to the ribbon period—the "knot of ribbons", or the "perky bow", or the bonnet strings.

Everyone knows the difficulty of ironing a made-up bow so as to restore the rounded loop without giving two creases on either side (*see* illustration).

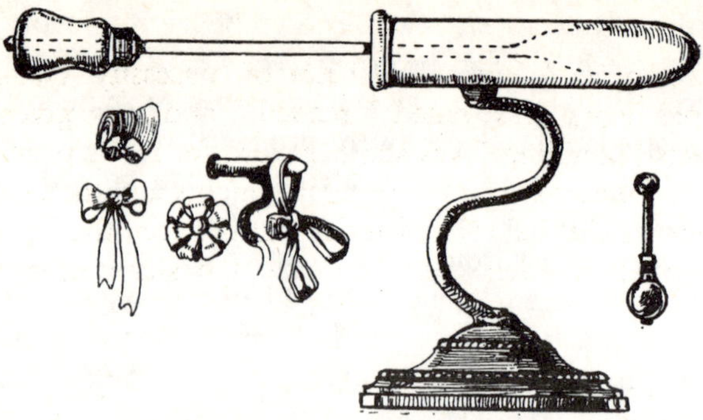

So the Italian iron was indispensable in a period which used ribbons lavishly. Another point in its favour was its cleanliness and easy heating. Most Italian irons were made with two pokers (or heaters) though few have survived with even one. The poke bonnet period depended for its charm on the big bow that tied under the chin and the ends that floated down to the waist. These bonnet strings could be run over the Italian iron without spoiling the gloss of the silk and the creases made by the bow could be smoothed out at once. It was the universal distribution of the poke bonnet that accounts for the remarkable number of Italian irons still in existence.

They had good use also in "getting up" frills. Everyone who has ironed knows the difficulty of getting the nose of the iron up into the top of a frill. With the edge of the frill towards you, the nose of the Italian iron could poke quite up into the tight gathers at the top of a frill and the "passing over" on the rounded iron gave an undulating even "waving" to the frill. The "Italian" was a handy little iron and very useful for all curved work, but it should not be confused with the goffering tongs, which gave a tight pleated finish.

The rose bow, or rosette, at one time so fashionable on shoes, would require restoration by hand poking with a small short Italian iron.

The French iron

The French iron much resembled the Italian iron, but with a rounded mushroom top, sometimes attached to a long stalk for heating in the stove. Sometimes the top only went to the stove and was fitted on to the top of the stalk. This iron's chief use was the rounding out of puffed sleeves and inserting ornamental puffs.

THE GAUFER

This iron belonged to tight frills not of necessity Victorian. The earliest goffered work was called "reeded" and was given its close "quilling" effect ("quilling" was another word for it) by packing the wet material over and under reeds. Other arrangements laid the strips between two upright boards that held the material taut between the "reeds" which were actually small wooden sticks, the size and shape of wooden meat skewers.

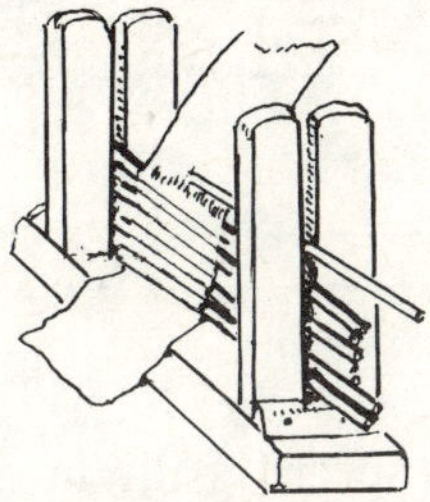

There was a great advance in the craft when metal "reeds" were used, as they could be run in hot, which speeded up the work and led to the invention of the Victorian goffer irons—or goffer tongs.

In the 1850's a wheel goffer was invented. It was simply two interlocking cog wheels, through which the ribbon could be run while the cogs, turned by a handle, pleated up the wet material. Most of the quilling and reeding was a wet process until the sixteenth century. Not until the Elizabethan ruffs and frills developed was heat used direct. The contemporary "monkey laundry" shows that process perfectly!

The "goffer irons" or "double tongs" remained in use until late Victorian times and in some districts until the Edwardian period. They were used in pairs; one pair heating on the stove while the second was in use. Being thin and light, they cooled and heated very swiftly and woe betide the finisher who neglected to test the hot tongs upon a scrap of waste material. Eight little black slits would result from a scorch, yet if the iron was not sufficiently hot the frill would be only crumpled, not stiff and crisp and corrugated.

Children's bonnet frills, petticoat frills and neck and sleeve ruffles were the first main gofferings; pillow case frills probably the last we remember. The last pair of goffer tongs that I had the honour to use were brought from a Welsh household, so it is reasonable that the delightful Welsh caps that Borrow found pinned to the curtains of the inn at Devil's Bridge were elaborately "got up" with a goffer iron. (The Italian iron would be used to give a fine undulating effect to a frill but it was not a goffer iron in the tightly-corrugated-pleating sense of the word.)

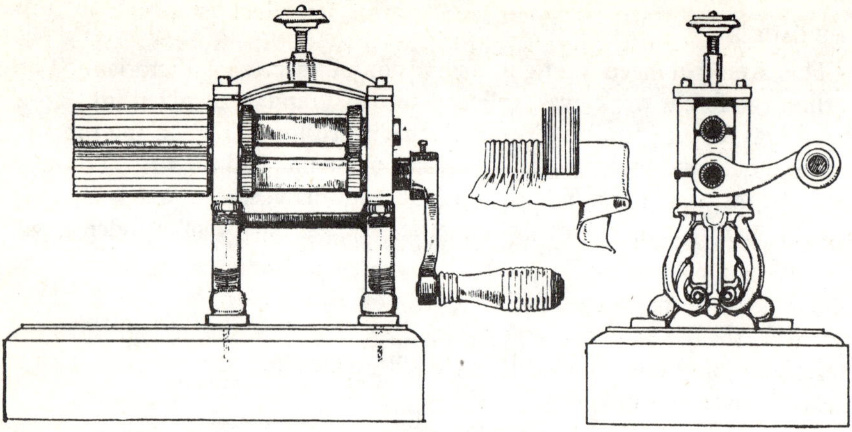

The wheel goffer of 1850

SPECIAL SKILLS—THE CRAVAT.

There have always been special skills in getting up special items of laundry. At one period it was the Elizabethan ruff; in Victorian and Edwardian days it was "bosoms", as men's shirt fronts were then called. Collars were always a test of skill, but the high cravats of George IV's time were most astonishingly difficult. The cravat was a fold of linen, cut on the cross, anything from six to ten inches wide, but it had to be folded over (making it three or four inches wide in the centre part) so that the double fold (unpressed) came under the chin, giving a smooth edge that did not chafe. The two ends had to be folded in again on both edges to make the flat band that crossed at the back, came around, and tied in a bow in front. The characteristic folds came below the chin only; the sides rose high around the ears. It was quite usual for a man to crumple and discard half a dozen cravats before he got the exact adjustment that pleased him.

By comparison the dress tie of today is simple, as it is separate from the collar. The cravat was collar and tie combined, and required great skill. The modern hunting stock is a little like the cravat in shape, but is soft and pliant. The cravat was stiff and could only be creased *once*.

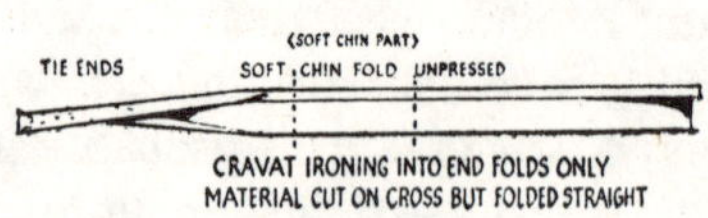

TRANSITION TO LAUNDRY AND BOILING

Washing, 1870—*the Transition Period*

The transition from Bucking to Washing and Boiling (as three separate processes) is explained in a note of 1857: "Boiling AFTER WASHING is considered necessary by some laundresses. Its effect is to extract any remains of dirt left in the PRECEDING PROCESSES, and ALSO TO TAKE OUT THE SOAP. Whether dirty or clean, without it (i.e. boiling) the clothes are supposed to smell disagreeably." (This would synchronise with the disputes over fish oils being used by soap boilers.)

It is impossible to say exactly when the old usages of bucking and washing combined. Rows of small houses each had its separate clothes boiler with a small fire below. The "copper" started wash day in the long East End streets, as well as in country labourers' outhouses. I remember heating such a boiler to obtain a hot bath, when I lived in Harford Street, Stepney, in 1928. The water took about half an hour to heat up, and one scooped it out of the boiler into the bath tub with a round, galvanized tin scoop.

These instructions, "Clothes, to wash and boil" from a book of 1870, show the old technique being carried over into the new boiling process: "½ lb. yellow soap, 1 lb. soda, ¼ lb. lime. Put the lime and 3 quarts of boiling water to stand overnight. Boil the soap and soda in 3 pints of water and add it.

"The clothes are to be soaked in a tub of this mixture for 24 hours and next day wrung out, *before being boiled in fresh soapy water*. (This is the new boiling process.) Then, if clean, they are to be well rinsed."

The feeling for the old divided technique is there, but the wash has now become one process.

THE COMING OF THE FREE STANDING "COPPER"

The laundry boiler that developed as bucking ceased, was usually a built-in cauldron of copper (and it is still spoken of as "the copper" though later it was frequently made of zinc). The brick surround was usually mortared and plastered with fire cement (like the brick oven) and the small firehole below was fitted with an ash pan and door, but the boiler differed from the bread oven by having a flue chimney, as it was usually heated by coal.

In the late 1800's mobile, free-standing boilers were designed, some models being set on wheels, but the best-known was the plain circular boiler, enclosed in an outer circular case, with a fire-box below and tin chimney behind. These boilers, with their fitted lids, were adopted by Soyer for the army cooks and used in the Crimea. They remain the "camp boiler" well known today. A few years later the circulating washing machine is coming!

A SUPPLEMENTARY CIRCULATOR

". . . A form of washing apparatus which is not, I think, generally known as well as it should be, for it is correct in principle and most

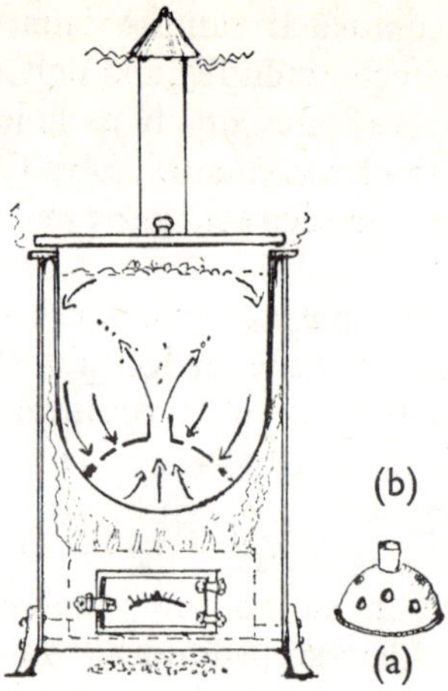

efficacious in use. By this means a constant current of boiling soap-suds is kept passing through the clothes until all dirt is washed out of them. . . .

The fire under the boiler being lighted, the space at a. boils first, and the heated water is forced up the tube b. and passes out in the direction of the arrows in a large spray, and keeps circulating up the tube and down through the clothes as long as the heat is maintained. The apparatus is made of galvanized iron, and costs but a few shillings, and neither wears nor tears the clothes."

DOCTOR MEDICINAE, 1885

PURCHASES FOR THE "PRIVATE LAUNDRY" OF THE LARGE COUNTRY HOUSE

While there remained enough large country houses, with their own wide domestic communities and big laundry buildings, items "for the laundry" were listed in the accounts with as much regularity as groceries.

The housekeeper would confer with the cook when she undertook the monthly replenishment of the storeroom. She would confer with the head housemaid for the cleaning materials and the laundry maid as to requirements for the washhouse. Stableman, groom, gardener and all the varied departments of the complicated community, each had their own specialized administration, the less responsible workers reporting to the one above, the driving reins of the teams being finally gathered up into the skilled hands of the head groom, the butler and the housekeeper. (A hierarchy that had held its unchanged tradition since the Middle Ages.)

Of course, inter-community wars arose, when some stable boy purloined the housemaid's beeswax, or the kitchenmaid pinched extra emery cloth from the harness cupboard, and skilled indeed was the housekeeper who never ran out of blacking for the boot boy, or did not find hoards of forgotten blue bags accumulated on the laundry shelves. (Laundry orders were usually despatched monthly and only revised yearly. But the housekeeper's "order books" for any household are safe keys to the political and economic life of the country, keys that attest to the general honesty or deceit, industry or idleness, thrift or dissipation of the people of the period.

Appearances may deceive and contemporary reports mislead, but the housekeeper's order book was the budget for the household, and the household keys were ever the keys of the chancellor of the exchequer.

A CATALOGUE OF 1790

Burgess of the Strand, Italian and oil warehouseman, stocked everything you could name and had an additional "Sundries for the Laundry" list. This included loose blue for washing, starch of several kinds, gum-arabic for stiffening (that would be for the large square bonnet veils of the period), scouring balls for removing wine stains (topical trouble) and "for those curios in lamp oils, for Music Rooms", they had oils that "can be depended upon to burn silently and without smell or smoke". (Some new air-conditioned lamps, both for light and heating, were invented at this period.)

This juxtaposition of lamp oils and laundry work is suggestive for, among all the household catastrophes likely to flood the laundry with washing, a lamp left smoking was the worst! Usually lamps were well supervised, and seldom (at first) used in unoccupied rooms, but with the advent of the oil-heating stove and the "Moderator" for cold bedrooms, greasy smuts could fill an entire room within an hour! The heat drove the dirt *into* all fabrics and, in some cases, the washerwoman had to resort to soaking the whole mass of the bed curtains in oil, to *loosen* the deposited grime, before she could begin to wash them.

THE WASHERWOMAN COMES IN

A clap book song—about the time of the Great Exhibition when hopeful amusement was aroused by honours being conferred upon certain traders and artisans for their excellent *work*, rather than their heredity worth.

Going out a-washing

"Toiling, boiling all the day,
Rubbing, slushing, sloshing,
Firsting, bursting, everyway,
Going out a-washing.

I gets my eighteen pence a day
(With grub and gin however),
As much as I can put away
To keep my strength together.

Weak folks say it is all a sin[1]
And at us get reviling,
But—there's nothing like a drop of gin
To keep the copper boiling!

I could take the starch out of a few!
In fact to none I'll give in,
For I'll get up He and She shirts too
Against any woman living.

Men's frills and collars, snowy white!
What's make them look so winning.
Men ought to bless us, day and night
For getting up their linen!

THE "WASH" PREPARES TO GO OUT

"Washing is in the present day seldom done at home, unless the family reside in the country, for drying ground in London and other large towns is wanting. The laundress, therefore, fetches the soiled linen on Mondays and returns it on Saturday. The charges for washing differ in different places. In London it is possible to get it done for 1*s.* per dozen, including everything; but this is not the price of *good* washing. Ordinary London charges are 2*d.* each the large articles of underclothing, except petticoats, which vary from 4*d.* to 6*d.* or 8*d.* according to trimming; 1*d.* the stockings per pair, collars 1*d.* each, cuffs 1*d.* per pair, tablecloths 4*d.*, kitchen do. 3*d.*, table napkins 1*d.* each, sheets 4*d.* per pair, towells 9*d.* per dozen, handkerchiefs ½*d.* each, fish cloths 1*d.* each, counterpanes 1*s.* each, curtains 2*s.* each, etc., etc. Servants are usually allowed 1*s.* 3*d.* a week each for their own washing.

"But many trifling articles may be washed at home even in London, and the house-mother who can do her own lace, or the costly trifles belonging to the baby, will find that she saves much more than the pence charged for washing.

"When washing at home. A woman is generally hired to assist the servants where there is no washing machine. Her wages are in

[1] Teetotal abstainers were waging war on the prevalent drunkenness of the period and (like all reformers) were the butt of ridicule.

London 2*s*. per day and she expects beer three times a day and gin-and-water at night. Everything is put ready for her before she arrives."

ROSS MURRAY, *Modern Householder*, 1870

This home washing using outside help continued for long, because public laundries were built for the lower classes (*see* page 244) and Ladies considered that their clothes would be carried down to these public washhouses and washed with the *same* water in the *same* tub as the washer-woman and her husband's own working clothes!

LAUNDRY LIST FOR FAMILY OF FOUR AND TWO SERVANTS. DATE ABOUT 1880

A Fortnight's Wash

2 prs. coloured wool stockings
7 silk hanks., 20 white cotton
20 neckcloths and collars
4 frilled collars and tuckers
8 night caps (silk?)
2 muslins
5 cambric gowns
2 flannel waistcoats
6 flannel petticoats
2 prs. white woollen stockings
5 coloured (calico) gowns
10 white shirts
10 white petticoats
30 shifts
26 prs. cotton stockings
8 pinafores
2 coats
2 cotton night caps
2 prs. trousers (pants?)
4 prs. drawers
4 fine table cloths
12 table naps
4 tray cloths
4 breakfast cloths
2 prs. fine sheets
4 pillow cases fine
20 towels
2 kitchen table cloths
6 glass and 8 kitchen cloths, 6 dusters
4 knife cloths, 4 kitchen hand towels
3 prs. common sheets
3 coarse pillow cases

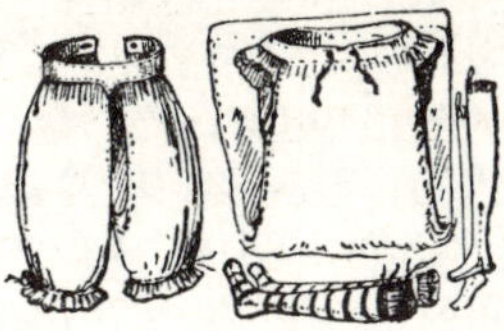

There are ten night caps, but nightdresses are listed with "shifts". Thirty would be about the right number for six people, for two weeks. Apparently the calico "drawers" are only changed once. If you allow two white petticoats for the two servants, that leaves two a week for the ladies and four for the children. The "4 knife cloths" need explanation: before stainless steel, knives were not washed up with the table service, but *wiped* dry and collected into a knife box (a good many long shallow boxes with sliding lids now called salt boxes were originally the knife boxes). This box was taken to the back kitchen or scullery where a manservant or a knives-and-boots boy cleaned them by rubbing them too and fro on a knife board sprinkled with brick dust. He then dusted them, and they were returned to the pantry, where the fingermarks were removed from the handles. Knife machines that cleaned a dozen knives at a time, by a rotary brush charged with emery powder, were used in all large establishments. It is a small detail, but knife cloths mark the pre-stainless steel laundry list as clearly as the scarlet lipstick cloth marks the present-day list.

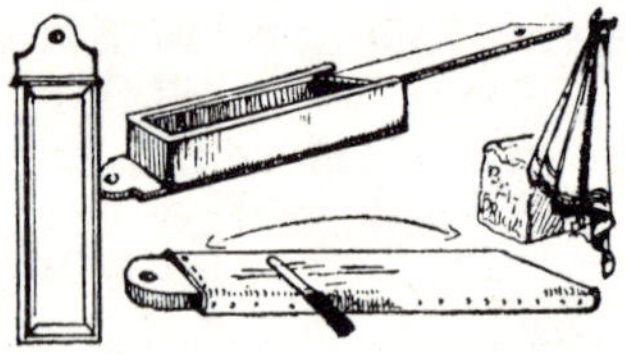

A CONTEMPORARY MIDDLE-CLASS COMMENT UPON THE SITUATION

> "Now before closing this subject, we must point out that the great want of the age in London is Laundresses. We feel convinced that if some respectable young women would club together to get the implements for the work, such as tubs, etc., etc., and really wash and iron *well*, returning the clean clothes correctly and at an early day, they would make their fortunes. At present the laundresses are inefficient, wash and iron badly, scrub out the clothes with brushes, burn them with chemical bleaching powders, bring them home by driblets, frequently retaining clothes from one week's wash to the next, during which time they are said on good authority to pawn or wear them. The cry of the need of good laundry work is loud and universal, and the *dread of infection from the miserable places in which London laundresses and manglers live is intensifying this desire*. That a fortune might be made by a good laundry, we feel convinced. For when ladies do things, they always do their best, induced to do so by a fine sense of honour. If ladies saw that the things were washed perfectly, dried in sweet open grounds, ironed well, carefully sorted, and duly returned to their owners, such a laundry would be a certain success in the present day, and if the new washing and wringing machines were used, would be still more profitable."
>
> *Quoted from a household book of* 1880

These were washing problems of the new urban middle class. Out in the country the farm and cottage still washed at home and the large country house continued to use its own specially-built private laundry.

WASHING LACE

"Of course, your Ladyship knows that such lace must never be starched or ironed. Some people wash it in sugar and water, and some in coffee to make it the right yellow colour; but I myself have a very good receipt for washing it in milk. . . . 'Well, ma'am, I had tacked it together . . . and put it to soak in milk, when unfortunately, I left the room; on my return, I found pussy on the table choking! . . . At first, I pitied her, and said, 'Poor pussy! poor pussy!' till, all at once, I looked and saw the cup of milk empty. . . . I believe I was provoked enough to give her a slap, which did no good, but only helped the lace down. . . . And then a thought struck me; and I rang the bell for my maid, and sent her to Mr. Hoggins, with my compliments, and would he be kind enough to lend me one of his top-boots for an hour? I did not think there was anything odd in the message; but Jenny said the young men in the surgery laughed as if they would be ill, at my wanting a top-boot. When it came, Jenny and I put pussy in, with her fore-feet straight down, so that they were fastened and could not scratch, and we gave her a teaspoonful of currant-jelly, in which (your Ladyship must excuse me) I had mixed some tartar emetic. . . . I could have kissed her when she returned the lace to sight, very much as it had gone down. Jenny had boiling water ready, and we soaked it and soaked it, and spread it on the lavender-bush in the sun, before I could touch it again, even to put it in milk. But now your ladyship would never guess that it had been in pussy's inside. . . ."

MRS. GASKELL, *Cranford*

This was (and is) a specialized craft and was highly paid in the days of expensive handmade lace. Today it can only be done for love and not for money. It is most tedious and difficult, as every single loop of thread has to be pinned (or sewn) and stretched separately. Some raised laces (and Irish crochet) had special small punch irons with which to raise the patterns, and bone pins, special shapes, to reform the leaves and flowers, as the work dried.

The washing was usually done around a flannel-wrapped bottle. Shaped collars and cuffs were tacked on to the flannel before it was sewn on to the bottle.

SPECIAL WASHING OF POKE BONNET VEILS

These were of lace, about a yard square, the top edge strengthened and often "worked" to take a fine draw thread, and the lower part of the "fall" sometimes of a beautiful and elaborate pattern.

The top edge was fastened along the top of the bonnet and allowed to hang down over the front so that it completely veiled the face. When the lady threw back her veil over the top it fluttered becomingly out behind.

The contemporary instructions for washing these delicate lacy squares was to "simmer them in soapy water, rinse and lightly stiffen with very clear starch or gum water. After stiffening they should be clapped between the hands and well shaken to clear the mesh, and the veil should be pinned out to dry flat, afterwards restoring the gloss by running the iron over it very lightly."

Nankeen Water Dye

Boil equal parts of anatto and common potash in water till dissolved. This "holland colour" was popular in early Victorian times. It was also obtained by boiling hay.

WASHING STRAW BONNETS

The washing of straw bonnets was a delicate matter, for they were usually constructed of the narrow English straw plait. This straw plait was in one length, of intricately woven, finely-split straws and the many yards needed for a large, face-shading bonnet were sewn together, round and round, shaping the bonnet from the centre of the crown outwards, and extending the oval brim forwards; a laborious craft.

Emigrant women were issued with a hank of the plait, straw needles and thread and a length of folded ribbon, so that they could sew their bonnets during the long voyage and wear them on arrival in Australia.[1] Salts of lemon and sulphur fumes were used to restore sun-burnt straw to its original creamy whiteness and bonnet dyes were sold to paint them brown and black, and restore the original crisp texture.

Panama and Leghorn straws were constructed by weaving and interlocking the fibre, and were expensive importations, but had advantages. In an advertisement of 1816 the firm of Frazers of Sloan Square, Chelsea, stated that they had now "Special Patent Peruvian Bonnets strongly recommended to Ladies for travelling, as they are the lightest and most durable ever introduced to the Public". They were "particularly for wear at the Sea Side, the Sea Air not having the least effect upon them. They are not easily put out of shape, *being worked from beginning to end without sewing*! Children may roll them on the grass without sustaining danger. . . . They [the Peruvian] are superior to the Leghorn, and *may be washed with soap and water*."

WASHING STRAW IN THE PLAIT

As straws are glossy outside and matt inside, the twists in a straw plait showed an uneven speckled effect. These plaits were called "singles".

[1] Voyage took about nine months.

To obtain a uniformly glossy straw the plait was worked in "doubles", that is, two of the flat split straws were lightly stuck together (frequently by being drawn through the lips of the worker) and plaited as a "double glossy" or "double matt", according to the fashion in demand.

In Buckingham and Bedfordshire straw-plaiting somewhat replaced the previous industry of lace-making. In both cases children began to learn the craft at three years old. It was one of those automatic occupations (like knitting) that have an almost mesmerizing effect. The work was poorly paid, but the entire population carried on doing it for years—only a few plaiters ever migrated to Luton to become bonnet makers.

The washing and bleaching of straw was a speciality of the "plait" district. They used tartar salts for bleaching (lime made the wood fibre too brittle). At Luton, after the plaits were sewn, the bonnets were "wet blocked" pressed and bleached with brimstone and sulphur fumes.

SPECIAL WASHING: THE GIFT CLOUTS FOR CHILD-BED USE

"But since, to Ladies, it hath Custome been
Linen to send, that travail and lye in;
To the nine Sempstresses, my former Friends,
I seu'd; but they had nought but shreds and ends.
At last, the jolliest of the three-times-three,
Rent the apron from her smock, and gave it me.
'Twas soft and gentle, subtly spun, no doubt,
Pardon y boldness, Madam; here's the Clout."

(*To a Lady with child that asked an old shirt.*)

Poems of R. LOVELACE

In villages nowadays the district nurse arranges supplies for a "lie in", but it is still a kindly gift to give pieces of old linen, such as sheets and towels which have worn thin and soft. Before sending these "clouts" they are boiled until every bit of starch is out of them and they are usually accepted as gladly as the good wishes they carry to the "Lady in the Straw". Because of convenient handling, and also because of the difficulty of washing and drying thick bedding, women, for centuries, were delivered on clean straw or reed. Sometimes it was a plaited straw bed, laid on the floor. Later it was the straw palliasse (which was used on all beds except the feather bed). These palliasses were warm and smooth and *very* hard! You still find a few in good small hotels in Scotland. They become so firm that one rector's wife had the bright idea of slicing them into cubes with a circular saw and covering them with felt, to make new kneeling hassocks for the church.

OSTRICH FEATHERS (LATE VICTORIAN)

After the hideous cruelty of obtaining white osprey plumes had revolted the public, the ostrich feather became popular, as it did not involve the slaughter and destruction of gentle harmless fledglings, and it did provide cash for the South African ostrich farmers. So the feathers were used lavishly as fringes and fans as well as hat and bonnet trimmings, and "feather dressing" became a specialized washing craft.

The unbleached feathers were often brown and the fronds of the plumes straight. Bleaching was done by the trade, but the feathers were regularly washed at home, using a soap lather and shaking the plume dry in the sun, or before a fire, while curling the fronds inwards by using an ivory paper knife or blunt table knife. When restored to the "foaming wave" shape that fashion demanded, the feather was "glossed" with a small spot of oil rubbed across the palm of the washerwoman's hand.

The three tightly-curled ostrich feathers that were part of the command costume at the Royal Drawing-rooms were white, and desperately difficult to fix on the head.

WASHING FEATHER BEDDING

The best feather beds were made of dry, clean plucked feathers. (Pillows were made of down.)

It is interesting that both the twelfth-century sailor and the eighteenth-century bargee slept in feather beds!

In case of shipwreck the early sailors "busily overboard cast their bags and their feather beds—and their best weeds, their kists and coffers, and cargo all, to lighten the ship". (And also, perhaps, because a feather bed floats strongly for a long time!) The bargees probably upheld the tradition as they were mostly country-bred folk and used to sleeping on feather beds. Also, only a compressible feather bed could fit in behind the sliding doors of a barge bunk and still leave space for the man and his wife to squeeze into the middle of it! (There were small air holes in the tops of the sliding doors.)

Now the best feathers and the finest down came from swimming poultry. (Feathers from *flight* birds, such as pigeons, must never be used, as the strong quills pierce the covers, and the "flighty spirit" engendered disturbs the rest of the sleeper.)

Bedding feathers, if clean-plucked, were never washed but "WONE", that is, shaken and dried (usually in the bread oven after the last of the cooking was done).

Soiled feathers, or feather beds that required cleansing, were washed in running water, under a fall of water if possible, or in tumbled water. I myself have seen beds and feathers tethered in sacks below the churned

39. Watergate to the Tower of London (White Tower). Behind, Old London Bridge is shown with the tide running strongly through the arches.

40 and 41. *Going batty*

"Batting" was a method of washing that seems to have depended on locality more than period. "Bucking", combined with batting, is a proces still in use all over the earth, and the bat shown in the 12th-century MS. is the same as that in use in the 19th century.

After bucking (or, later, soaking) the clothe were laid over batting stools, or upon smooth stones, and the dirty portions were rubbed with soap and beaten with flat smooth "bats" or "batting sticks".

The worker usually grasped the bat with he right hand and kept up a continuous poundin action, while with the left hand she tossed and turned the clothes under the strokes. Bats wer usually made of hard ash wood, and were abou two feet long and two or three inches thick (fo weight). The width varied considerably, as som workers affirmed that a narrow bat conveye more force under the blow. Others believed that wide bat also caused a suction, when lifted after th blow.

42. This redrawing was made from one of the man mediæval MSS. which suggest that the "blankets supplied by good hostels might take the form clothing to be used by soaking wet arrivals.

waters of a working mill. The sacks were loosely filled and repeatedly trodden and stirred. If very soiled, the beds would be soaked in a tub of strong ley, before being laid to wash clear. Feather washing was a job best done in March, as wind and shaking were necessary to re-dry and toss-up the feathers. If set to dry under a hot sun they might ferment, and "cake up all stuck together". After drying, the feathers were loosened up, by beating with a light stick and also by shaking to and fro, end to end, between two washerwomen. (The action was exactly the same as that used by costermongers when shaking the tissue paper covers off a sack of oranges.) It was a rocking tossing action, difficult to describe, but fanning the air from end to end of the sack while at the same time lifting the load.

But, despite the washerwomen's best efforts, *washed* feathers were never so light and resilient as those which had been properly "wone".

WASHING HORSEHAIR AND UPHOLSTERY

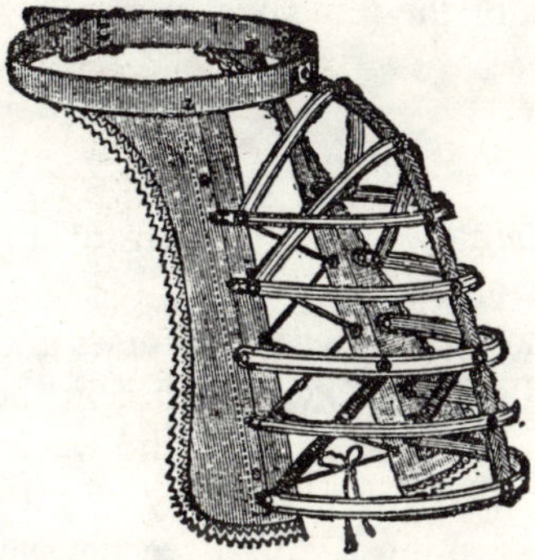

A calico and horsehair bustle that folded upwards as the wearer sat down[1]

Horsehair and cow- and goathair washing were seldom done at home —except possibly the horsehair mats for cider work, but that was a special and localized industry.

Horsehair (much more common in the old farming days) was collected and sold direct to the hair workers. Cowhair was chiefly the short pelt hair drained out of the lime vats during leather dressing. This was used in plaster.

This "processed" hair might not, by law, be sold for household use. This was important to the household washerwoman because by the fifteenth century the hard benches and stone window seats had acquired padding (had the costume fashion of the period fostered this?). Therefore

[1] A Jubilee bustle was fitted with a musical box that played "God Save the Queen" so that the wearer could *not* sit down.

the upholsterers' craft was flourishing, and many kinds of corrupt bedding were offered for sale. Microscopes had not yet discovered much, but plagues had taught people how easily cloth and bedding carried infection. So the law laid down that *no* sort of "mattresses of neats hair, deers hair, goats hair, etc. (*which is wrought in grease*—i.e. the lime vat), may be made for sale, for, if foul they give out, by the heat of a man's body, a savour so abominable and contagious that many are destroyed thereby".

Horsehair was used at various periods to pad or stiffen tailored clothes in the time of Elizabeth, and later padding inside the trousers was made fashionable by King James.

The very fine strong horsehair cloth, used to cover Victorian chairs and sofas, was never made at home. When on furniture it was washed over with a damp cloth and then polished with furniture polish, or a spot of oil to bring up the gloss (and make sliding off it easier!).

Its last uses were in the manufacture of the spring braid that held out crinoline frills and later to pad the Victorian bustle. In spite of its many uses horsehair was one of the few substances that escaped the household wash.

Washing riding breeches

When riding and driving were *daily* means of travel, much heavy washing reached the household.

The stable yard (as now) dealt with the horses and carriages and harness, but blankets and travelling rugs were washed in the laundry room, and in country places and on small farms, etc., the wash probably included the wool combings that stuffed the upholstery of the family traps and gigs. These instructions for cleaning Riding Breeches would still be understood in a modern saddle-room though they date from the late eighteenth or early nineteenth century.

> "*For leather breeches*. Brush well and damp with clean water. Then apply the mixture *all over* very thoroughly but lightly. Isinglass $\frac{1}{2}$ oz. Powdered pummice 1 oz. White soap 2 oz. Pipe clay 3 cakes (?). Starch 1 large spoonful. Sweet Oil 6 spoonfulls. Mix well with boiling water to a thick cream. Let the breech dry slowly and thoroughly, then dust well with a cane, stretch to proper shape on breech trees and iron with a box iron (take care not to scorch).

To clean white or porpoise tops.

> 1 oz. white copperas in a bottle of rainwater. Add 1 oz. oxatic acid. Apply with a sponge and brush down well."

About 1850 *"Properts powder" is advertised.*

THE SOCIAL STATUS OF THE LAUNDRY EXPERT, 1824

"Dame Crawford, an old woman; was a Mighty Notable Body, who picked up a good maintenance, by washing and ironing in different houses of the town; and filled up the odds and ends of her time in settling her neighbours' concerns, and retailing the news of one house to the ears of another."

S.P.C.K. Tract of the Period

This tract was designed to promote total abstinence, but as it was intended to interest the working-class girl of the period, it had to give pictures she would recognize as accurate and reliable.

The poorer "working classes" were the source of servant supply for the new "urban industrial class". Not the very rich, whose hierarchy of professional specialists, from hopeful kitchenmaid to omnipotent butler, had their own fixed social code; nor the old "rural estates" whose retainers were of family tradition and sojourned with them in their new town houses, but the small "Tradesman", the "Publican", or "Retired Family", who only employed one or two "helps" and who were the employers of the "general servant" (an outlet for orphanages and the origin of the skivvy, so grimly portrayed by Dickens).

The value of "Dame Crawford" is that she acts as a servants' agency, and in describing the "likely places" (i.e. possible vacancies) she gives a very fair sample of domestic opportunities and, incidentally, shows how the arrival of cheap cotton fabrics, and the subsequently voluminous and intricate clothes of the period, raised the status of the woman "skilled in fine laundry work".

As the would-be servant is only just 15, Dame Crawford first describes a "kitchenmaid's" place:

"There is a kitchenmaid wanted, she'll have to do all the washing-up of all the pans and dishes after the cook, and clean the kitchens, and it's a desperately hard place, though the last girl told me there were some pretty good winnings by way of perquisites. The cook herself usually takes all these things, but the kitchenmaid managed to get a few for herself."

This "place" is obviously in a large household where it was customary for the cook to take over any by-product, such as mutton fat, or left-over joints; the parlourmaid the candle ends and soap (for floor polish?) and the footman the ullages, etc.

The next place suggested was as "general" to an old lady. (Reading between the lines, this old lady may have been the widow of some professional man, who had seen better days, and "knew how things ought to be done". She is now poor enough to live cheaply, old enough to live quietly and gentle enough to share the company of her servants, as did her Elizabethan ancestors.) This is not a prospect to appeal to the working-class girl, "The situation will hardly keep you in shoeleather! and its so shut up and DULL! Betty Hacket, the girl who is leaving, says the Mistress is not bad-tempered, but so faddy and tiresome, will always have things done exactly *so* and she often sits in the kitchen, so that there's only one fire, and one candle between them! and the wages not £3 a year! and nothing but sheeps' heads and cold 'taters for Sunday dinner!" (The old lady also reads improving books to the girl while she is sewing, which seems to be the last straw!)

So Dame Crawford's next "place" is at a public house, an inn—the "Sow" at Dolby. It's a capital place. She will have to draw the liquor (which means long hours and late nights) but she is paid £6 a year, and the last girl got twenty shillings in tips for showing the gentlemen into the parlour during the races. (This is a good job, and has its parallel today in jobs demanding youth and good looks.) The employment did not last long enough to save money for retirement, and left the worker, now "past her prime", "untrained for other employment". Therefore, the Dame produces her trump card! "Go to Squire Shangering of Holden, it's where *I* have ironed these last ten years! Madam Shangering does not fancy her things unless *I* iron them myself!" If the girl is willing to learn, Dame Crawford will get her the place. It's as "general". Mrs. Shangering rings her bell at 6 and the girl must have breakfast laid by 7, and after the Mistress has had hers, while the girl is upstairs doing the bedroom, the general has hers, and washes up, and does the housework, and the cooking, not much, but *good*, and done under the mistress's own eye, and fault-finding! And dinner must be ready precisely when the cuckoo clock announces ONE. And afterwards, the girl has to clean up the kitchen and change her working dress and attend the mistress on her afternoon walk. Then after tea, she must sew household linen till bedtime (pre-sewing machines and ready-made bedding).

That was the girl of fifteen's daily work, but on wash days Dame Crawford comes in for the day and the pair work from early dawn till nightfall, and so the girl learnt to wash, iron, plait, stamp, clap, do clear starching, and to pull and fold, and press, and "do all the troublesome" business of laundry work, which some girls detest so much. However, the paragon of fifteen wanted to learn the trade, so served the apprenticeship for three hard years, by which time the Dame had taught her all she knew, and the girl (now seventeen) could herself "go out and work by the day", as a "skilled laundry woman", earn good wages and be independent![1]

[1] Contrast this with the washerwoman on page 297.

EXTRAS FOR THE LINEN CUPBOARD

Lavender Water (for ordinary use)

"Half a pint of spirits of wine, quarter of an ounce of oil of lavender, two drachm and half a drachm of essence of bergamot, one drachm of essence of ambergris. Mix all well together."

Lavender Faggots (for clean-washed linen)

"For making these, we must have the stalks fresh and green, while the lavender is in flower. About twenty head of lavender should be placed evenly together, the leaves and small buds that grow beneath the head being first removed. One end of a narrow ribbon, of any bright colour, should be tied round the whole tightly, close under the heads, so as to form a bow and leaving the remainder of the ribbon about a yard long. The stalks are then bent backwards over the heads of the lavender, and the ribbon being first doubled, or folded over, to make it narrower, must be wound round the faggot spirally, passing it, alternately, over two stalks and under the next two, until the heads are covered. The end of the ribbon is then cut off and fastened in among the heads, by tying another ribbon in a bow round the stalks, which should be cut off about two inches below the last bow."

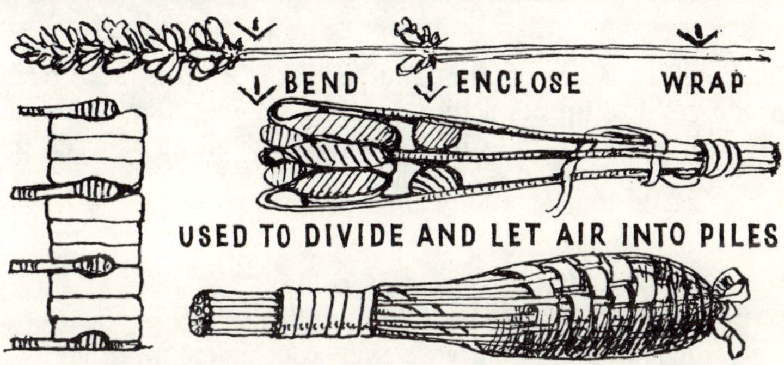

Lavender faggots were used to space out linen, and served to let air in between the close stacks

Eau de Cologne (called Cologne water)

"One drachm orange flower water, one drachm essence of citrone, four ounces of essence of melissa officinalis (the bee balm), one ounce of civet, three ounces of bergamot, one ounce of lavender and one of musk, four pints of spirits of wine.

When the chemist mixes the essences for you warn him not to use potash, as this would burn materials. When you have the mixed essences put them into two bottles and fill up with the spirits of wine, shaking well." The price quoted for this amount in 1850 is about 1*s*. or 1*s*. 6*d*.

"Wash on Monday, the best day.
Wash on Tuesday, slight delay.
Wash on Wednesday, no great blame.
Wash on Thursday, wash for shame.
Wash on Friday, wash for need.
Wash on Saturday, sluts indeed."

OUR EMMA

DOMESTIC CLEANING

"'My first aim will be to clean *down* (do you comprehend the full force of the expression? To *clean down* Moor House from chamber to cellar; my next to *rub it up* with bees-wax, oil, and an indefinite number of cloths, till it glitters again. My third, to arrange every chair, table, bed, carpet with mathematical precision. Afterwards, I shall go near to ruin you in coals and peat to keep up good fires in every room. . . .'

"'I trust you will look a little higher than domestic endearments and household joys?'

"'The best things in the World!' I interrupted."

"Three women were got to help; and such a scrubbing, such a brushing, such washing of paint and beating of carpets, such taking down and putting up of pictures, such polishing of mirrours and lustres, such lighting of fires in bedrooms, such airing of sheets and feather beds on hearths, I never beheld."

Jane Eyre

SCOURING

"No scouring for pride:
Spare kettle whole side.
Though scouring be needful, yet scouring too much,
Is pride without profit, and robbeth thine hutch.
Keep kettles from knocks, set tubs out of sun,
For mending is costly, and crackt is soon done."

TUSSER

WASHING-UP WATER

The early mediæval equivalent of a modern sink was a wooden bench holding tubs, or it was a stone slab hollowed to carry free-running water (as in Gloucester cloister and many other places).

Sometimes a stone shelf supported the tubs, and would be placed near a hole or "sink" into which the dirty water could be emptied. The same word is used today, when country people dig a "sink" or "sump" for the same purpose. A well-made "sink" will last as long as a small

Section diagram—a sink or sump

country household needs it, once a balance is established with the vegetation and subsoil.

It was the multiplicity of these "sinks" (they were used by every small cottage) that caused such insanitary complications when the villages became congested towns. The trees were cut down, the reduced vegetation could no longer cope with the increased discharge, and a soured and saturated soil clogged the land with insoluble grease. The texture of the soil was destroyed, so that in places like London where the town was on water-retaining clay the very earth stank!

The first obvious development of working tubs and benches was to tilt them slightly inwards, so that spilt water did not drip down the legs

A slate trough supplied by pump

of the washer-up. This led to a drain hole at the end of the slant, and from this the "trough" sink evolved, remains of which can still be found in old dairies and back kitchens.

The indoor tap usually stood over a stone sink, shallow and flat-bottomed, but wide enough to stand the bucket and tubs upon.

A slop-stone was a stone slab, hollowed out to form a shallow flat-bottomed trough. The front of these stones are usually worn down into a curve from the whetting of centuries of kitchen knives! In a large establishment there would be separate washing-up places in the butler's pantry, the still room, and the scullery, etc., but in a working household most jobs gravitated to the slop-stone. The curious may trace the knife cleaning, the vegetable scrubbing and peeling, the ham soaking, etc. The wooden tub for washing-up crockery stood on the flat slop-stone. There was a lighter brass or tin basin for rinsing the hands, or doing special jobs. Here the cream churn came to be "scalt", and under the sink the pig pail and hens' tin awaited contributions.

Following and contemporary with the slop stone was the heavy earthenware sink, usually brown or yellow, the front decorated by hand strickled ornament. A slightly superior sink was of white glaze stone-ware, with an impressed decoration and sometimes a built-in overflow. All these sinks had two flat sides, for building into the wall and contacting the draining-board but they remained wide, flat, and shallow enough to be used as a "wet working bench". For washing-up a deeper bowl or tub stood *in* the sink.

Except in exceptional positions (hotels and schools, etc.) it was not till comparatively recently that sinks were designed deep enough to prevent the use of the extra wash-up tub.

This "slop stone" still remains in old houses. It was the sink portrayed by Rowlandson and Dickens and was used as a rough work table by generations of cooks. They used it to gut fish, clean game, chop up vegetables and break soup-bones (as dents in the stonework show). Here the cumbersome iron cauldrons and pans were scoured with sand.

The lead of the slop stone drain pipe came up inside the stone hole, and was hammered flat into a circular stone groove. The front of slop stones is usually worn to smooth oblivion by the sharpening of many kitchen knives! (Lately slop stones have been bought up by gardeners for rockery plants.)

The brown stoneware sink followed the slop stone and carried its name and shape for years. Gradually this sink grew deeper and cream coloured and decorated sinks arrived. The white sink came in about the same time as baths ceased to be painted tin and became porcelain enamelled. The white sink was deep enough to be filled with water and used as a tub.[1] Contemporary with them was the wood and lead sink, that foreshadowed the stainless steel of today.

Thick sheet lead was rolled over a solid wooden foundation (with the clarity of childhood, I can still see the grain and knot-holes of the wood below, raised like a shadow on the dull surface of the lead, so closely had the soft heavy metal been beaten down). Joins in the lead were paired copper rivets, and the whole must have weighed a ton. The top portion, with cold tap only, was still the working slop stone, upon which the great beef marrow bones were hacked to pieces to make soup.

A form of sink that followed the tub sequence was the milk cooler. There were also built-in milk coolers of marble, very expensive and beautiful. They were four or six inches deep, with drain holes for letting out the skim milk after the cream was removed, and for washing with water, hot or cold according to the weather. The last I saw of these was at the Tempest's model dairy at Broughton Hall in Yorkshire.

Basic requirements for all primitive washing places. Pails to carry, or spring or pump to provide water. Stand at convenient height for work. Wooden tub for washing pots and pans on (or slate trough) for soaking and steeping. A "sink" *or drain to remove water.*

[1] The washing up of china was still done in a tub of soapy water, carried on to the table and sometimes padded with a soft cloth to avoid accidental chips, though every cup was dipped in separately, and delicately held by the handle.

MOPPING FLOORS

This was general usage, but the North Country excelled in the technique—probably because of the larger acreage of stone floors. In the Midlands and South wooden or tile floors were more usual and were scrubbed.

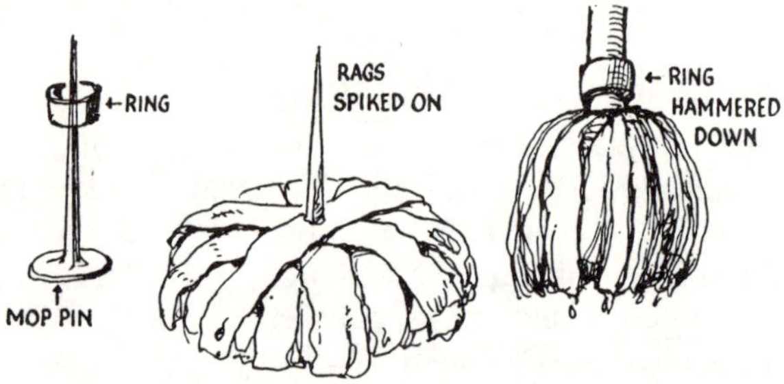

Mops are now bought ready made, but they used to be home-made: of old rags, sliced up, and spiked onto a long "mop nail", which was then driven up into the iron ringed "mops-tail".

The special mop bucket with a wringing cone does not seem to have been invented till the 1930's. Before that date two buckets were in general use—one containing the soapy (or soda) water, and the other the clean water—in which the mop was wrung out. To get a really *dry* finish the expert would trundle the mop outside, making it spin around as it rolled down her forearm and throwing off the water in a joyous catherine wheel! It was the skill of a good mopper to leave the floor not only clean, but almost dry. An interesting trick, in wet winter weather, was to put a few drops of paraffin on the well-trundled mop, and give a last quick wipe over with this. On the lithographic principle, the oil went out onto the stone, in a thin film, and the water was driven up into the mop. It worked, but left the damp floor very slippery.

The finish of a mopped floor depended on whether the surface was of tiles or bricks.[1] Skim milk gave a gloss, and weak starch (saved from the weekly wash) filled the porous bricks, but the common "cheat" for brick floors was the "red raddle" earth, used by shepherds to mark sheep. Red raddle water, mopped over the floor as a last finish, gave a fine level red, but, if stepped upon before it was dry, it "trod up" and "carried about".

Years ago I remember scrubbing down a long flight of wooden backstairs and rinsing them, till they dried snowy white. Then I mopped the big old-fashioned kitchen floor with red raddle till it glowed. Feeling

[1] Where holystone was used this "got into" the water and put a matt finish over flagstones.

proud of the job, I opened the window wide to let all dry . . . and the cat came in! He walked all across the red floor and up the stairs, bloody footed, four red paw marks in the middle of each white step. (These things are sent to try us.)

Clogs or pattens were always worn for swilling or mopping.

LIFTS AND WATERBOARDS FOR SWILLING

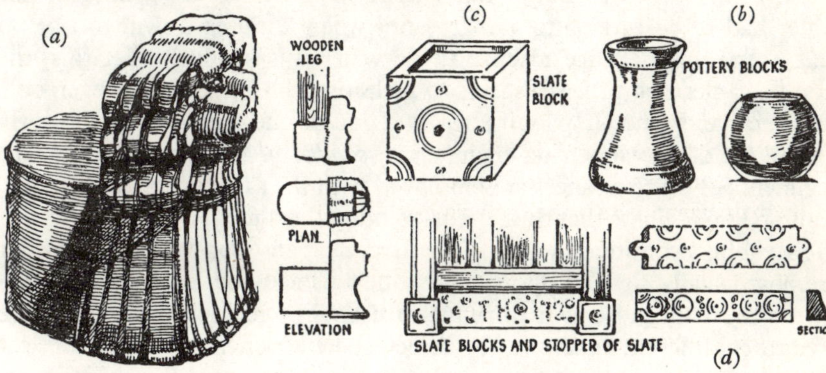

Lifts or raisers were solid squares of pottery or stone that took the feet of the heavy wooden chests and dressers and raised them above the wet. Sometimes these lifts combined the office of "break water" and "mouse excluder", being shaped with a cunning overhang that defied both. Sometimes these "pot foots" or "raisers" were designed with dog's heads or ornamented with coloured glaze. The slate blocks were usually squares, with ornamental circles strickled on them.

The brown Buckley dogs that raised their heads in front of their solid stands, not only served to keep the wooden legs dry, but also covered up any that had become battered or worn, and an extra slat of slate or tile on the platform behind the ornate head levelled up any unevenness of flooring (*a*).

Squared slate blocks were slightly hollowed on top to fit the wooden posts (*c*).

Buckley and Staffordshire (?) pot stands, variously shaped, also acted as mouse excluders (*b*).

The "whorle" decoration scored upon the slate "stoppers" centred round a drill-hole that sometimes went right through the slate and gave ventilation. Initials and dates were inscribed in the same way.

In stone- and brick-floored rooms there were special *waterboards* set along the walls "against the swill and mop water". Usually they were of the same material as the floor itself; slates might be used around a slate floor, and tiles around a brick floor. (These protectors were rather higher than the usual skirting boards used on wood floors.) It is interesting to find that curved adaptations of these old waterboards are now generally installed around all modern tiled floors (*d*).

SCRUBBING

This never used as much water as it should have done, because the water had to be carried to and fro and, when kneeling down, to rise up and walk some distance to change the water was irksome. Yet this, the first floor-cleaning process, seems to be lasting the longest. For even outside the handsome shop buildings of London one still sees in the early morning elderly women on their knees, *scrubbing!* In city offices, whole regiments of office cleaners are employed with the same primitive brushes, pails and floor cloths that their great-grandmothers used, and, in a hospital, the scrubbers continue to work. The larger expanses of ward and corridor are now usually cleaned by machine, but on stairs and kitchens and elsewhere the pail and brush continue in use. The technique varies, so we give three different examples, by three expert exponents.

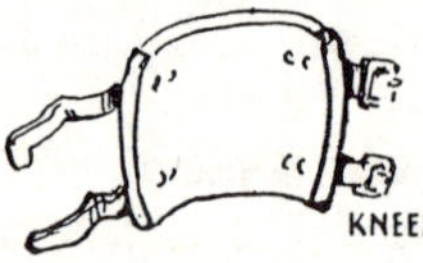

KNEELER

SCRUBBING MAT

The first (male) was an ex-convict who scrubbed stone passages. He had two water pails, one of soapy water and one of clean disinfectant water. He used a stiff, square fibre brush and a coarse hessian cloth, and he wore strapped-on knee-pads of leather lined with felt. (He whistled as he worked.)

The second was a nun in a convent who scrubbed long refectory tables and a hard wood floor. The tables were scrubbed with soap powder and rinsed with a mild bleach. The floors were scrubbed with a harder brush and silver sand. They were done in sections, and each patch was rubbed dry before starting the next. (She prayed as she worked.)

The third expert (very female) was an East End charlady, who weighed twelve stone (but was always called "Butterfly" because in her youth she had been apprenticed to a tight-rope walker). She scrubbed the cork lino of the bathroom, the wooden floor of the surgery and the lino of the kitchen, with fine impartiality, using one brush and a tin of soft soap.

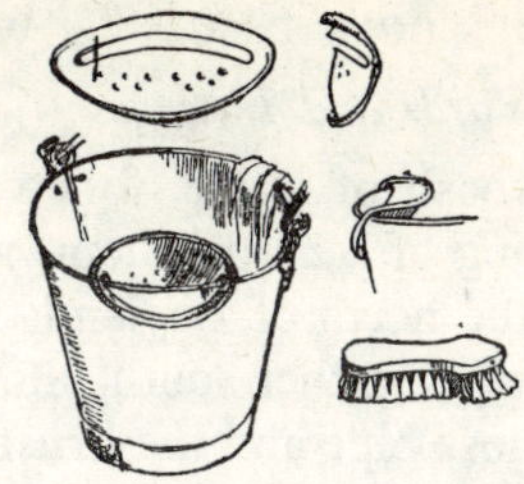

A cunningly designed gadget that fitted over the rim of a bucket to hold the soap out of the water

The cork lino used to rise in waves after her, as it "hadn't ought to have been wetted", but "if you didn't wet it, it wouldn't come clean". The surgery was a wooden floor and a thankless task, as the patients always walked over it before it was dry. She used to bring the Sunday picture papers to lay down in trackways, from door to benches, so that dispenser and "duty surgery" were frequently stuck spellbound in mid-passage, enthralled by press photography, or bent, circling concentrically like water beetles, deciphering some enthralling caption. (Butterfly had a good voice and she sang music-hall hits as she worked.)

These three examples cannot cover the subject of scrubbing, but they are representative.

Postscript. In the account book of one SARAH:

debit to W. Eddy, 1840 [My Grandfather]
1 bar sope
1 wail-bone brush.

"WASHING-OVER"

(A distinction rather than a difference.)

Kamptulican, the precursor of linoleum, was a mixture of rubber, paint and gum, solidified with pounded cork, and was comparatively expensive. The thick cork lino that followed was also expensive, especially if inlaid in colours. It was ideal for nurseries, as it did not splinter like wood, nor soak up dirt like a carpet and it could be washed, though it was usually wiped over and only given a real scrubbing when very dirty. The early linoleum (rather thicker than today's) had a glazed surface easily damaged, so was usually polished and only washed over occasionally. In consequence some very old lino, that had been down for a long time, became quite shaded, being dark brown below bureaux and around the skirting-board, and quite bright, with the pattern showing, where walked upon. Today all the many and various floor coverings insist on each selling their own specially-adapted type of cleaner (which is excellent business, but makes them too complicated for any book notes. They develop and change so rapidly that only TV advertisements can keep up with them).

OTHER HOUSEHOLD USAGES OF WATER

Swilling Yards and Passages

The swoosh of water, followed instantly by the clatter of a pail and the scouring of a hard broom, was the regular sequence of sound, heard daily, in the north of England. (It was usually preceded by the clanking of a pump.) Further south, the clatter of the pail was exchanged for the hiss of a hose pipe and the brushing sound was more intermittent.

Dairy farms and stables carried on the tradition of the swill-down (and in some it still persists.) But around many old houses the cobbled yards are weed grown, and the searing destruction of the flame-gun leaves the cobbles, that used to shine and sparkle in the wet, dull and lifeless under a fine film of ashes. Some old paved yards have grown mossy, and the flagstones have disappeared below years of unswept autumn leaves.

Down west, the Budleigh-pebble-sets and the long sloped passages are vanishing. The new farms have smooth new cement flooring and "available faucets". Swilling is done less, and the practised skill of it becomes rare. The older-fashioned "bucket swill" used less water than the hose, and the method was well formulated. First, the yard was dry swept, and the gutters and drains "set clear". Then "first water" was thrown down and "first brushing" was done *against the slope*, pushing the water back and brushing till all the dirt was loosened. The brush was then "dipped" and the loose mud swept down to the gutters. "Second water" was then thrown over, with a sideways sweep along the surface and its flow instantly "followed down" by the coercing broom. This removed the residue of loose mud. The broom was then rinsed, the buckets refilled and "last water" was run down over the stones, and, as it drained down to the gutters, the broom followed the flood, down the gutters and down to the drain gratings. Finally, if it was a stable yard or cow shed, this "last water" was allowed to dry off before a couple of buckets of mild disinfectant were watered over the whole.

The yard hand must acquire enough skill not to dislodge stones, or stop up drains. A long ladle dipper usually hung up handy, for, every week or so, the sunken "catch pot" of the surface drains needed to be cleared out (*see* diagram, page 131). The grating was lifted out and its underside washed clean at the same time.

After Swilling Came Sanding and Stoning

"Hearthstone and Flandes brick." (London street cry.) This craft seems to have been practised in the 1700's, but reached its peak about 1850. It continued in use well into the 1900's and there are vestiges of it today in some stone districts.

The "stones" were sold by street vendors. They were also a stock-in-trade of the unhappy children who attended the new ragged schools of the industrial cities (the small pieces sold for less than $\frac{1}{4}$*d.* each). In Lancashire in the 1900's handcarts used to come around exchanging "jam pots or rags" for pieces of hearth stone. The stone was white or yellow. It was mined in Surrey and also in France. Both kitchen and parlour hearths were whitened, as part of the ritual of fire-lighting. After doing the grate, and removing the ash, water was brought, with a cloth and a small tin containing the stone. A damp duster took up the last of the dust, then the hearth was washed over and the old stoning wiped off. The clean hearth was then rubbed over with the stone, working round and round in small circles. The clean wet cloth was then folded smooth and the "stone" smoothed out to a flat finish and left to dry. In the north, stoning became a cult. Doorsteps and windowsills and every scrap of domestic stone work was rendered snowy white, or, if the fashion changed, bright yellow. Down the long stone passages of inns the sides only would be stoned, the tread-way left plain. In the tap room the oak settle by the fire, the table and wall benches and even the spitoons had white mats of stoning.

These "finishes" did show that the place had been freshly cleaned and, in kitchens, it served to take up spilt grease. In the washhouse, after the weekly wash was finished, tubs and coppers were set back into place and the fancy patterns stoned around them, showed that they would not be moved again for another week.

How strong is the urge to enjoy one's handiwork! All men may be poets, and every woman is an artist at heart to enjoy that little lively finish to a hard day's work; that instinct which constrained her to create anew, each week, a swift intricate pattern for a water tub to sit upon!

BOTTLE-WASHERS FOR BOTTLES AND CASKS

"As violent as botel in the spence."

CHAUCER, *Somnours Tale*

Bottles and casks were scoured within by chain brushes. The chain had wooden, lead-weighted, beads, set with stiff bristles. The end of

the chain was attached to a long wire and "stay" to prevent it from falling completely into the bottle, where, becoming entangled, it would be impossible to extract.

The size varied from a light chain with beads the size of peas, suitable for glass bottles, to heavy chains with iron beads weighing up to a quarter of a pound each and used to scour large casks.

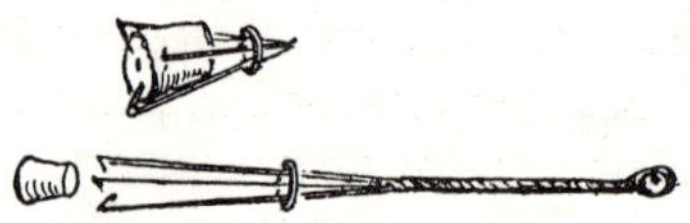

When glass bottles were more valuable households kept a wire "cork extractor" to pull out sunk-in corks. The sharp prongs harpooned the cork and gripped it firmly as it was withdrawn through the narrow neck.

STEEPING IN WATER

This usage was much more common for many more matters when cauldrons were few, and used on open hearths, because steeping could be done in tubs or pots, or open water. Industrial workers continue the usage, perhaps more than domestic workers, since skins, horns, hair, various forms of lime and plaster, fibres such as flax and hemp and many other materials are steeped and soaked.

But the greatest change from steeping is probably in food preparation. Steeping was a slow process and today all is for speed. Also, today, we freeze, tin, bottle and compress many goods that had previously been dried (and modern dehydrating has somewhat different results). All this applied especially to winter stores and shipboard provisions.

Steeping was not the simple matter of putting an article into water to soak; for some things, if soaked suddenly, swelled and broke, or the outer layer soaked and swelled, forming a waterproof casing that kept the interior dry and somewhat compressed. For such cases the goods had to become damp slowly before immersion. Some steeping was to loosen particles without disturbance; some, as in salted goods, to enable the salt to be washed out. The old folk understood this difference between steeping to loosen particles in suspension, or to remove them in solution.

This involved a study of the density of the steep as well as its temperature. For example, a thick steep of water and honey could be made to penetrate a bladder or a leather bag that had stiffened. Wood vessels were steeped before use, to swell them watertight. When country children walked to school their wet winter boots were steeped overnight in warm mutton fat to drive out the water (and if the shoes were set in a draught or warm dry place it very soon did so).

The easiest way to study the process is by examples.

Food—Hams were the classic steep. A well-salted ham was steeped at least twenty-four hours with frequent changes of water. Before curing, green hams, tongues, etc., were steeped in a solution of salt and water to draw out the blood and lymph and then, sometimes after washing, given a steep in honey water to make the salt "take" more evenly. Steeps of water to which beer or cider were added were used for hares and game. Tough meat was given a steep of water in which sorrel had been bruised. In autumn, pumice from the cider press was a steep for hams or boiled bacon. Hung beef and harberden were all steeped. (The steeping of chaff and corn products is explained under Drinking Water.) Mead was the result of steeping the broken comb and skeps from the hives (and the bag from which the honey was dripped clear).

Dried peas and beans are good examples of damping before steeping. In peas and beans there is a tiny hole through which the seed gets water, and if they are submerged in spring, the seed soaks up the water so swiftly that the pea sprouts before the outer skin has had time to soften (hence a mess of burst peas and loose skins).

The dried peas and beans of winter were a very important part of mediæval diet and the clearing out of the last of the grey peas before Easter was a domestic ceremony. They were steeped, drained, and fried in butter and called carlings. The second Sunday before Easter was Carling Sunday. (Smollett calls this dish "scaldings" when served on shipboard.)

Cheeses were variously steeped. For some forms of soft cheese, the curd, tied in a bag, was steeped in salted water. The calf's stomach, the cock's crop and other substances from which rennet was made, were steeped, so was tripe and other intestinal interests. The noble haggis was steeped before boiling, lest it burst. To a cook, steeping was a very thoughtful form of soaking. (The washerwoman steeped much of her work.)

What dry-cleaners and laundries do today when they study stain removal, the ordinary housewife has done for years. Each washerwoman had her own special steep; butchers' wives steeped in salt and water; sailors' wives (for tar) used hot lard first, and steeps of soda water; afterwards painters' and printers' wives steeped in paraffin first and then submerged completely under soapy water. The parlourmaid steeped wine stains on table cloths in buttermilk, other stains required steeping in urine, salts of lemon, chloride of lime, etc., and all these had to be timed carefully or the steep dissolved the material. Steeps for linen could not be used for wool. Men's socks were never washed till they had been steeped in hot water and oil (to keep the knitting soft and prevent matting). Sheep skins were steeped before curing. In the harness room, hardened reins and straps were first soaked in water and then steeped in neat fat oils or mutton fat. The washing of shellfish, gritty corn and earthy roots in running water are all forms of steeping in water.

MANUSCRIPT WATER

The Venerable Bede has a curious note about the water in which the trimmings of Irish manuscripts have been steeped. He says that it reduces swellings and helps to cure poison in wounds. Bede puts this down to the anti-venom of Irish influence, but the gelatinous water may have contained some natural curative culture. Parchment was cleaned by repeatedly dashing it with boiling water (while it was stretchedly taut on wooden frames) and rubbing with "white stone" (lime?) to complete the smooth surface.

THE RELIGIOUS ASPECT OF STEEPING BEANS AND PEAS

The most curious reference to the steeping of beans and peas comes in an English version of Quodragesimale Spirituale taken from the French of 1565. Here the steeping of beans in water is made an allegory of the Lenten meditations before Confession:

> "When we would have beans or peas sodden, we lay them in a steepe; otherwise, they will never seethe kindly, and cooks should know that as River water, which continuously moveth and runneth and floweth is very good for steeping of pease and beans—so we must take as the running water our heartfelt tears of contrition."

Here is an excellent example of steeping mechanics—if you put peas to soak in a jar or basin they will swell up, and jam into a tight mass. Pease pudding is but a close-packed ball of peas, seethed in hot broth till they are swollen into one round close green ball.

EARTHENWARE AND WINE JARS STEEPED IN WATER

Before use, the heavy kitchen pots had to be "tempered". This was a form of steeping that varied according to the use of the pot. Baking pots were slowly heated to get the water from the clay, then greased and cooled slowly, so that the grease was absorbed into the porous pot. Otherwise the water in the clay, being imprisoned under the glazed inside surface, made steam and blew off or cracked the glaze.

New wine jars had to be steeped in running water (mouth of jar up stream, bung hole open) till the smell of the kiln was washed away, otherwise the clay flavoured the wine. Jars and pans that had held malted liquor and were "beer strong" might be steeped for weeks, but still not be safe for hot liquids as they held the flavour.

WOOD STEEPING IN WATER

All barrels and cooper-ware required steeping before use. Barrels and tubs that have been "standing dry" leak like sieves till well steeped to swell up the joints.

Large clean stones were used to sink the wooden tubs as they had to be completely submerged or they swelled unevenly and became warped.

Also, before using a wooden trough for pickling, or salting, or brewing, the vessel had to be steeped till completely saturated. Otherwise the wood would absorb the liquid, and there would not be enough pickle to cover the meat. Steeping to remove salt from wood was almost impossible, so all milk and dairy work had its special cooperware. The special cheese tubs and moulds (where salt was used) were steeped separately in *running water*.

STEEPING THE HONEYCOMB TO MAKE MEAD

Mead was made from the washings out of the old straw skeps, and by steeping the comb and the linen bags, in which the comb was crushed and tied up to drip out the honey. After the clear honey was all extracted the sticky bags, spoons, dishes and all the honey apparatus was steeped in a tub of warm water. From this steeping water was made the "barrel mead" of daily use.

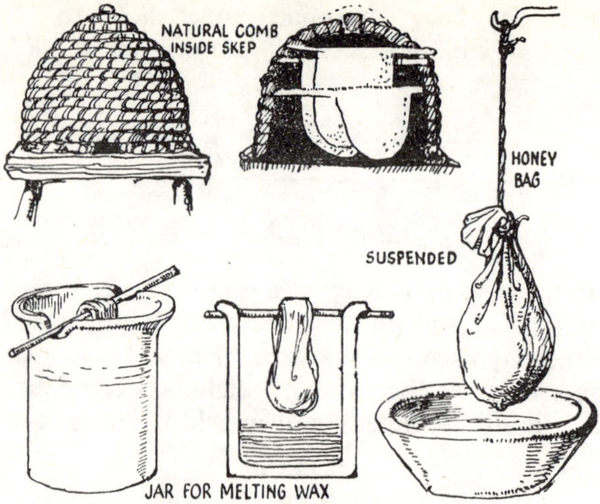

None of the older recipes for making mead use any outside ferment. The steeping water itself fermented naturally and this provided a puzzle (mentioned in *Food in England*). Apparently the old skeps were made of rye straw and the fermenting agent came originally from this. Once the fungus had infected the tubs and barrels the fermentation became automatic.

The mead that we ourselves made from this steeping of honeycomb was almost colourless, quite clear, but with a fine very light head of foam. (More like the light foam that drifts along the sea shore than the stronger, heavier foam on beer.) It was more strongly intoxicating than to be expected from its light mild texture. It was a very happy drink—not very sweet and depending for its aroma mainly upon the "bush" of scented herbs which lay in it, and with which it was stirred frequently while working. This "bush" was kept and hung up in the air so that the living fungi embedded in it obtained oxygen and stayed alive. It could be taken down and used again both to start a new ferment, or to enliven one that had become stale and flat.

STEEPING FEATHERS

No laundry was needed for "wone" feathers. But, beside these superior feathers, were quantities of feathers hurriedly plucked, dirty with grease, mud, and blood. These were steeped, and when clean, fetched a fair price.

First they were put into a tub under running water, held down in a net, and stirred to remove mud. Salt steeping was next, to remove blood, and they were again washed under running water. A ley steep followed, to dissolve any grease, and after a final washing under running water, the feathers were dried out. The simplest way (especially in winter

when the influx of feathers was greatest) was to hang them loosely upon a stretched net, in a through draught, with a sheet laid below to catch the feathers, as they dried out and shook through.

The packing, or "laying", of the feathers was, at all stages, important because space was needed in the steeping tubs to stir them around and in the rinsing tubs, for the running water to swirl them around. In the drying net, they needed to be laid out in a thin layer and shaken loose frequently, because close-packed, damp feathers heated easily and within twenty-four hours could have rotted into a stinking mass.

From a very early date the regulations governing feathers and hair, etc., sold to the upholsterers were stringent.

MEAT STEEPED IN WATER

The classic example of mediæval faith in steeping was for carrion.

"Si une berlyz murge sudeyment il mettent la chas en ewe aufant de dure com et entre mydi e noune. Et pus le pendant sus e kant let ewe escule le fount saler et pus ben secher."

Steeping in vinegar was a later effort, and among eighteenth-century "advice to fishmongers" it was suggested that immersion (steeping) in a solution of chloride of lime will keep "doubtful" fish over the weekend.

We hold no brief for these practices, but it is an historical fact that they were carried out.

COMMERCIAL STEEPING OF RABBIT SKINS

The Skinners of London presented a Bill to the House against the felt hat makers, because "during the present war with France, the felt hat brims are enlarged, and for these the fur steeped from hare and cony skins is used, so that if the export of the felting fur is prohibited, the yearly value of the rabbit warrens of the nobility will abate, and the loss of the steeping work will be an inexpressible loss to hundreds of poor families who labour every day at the vats and thereby live comfortably."

SHEEP SKINS STEEPED, WET AND DRY

The skins are steeped in water till soft and scraped clean of fat before being drained and steeped in an old bran pit, which rough dries them. They are then folded with the fleece inside and an alum paste is spread over the damp skin side. The alum paste is thick, and the skins only so damp that they should barely drip, when piled up. This is called the alum steep and is another example of the variety of steeping processes.

STEEPING LEATHER IN THE "TANNIN" BATH

> "There is sufficient foundation for the opinion of the common workman, that, in the slow method of tanning, the process has been unnecessarily prolonged by defective methods of steeping. . . . The want of progressive infiltration of the astringent liquors (i.e. tannin) through the skins."
>
> *Early trade note*

Another excellent example of selective steeping. If the skin is put directly into a thick solution (or strong tan) the surface is blocked or closed, and the tan does not penetrate. The skill is to fill the skin with the lighter, more easily absorbed solution, which holds it open so that the heavier solution soaks in to replace it.

Tan steeps were oak bark, galls, Leicester willow (stronger than ordinary willow), common elm and sumach. The willow was the most waterproof (sally willows—salicylic acid).

A NOTE ON COMMERCIAL STEEPING OF LINEN FOR PAPER

The tax upon imported paper was discussed in Parliament in 1600 as it was pointed out that English paper was made by "steeping the rags collected by scavengers off the dump heaps of the city". The cost of newspapers and the Bible and other educational works are all quoted.

SALT GHOSTS AND SALT CELLARS

> "Salt, hath . . . properties for to shew the weather, for, in fair weather, it will lie dry, but apt to dissolve against wet into its proper element. On boards that it hath lain upon, and got into the pores of the wood, it will be dry in fair and serene weather, but when the air inclines to wet it will dissolve, and that you shall see by the board venting his brackish tears . . . and salt cellars will have a dew hang upon them, and those made of metal, dim against rainy weather."
>
> WILLSFORD

Salt has always been troublesome to store on account of its propensity to become brine. Andrew Boorde gives sensible instruction for table salt to be kept in bowls and crushed and served with a bone spatula. The elaborate mediæval salt cellars of silver would be cleaned daily, as were the small Victorian salt cellars. In old kitchens salt was sometimes kept in jars on the hearth stone, or placed in the cooling bread oven. The wooden salt boxes hung up in kitchens were very specialized woodwork. Iron nails rusted, copper nails were subject to verdigris, so that all joins had to be wood pegged, or dove-tailed, and the hinge made of leather.

Transport of salt was expensive and difficult, and salt was usually a summertime purchase and had to be stored. Anyone in an old house who has a bacon larder, or salting trough, knows how impossible it is to keep them dry. Centuries after the last pig was salted down the walls continue to flake and drip, and the wooden troughs and shelves become clammy before rain.

This old "salt damp" probably accounts for the ghostly "blood stains" that can never be wiped off the boards, the "blood stains" that come and go as prognosticators of fatalities. Salt sinks in, and the reddish-brown tint shows when damp, but fades when the crystals dry out again. One does hate to lay a good ghost story, but some do require "salting".

SEDIMENTATION

This process, using water to grade materials held in suspension, is common to many industries and is often used in household jobs.

Here are two examples: 1 Trade, 2 Domestic.

(1) Carborundum or emery powders used for fine grinding and polishing of optical glass. In its simplest form the apparatus is little more than a row of glass jars and a timetable. The powder is stirred into the first jar and left to settle.

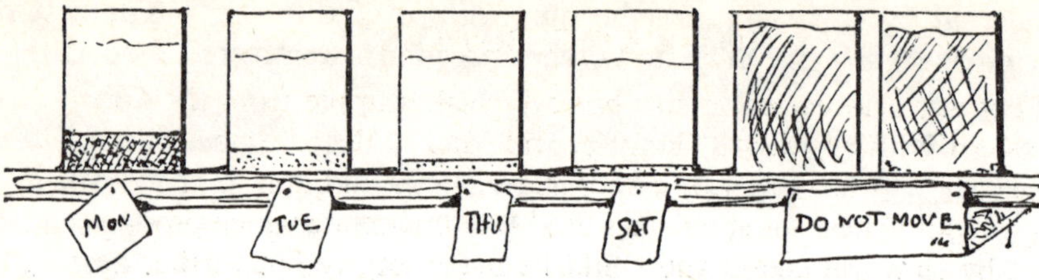

Next day (or at a studied interval) the water, still cloudy, is poured off the sediment into the next jar. It is left to settle again and gently poured off until, after a very long "standing", no more particles are left in suspension and a graded set of powders are left to be dried off. Combinations of deposits and long variations in time of settling can make this simple process quite complicated. The results are surprisingly predictable and accurate.

(2) Domestically the old-fashioned mixtures of whitening and rouge used to clean silver, or bathbrick and chalk for tins, were made by the same process.

A reversal of the process is still the quickest way to float the twigs and leaves from carelessly gathered blackberries!

It would be unnecessary to labour such simple water processes save as a reminder of the enormous number of water usages that we take for granted and never notice.

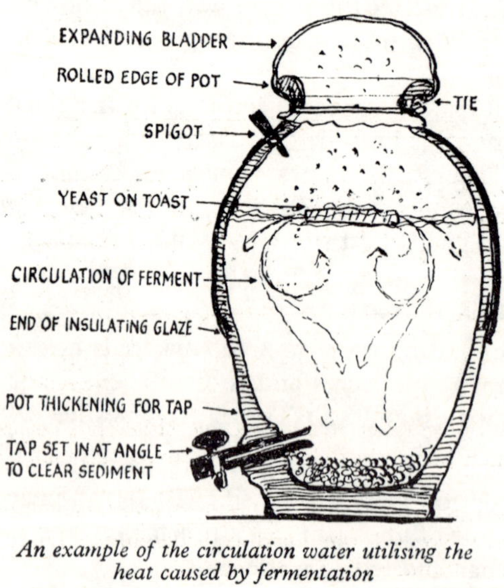

An example of the circulation water utilising the heat caused by fermentation

HOT-WATER BOTTLES

"Foot warmers varied in size but a typical example from the Great Western Railway was 18″ long, 9″ wide and 3″ deep. Some railways covered foot warmers with carpet material. In addition to hot water for providing heat some railways used sodium acetate which produced heat by chemical action and could be made to give out further heat by vigorous shaking after the effects of the first action had worn off."

Public Relations and Publicity Officer,
British Transport Commission

The warming-pan pre-dated bottles (except in special circumstances) and so, to appreciate the early hot-water bottles you must first understand the usage of the earlier warming-pan.

I consider myself fortunate in having owned *and used* warming-pans. The warming-pan in use did not ornament the hall wall, it hung conveniently near the kitchen fire and was kept in good repair. In the private household it was a comfort; in inns and post houses it was indispensable, as beds made up ready for the traveller were kept aired by the constant use of the warming pan, with which the chambermaid was supposed to "run" through the beds daily. At night, before going to bed, the warming-pan was filled with hot cinders and it was then pushed in at the side, or foot of the bed, swung up and down and to and fro, till every inch of the bed was heated, and the sheets ironed hot and smooth. The whole bed was warmed through-and-through.

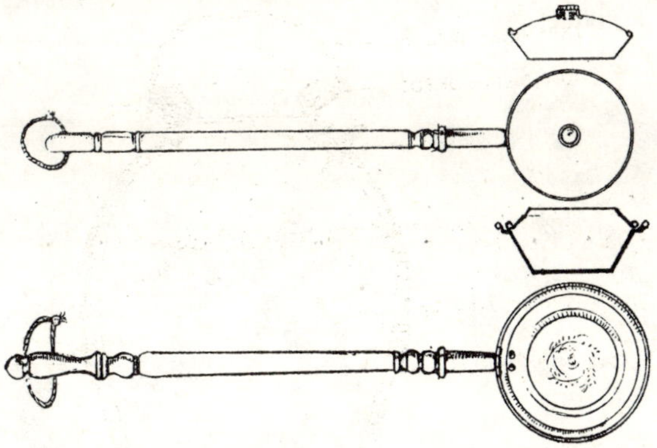

"A warming-pan, whose office it is to receive either hot coales or an iron heater into it; which being shut close with a cover, the maide warmes her Maisters bed."

The replacing of the "iron heater" by boiling water (even with a screw cap on top) must have worried the maid considerably. These first water warmers can still be found in antique shops.

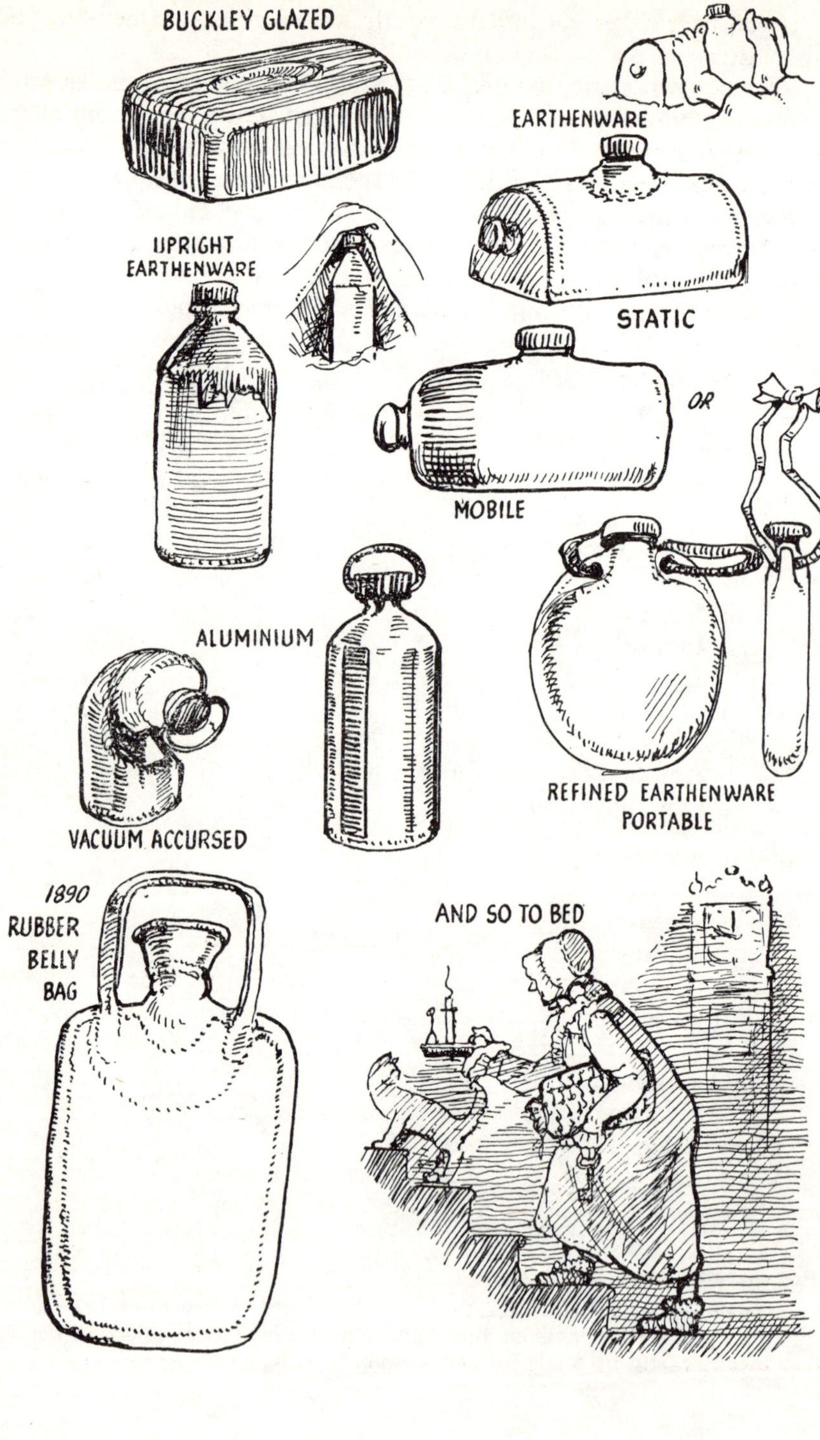
BUCKLEY GLAZED
EARTHENWARE
STATIC
UPRIGHT EARTHENWARE
OR
MOBILE
ALUMINIUM
REFINED EARTHENWARE PORTABLE
VACUUM ACCURSED
1890 RUBBER BELLY BAG
AND SO TO BED

(If you have never got into a properly warming-pan-warmed-bed you cannot dream of the enveloping warmth thereof!)

A hot bottle is static, the bed clothes lie prone upon it, it is insulated by blankets, immobile and isolated! If the hot spot is at the top of the bed, you must thrust your feet down to untempered chills. If placed at the foot of the bed you grope for it and stub your toe. Two hot bottles, though adequate, complicate repose, and even so, they only warm the central strip in the bed, all the outlying regions still remain cold. Now with a well-swung hot warming-pan, *all* the bed is warm. As you open the bed the imprisoned warmth billows up. As you slide down into the depths released pockets of warmth envelop you from all sides, every movement you make causes breaths of warm air to fan in from all around. A warming-pan-warmed-bed is completely full of evenly warmed air! No wonder that the static heater was considered inadequate and the older generation, accustomed to be bedded down by a warming-pan, insisted that the new water-pan also be mobile! So that the earliest hot-water bottles were copper pans, shaped *like* a warming-pan and mounted on long handles for use in the same way.

The copper water bottle was often called a "heater" or "airer". Afterwards a Noah's Ark shape developed, that, as it raised the covers slightly, was supposed to shed its heat further afield. Stone hot-water bottles were of thick pottery (stone ware). These varied in shape; their weak spot was the stopper, which had in each to be individually built into the clay when making the bottle. So that it was almost impossible to replace a broken or lost stopper. Also the rubber washers (at first they were leather) that insured a tight fit, were apt to wear thin or slip. However, the old stone hot bottle stayed hot for long hours, was very solid and hard-wearing, and its descendants of "improved design" continue in use today ("at all good chemists", etc.).

The rubber bottles that replaced them were at first just belly bags, with small stoppers and long loop handles. They were almost seamless and their abdominal gurglings were fearsome.

The stone bottles had only whistled and chirped as they cooled, sucking in the air through the lumpy screw stopper.

Bottle-shaped spun aluminium hot-water bottles came into general use during the war. If not carefully "bagged" they were dangerous bed fellows and, unless fully filled, created such a vacuum in cooling that their thin metal twisted and caved in, as if they had been chewed by dragons.

Of course, many other heaters were used; the hot tiles set at the back of the stove and flannel wrapped, to set under the seat and warm the pony trap or family coach; the hot sandbag, the hot brick, taken from the oven, encased in an old blanket and carried up to bed; or the "oven shelf", wrapped in brown paper and "slipped into the bed before you climb into it, my dear"; all the dear warm comforts of the old and sleepy! But as they did not use *water* they do not belong to this volume.

We have it on good report that special bricks were made in Buckley for use as bed warmers. These bricks were flat, like thick tiles, and glazed all over, so that they slid smoothly between the sheets.

The potteries at Buckley did turn out a lot of excellent domestic ware —wine jars, bread panshons and milk pudding dishes (the late Mrs. Gladstone would use no other). So it is likely these bed warmers were a local invention and a good one. The closing of these small potteries, that each catered so well for the special needs of their own locality, has been a loss to English education and ingenuity.

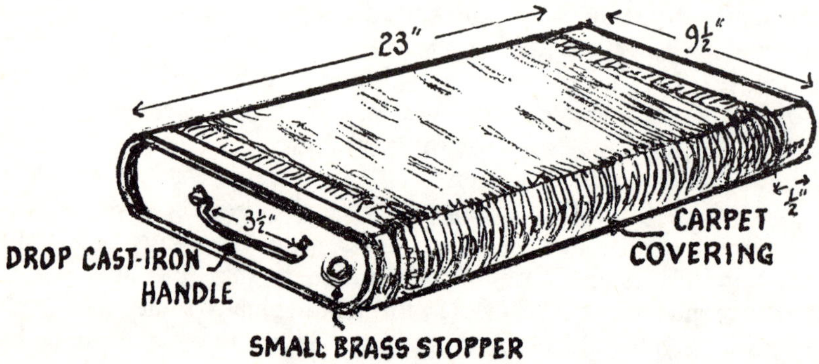

The railways used hot-water bottles for many years. They were called "foot warmers", were of copper or zinc, shaped like narrow tombstones, and covered with appropriate carpet covers. In winter, great loads of these water heaters were trundled on trucks along the platforms and heaved into the carriages, one to each carriage. "Mind your feet, please", and the two rows of seated passengers obediently raised their feet as the welcome heater slid in along the floor. (I always believed they were filled off the engine, but that may have been the invention of an exasperated parent.)

THE WATER BED

This was the gigantic rubber hot-water bottle upon which (before electric blankets) hospitals placed their cold, sub-normal or shocked patients. Speaking from experience, they were grim! For the fat and heavy, who could hold their own, a water bed may have been cuddlesome, but my long thin corpse lay quivering upon the resilient convex rubber curve expecting to slide off any moment (and if one dared to stir, the wretched thing chuckled "Punkle Punkle—toot" and quaked below you).

A water bed may have had its uses, but, culinary, I've never laid a garnish on top of a blancmange since; I know what it feels like.

CLAVIER WARMERS or "comfort for organists".

When cathedrals were heated only by coke stoves organists remote in the cold organ loft became petrified, so a complicated arrangement of small pipes blew air from the bellows across the top of a steam heater set below the pedals. (Then the chant *Tonus peregrinus* would be appropriate.)

DRINKS

"He gave you fine senses, wherewith to serve him.
Therefore he badeth earth, to help you each one
With wool, with linen, with needful livelihood
In moderate measure that ye may be at ease,
He, of his courtesy, set for common use
Things three, No more; but these three are needful.
The one is clothing, to save thee from chill.
The one is meat, for thy healths sake,
The third is drink, when thou driest."

PIERS PLOWMAN

There is no social guide to getting drunk, the only prestige involved is what you do it on, in which century.

Always the simple ingredients for mead, ale, or wine have been at hand, and a strong brew was easily made, very cheaply, when every hut had its own beehive, and every housewife grew her own bread and brewing yeasts. The brewing yeasts she preserved alive, from one brew to the next, hung outside the door in the fresh air, embedded in the "little broom of birch twigs" with which she stirred and whipped up the fermenting liquor. Thus this "brush" became the time-honoured sign of every ale house (*see Food in England*).

Distilling did not become common household usage till the seventeenth century, but for the whole of the next hundred years distilling was a fashionable domesticity. More elaborate copies of the great trade stills were erected in special pantries reserved for the skilled craft, and the names "still room" and "still room maid" remain today. Because, at this period, mankind was specializing in the importation of foreign wines (this is when some of the important "cellars" were first laid down, to mature the wines for the hard-drinking Georgian period). Because of this the "ladies' delight" was chiefly in the distilling of "waters", scented, or medicinal, and probably very potent, and the subtle, delicate flavours used in some seventeenth-century dishes were essences distilled from flowers and blended elderflower, rosewater and orange-flower flavourings were used in recipes for creams, where today one would read only "vanilla" or "almond".

GELATINOUS DRINKS

Calves foot and Irish moss and almost all jellies were used to make drinks by dissolving them first in hot water and then diluting with cold. There is great difficulty in placing the colloidal solutions among drinking waters. Primitive mankind probably brooded upon the phenomena of his cooling broth; how it became a solid jelly overnight—why? He knew water changed into ice or could be boiled away as steam, so he was prepared for changes, but the different textures must have caused him to think. In broth, he saw a solid, opaque mass of animal gristle dispersed into boiling water, to become a larger mass of less solid jelly. He early learnt a lot of the technical side of glues, and could see a colloidal fracture differed from the splintery breakage of ice. He saw that the density of jelly varied, but the density of ice did not. (It thickened or thinned but the texture of the ice was constant.) The liquescence of decay; the viscosity of fungi and roots, and the soft and hard gums that exuded from trees. All these things must have suggested animal substance, a form of life. For although he could split a stone with fire, or explode a damp slate, yet he could boil a pebble in an iron pot till kingdom-come and not change either.

The difference between the textures of meat-formed drinks and grain-formed drinks showed more when both had cooled to a solid form. The solidifying of milk when it went bad in hot weather. All these were known to the peasant, and doubtless he "sorted the facts" in his own mind, but we do not know what explanation he reached. (Again we have the problem of the penetration of knowledge.)

The addition of vegetable substances to meat broths may have been the accidental result of some leaves or roots making the meat tender.

For interest, we give a beef tea of the twelfth century and you will find it but little changed today.

The piece of beef (after slashing?) was laid over a criss-cross of birch twigs at the bottom of a deep "glass", i.e. a thick earthenware cooking pot. The twig arrangement, reminiscent of the drainage arrangement at the bottom of a bucking tub, was to prevent the meat sticking to the pot and allow the juice to drip out. The "lythe" salt was added and the pot closely covered with waxed cloth or wet parchment and set up to the neck in a cauldron of water, slowly brought to the boil and left for hours, till all the beef juice was extracted.

It was then thinned down with hot water (and doubtless "pepir" added). Thus—beef soup, later beef tea.

The birch twigs do give a slight aroma, but were probably chosen for their waterproof springiness, not flavour.

DISTILLING

DISTILLING PRIVATELY

"The knowledge of stilling is one pretty feat
The waters be wholesome, the charges not great.
What timely thou gettest, while summer dothe last
Think winter will help thee to spend it as fast."

TURNER

The distilling craft dates from remote antiquity and seems to have been continuous in England. The alchemist and the affluent carried on the craft through the Middle Ages, and its most prevalent period seems to have been from the sixteenth to the eighteenth centuries. After that time the still-room remained as a household craft, used chiefly for making scent and essences and cordial waters, and the distillers that produced spirituous liquors were taken over to a great extent by the trade—one exception being the illicit stills concealed in the Highlands and remote districts.

The apparatus, therefore, varied, according to its use, from a plain copper boiler with a long, straight spout, cooled by wet cloths, to elaborately designed stills with "warm" pipes and conducted water. The size varied, in the same way, from huge brick-built boilers capable of holding several gallons, to smaller types. The still could take as much room as a cider press (and they vary considerably) or lie as small as a pint pot. We quote as an example instructions for a typically large seventeenth-century still. It gives a good picture of the stone outhouse (the still-room) and describes much of the interesting tackle required. The most important point, as the expert explains, was "a sufficiency of water".

SEVENTEENTH-CENTURY INSTRUCTIONS FOR THE PRIVATE STILL-ROOM

"I hope my pains will not prove unacceptable to such persons of Distinction as keep a Still in their Families for their own Private Use."

"The still should be built in an outhouse, and a wet blanket kept at hand in case of fire. The still room should be large enough to accommodate the tubs and barrels needed for storage and the floor should be paved with stone flags, with a drain to carry off the wash, and all occasional slop which will be made by washing your casks. A sufficiency of water must first of all be apprized of; though it matters not if the water for stilling be soft or hard, if you have but plenty of it. The pump, or pipe (that delivers the cold water), must be set close to the worm tub (i.e. the condenser portion of the still)."

Instruction is then given for building the brickwork which supports the boiler portion and the fitting of an iron fire-box below this, with a chimney or flue. "The worm tub must be placed very near the still, and be firmly mounted on a strong wooden frame to support the great amount of water needed to keep the worm itself cool". The water runs through the tub over the "worm" or condenser tube and there must be a good depth of water and fairly swift flow, as the worm is continuously heated, and must be continuously cooled.

It is interesting that among the appliances there is a "movable wood gutter" which conveys the water to the cooling tubs, because it is certain that these long wooden ducts solved many of the "filling" problems of earlier centuries. One is shown at Tottenham Pump (*see* Plate 11).

The expert also recommended a large cauldron or tank of static water be kept near the still for any emergency, as it is *quicker* to bale the water from an open tub than have to pump it up and—"the still may accidentally become dry and prove dangerous" (a mild way of describing the explosion!).

For preparing the fruit juices before distilling a "strong and steady wooden press", "fixed very steadily and with 5 or 6 hair (horsehair) cloths or mats to wrap up the layers of the fruit" was recommended (this is exactly the cider press of today). The expert also describes the thread needed for the "Pres Skew" (press screw) and insists that the spout which delivers the juice from the base of the press be of lead (copper would, of course, be acted upon by the acid).

The thirteenth-century press (page 270) is very much the same (only an earlier model). Tubs, funnels and casks are listed as needful and a small "Tinpump" (exactly like a modern foot pump) to draw the spirits out of stone jars. A "pewter-crane" or scoop is needed, and a "Valencia". This is a pipette of pewter about 2 ft. long, where, by putting your finger on the end, the liquor is sucked up into a gim crack[1] for tasting. It was recommended that "there should be hung against the wall, a Hippocrates Bag"[2] (this was to hold spices that could, if necessary, be dipped into the liquor to improve the flavour etc.). A "flannel sieve" is another necessary bag (like a jelly bag) to hold isinglass, etc. The expert then could insist that "some powdered alabaster" be kept at hand, to clear any "foul liquors". He explains that the powder, "by filling the pores of the flannel bag, the goods run clear, leaving the sediment in the bag. Nor do the goods contract the least ill flavour from the said Alabaster powder". He does not here mention any chemical action between any acid and the alabaster, but

[1] Gimcrack or gim-crock?

[2] Spices of all sorts, and some "grains of paradise" were much used to enliven spirits and wines.

gives directions for holding the mouth of the bag open "upon a hoop of bent willow".

Other items are "a poker, fire shovel or rake for the fire, a cooper's handsaw, edge and gimleck,[1] a hammer and a pair of scrutching irons (?), tarriers[2] (tarras), bung borers and forceps, and a box of bungs".

The sealing paste for the joints of the still is to be compounded of wheat and rye meal, bean meal, "made into a paste with water, and it must be laid on well and smoothed out with a wet hand, and keep a piece of the paste as big as a small apple in case of leaks". One feels nothing could go wrong in that seventeenth-century still-room!

DISTILLING FOR THE TRADE

Distilling in quantity for the retail trade developed so enormously during the seventeenth and early eighteenth centuries that, as a contemporary says, "Brandy shops are in many places as numerous as ale houses". Also, typical of this period, he notes that "It has now become customary for distillers to furnish their customers with gilded and painted casks and to provide bottles and brass cocks marked with their own names, and to insist that retailers selling their liquors exhibited these forms of advertisement". In all of which we see the coming of the modern brewing methods.

In spite of legislation, liquid measures continued to vary between districts, and county measures contrasted much, both in name and content, from the Standard London Measure. Also, in London it was prudent to distinguish between distilling for the trade or for a private gentleman. "Because the private purchases requires personal attendance and a long credit, and this should be remembered when making out the price!"

Another point to note in this period—"some gentlemen (having, we suppose, still got their own county seats and their own still-room experience) may insist on the full proof strength of brandies (either French, Spanish or English); for these people (though not one in twenty really understands what he is talking about) you must supply goods which are of high proof and better flavour and charge accordingly".

Citron Water

Pare thinly 5 dozen lemons and put them into 5 quarts of French brandy for 14 days, then make the juice of the lemons into a syrup with 3 lb. of sugar. Boil 15 gal. of water with 40 lb. of sugar and put into a tub; work it with barm for 2 days, then put in the brandy, peel and syrup and close up the cask and let stand 3 months, then bottle it. It is more a cordial than a wine.

[1] Gimlet.
[2] "Tarriers", trass—a form of cement.

Stum

Take a 5 gallon cask, well soaked in water (*see* Steeping), set it to drain, then take 1 lb. of roll brimstone and melt it in a ladle, put as many rags to it as will soak up the melted brimstone, and burn these rags in the cask. Cover the bung hole but let it have a little air so it will burn. When burnt out, put in 3 gal. of strong cider, 1 oz. of common alum, pounded, and mix; roll it about five or six times a day for 10 days. Take out the bung and burn more rags in the cask (hung on a wire) as near the cider as possible and then bung the cask again, and roll it about well 3 or 4 times a day for 2 days, and let it stand 7 or 8 days and the liquor will be so strong as to effect your eyes by looking at it.

When you want to force a pipe of wine, take a quart of this stum, heat ½ oz. of isinglass and put it in, whisk together till dissolved, when it will be a jelly; break the jelly, and add a pound of alabaster to it; dissolve a little in the wine, then put it in the pipe and close up, and in a day's time it will be fine and bright.

STARCH DRINKS

Pananda—for an invalid

Varied in type, the basis was wheat bread dissolved in water. We give two recipes.

Put water (about 2 pints) into a pan with sugar wine, nutmeg and lemon peel. Boil up and add finely grated white bread till it thickens. Let it cook till clear and drink when cool. (It may be necessary to press and strain off if it is to be a thin drink, or it can be eaten with a spoon if wanted thick.)

Pananda for a Cold on the Chest

Boil fine white bread in water, very fast, beating it well, till it becomes smooth and thick. Add sugar, butter and rum; eat hot in bed!

Starch Jellies (drinks made from them)

Tapioca water was one of the many "starch" waters that was classified as a jelly water for invalids. Wash the tapioca, and soak in fresh cold spring water at least 5 hours, then simmer till clear and allow to cool and set firm. To make the drink, beat up a slice of the jelly in cold water, adding lemon juice and honey (or sugar).

Water Gruels

Gruels varied from other starch drinks, being definitely thicker, and served as a "spoon food".

Various forms of oatmeal, or barley, usually replaced the more glutinous wheat, and the gruel was usually darker in colour and more "solid".

Gruel was sometimes thinned down to a drink, for which we give one recipe.

One pint of boiling water; tablespoon oatmeal (fine). Mix in a basin with a little cold water and pour the boiling water on to it stirring well. Boil all up and immediately strain through a sieve, adding salt and butter (if to be drunk hot) or wine or sugar if to be taken cold.

These oatmeal drinks, usually made with beer or lightly laced with brandy or rum, were useful in the days of horse travel, when riders, tired, cold and hungry, needed something hot to "carry them on" till they had got their boots off and supper was on the table (see *Food in England*).

Barley Water

One of the oldest "waters" and still popular. Two ounces of *fresh* barley boiled in 2 quarts of water till the grain is white and soft. Strain the water off. Add lemon if liked, but it is pleasant and has a delicate flavour of its own.

The same barley may be boiled again with only 1 pint of water and a spoonful of red currant jelly. This gives a pinkish, sweet drink for children and is wholesome.

Pearl barley may be used, but the fresh barley has a more subtle flavour.

CARRIED DRINKS

"The Shepherds homely curds
His cold thin drink out of his leather bottle."

Henry VI

This "cold thin drink" from the wet wooden hoggin or porous leather bottle could have been water, whey, or buttermilk. Buttermilk is still offered to travellers at any Welsh farm on the hills and, when fresh, the cool, slightly acid drink is very refreshing. Or it could have been whey from the cheese vat, or one of the light harvest ales, or meads, or sugar beers, which are little more than slightly fermented barley water, being made from the *last* washings of the straw skips, or the wrung-out bags in which honey was strained. Or the "cool thin drink" could be one of the many forms of water gruel that had a cereal basis. All could have utilized the well-known flavouring of herbs, such as gale (bog myrtle), balm, briar, rosemary, burnet or coltsfoot. These old drinks far outnumbered the soft drinks and mineral waters of today, and were a substitute for them.

Ale, in all its forms, from the light drinking ale, quickly made and quickly used, to the strong and matured ales of rich potency, depended upon the water used almost as much as the brewing methods. All breweries had their own special springs and wells. In the author's own district there were five different wells, each giving its name and character to a special brand of ale; but all have been closed down, being replaced by one standard product brought from a distance by lorry.

The whey and buttermilk need no explanation, but the types of water gruel are interesting as they vary from the cereal jellies based on the sediment washings of chaff, to the Scotchman's "cold brose" and the Welshman's hot "potes pigtegill". Brose (the name is now loosely used for broths) was originally a form of aerated, slightly fermented, oatmeal drink, made by putting a handful of loose oatmeal into the hoggin, filling it up with water from some mountain stream, and carrying it, swinging and bumping as you walked, or rode, for several hours. The churning action, and probably some bacteria, long developed in the wood, produced a cool thin gruel, slightly sweet, slightly acid, and reasonably sustaining. Crushed fresh barley could be used, but the operative item was probably the hoggin, previously used for ferments.

The same phenomena turned up in some gourds used by African natives to carry milk. Instead of the milk turning sour, these gourds produced a delicious thick cream, very beneficial to patients in a Johannesburg hospital, where fresh milk was proving difficult in the dry season. Unfortunately, a well-trained nursing sister sterilized the gourds, and the bacteria had to be painstakingly redeveloped with considerable difficulty under official conditions. It is the same old story of certain storerooms and caves "making" the cheese; it is the bacteria that survive in each case.

BROSE

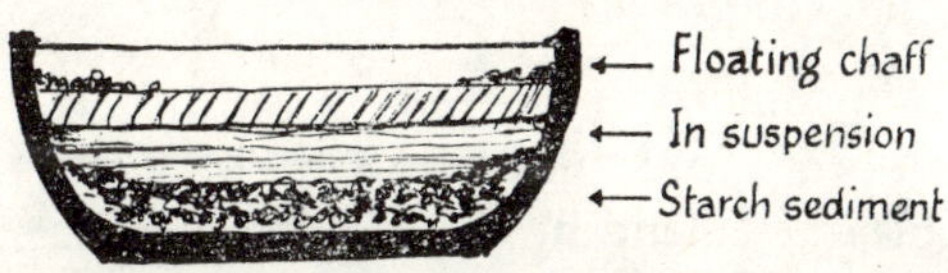

The chaff-water-brose was more complicated, and the process was also carried out with bran and other by-products of the millings. The water in which chaff was soaked was well shaken up and then left to settle.[1] After the grains of cereal dust had swelled, and the wood fibre of the husk softened, the saturated water was drained off and boiled down, thus checking fermentation at the required stage, and the boiling and thickening process continued to give either a drink (usually laced with spirits) or a cereal jelly (usually served with cream and sugar). This last form was a flummery (*not* to be confused with fermenty). Either could be eaten or drunk, hot or cold.

The "potes pigtegill", or "brewis", of the Welsh, was invariably served hot, but again, the basis was cereal. Originally broken oat bread (bara cierch) was crumbled into a bowl over a modicum of fat (bacon

[1] See page 328

fat, butter, or dripping), and after the boiling water was poured on, this fat was given time to rise and permeate the expanded cereal. Seasoning and cheese were added ("brewis" is made a different way in every household), and the result was more a thick broth than a thin drink. But the interesting variety of the old water and cereal drinks and dishes would fill a complete cookery book. Today barley water is the only one left in general use.

Toast Water. That golden drink of the Victorian childhood, that ceased to be flavoursome after the fine white loaf replaced the wholemeal, was boiling water poured onto well-toasted bread, allowed to cool, and strained off into glasses.

MEAT DRINKS

These were *not* soups. They were not boiled. They were made by pouring water (hot or cold) onto the meats and pressing and straining off the liquid.

These drinks are definitely drunk from a cup, not eaten with a spoon from a bowl.

We give these examples from a recipe book of 1806 by Elizabeth Raffold.

Chicken Water

Skin half a fowl, break the bones and slice the flesh thinly, put it into a jar and pour over a pint of boiling water. Cover close and set by the fire for 3 hours, and the water will be ready to drink.

Beef Water

A pound of lean beef sliced thin into a jar with a quart of boiling water poured over. Cover and stand by the fire, but it must not boil and must be drunk when it is milk warm.

MEAT DRINKS THAT WERE DEFINITELY BROTHS

Though made in water these belong more correctly to a cookery book, but we give four examples to show the type.

Strong Broth of Mixed Meats (*about* 1800)

1 hock of beef. 1 neck of mutton. Break all bones and take both joints into pieces.

(In earlier centuries the cook would have been instructed to "take an axe and smite all into gobbets". Today the cook would gently ask the butcher to "please bone the joints".) Pack bones below meat into a thick pan, and cover with cold salted water. Boil up slowly and skim well. When part cooked, add one onion stuck with cloves, a quarter of nutmeg broken up, some sweet herbs and a couple of crushed black peppers, all tied loosely in a bag and hung in the water. Boil till all the strength is out of the meats and into the water, and withdraw the spice bag when enough. Strain for use and skim off fat when cold.

Beef Broth (*about* 1700)

Crack a hock, add a gallon of water, 3 blades of mace and a bundle of parsley and a crust of well-browned (i.e. slightly burnt) bread. Boil all "till the sinews be softe and tendre", then chop them up; add diced toast and seasoning and serve.

N.B. The cracked hock bone would be boiled clean of meat and the soft sinews could be detached easily. This period seems to have appreciated gelatinous gristle and the translucent cubes of sinew would be cut the same size as the cubes of toast.

Cock Broth (*Cock a leekie*), *an early recipe*

Chop up the cock, and chop up leeks, and add salt and pepper and a few marigold flowers. "Boil till all is in the water" (i.e. meat off the bones and leeks in shreds), beat and strain. Put back any meat left whole into the broth.

Sheep's Head Broth

Chop the head and add barley and onion and boil all together till bones be clean. Then *strain off* and put in small cut-up turnip and carrots (not too many) and cook till done.

The old cook book, from which these are taken, advises them to be made in thick earthenware pots raised high over the fire and covered close so that they can "do softly for some time (probably left on the fire overnight), then the broths will be good."

WATER SOUCHET OR SOUCHY

A clear fish soup, sometimes flavoured with herbs, tarragon, fennel, parsley, etc. It was served to guests at Greenwich before they had freshly-dressed whitebait.

WATER AND WORTS AND WORKING FERMENTS

An Important Explanation

It is difficult to divide the soft drinks from some of the fermented ones. Their basis was water, boiled with the flavouring ingredients (nettles, dandelion, spruce, etc., and often the sixteenth-century hops). When the water was cool enough to "see your face in it" (a universal test) the yeast, barm, or whatever "working" material used, was put into this water. If it was a yeast type of plant it grew in the water, feeding upon the sugar content, till all this nourishment in the water was used up. This was the "working" period, because, during this time, the yeast was alive and growing, and the slight hiss of escaping gas and movements in the liquid showed it was "active". When this "working activity" ceased, the cause might be the death or "sleeping" of the yeast plant (through cold, or other accident), or simply that the nourishment in the liquid was all used up so the yeast plant became dormant.

To find out the cause, the housewife sprinkled a little more sugar near the plant and watched the reaction. If it began to hiss and work again, then the sugar in the liquid *had* all been used up, and the yeast was alive and hungry! If there was no reaction, the yeast plant was dead, though the liquor might still be full of unused sugar.

This is a very simple elementary explanation of a very involved process. In households used to making "home brewed" the brewer understood all the complications that could occur between changes of the fungoid fermenting plant, and the nourishment provided in the water.

Some yeasts (for example, most bread yeasts) could be grown in jars or tubs, and provided they were kept warm and fed, flourished well, being provided with air, frequently "let in through the bladder cover of the jar, through a goose quill." But most wine, and some ale, yeasts required continuous fresh oxygen, so were hung out in the fresh air, usually in the *intensities of the bush or besom of loose twigs with which the winemaker had stirred up the liquid.*

The sticky yeasts clung to the twigs and packed into the brush, where they remained, well aired, and slightly damp, till they were next required for use.

Moreover, if a brew had gone flat, or dull, the brush could be taken down and the brew well beaten up with it, so that the brew began to work again and the brush was refreshed and rewatered.

This was the origin of the tavern sign of the stuck-out brush. Anyone seeing such a brush by the door (even if it was not a tavern) would know someone had been brewing and drop in to sample the new barrel.

For many meads and metheglins the brush was made of scented shrubs, bog myrtle, rosemary, or sweet briar, etc., to give the subtle aroma.

Thus, the true meaning of "Good wine needs no brush" went beyond the obvious outer sign of the tavern.

"Of the Bowe and braches of the Byrche ben Besomes made."

—BART. ANGLICUS.

The besom was usually made of birch, as the twigs were springy, and wet resistant. It was the common type of broom for centuries, and remains

the gardener's favourite. The binding was usually of ash strips. A log of ash, cut across both ends, was laid under running water, the grain of the wood down the run of the stream (*see* steeping, page 320). After a month or so, the outer rings of the wood could be knocked loose, and peeled up in pliant strips (like very thick wooden tape). The log was then replaced till the next layer was loosened. The head of the besom was wedged tightly into a rounded groove (later an iron grip) and bound for several turns with the ash strip, the end being pushed under. Released, the besom stretched the binding into a firm smooth ring. This white binding on the dark besom is shown very clearly in early illuminated MSS.

MEDICAL WATERS BETWEEN THE SEVENTEENTH AND EIGHTEENTH CENTURIES

One might describe the characteristic "waters" of this period as a mixture of astrology and distillery. The whole flavoured with a spice of witchcraft and modified (when required) with a slight sweetening of Christianity. On the whole, medicine improved rapidly during this period, but there were some extraordinary brews!

Several thousand pounds were offered and awarded in the late 1700's for a cure for consumption. A woman won with calcified snails, the shells of which, with charcoal, seem to have been drunk as a form of lime-water. The small white "dew" snails, gathered from meadows and dissolved in warm milk, were a rural remedy till the late nineteenth century and, like the elvers' jelly of the Rhynes, may have supplemented some diet deficiency after the restrictions of the winter.

This use of "mineral waters" continued (*see* springs, holy and otherwise), but plants were tested in abundance and the increase of interest in distilling of "essences" was helped by the improvement of apparatus.

An old gardener friend expounded the whole matter to me thus: "Plants do take up minerals from the soil, and some plants do take more of one mineral than another. Watercress—now that seems to take up iron from the water, and broom, now, shepherds used to gather it for sulphur for sheep. But nowadays [this was about 1920] the chemists are so clever that they take the mineral *direct* from the soil, to give to you, so the plants are not much used. All the same, we older folk do think that as plants is in line *below* animals it *might be better to let the plants digest the minerals first, before we, as animals, takes them.* There's no short cuts with growing things, and as we all come up from the soil, and go back to the soil, *it's maybe better to do it in the right order.*"

God rest him! He was one of the most thoughtful men I've ever known, and taught me more than can be told.

MEDICINAL WATERS OF THE SEVENTEENTH CENTURY

(Owing to the ornate eloquence that medical etiquette demanded during this period, we regret being unable to quote more than one example in the original.)

Dr. Stephen's Water

"This water discurses wind and vapours lodged either in the first passages, or included between their tunicks, or in the interslices of the muscles; and that, either primarily, and safely by its discursive and carminative virtue, which has an immediate effect upon the primae viae, by attenuating viscidities, and rarifying and discursing those vapours therein included. Or, secondarily, by impregnating, and communicating, the said qualities to the sanguineous fluids, which, being thereby conveyed, and carried along, with the blood, and distributed by the arterial capillaries, amongst those muscular or membraneous parts, must necessarily rarifie, and discurse those vapours pent up therein, and throw them off by the secretory ducts.

"The nerves also may contribute to the work, by the grateful effluvia arising from those aromaticks, they are immediately affected therewith, and an elasticity of springiness, is added to their fibres; and this may be partly assisted by the pungency of the salts, which arise with the oyle in distillation, from several of the ingredients, which thereby may vellicate the nervous fibrillae, and so cause their vibrations to be more frequent and strong, and partly by a fresh influx of animal spirits, which those sensitive organs receive from their most volatil and subtle parts. The nervous system is thereby invigorated, and enabled more forcibly to agitate, and throw off, the contained wind, and so help forward its other expulsion. By the same reasons may we account for and know the method which nature takes in removing obstructions of the nerves, and also those of the cutaneous glands; which here would be needless to lay down, as requiring more time than I am willing to spend upon this subject as designing shortly to treat more amply of nervous diseases, their cause and cure in another work of another nature to which I refer the reader.

"It will be the best season to make Dr. Stephen's water (which is in great demand in London) in June or July, when the herbs are in their full prime and must be drawn over with a very moderate fire and no longer than it is proof. It will be abundantly better for keeping. Often it is made up and dulcify'd with fine sugar. Let it stand 5 or 6 days in an open headed vessel, with a brass cock in it, and when it is perfectly fine, draw it off gently into the cask you intend to keep it in all year. But, forasmuch as you must have standard bottles for keeping and selling small quantities of Dr. Stephen's and other fine cordial drams, you must, when you fill your standard bottles of Dr. Stephen's water, put to every gallon thereof 2 leaves of gold, dissevered with the feather end of a quill, and shaken well up when you pour it out for sale. Some few persons chuse to drink it and other fine cordials undulcifyed."

The Recipe

"11 gls. rect. proof malt spirit.

Thyme, mother of thyme(?), sage, pennysojal, pellitory of the wall, rosemary, red roses, chamomile flowers, origanum lavender, mint of each 4 handfuls.

Ginger, galingale, cinnamon, nuts, aniseed, caraways, each 2 oz. 5 lb. sugar and 2 leaves of gold to the gallon."

SNAIL WATER. FOR JAUNDICE 1700

"Take a peck of shell snails, lay them on a hot hearthstone before the fire till they have done hissing and spitting, then wipe them from the froth and break in a mortar. Have a quart of earth worms, slit and scoured clean with salt and water and heat them with the snails. Then take angelica, celandine, woodsorrel, agrimony, bearfoot, barberry bark, great dock roots of each 2 handfuls, rosemary flowers a quart., 1 lb. of hartshorn, turmeric and fenugreek 2 oz. of each, $\frac{1}{2}$ oz. of powdered saffron and 3 oz. of cloves fresh beaten. Shred and in-fuse all in 3 galls of ale, then distil and draw off. 3 spoonsfuls in a glass of sack before every meal and use moderate exercise."

Palsey Water used cowslips, borage and buglos, and lilies of the valley, rosemary, sage, and lavender, etc., and these were digested in the sun before distilling.

Alexiterial Milk Water used meadow sweet, flowers and groats, mint and wormwood and rue and angelica. 3 gal. of milk and lukewarm distilling.

Black Cherry Water

"When cherry brandy was made by pressing, the stones were sold to the druggists to make black cherry water, and the druggist commonly gave as good a price for the stones as the cherries themselves had cost. This being in London, whereto came the Kentish cherries in quantity." (Brown sugar, cloves and cinnamon were added to old recipes for cherry brandy. A raspberry brandy was made, but in less demand than cherry.)

Golden Cordial

This was made of angelica and liquorice with rose water and sugar, and, in the best cordial, English saffron to give a good golden colour. But cheaper cordial used burnt sugar.

Ratafia Water

(This was used as a flavouring—though classified as a medical water.)

The distillation was of "Nuts and bitter almonds, and Lisbon sugar and brandy infused cold for 7 or 8 days before draining off for use.

"The nuts and almonds, by their opening and cleansing quality, may prove a good evacuant, for the bitter almonds oyl, as it undergoes no torture by fire,[1] retains its unctuous and softening quality. For by its oleaginous quality, the fibres that compose the urinary glandules and canal are lubricated, softened and released; and by their penetration, virtue; which certainly they receive from some saline particles wrapped up in, and as it were, lying dissolved in the oyle; they scour off such vicious humours, or calculousses, concretions, as may abstract the said glandules, and hinder the free emission of urine."

Colours for Waters

Both archill (used also for cheeses) and sanders were used to give red, and also elderberry juice. These were pressed through a "harden" bag.

Surfeil Water

Herbs. Centuary, marigolds, mint, rosemary, margent, scordu, rue, carduns, balm, dragons, St. Johns wart, each 8 handfuls.

Roots. Angelica, butter bun, peony, scorzonera, of each 1 lb.

Drug. Calamus aromaticus, galingale, angelica seeds, carroway seeds, 4 oz. ginger, 2 oz. red poppy seeds, 2 oz. oils of sugar.

[1] Cold drawn oil.

Ros Solis. An infusion of rose leaves and spice with brandy and sugar.

Lime juice is said to be unwholesome, but that may be from prejudice against vitriol, which is known by all practitioners in physic to be most wholesome and a safe medicine.

To make it, take double the quantity of water you intend to make juice and put 3 or 4 lb. of limestone[1] to it and stir till dissolved.

Pour off gently as much as you intend to make up, and to every gallon of this lime-water add 1 dozen priced lemons sliced, stir, and infuse till the next day.

Strain off, and to every gallon add ½ oz. of oil or spirit of vitriol; mix the same a little and then mix the whole.

The usual proportion used is 1 lb. of limestone to a gallon of water.

1600.

Horseradish Water. The leaves of scury grasses, brookline, watercress and horseradish root, arum root (fresh). Winter bark and nutmegs, lemon peels and French brandy.

Dr. Butler's Treacle Water. This was hartshorn shavings, boiled roots of elicampane, gentian, cypress tormentile, blessed thistle and angelica, borage buglos, rosemary and marigold flowers, citron peels and cowslips, clove July flowers (gilly flower?), lavender, marjoram and Venice treacle.

Fever Water was red wine and milk dubbed together.

Walnut Water was made of green walnuts and water of balm leaves and liquorice.

Cranberry Water for the Sick Room

Put a cupful of cranberries to a cup of cold water and break and soak them. Boil 2 quarts of water with a large spoonful of oatmeal and lemon peel if liked. Add the cranberries to the boiling water and a little sugar, but do not destroy the acid tang of the fruit. Strain and cool. This, essentially a fruit drink, was sometimes laced with a little white wine.

A Cold Water Caudle

Caudles were usually hot and "restorative". This seems to have been designed for feverish cases.

1 quart of spring water, boiled and allowed to cool, beat the white of an egg and a little lemon juice and white wine.

Mint Water (Peppermint?)

"Take mint 2 handfuls, proof spirit 2 gallons (?), water 1 gallon, distill and dulcify with sugar 1½ lb.

"This water wholy partakes of the nature of mint and is used against

[1] It is not clear what form of limestone is used.

vomiting, hiccough, wind in the stomach (or bowels), gryping of the guts, megrine headache, etc.

"It effects by the tenuity and subtility of its parts inciding, attenuating and discursing all vicid humour and vapours lodged in the stomach or guts. All (the listed deseases) spring from the phlegm lodged in the first passages—which being agitated emiss vapours thence to the head or parts that always sympathises with the stomach."

(The virtues of this water are much condensed.)

China Ale

(This, in 1700, was a name for "ginger" beer.)

"To six galls of ale $\frac{1}{4}$ lb. of China root sliced and $\frac{1}{4}$ lb. corriander seeds. Hang them in a tiffany,[1] or loose linen bag, in the ale till it has done working and let it stand 14 days before you bottle it. This is good, but there is a common sort vended about town that is nothing more than very (cheap) beer put up in small stone bottles with a little spice, lemon peel and raisins and sugar."

The cheap beer was probably one of the "watered beers"—that did *not* mean water added to the beer, but to the liquid drawn off from the brewing tubs. The tubs were refilled with water, the utensils used in the previous brewing being rinsed in this water, and enough fermenting medium would be left at the bottom of the tub clinging to the plants and herbs put in for flavouring, to work slightly and be used quickly. It would have little strength and flavour, hence they "gingered it up" with spice, raisins and sugar to sell off—bottled.

Ebulum

This is an example of a better type of this "second water" beer. For it was "second water" on to the reside of a *strong* beerwort. This strong wort was not drained off too finely, and an equal amount of warm elderberry juice was poured on to it, and stirred, before being strained off into the cask in which the new mild "working" was carried on for a year (at least) before drawing off and bottling.

A note says, that (because the original wort was strong) there should be no need to add any extra sugar (that is, there would be enough food left for the residue of the fungus to feed upon), but a few spices could be added to the cask, and when well kept and bottled off clear it was "often preferred to port wine—and had a very healthful quality".

There was also a white ebulum, but we do not know if this used the flowers or the berries while still green.

[1] Tiffany was a loose net, the word usually applied to the silk net or gauze used for dresses, but seems to have been used also for a domestic fabric, somewhat like a milk syle cloth.

Tea Water

A Victorian name for excessively weak tea was "water bewitched". The time required for the water to stand on the leaves varies. According to the priests who brought the first tea back from China, "as long as it took to say three Pater Nosters slowly". Tea leaves were easily (though expensively) adopted, because the country people had made leaf decoctions for years. Sage, catnip, horsehound, raspberry leaf, blackberry tips, dozens of plants supplied "tea leaves" (fresh or dried), so that the foreign tea leaves were only a new variant. It was, at first, a new drink adopted by frequenters of coffee houses; working people still drank salop and other watery brews. However, once thoroughly adopted, foreign tea became a revolutionary trade. Special tea clippers were built, special china was designed. Every watery hot drink became a "tea", even spa waters were designated "limestone tea". Laws had to be passed to prohibit servants from selling the used tea leaves, as an illicit trade was springing up in which such tea leaves were dried and re-rolled, supplemented by a few common English leaves (blackberry tips made the brew look darker) and resold for use. Teapot shapes varied as opinions on "infusing" changed. The shallow rounded pot was popular as it gave a wide space for the leaves to expand. After tannin was "discovered" the more globular shape followed, as this shape allowed the spout to be inserted above the tannin level (also it copied the new and now popular chinese designs). China pots with fitted infusers were popular with the rich, but the poorer folk wanted value for their money and liked the hot water to stand and stew on the leaves, to get *all* the strength out.

One ingenious patent tea-pot (used in the early 1900's) had an air lock release that pulled out and allowed the water to fall down away from the leaves and so avoid brewing too long. One realizes the importance of tea in the late 1800's because councils and municipal waters and special springs and rivers are recommended as "brewing good tea". A century before "the water is excellent for brewing" . . . would have meant brewing ale.

KETTLES

For water to be heated over anything but solid fuel was a revolution that entailed swift fundamental changes in design. We are so accustomed to oil lamps, spirit lamps, Primus stoves, gas rings and hot plates, that we take the bottom heat principle for granted, but with solid fuel the side heat was frequently more important than the base heat.

The inverted angle

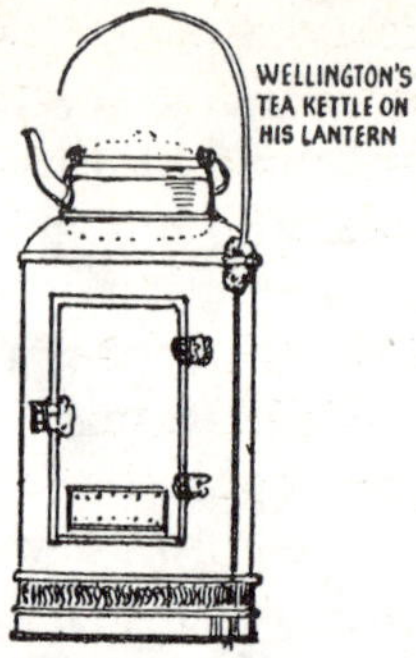

If you study the old water heaters (the kettles and cauldrons for wood and coal fires) the slope is outwards from a small base to a wide top. In the "muller" design (for extra swift heating of liquid) the base was simply the point of a cone thrust down into the fire. This early type of quick-boiling kettle shows how *swiftly* the design changed. These sketches of the inverted angle are simple and obvious, but the principle involved accounted for some extraordinary mental howlers in some of the earlier boiler designs. We are not guiltless today, as most of our electric kettles are simply the old base-heated kettle adapted to take the new internal heater.

Left, the double saucepan, 1861. *Right, a quick-boiling kettle (the tubular),* 1890

Water was measured out scantily on sailing ships and though a few voyagers took a small stove "for use in the cabin", the general habit was to apply to the galley (or doctor) if hot water was necessary. It was the steam locomotive that seems to have introduced the tea basket and small travelling spirit kettle. Kipling takes it for granted that the English travelling by train in India should boil water and brew tea in their carriages.

The Electric Kettle Arrives

A small electric water boiler was exhibited at Crystal Palace Great Exhibition. It was a simple affair of metal wire wrapped around an inner container capable of holding water.

The arrangement was a prototype of the coiled wire element of an electric fire, and the inventor, Mr. Fox, claimed that he could boil a pint of water in ten minutes and pointed out that "when electricity is supplied in every home the contrivance will be useful".

THE TEMPERANCE MOVEMENT—A NOTE ONLY

> But while he was gentle he was firm. He did not refrain from reprobating intemperance because one of his deacons owned a distillery.
>
> Longfellow. Kavanagh, 1834

The main hard drinking of the Georgian period was on expensive wine, and this, together with extravagant gaming, absurd wages and other extravagances, destroyed many of the nobility and brought their estates to ruin.

In contrast, the hard drinking of the Victorian period was mainly coarse spirits, and drunkenness was at its worst among the industrial workers, where it reduced whole families to abject poverty. Their drinking was induced by their bad living conditions, and in some towns almost every other shop or house sold beer and spirits. Men coming off work, tired and hungry, turned automatically into the nearest bar where credit was allowed and very little restraint attempted. To be half drunk every night, and dead drunk every Saturday, was "just the custom". No sort of birth control was considered, except the women's gin (which got the nickname "Mother's Ruin" on this account).

Some of the first fish and chip stalls were started up close to factory gates, in an attempt to supply the workers with hot food they could eat as they walked home, and so mitigate the effect of drinks upon an empty stomach.

Because this book only concerns water we give only one example of a "Reformer", or "Water Drinker", though the movement was general and everywhere, or almost everywhere, was backed by religious feeling (rather than the State control that enforced prohibition in America). As an example we give one Joseph Liversley, an orphan, who worked as a weaver in a damp cellar. He seems to have been immune from the general trend (perhaps instructed against it?) and at 21, when he unexpectedly inherited £30, married. That was in 1815 (the Corn Law period), and after twins were born, the family almost starved. Joseph used to go to the local market after work to buy cheaply food the stall-holders did not want to carry away. He used to buy very cheaply the cut cheeses, or those left unsold at the end of the day. These he would retail to the less provident workers, who had spent their evenings drinking! He did so well at this, that eventually he gave up the ill-paid weaving and used to trade in all the local markets. In large markets like Wigan, or Chorley, he came in contact with the farmers themselves, and took to visiting their farms direct. As (by comparison) the rural workers had far more food, and he could sometimes take advantage of a glut, he was soon in the lucrative position of "middle man", and being frugal and saving, he became a well-to-do public figure. In 1844 he started the *Preston Guardian*. It is said that it was at an official luncheon he first conformed to polite custom and tried the official whisky. He disliked it and it made him ill! As he could account for his personal success by never having wasted time and money on beer and spirits (in every other way, he had shared the handicap of poverty) he was an excellent example. At first the "Pledge" was only "to abstain from getting drunk", but as it proved impossible to decide when one crossed the line, it proved more reliable to "pledge not to drink alcohol at all", in fact to pledge "total abstinence", and the word "T.Total'er" came into use.

The movement did wonderful work and better supervision in the public houses had influence. Today the "alcoholic" is regarded with a sympathetic medical eye, and considered an exception, and there are few public houses that will serve unwisely. But the few old people who can still remember Victorian days will remember the scorn and consternation that could be caused by a T.Totaller at a dinner party! If the unfortunate eccentric could produce a "liver" or a "diet", sympathy was allowed, and perhaps barley water provided (and the unaccountable T.Totalism of a few noble English families would be hurriedly mentioned to cover the general embarrassment). But in those conventional days to be a T.Totaller was hardly proper, and to be a vegetarian downright indecent!

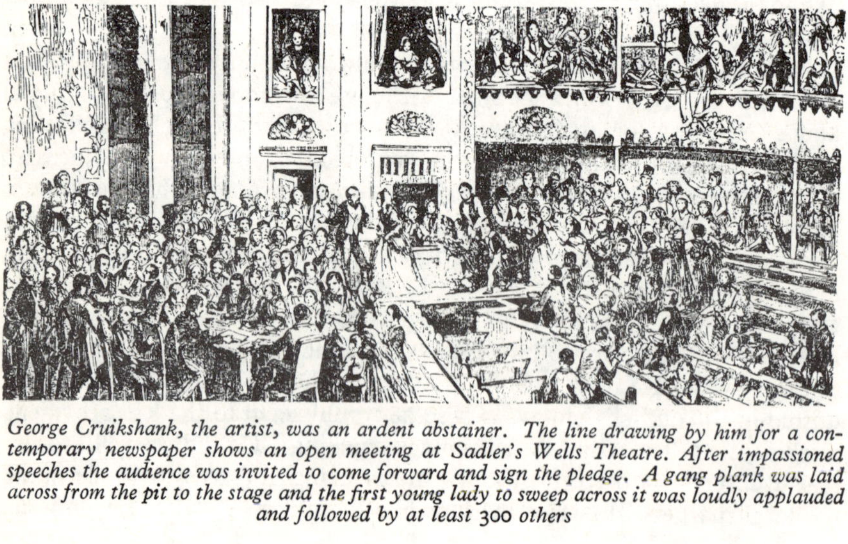

George Cruikshank, the artist, was an ardent abstainer. The line drawing by him for a contemporary newspaper shows an open meeting at Sadler's Wells Theatre. After impassioned speeches the audience was invited to come forward and sign the pledge. A gang plank was laid across from the pit to the stage and the first young lady to sweep across it was loudly applauded and followed by at least 300 others

PLANTS AND PERSONALITIES PERTAINING TO WATER

RUSHES AND REEDS

The water rushes, or sedges, or reeds (the names are used loosely in common speech), include the eight-to-ten-foot-high river rushes and the smallest bog reeds only a few inches high. Water rushes are a class of plant of much complicated interest.

Reeds and rushes have little fodder value. Sheep enjoy the brown tassels of the mountain rush and in hill districts the green rush is used as waterproof thatch for ricks, and so is the plaited marram grass whose creeping roots are used to reclaim sand dunes and salt marsh lands.

Fen Reed or Norfolk Reed (Phragmites communis)

The common river reed grows along and across rivers and shallow waters in a dense mass. Ultimately, by accumulated decay it gradually forms marsh and dry land. The Saxons built whole settlements of reed huts, made tracks across the peat bogs with bales of this cut reed and, so history tells, defended their last eastern stronghold by firing the dry rushes around it. Today the draining of the fens has reduced the acreage of "reed ronds" (as the plantations are called), but acres are still cut and stacked and used for many purposes. This is the finest thatching reed, which stands fifty years, and is stacked till the leaves drop off, before use. This clean circular reed takes on the gloss and sheen of a pigeon's wing and sheds water like a duck's back. When "raised" by expanding frost it requires to be "beaten in" and any sign of moss should be pared off, as that would retain water. Most old churches show the stone courses that mark the first higher-pitched roof of thatch, and the gabled edge that originally held back the butt ends of the thatch; now it stands up naked and thin, in front of the deep gully necessitated by the shallower roof of slate.

The leaves from the reed are used to stuff firm hassocks and upholstery. In some districts they replace the more valuable straw in making the "straw palliasse" or under mattress used on old beds.

In sixteenth- to eighteenth-century herbals it is noted that a "bird called a starling (Sturnus vulgaris) has eager attachment to this reed, and roosts upon it in flocks. By the extraordinary circumstances attending this bird's violent passion for this reed, bushels of (the birds) are destroyed by farmers within one night". As the cutting of the reed for thatch reduced the number of starlings, so now with the reduction of the reed beds, the starlings seem to have transferred their "violent passion" to Trafalgar Square.

Great Reed Mace (Tryphalati folia)

Commonly called the Bull Rush—though that is the official name for *Scirpus Lacustris*. This was sometimes used as a torch, being soaked in oil, several tied in line, and one lit from the other as they burnt. They lasted some time, but made a smokey flame.

Reed mace (the soft brownish panicle of many reeds) was used to fill working boots in cold weather. The fibrous woody texture would certainly be a warm padding, and tramps, changing their socks by running water (or lacking socks to change) would be as likely to see the reeds as many foot travellers and footsore field workers have done for centuries. (I believe something of the same sort is used by the Laplanders and Finns.)

The Mud Rush (Isolepis savii)

This became fashionable in the 1890's as a London window plant. The roots (common enough on bogs) were brought in by gypsies and sold as "Isidores" by the trade. It was quick-growing and soon filled a watered bowl with vivid green. (Rediscovered it might well supplant the gloomy rubber plants of today.)

The Scented Rush (Acorus calumus)

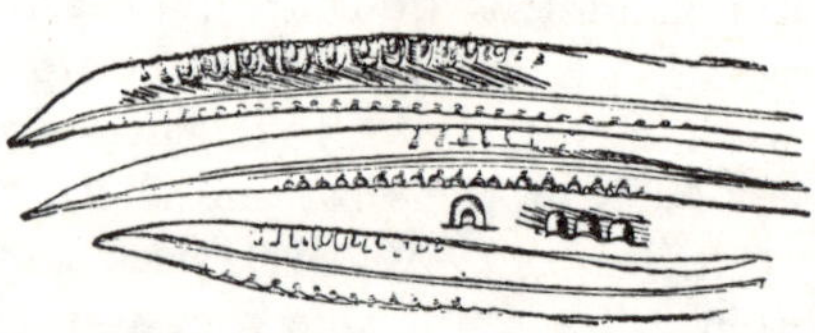

The scented rush

"O please! There are some scented rushes!" Alice cried . . . "Such beauties!"

"You needn't say 'please' to *me* about 'em," the Sheep said. . . .

"No, but I meant please, may we wait and pick some?" Alice pleaded . . . so the boat was left to drift . . . till it glided gently in among the waving rushes . . . Even real scented rushes, you know, last only a very little while and these, being dream rushes, melted away . . . as they lay in heaps at her feet.

Alice Through the Looking Glass

The scented rush was one of those gathered to strew over the floors and under the dining-tables in times when chairs and tables had long cross stretchers at floor level to hold them down underfoot. The wavy-edged leaves of the scented rushes that grow along the Thames by Hampton Court can still awaken dreams as the boat drifts among them.

The Rush that Made Rush Lights

This round green rush with little brown tassels which the mountain sheep nibble, has a white pith that was for centuries found to be of exactly the porous texture to absorb wax and provide tapers. The rush is also used in Breconshire to thatch stacks. It grows best by shallow moving water on hillsides. In autumn the rush gatherers went out with old knives to cut the longest and thickest reeds, which they either carried home in bundles, or sat down and peeled on the spot. Once the knack had been acquired rush-peeling was child's play. Starting at the base you split up the green "rind", running it up over your thumb-nail till the soft white pith curled and swung loose. One strip of green rind had to be left on to hold the soft pith strip. Too narrow a green strip left the rush too brittle; too wide a strip made too much ash when the waxed pith burnt. Rather *less* than a quarter circumference was ideal. If reasonably dry the "dipping" was done at once. A mixture of tallow and beeswax was melted in a long dish and each rush was pulled through it and laid down or hung up to dry. The round tables with swivel tops set on a small square "colonnaded" cage are old rushlight tables, the rushes being laid in sheaves through the carrier space and pulled out to insert in the rush-light holder on the table.

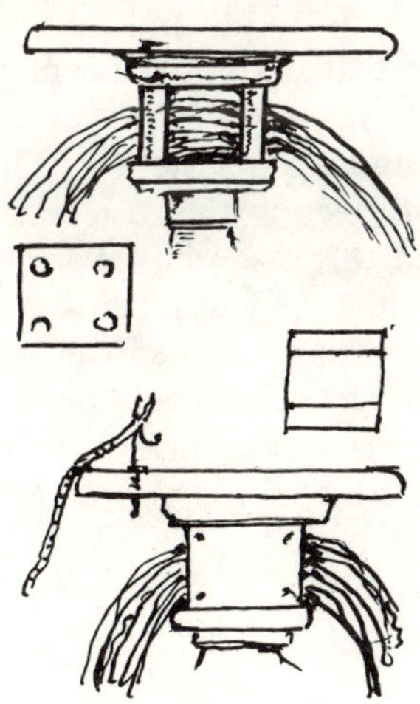

Rush-light holder

The small galleries under Pembroke table-tops were made to hold bunches of rushlights, which could be easily pulled out as they were needed. The galleries under polished parlour tables had four pillars, common cottage tables usually had a plain box for the same purpose.

The swivel top allowed all the women working round the table to swing the single rush light to their side for any special need (such as threading a needle) and to reach for a fresh rush light if the one in use was burning out.

Long after tallow dips, candles and, later, oil lamps and tapers came, the small rush lights remained in use. Because in rural economy they cost nothing! Everyone kept bees, so that beeswax and a little tallow fat could be had easily and the rushes were there for the cutting. The rush light in the country was free of charge, and even when purchased from a city chandler was the cheapest form of lighting we have ever known!

Rush Rings

This is the same small rush that was plaited into rings by country lovers, to forestall the wedding ring, so that being wed "with a rush ring" might imply scorn. The gypsies also used this rush to plait "tokens", used as a sign or signature of the sender. Each family had its own pattern. A rush token containing a sprig of heather, a certain bird's feather, or a head of corn, could tell where the maker had been (and perhaps what he'd done). Some of the old tramp signs on high road, or by door-post, gave their silent message in the same way. A river rush or small water plant, faded and fallen by the dry roadside, would not be noticed by anyone except a searcher on the look out for it. Then its position (right or left and pointing up or down) could tell him on which side of the next river bridge the police were searching, or his pals were camping.

The "Plaiting Rush"

Several types of reed provided leaves that were used for mats, trundle beds, chair seats and under thatch, etc.

The rush chair seat is too well known to need description. The strength and neatness depends on the tight twist given to the rush leaves and the interlocking of the joins. A trundle bed was made in the same way, but with a thicker rope, and often, if the floor bed was being woven for a "fine" bedroom or some special child-bearing, the bed would be woven with a loving intricate weave. All babies were delivered upon these straw or rush floor beds. A woman in labour was spoken of as "the lady in the straw" or as having "been brought to the reeds".

Therefore, that carefully-carved stone rush mat on which the knight rests upon his tomb, recalls that it was upon just such a mat of plaited rushes he was born into this world and so, sleeping quietly, he awaits his next rebirth into heaven.

(You must walk as they walked, by river path and mountain track, before you see the things they saw and understand their ancient usages, *see* page 57.)

Reed and willow have entirely different constructional uses. Willows, used individually, are plaited and bent to shape, the strength coming from tension and a firm design, so that even strong hurdles and fish traps remain light in weight. Rushes are more usually bound into rope form and sewn together, so that rush constructions tend to be soft and heavy.

In building wattle (willow) and daub work, the supporting strength is the wattle, clay being daubed into it. Reed and straw are incorporated in the plaster or daub.

The drawing shows the only tool common to willow work. Used to bend rods, it's curiously called "The Commander". The noun-name is always used as an absolutely dominant pronoun. *The* Commander, *the* Ruler, *the* Governor, *the* Boss, etc. Never by any worker have I heard this object referred to as *a* tool. In a craft, mainly dependent upon hand labour, the Commander is used to force the most stubborn work to bend to ruling.

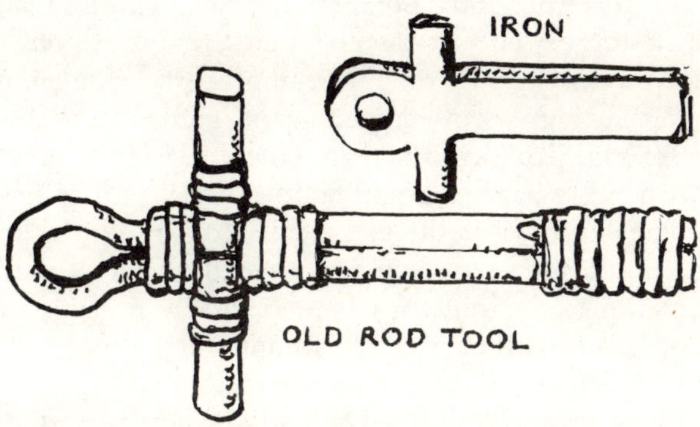

The form is as ancient as the willow; and so exactly resembles the token of command (the ankh) *held by ancient Egyptians, whose life and work depended upon river rods and reeds, that it is at least interesting to compare them.*

In a shed, where men were making "crans" (i.e. the standard basket measure for herrings) I watched how, under the lightest tap of the Commander's handle, Whitehall itself (as represented by the stamped and crowned slat from Her Majesty's Office of Weights and Measures) slid down obediently to its proper place. A small item but of too much interest to omit.

Comfrey

It used to be called Saracen's Root and tradition says that the Crusaders brought the knowledge of its use from the East (though it was used by the Saxons).

Comfrey has small flowers, profuse, thick leaves, and deep fleshy roots. A good fodder plant.

This interesting plant was until recently in the *British Pharmacy* and it is still called "All Heal" and "Boneset". It has been used successfully in modern plastic surgery and its content is now we believe on the market as a proprietary product.[1] The root has the property of retaining masses of water, and producing, when mashed up, a glutinous healing substance that looks like mashed turnip and has the consistency of white of egg. This plant, when broken in March, pours out clear water-sap.

It could be eaten raw, or the extracted juice drunk "by those bursten within", and is still used by the gypsies as a cure for gastric ulcers.

For bone-setting, the pulp was squeezed dry enough to enfold the broken limb, around which it set, without warping, to the firmness of plaster. In early spring, when the root was full of water, it was used fresh. When the plant was in full growth and the leaves and flower shoots contained more of the healing element, an infusion was made of the leaves and flowers and drunk. The sap was also used as a curative water for bathing flesh wounds or bruises.

Angelica A. Archangelica (officinalis)

Some herbalists class Angelica as a garden plant, but it has been growing wild for centuries. It is one of the plants that "locate" old dwellings as it is found in streams on the "infirmary" side of old abbeys, or by travel hostels and inns. It grows up to four feet high, has vivid glossy green foliage and, from June to September, umbels of small white flowers. Parkinson, at his later date, continues its earlier uses, and adds "distillations" and "cordials" "within the compass of the gentlewoman's skill

[1] *Allantoin.* Allen & Hanbury—v. The BMJ advt.

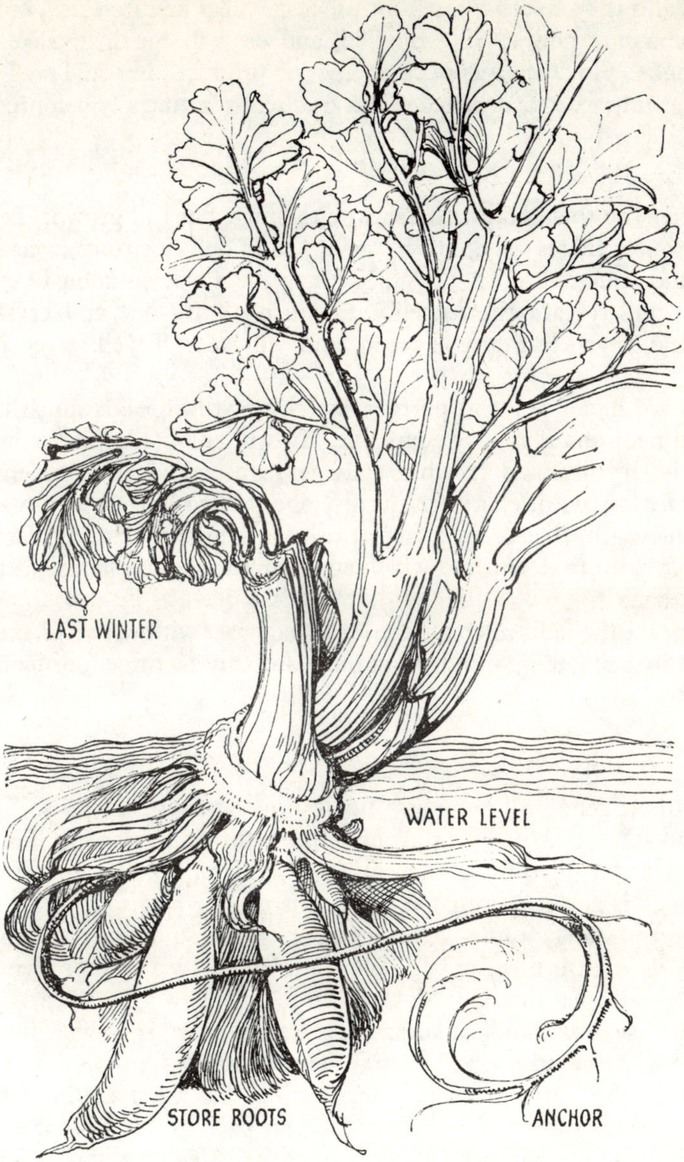

who help their own family and their poor neighbours that are farre remote from physitian and churgeons". (So it was still a "medical" plant.)

It seems to be an "angelic root" in use all over the northern part of Europe and as far north as Lapland where, according to A. Pratt, both plants and seeds are very popular. The young stems may be eaten like celery, and the smooth white root tuber can also be eaten raw, or cooked. The stems are now usually candied, and used in cooking. Like saffron, our English Angelica was once a superior product, and sold well abroad. Now we import it ready made (and frequently artificially coloured).

To Candy Angelica

Gather the thick hollow stems when young, but full grown. Peel them (as the outer ridges are apt to be stringy) and boil in strong sugar solution till tender but unbroken. Drain, reduce the sugar solution to "candy" degree, and replace the Angelica to finish off till dry and crystallized. It should be a clear bright green, and will keep if well stored in a dry box.

It is a difficult plant to portray, as its growth depends much upon its environment and it is very adaptable. In winter bundles of "store food" (looking very like smooth white sausages) are embedded in a dense mass of hairy roots with, characteristically, one or two long rope roots a yard or so in length, that seem to act as travelling anchors during flood time; or as life lines to deep water when summer leaves the plant high and dry on the bank.

In spring the old brown winter leaves contrast with the vivid green new growth that shoots up rapidly and the plant may be three foot high before it flowers.

SPHAGNUM MOSS

This is a genuine "bogmoss". (As peat lands are of an acid nature, fens and salt marshes, being alkaline, grow different plants.) This extraordinary water plant has a long, interesting history of service to mankind. Its foliage is so formed that it imprisons the air and so it floats upright through the water, from a great depth. It grows so densely and so closely interlocked that it fills the bog hole completely, even when in winter it is full of water. Yet the moss sinks down to a shallow grey layer as the bog water drains away, and, in summer, the same moss is a thin, dry, silver-grey border around a small central damp patch.

It has, when dry, a feathery texture and has been used for bedding for centuries. Recently it has been brought back to this same use, for hay fever and asthma sufferers who are allergic to feathers and dislike foam rubber. Also being so absorbent (it can take sixty times its own bulk of water), having antiseptic qualities, and acting as a deodorant, sphagnum is still used for a medical dressing. (A chemist near Harley Street used to compress the mass into large soft pads, like grey felt, for use with rubber sheeting for incontinents.) The broken moss dust, together with bracken dust (from the transport of stone ware) used to be incorporated with linseed oil to produce cow cake. At present it is being used by gardeners to pack plant roots.

The sphagnum harvest was usually in late autumn while the moorland was still hard enough for transport by sledge, or panniers on ponies. The moss was lifted out by long-handled scythes, or pulled out by a sunken rope dragged across by two men on opposite sides of the bog hole. It was left to drain and shrink before packing and taking away for baling. An ordinary hay baler was often used for the job. Bracken was packed around the grey moss before baling as it was tougher to withstand the pull of the rope.

WATER IRIS OR THE FLEUR-DE-LIS

The common yellow iris (by country people it is still called "the water flag") grows best in shallow river water and so is the ancient sign of the river ford. The long crawling roots, cracked and broken by horses hooves or the feet of travellers, float away downstream to catch and root again. Therefore, if the number of irises increase as you walk upstream, you are probably approaching a ford. As the broken roots cannot float upstream against the current, the iris beds often end abruptly just above the ford.

It took me many mediæval miles and many solitary years before this simple fact showed itself to me, but it must have showed itself to generations of ancient travellers who had passed along the river paths before me.

Thus the water iris, the Fleur-de-Lis, becomes the sign of the traveller, the small sturdy gold flags guiding him safely across the ford. So, the conventional iris, folding their wooden leaves in prayer in our ancient chapels, were set to comfort the traveller who reached the last ford of all—the ford of Jordan.

MARSH CINQUEFOIL (*Comarum*)

This dark red-purple flowered plant seems to be vanishing. It is many years since I found it by a stream in Yorkshire, where it was probably used as a dye for wool. (It gives a deep orange shade—more reddish then the yellow dye obtained from soot.) It may have been one of the vegetable dyes used to colour cheese.

Fleur-de-Lis

GYFFIN 13th Cent.
MOTIF FROM 13th. CENTURY
FONTS

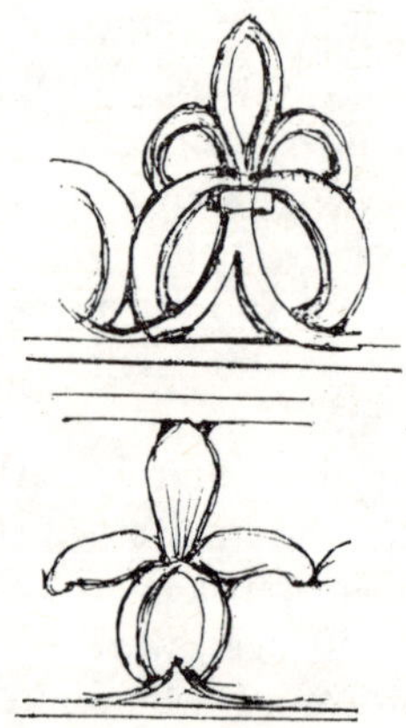

(*see* page 425)

FENNEL (*Peucedanum officinale*)

One of the water plants that also grow on comparatively dry lands, and abundantly upon salt marshes, where it seems to change its curious scent to a more sulphurous stink.

Its flavour seems to have been more popular in the fifteenth and sixteenth centuries when it was used medicinally and also as a condiment for fish. Fennel sauce is still served with salmon. It does not dry successfully and so should be used fresh.

SEA HOLLY (*Eyringo*)

Now grown in gardens for the blue beauty of its foliage. Though when wild it grows on dry shingle, its stems go deep below to the damp places of high tides, and store food for the plant, so that it appears to "grow on drie and stoney ground".

These underground stems were the *eyringo* root of old recipes, and were so aromatic and popular that they were classed with oysters as the stable product of Colchester, and everywhere commanded a ready sale to confectioners. Today, popular seaside resorts have destroyed acres of sea holly, and also the long-horned poppies, and all the other lovely plants that lie dead and buried under miles of cement promenades.

WATER CRESS (*Nasturtium officinale*)

This plant has been valued for years both as a salad and also as a dressing for skin complaints. The stalks and leaves were pounded up to a green paste and laid over the scales of a dry eczema. An old "wort wife" of great repute among the Scarborough fisherfolk used quantities of water cress, together with broom blossom, macerated in hog's lard till the resultant ointment was a deep yellowish green. Septic wounds were washed in well-boiled honey water and the ointment laid on "to give a quick heal" after the discharge ceased. It probably formed a waterproof bandage which was very serviceable for men returning to their boats. For them the ointment had a basis of beeswax, put on warm, as being a more durable plaster.

HORSETAILS (*Equisetum telmateia and E. palestre and E. limosum*)

All these prehistoric-looking plants grow wild, abundantly and most vigorously in or near water.

These tough, rough plants have been of great use for centuries, and at one time had considerable commercial value. They scoured pots and pans, and polished armour. When pewter was in everyday use they scoured that, for pewter in daily use had not a dull grey surface but shone with a watery lustre.

Horsetails and sharp river sand were common scouring agents for wood, stone, metal, etc., right down to, and during, the eighteenth century. When supplies gave out and Dutch influences came in, horsetails were imported under the name of Dutch rush. With the sale of prepared abrasives many of the old natural scourers (Dutch rush, cuttlefish bone, bath brick, water of Ayre stone, etc.) went out of use.

Now the horsetails rasp only the painted panels of old canal barges, a few of whose artists still prefer the surface it gives to the new waterproof emery cloth of the ship's chandler.[1]

Water musk is larger than garden musk

May flowers or ladies' smocks (*see* page 298)

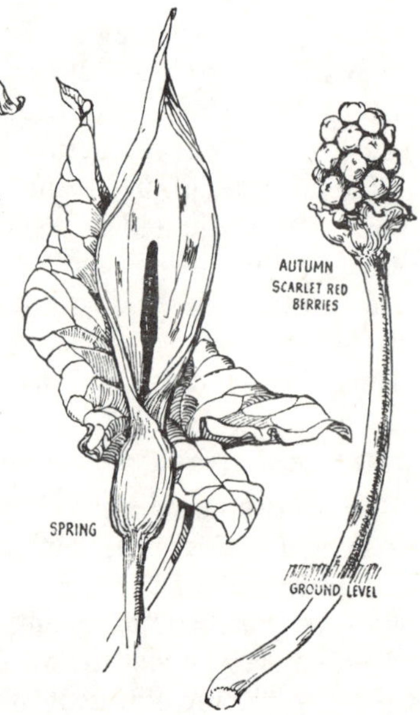

Wild arum

FERNS

Always thought of as "water plants" ferns had a tremendous vogue in the 1850's.

Till this date they had been regarded as slightly magic plants—almost as suspect as fungus, since they grew without flowers or visible seed, and the curious development through spores that needed the spray of water to grow was not commonly understood. Earlier, bracken was called "fern" or brake, though it will grow on a dry hillside and has a different growth.

The Fern Case or "Water Case"

The period that played fountains on the dinner table, sprayed conservatories with constant jets and built "mossy dells" and "rustic water troughs" developed most delightful fern cases.

[1] The following extract from the book by M. T. Cook, *Applied Economic Botany* (1919), will explain the sharp flints in the stems of various species of *Equisetum*. "The aerial stems are derived from an underground stem and may be branched or unbranched,

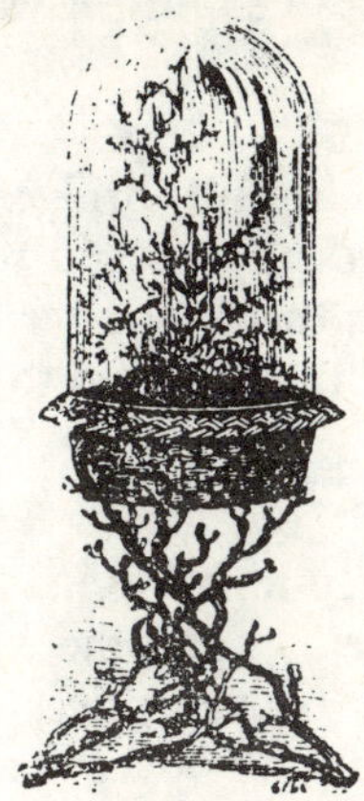

These were set into windows, so that the light filtered through them, much as electrically-lit tropical fish tanks are placed today. The fern cases were constructed with great care as they had to be waterproof.

Well-drained peaty compost was set about with suitable rocks and the ferns planted in shale, rotted slate, or river sand. The whole was well watered and then closed up!

In the humid air and filtered light the ferns throve exceedingly, requiring very little attention.

THE WATER BEE OR GINGER BEER BEE (*A Fungus*)

The old type of ginger beer was water treated with the "water bee" or "bee plant". It was, correctly, a fungus, in appearance white and slightly woolly, and varied in size from a honey bee to a cockchafer. It was a yeast that grew entangled in a web-like bacteria.

When this yeast plant or "bee" was placed in water and fed with sugar, it fermented the sugar and formed carbon dioxide (gas). The gas, being lighter than air, entangled in the bacterial web, caused the bee to float upwards to the surface of the water, where the gas escaped and allowed the bee to sink down again. The constant going up and down of dozens of small bees and the faint buzzing of their escaping gas made a very life-like action.

The bees worked harder in sunshine and turned the water into a honey-coloured syrup. Many people thought of their "water bees" as live

hollow-jointed, fluted, with well-marked longitudinal ridges and furrows and *infiltrated with silica,* which makes them round and rigid". *Letter from the Royal Horticultural Society.*

insects, and grew quite fond of them! The glass bee jar in the window was the cottagers' goldfish bowl. The ginger flavouring was added after the fermentation was complete. The water was poured off the dormant bees, and a fresh supply of water and sugar poured in.

BEAVERS

"The church, mill, bridge and salmon leap, an orchard with a delightful garden, all stand together on a small plot of ground. The Teivi being the only river in Wales which has beavers . . . though in Scotland they are said to be in one river, but very scarce."

GERALDUS CAMBRENSIS, *twelfth century*

THE FROG

"The Frogge highte Rana and hathe the name of noise and cryenge of his voyce . . . and the Male in tyme of love, whan he cryethe for the female; (for every beaste that hath voyce cryethe in tyme of love) —multiplyeth his voyce when he dompe his nether jowe some deal in the water and stryketh the upper jowe."

BART. ANGLICUS

The "Frogge" does croak in water, as described. The male is needed to fertilize each egg, and the female deposits her spawn among roots and reeds. The "combined operation" has to be carried on in shallow water.

THE TOAD

"There is a maner frogge that maketh a hounde stylle if he convethe yt in his mouthe."

BART. ANGLICUS

The toad, "venemous in himself", is never bitten twice by any animal! The rash destructive pup who retrieves one is "stylle" one instant and spends the next half-hour wiping his mouth.

BORASC OR TOAD STONE

"You shall know whether the tode stone be the right and perfect stone or not. Hold the stone before a tode, so that he may see it, and if it be a right and true stone, the tode will leape toward it! and make as though he would snatch it. He envieth so much that man should have that stone."

LUPTON'S *Notable Things*, 1569

THE LEECH

"The Leche is a worne and loveth and sucket blod."

BART. ANGLICUS

These unpleasant creatures were such a common form of blood letting at the time when blood-letting was popular that the doctor was called "the Leech". Till about fifty years ago most old-fashioned chemists used to keep a few leeches in a jar for occasional customers (who had gumboils or black eyes), as the leech was a form of "cupping".

THE FISH

"Fish conceive of dew, and when the moon faileth some fishes be void, and the waxing of the moon increaseth their humour, and their humour vanisheth when the moon vanisheth. By night shell fish come to cliffs and conceive pearls of the dew of heaven."

MERMAID (*Mediæval*)

"The mermaid is a sea beast wonderly shapen, and draweth shipmen to peril by sweetness of song. And some men say that they please so shipmen with likeness of songs, that they draw them to peril and to shipbreach (but the sooth is that they are strong whores that draw men that passed by them to poverty and to mischief). And Physiologus saith that it is a beast of the sea, wonderly shapen as a maid from the navel upward and a fish from the navel downward, and this wonderful beast is glad and merry in tempest, and sad and heavy in fair weather. With sweetness of song this beast maketh shipmen to sleep, and when she seeth that they are asleep, she goeth into the ship and ravisheth (him) which she may take with her, and bringeth him into a dry place and maketh him lie by her.

And some sea men caught one and brought her with the ship and fastened her to the quay (intending all to shew her) but for her piteous wailing they were constrayned to let her goe."

BART. ANGLICUS

SUNDRIES

WRITING FLUIDS

"'Tis to the Press and Pen we Mortals owe
All we Believe and almost all we know.
All Hail; the great Preservators of these Arts,
That raise our Thoughts and Cultivate our Parts."

The Instructor, 1810

Inks

For centuries rain water has been the basis of ink. The earlier inks depended more upon fine matter held in suspension than on solution. The content was, in most cases, stored solid and ground down for use as needed, exactly as artists' Chinese and Indian ink blocks are used today. Sometimes the block was rubbed up on the wet palette (the china palettes of the oriental artists were beautifully designed for this purpose), or the ink was ground down under a maul, as for printing press work. In some cases the fixative medium was incorporated in the block, sometimes it had to be added separately. The old hand-written script inks were usually bound with some form of gum water. With later block printing an oil binding became more usual, for as the shadow printing in any old black letter MS. proves, an oil ink does not dry out as quickly as a water ink.

Almost every scriptorium or household treasured its own special recipe for ink, so that it is sometimes possible to locate an MS. by the locality of the special ink.

Various vegetable and animal substances were used and sepia was an early acquisition. Some of the oldest vegetable inks have remained clear and unfaded for centuries. Galls from the oak were used for some early inks. There is an "ink horn" fungus, which in its black liquidereal state makes a dark brownish ink, very like the genuine sepia. I can find no authentic record, but the name and appearance (exactly like a mediæval ink horn with a quill stuck into it) suggests its use. However, as it would be impossible to give all the various known writing fluids, here is one representative mediæval ink.

It is made from rain water, blackthorn bark and pear tree gum. It is one of the most pleasant recipes, for the white flowers on the sooty blackthorns are very like a new manuscript. So like, that when in April the blackthorn whitens against the grey stone walls of a castle, or on the dykes of some monastic water meadow, it seems to write its own history.

Fine Writeing Inke

During the winter the dark bark loosens and when it feels "dusty" and blackens your fingers cut the twigs and steep them in a noggin of rain water. Fill the water as closely as you can pack the twigs, weight them under with a stone and leave them till the black powdery bark peels off. Then lift out the bare white twigs and refill the same water with more twigs again and again until it is "black as ink". Let it settle undisturbed, pour off any clear surface water and evaporate the accumulated black deposit into a dry, hard cake. Pound, sift this through fine linen, and grind down with pear-tree gum dissolved in a little hot water.

If the ink rubs off, you have not used enough gum; if it cracks in drying, you have used too much. The parchment should be rubbed over with finest pumice or sand to give a surface "bite". A small ivory paper knife, held in the left hand, follows the script across the cockling parchment, holding it down steadily under the pliant quill.

In later centuries households ceased to brew their own inks and it was purchased by the gill or pint and frequently proved far more fugitive than the simpler earlier brews.

Here is a writing ink, such as might be sold from the barrel shown on the plate.

Ink of 1872. *Powder*

Oak galls, 4 oz. sulphate of iron, 1 oz. gum arabic, 1 oz. sugar not quite an ounce.

Mix and pulverize finely and store in three packets. Pour boiling water (1 pint) on one packet, let it stand a few hours.

A fireproof ink is noted about 1850. It consisted of ten parts platinum chlorate, twenty-five parts oil of lavender, fifty parts varnish and a small quantity of lamp black. This ink was used on fireproof paper compounded of wood pulp and size that had been treated with borax and mixed with asbestos fibre.

To make Japanese Writing Ink

1 oz. gum arabic and Roman vitriol, 1 lb. of oak galls well bruised, 5 quarts of small beer (sour) set in a warm place and shaken often, then pour off onto an ounce of ivory black.

To Remove Ink Stains—1850?

Mop it up as soon as possible and wash with skim milk (London milk will do as it is). Salts of sorrel and vinegar are also suggested. The variety of stain removers tried show the variety of inks invented and the reflection on London milk suggests pump water.

Ink Pots and Pounce Pots

Wedgewood and Bentley invented, and put upon the market, a terracotta inkstand "made on an air lock patent, to keep the ink closed from the air which thickened it". The inkwells "could be bought separately or were sold together with their sand box, making a complete inkstand".

This sand box or "pounce" was used to dry the ink before blotting-paper came into use. Some of the antique pewter "pepper pots" now on the market were originally pounce pots, made to go with the circular flat-based pewter ink wells, with encircling holes for quills, so long associated with the bank and the Law. With the steel nib and separate handle pens laid down in troughs, or on a staircase of hooks, the presentation office inkstand became an important architectural feature in the board room before fountain and ball-point pens inscribed less majestic periods.

The sand or pounce box was used to dry the ink before blotting-paper was made. Among "sands" we have found mentioned DUST of OARE, which we have been unable to verify. Oare was the Kentish brick-making village, so it may be a form of brick dust?

Inke Horne

"A standish (has) both Inkeplace, sand box, candlestick, and a long box to lay wax, pens and knife in, allfixt together."

"An Inke horne (portable) be long and round and some have a screw at each end, one for inke, the other to put in the pens. Others have the inke and a sand box at the end and a wafer box at other.

"A *pockett* Inkhorne (hath) a round belly and the penner screwed on it. This is onley for a private persons use, which is not much used to writting but keepeth it about him for occasion when it is offered."

Holmes Armoury

Quill Pens

Scrape off the outer film, cut the ends off and put the barrels into boiling water; wherein is a small quantity of alum and salt. Let them remain ¼ hour and then dry off in a cool oven.

Metal Pens

Metal pen nibs came into general use at about the beginning of the nineteenth century and provided a problem for the ink-makers, as many of the fig tree juices, tree gums, etc., would not run. The colour was formerly applied either in the water or was laid on wet afterwards, somewhat in the technique of mural painting (which used plaster tinted with coloured water). A delightful note on these coloured waters suggests that strips of linen be soaked therein and dried, so that afterwards, when a colour was required, a piece of the linen could be cut off and soaked until the right depth of tone was reached. The older inks did not flow easily and the new ink corroded the metal. Hence an outcrop of pen wipers.

Wafers made with Gum Water

With these wafers, letters were sealed before envelopes came into more common use. Beat a little fine flour, white of egg, isinglass and a very little yeast together, and thin out with gum water. Colour as you choose, and pour onto tin plates and dry on a stone, then cut into pieces for use.

Sealing Wax was made of beeswax rosin and turpentine, melted together and coloured with vermilion verdigris, smalt, ivory black. Important when Seals represented authority.

WATER COLOUR

Where colour was required for the earliest MS. it was water colour. The white ground was variously made of some fine chalky medium which was bound with a size of egg white or gum.

Instructions of the period advise that a strong solution of the colour be made in soft water. Scraps and strips of linen cloth were soaked in this solution and then dried. When a coloured water was wanted to paint onto the white gesso ground, a piece of this cloth was cut off and soaked till the right tone was obtained. This method gives the very even matt colour of MS. illuminations and is a development of the wet plaster tempera work used on walls. A note added to the instructions suggests that in order to preserve the strips of linen from damp the illuminator should take them to bed with him.

If these colour strips had been prepared in a gelatinous or sea-weed "size" they would be very susceptible to damp, so the devout brother is advised to take them to bed with him. We hope it cheered up the dormitory.

QUILLS

Appropriately, most quills were from water fowl, perhaps because their naturally slightly oiled plumes were more water-resistant than land bird quills. The goose quill is still used by artists for certain scripts and has not completely left the courts of law. The quill is still the unit of measurement for some of the best water colour brushes. Swan, goose, crow and

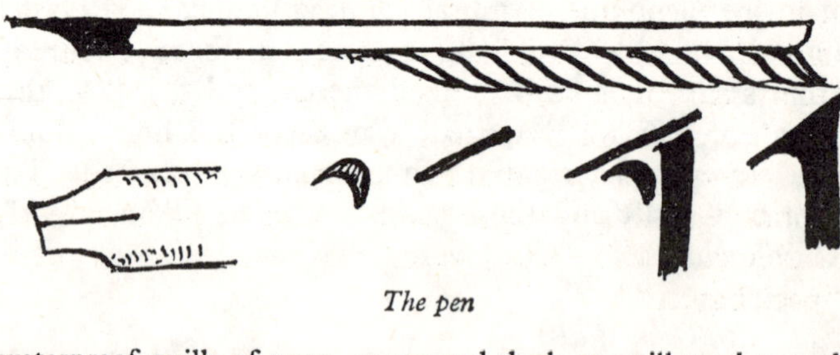

The pen

The waterproof quills of swan, goose and duck are still used to make fine water-colour brushes. The smallest is the crow quill; and one very special brush is made from the single curved feather found only on the back of a drake.

duck quills are standard sizes, and certain special quill feathers (that which curls stiffly on the back of the drake is an example) are also treasured for special crafts.

Instructions for "making your pen" preface all books dealing with ink scripts. The diagram gives the usual method.

A WASH BARREL

The old measurement for shellfish, notably oysters, was taken from the size of the tub, conveniently deep for washing off the sand. Another measurement was the wash barrel, which was used in the splitting and salting of fish. As with shellfish, experience taught the exact size that would take enough water to soak the fish, without packing them too close together at the bottom, or making them float in too thick a layer on the surface. Thus a "wash barrel of mackerel" (or herring, etc.) was the number that could conveniently be rinsed and soaked clear of blood before drying and salting.

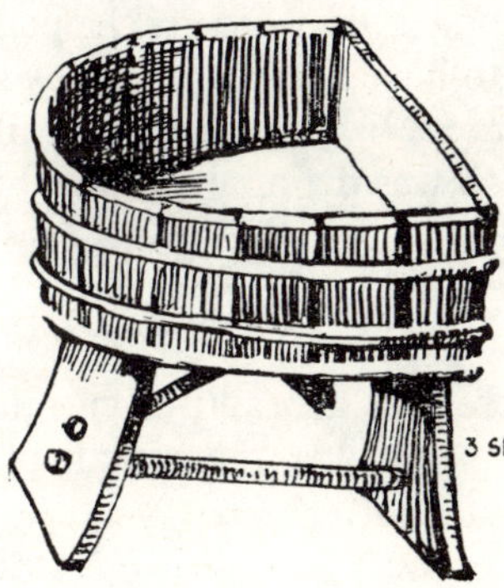

A WASH OF OYSTERS

Most shellfish were washed in sea water to rid them of sand and mud. The amount of shells that could be "thrown about in the tub" and rinsed clean varied with the texture of the mud and skill of the washer, but the average naturally became a local standard of measurement, "a washing". A bushel tub was a handy size (a "strike" was the stick drawn across the top of the bushel to level or "strike off" the measurement).

A "wash" of oysters was officially ten "strikes"—but a "wash" of cockles, or mussels, or any other fish, was an individual (and usually local) measurement. (Like a "peck of peas" it depended on the local size of a "peck basket".)

DRINKING VESSELS

Drinking cups of precious metals, banded horn, or finely-decorated wood, were, like the linen cloths and embroideries, of curiously fine quality in contrast to the comparatively crude furnishings and trestle-board tables of the early Saxon hall. These costly items were handsome investments, easily stored and portable, on the same principle as that of nomads and warriors, who concentrate their valuables in personal jewellery, silken rugs, etc. It requires a very stable civilization to risk unwieldy stores of cash, or to invest in anything but personal goods.

Ships or oxen represented working capital. Gold and silver cups testified to accumulated wealth (and were always enjoyable in use!).

Disc—dish. Bolla—a bowl. Knoep—a cup. Crocca—a pot of earthenware such as country people still call "crocks" and we call crockery. Flaxe—a flash or flagon.

This list of Saxon utensils is taken from T. Wright's *Domestic Manners and Sentiments.*[1]

A Clack Dish

This was a beggar's bowl for receiving drinks or soups and almost any sort of food. It had a wooden lid which if clapped on the bowl was a sign it was empty. It seems to have been confused by some with the clapper of the leper, which was more like that used by children scaring crows from the corn. The clack dish was definitely a *bowl*, but I've been unable to find an example.

The Carafe

> "Then at every plate there was a beautiful cut-glass bottle, something like a decanter . . . and over the mouth of it a tumbler to match."
>
> "NOBODY" S. WARNER

What we now think of as an old-fashioned bedroom water bottle and glass, seems to have been a dinner-table water service in New England (*see* page 199).

SOME DRINKING CUPS NAMED

"Of drinking cups, divers and sundry sorts we have. Some of elme, some of Box, some of Maple, some of Holly, etc., Mazers, broad-mouthed dishes, noggins, whiskins, piggins,[2] crinzes, ale bowles, wassell

[1] Early English Text Society.

[2] Andrew Boorde states that a "*pygge* is a cock slewed and made in a jelly, and a cockerallys is stewed in gootes milk and suger, almond mylke in the which ryce is sodden and rabettes stewed".

(This may account for the "cockerys" at the wedding feast after the Tournament of Tottenham.)

Whether the white broth being served in a small table tub gave the name to the tub is conjectural; such a small tub is still called a "piggin" in some parts of Britain. Today we have punnets and cartons, etc.

bowles, court dishes, tankards, karmes (from a bottle to a pint and gill). Other bottles we have of leather (but they most used amongst the shepherds and harvest people of the country). Small jacks we have in many ale houses of the citie and suburbs, tipt with silver, besides the great black jacks and bombards at the court, which when the Frenchmen first saw, they reported at their return with their (own) country that 'the Englishmen used to drinke out of their bootes'.

"We have, besides, cups made of hornes of beasts, of cockernuts, of gourds, of the eggs of Ostriches, others made of the shells of divers fishes brought from the Indies and other places, and shining like mother of Pearl. Come to Plate; every taverne can afford you flat bowles, French bowles, Prounet cups (punnet? posset?) beare bowles, beakers; and private householders in the citie when they make a feast . . . can furnish their cup boards with flagons, tankers, beere-cups,

wine bowles (some white, some percell guilt (gilt), some guilt all over, some with covers, others without of sundry shapes and qualities)."

HEYWOOD, 1635, *Philocothonista*

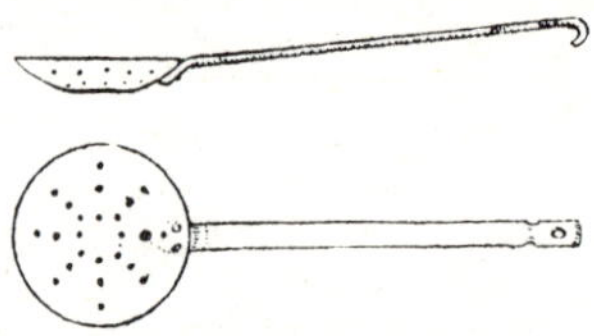

"A scummer is a rond plate of Tyn or Brasse or Copper or Silver, 10 or 12 inches in diamiater, set orderly with holes that a rush may goe throgh. With this instrument cookes take away all filth and scume from off a Boiling Pott. . . . There is other little Instrument of this nature used by cookes called an egge slice; made much the same manner, but more ovall; with this they turnne any thing that is fried or stewed. . . ."

Holmes Armoury, 1649

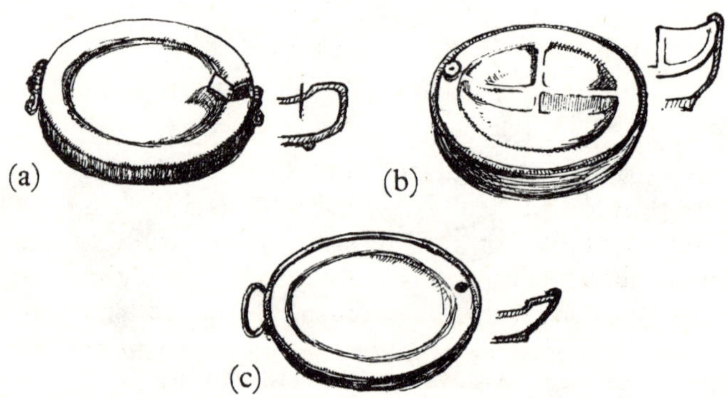

Hot water dishes. (a) All pewter, 1600; *(b) Pewter with pottery plate top,* 1700; *(c) Block tin and pottery,* 1900

A LADE GAWM

The handy or small open-handled tub was also called a lade gawm. Lade being the word for lifting or ladling up water—and gawm is derived from "gallon".

The size of these small tubs varied considerably but was never more than one person could conveniently handle.

LAGENS ASEEN—A BUCKET OF ASH WOOD

Wright also describes a small strong wooden bucket that was called a "back-bucket". It is depicted by sickbeds, and was frequently buried with the corpse. It was probably an early form of bed-pan.

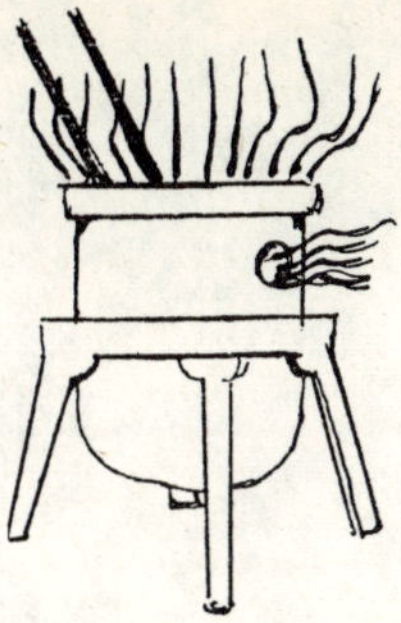

"A furnice for closing of the mouths or necks of glass bottles. It is of cast iron set on a BRANDANT, and above the furnice top is set a strong paire of Tongs with broad ends, so that the neck of the bottle being made hot, with the tongs is squeesed together."

Holmes Armoury, 1649

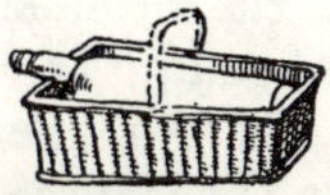

NELSON'S BOTTLE BASKET

BOTTLE BUOY

"Magilamus, performing the first voyage about the world, falling with this port (St. Julian) had their a mutiny against him, for which he executed divers of his company upon a gibbet close by the sea. Which gibbet, being of firwood, as found there, sound and whole, 50 years at least upon our time of coming thither. Of which (gibbet) wood our cooper made tankards, for such of the ship's company as would drink in them. Whereof, for my own part, I had no great liking, seeing there was no such necessity."

Journal of Capt. Blanck to Cape Verde, sixteenth century

The "bottle buoy", so often shown in old seascapes, had been frequently a real bottle, for such cooper-made wine bottles and flagons were common usage up to the eighteenth century. The wood withstood changes of temperature, and the strong banding the pressure of fermentation. When befouled, or infected by bacteria, the bottles were easily converted into floats by inserting a crossbar or wedge stopper. Because the shape seemed suitable, some later were definitely made up for buoys, and in these the wedge stopper must have been built in during construction. This wedge principle recurred later in glass bottles sealed by glass marbles, which pressure from within wedged up tightly within the narrow, rubber-ringed neck (*see* plate 3).

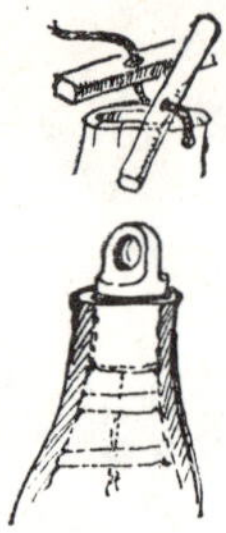

WATER LIGHTS

Before gas and electricity piers, ornamental waters and some official waterworks had to be lighted by candles or oil. Lighthouses used both oil and candles, and reflectors were well thought out. The illustration shows a nine-candle-power fitment. Each candle burns inside a draught-proof glass globe and the set is arranged on an iron frame twelve feet long by five feet high. The inventor affirms that even a small wax candle placed within a glass globe (over water) produces a "very luminous Ball of Fire, specially if the glass is clear and well polished".

WATER LIGHTS

Water lighting for piers and jetties, 1700–1800

"The candles are placed in draught-proof bottles arranged securely on iron stands. . . . Even the light of a small wax candle placed within each globe, produces a very luminous Ball of Fire, specially if the glass is clear and well polished.

"The whole illumination of two such globes, extending 12 ft. long and 5 ft. high appears (over water) as if it were one Body of Fire!"

It is recommended for lighthouses, or piers. It "is easy to keep in order".

Advt.

These, utilizing the reflecting power of water, were made for both practical and ornamental waters. The note is taken from an advertisement.

The ornamental form adorned pleasure gardens; adaptations were used as harbour lights.

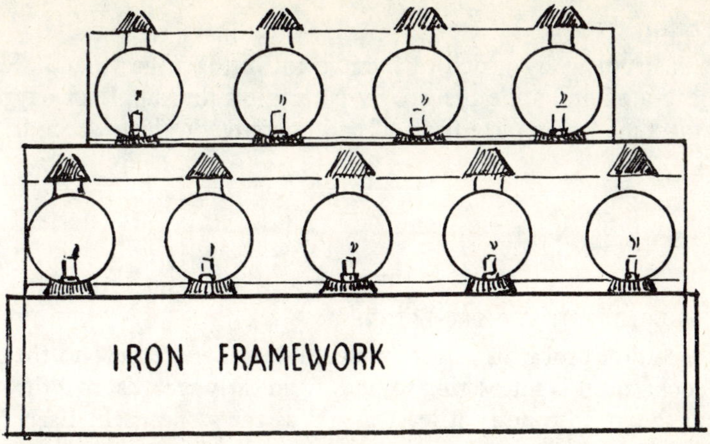

WATER FIRE EXTINGUISHERS

In 1865 a "compressed" fire extinguisher was on the market in London. It was a French invention, patented by an English firm in Chancery Lane. It depended upon the fact that water under pressure will absorb carbonic acid gas to an almost unlimited extent, and thus, if the charged water be confined to a strong container, it can be released (i.e. squirted out) in a strong, easily directed stream on to the centre of the blaze.

The patentees advertised that six gallons of the extinguishing mixture, under a ninety pound to the square inch pressure, could be easily carried by anyone and could be sprayed out a distance of thirty or forty feet.

A development of this idea was the sale of strong glass bottled extinguishers, usually coupled in pairs, that could be thrown by hand to break on the fire. These round greenish bottles in their carriers can be seen in some old Victorian prints, and are sometimes erroneously explained as being carafes or cruets, in spite of the fact that they were usually kept on staircases.

Chemical Action Supersedes Water (*in* 1856)

"There is reason to believe that the fire which destroyed £100,000 worth of property last Monday at London Bridge (Mr. Alderman Humphrey's warehouse) and which was only a repetition of one that had occurred in the same vicinity a few months before, might very probably have been immediately extinguished at the precious cost of £4 or £5, for a machine which has been long known and tested."

The Times City Article, June 1857

FIRE ANNIHILATOR

An instrument by which carbonic acid, nitrogen gases and steam are generated and stifle the fire by cutting off the supply of oxygen. The machine is complete in itself and operative in thirty seconds.

WATER AS LUBRICANT FOR GRINDSTONES

The technical problems of mechanical lubricants are beyond the scope of this book, but it is interesting to find, from early records, that the use of water on the grindstone is at least as old as the stone itself. Early MSS. show stones of such large diameter that the grinder has to sit on a special scaffold to reach the top and the labourer turning the handle works at shoulder level. The water is in the trough below, through which the stone revolves.

Grease and tallow lubricants were valued as medical agents after they had become blackened (and therefore "contained the metal"). The black grease from the church bells was especially efficacious, as it had previously been blessed, so both spiritual and material qualities were present.

While manpower was still used the grindstone had to remain large to provide circumference speed

WATER DIVINING OR DOWSING

"This much-despised and maligned Rod, which has been a puzzle from the days of Moses, may be regarded as one of the most beneficial and remarkable discoveries of the nineteenth century."

The transition from "an accepted miracle" shows mankind's thought through several complete sequences. In the religious sequence, Moses striking the rock with his rod is "entirely an Act of God" and unexplainable. In the materialistic sequence, "it was the work of quarrymen directed by an engineer".

The quarryman's earliest tool, the rod, remains in use, called (variously) a "jumper", because it jumped round and round under continuous strikes from a sledge-hammer, utilising the rock chippings it caused to grind out a circular bore-hole as it went down. At intervals the debris was extracted from the hole on a greased stick or weighted tuft of wool. Water was usually supplied during the boring process to help preserve the temper of the jumper's cutting end. A sand abrasive and bow drill might be used under some conditions. The depth of some bore-holes, providing water for hill-top castles, testify to the "use of the rod"; and the "artesian" gush of released water was often quite "miraculously powerful".

Elsewhere we describe the primitive raised aqueduct; but few realise that "surveying" was done to conduct water through cuttings or boreholes.

The legend of St. Fechin, who ordered the building of a water mill, confident that by the time the stones were set the water power could be provided, is an example of this sort of surveying that may well have been considered "divination".

The hazel twig, which seems to have been used in the fifteenth century, provided a less material sequel of thought that depended upon some subtle mental "affinity", which might be plain "sorcery". This thought had a religious sequel when a Jesuit Father "believed pious men might have the gift", their occasional failure proving it could not depend upon the "infallible devil"!

Another kindred sequence was the "Influence of the Planets" (the heavenly bodies being a special science during the fifteenth to seventeenth centuries). In 1797 this sequence echoed the medieval belief in the continuous striving of all elements to seek their own level—the "waters below the earth and the waters above the earth". Thus "the aqueous molecules exhaled from the soil ascend, and, finding entrance into the stem of the branch, accumulate there"—like sap rising up a tree in the spring season—"and augment its weight by repelling the air, the ejected matter, returning into the weighted end of the rod, making it dip towards the soil". . . . "This effect is perhaps the cause that branches of trees growing by water droop towards it—i.e. the water sends up aqueous particles which penetrate the branches and weight them, causing them to dip down, thus bringing the branches as much as possible parallel with the columns of ascending particles of water"—a very interesting theory, as about this period of navigational development the capillary attraction, that caused ships drifting far apart to collide, was giving people new ideas of invisible "columns" or "lines of attraction".

It is necessary to see the sequence of thoughts, not with the imagination of the scholar, but with the *material observation of the peasant.* The peasant saw lightning come from the sky and plunge into the earth; he saw it travel through a tree, blasting it, or through a man, killing him. The peasant *saw* roots, in the blind dark, reach towards distant water, and mating animals and insects follow "invisible lines of attraction". So that a "line" from a planet, travelling through a man back to earth, was to him possible though not perceptible?

This faculty of observation perhaps accounted for the most interesting theory: that *the human eye could see the water below the rock*—as a gannet, high up in the sky, could see fish far below the sea—the eye itself being a mechanically comprehensive organ (as a mirror is capable of reflecting all a room, but we are capable of using only one aspect in the mirror).

The theory held that the human eye, as a mechanically perfect organ, could penetrate the rocks, but the human brain, being of lesser range, could only receive a limited supply of information from the eye. So, though the eye *saw* the water below the rock, the brain could not receive the information *visually*; therefore the message was transmitted through the motor nerves to the brain, which, in response, forced a movement down arms and hands, and pointed the twig downwards.

The fact that all diviners affirmed "the movement of the twig was *automatic and as much beyond their control as their heart beats*" served to prove this theory, which was backed up by a boy diviner, working in Mexico, who affirmed he could see the water below rocks, but "not as he saw with normal eyesight". The American Institute of Mining Engineers considered that "traces of minerals in the diviner's body might have magnetic reaction with minerals underground."

The whole controversy was hotly debated during the 19th century; development of powered industries made the location of water urgent, and it was a period of social and intellectual debates and conversations. Quite definitely, water divining became an accepted fact, and developed as an accredited trade—though some families still held it as a mysterious "gift", and children of three years old were found to be "natural diviners". An example of a trade exponent was one Mr. Chesterman, who actually took pupils to learn the art and advertised openly.

Underground springs found
Estimated yield and distance from surface supplied
Mr. H. Chesterman, Water Expert
Cleveland Place,
Bath.
No Water — No Pay

Mr. Chesterman, himself an engineer, worked out a mathematical formula for estimating the depth of the water, by measuring the distances at which the "current" could be felt, either side of a central line, at right angles to the flow of the water. This developed research into "the transmitting of electricity", and diviners studied the insulating effects of standing on glass, etc.

Through all this scientific activity passes one pleasantly unworried exponent—a certain Bill Stone, an estate worker at Bolingbrook Hall. He had no "temperment". He kept the unhurried placidity of the man who knows his own mind. He would chat affably while walking around with his twig. He said he "didn't need to concentrate", he "just let the thing work himself". "He rather inclined to the mineral and magnetic theory, because the doctor told him he'd 'a lot of *iron* in his system which might account for the strength of the electricity'. No, he didn't understand it—*he just found water*; and as he'd found it on the estate after they'd lost £100 on *not* finding it, he thought his power was *A good thing*"—and there speaks again the continuous peasant, placidly secure in his own experience, and completely unburdened by the varied explanations of the scholar. Today scientific research seems to have elucidated this centuries-old puzzle. The tracking of buried bombs and locating of submarine objects now cause no surprise; the cause is known to the few, the explanation is as far beyond the comprehension of the many as ever it was.

NOTES ON RAIN SIGNS

"O! it ain't goin' to rain no more, no more!
O! it ain't goin' to rain no more—
How the Hell can the old folks tell
That it ain't goin' to rain no more?"

Song

BAROMETERS "*When made of water require a column thirty-three feet high*"

The country people have dozens of water barometers which they have learnt to read from observation and experience. Thus the old bladder covers, fitted over jars in the store-room, were considered quite reliable by the housewife, as they were as sensitive to damp and pressure as any other type of drum.

Seaweed hung by the door owed its "reliability" to the salt and damp which altered its membrane texture.

The salted bacon and ham hanging up in the kitchen made a good weather indicator, sparkling with salt crystals in dry frosty weather, or becoming pearly when the air was damp. Then, too, "When the spotted toad is seen on his four legs walk on the green" also foretold rain water (but why he should change his gait was controversial).

Excessively dry weather brings toads and hedgehogs into dwellings in search of water. When a hedgehog is suckling she will become desperately brave to obtain water (or milk) for her little ones, and spilt milk in the dairy, or milk left in the cat's saucer, may save their lives. (So it is merciful to put some water out for these useful creatures.) The toad is more likely to walk up when the yard is swilled, and in drought the clatter of buckets will bring many wild things very close. So, if they have been coming to houses for days and suddenly stop doing so, country people know that they have felt rain coming and are waiting for their own supply.

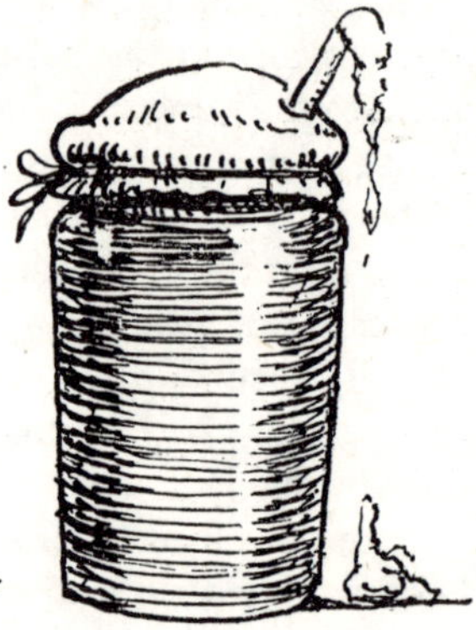

The yeast jar boils over

The vacuum above his mercury told Torricelli about the weather. The ale wife judged it by the working of her brew, the spinster by the working of her thread.

The wind in the ears of the ploughboy, the song of birds in the trees, the ghostly voice of the parchments stirring and stretching in the scriptorium that was understood by the scribe—all damp-induced tensions of everyday things told their owners that rain was coming. These few random signs are chosen from hundreds because they have reasonable explanations connected with water.

But very often the knowledge of weather signs was reversed. For example, the mediæval shepherd, choosing which of his ewes would be likely to withstand the winter and which had better be killed off and salted down for Christmas, went out to pasture early in the morning to see upon which animals the hoar-frost hung longest, and from which it most quickly cleared. The sheep with the warmest and most vigorous blood were kept, the old and cold must die.

STEVENS' PROGNOSTIC FOR RAIN

"These are the general prognostics of rain—When cattle snuff the air and gather together into the corner of the field with their heads to the leeward, or take shelter in the sheds—when sheep leave their pastures with reluctance—when goats go to sheltered spots—when asses bray frequently and shake their ears—when dogs lie much about the fireside and appear drowsy—when cats turn their backs to the fire and rub their faces—when pigs cover themselves more than usual in litter—when cocks crow at unusual hours and flap their wings much—when hens chaunt—when ducks and geese are unusually clamorous—when pigeons wash themselves—when peacocks squall loudly from trees—when the guinea-fowl makes an incessant grating noise—when sparrows chirp loudly and congregate on the ground or in a hedge—when swallows fly low, and skim their wings on the water, on account of the flies upon which they feed having descended so low—when the carrion-crow croaks solitarily—when water wild fowl dip and wash vigorously—when moles throw up hills industriously—when toads creep out in numbers—when frogs croak—when bats squeak and enter houses—when singing birds take shelter—when the robin approaches near the dwellings of man—when swans fly against the wind—when bees leave their hives with caution, and fly only short distances—when ants carry their eggs busily—when flies bite severely, and become troublesome in numbers—when earthworms appear on the surface of the ground and crawl about—and when the larger sorts of snails appear."

Book of the Farm, 1871 *Edition*

RAIN WATER AND ST. SWITHIN

"Saint Swithin's Day if it does rain
Forty days rain will remain.
Saint Swithin's Day if it be fair,
Forty days 'twill rain na mair."

St. Swithin was a Bishop of Winchester about 850 who desired to be buried outside under the green grass rather than, as customary for church dignitaries, inside the choir. So it was done, but later, after he had been canonized, the monks arranged for his body to be reburied inside. However, they were prevented by torrential rain that lasted so long they took it to be an omen and let the bones rest. Whereupon the weather instantly improved, so they compromised by building a chapel *over* the bones.

Curiously, St. Swithin seems to have duplicated St. Paul's Day, January 25th. Robert of Avesbury's history mentions:

"Clara dies Pauli bona tempora denolat anni,
Si nix vel pluvia designant tempora cara
Si fiant nebulse morientur Bestia quaeque
Si fiant vendi proetisbunt proelia gentl."

By 1676 the well-known "Shepherd's almanack" cheerfully admits that 12th January and the 25th are "disputable dates".

RAIN SIGNS

"On hosiers' poles, depending stockings tied
Flap with the slackened gale from side to side."

GRAY

(As the rough wool absorbs the damp the legs sway slowly; when it's a dry breeze they kick about briskly.)

WATER AND CORNS

"He first that useful secret did explain
Why pricking corns foretell the gathering rain."

GRAY'S *Pastoral*

Because of the alteration in "pressure" (the weight of the air that presses down the mercury in a barometer) some people can feel the oppression of a coming storm. The pressure from within their bodies responds to the altered pressure from without. The cry "I know it's going to rain because my corns shoot" is true. The soft porous skin of the foot can expand to the changed pressure, but the hard-textured corn cannot do so and the tension between the two different textures causes the nerve end to "shoot". A sprain or the scar tissue around a newly-knit break act in the same way, being very painful but thoroughly reliable barometers!

"HYDROMAIN"—HYDROPHOBIA

In 1787 there was agitation in Parliament over the increase of hydrophobia. "A considerable, if not the greatest part of the dogs are kept by inferior sorts of people. The bites of mad dogs are now become more frequent than ever, and there is the greatest reason to apprehend that the infection and pestilential diseases now raging amongst horned cattle are extended by means of the said animals."

Question in Parliament

A CAUL

"A child's caul to be sold, enquire No. 2 Greystoke Place, Fetter Lane.

To persons going to sea, a child's caul, in a perfect state, to be sold cheap, 5 Duke St. Manchester Square."

Advt. The Times, Feb. 1813

Persons going to sea (and sailors themselves) put great faith in a child's caul against drowning. How much was superstition (based on the idea of the head rising through the waters of the womb) or how many inflated pigs' bladders were sold as water wings no one knows, but to be born with a caul was considered very lucky.

A WATER GAME

In a thirteenth-century MS. is mentioned a greasy pole, in which the player was given a candle (which he must keep dry). He had to light this from another candle burning at the top. The pole was set above a large tub of cold water!

THE OLD EGG TEST (USED TODAY WHEN MAKING BRINE FOR PICKLES, ETC.)

> "Aristotle saythe that salte water of the sea is more hevy and thycke than freshe water . . . and the taken therof to knowe it is so, is this, for an egge floteth in salte water and synketh downe in freshe."
>
> BART. ANGLICUS

THE LOG

The ship's log, in its simplest form, is a log thrown out ahead of the ship, to float on the water and be a fixed point by which the time taken by the ship in passing it can be measured. The words "ship's log" have now transferred from the instrument in use to the chart, or record, that reports its findings.

CLEPSYDRA

The water-clock and the sandglass have been well documented by experts. They are man's timing.

Water's timing is of the ocean, and by it the smallest invisible water bud lives or sleeps. And because all life came by this timing vestiges within our new frail humanity still respond to it. So that the turning of a river tide in the night can wake us and the outgoing tide of the sea draw away those who will sleep for ever. The timing of water is the pulse of the earth, and who knows where beats the heart of it?

Ford Jordan

BIBLIOGRAPHY

This list of books does not include the reprints of the Early English Text and other Societies, nor the well-loved novels, nor the dozens of S.P.C.K. and other tracts that are such copious sources of information. But it does give me the opportunity to thank my real references, the kindly labourers, engineers, master-plumbers, hill farmers and river and marsh men, who have made this note-book. Bede's "brother Badudegn" who had a stroke while washing blankets in the eleventh century, the warden of a youth hostel who had to unfreeze blankets last winter, the surveyor who splashed up the Elan reservoir streams in the rain and the many landladies who have so often "dried me out"—all are here. All my thanks are here—to every one of you.

Accomplist Housewife, 1754.
BARTHOLOMAEUS, *De Proprietatus*, 1495.
Bath Poems and Guides, 1748.
Baths and Wash Houses for Labouring Classes, etc., 1845.
Baths for the Million, etc., and Parliamentary reports, 1845.
BAYNES, *Early Church Social Life*, 1927.
Builders dictionary, 1734.
Builders price book, 1775.
Catalogue of Mineral Waters (and other trade papers), 1911.
CHURCH, G., *Soap Working Materials* (various dates).
COULTON, G. G. C., *Life in The Middle Ages*, 1910.
COULTON, G. G. C., *Medieval Panorama*, 1938.
CROMBIE, A. C., *Augustine to Galileo*, 1952.
DACRES, *Elements of Water Divining*, 1660.
Earth and Water Closets—Trade Prospectus (various dates).
ELYOT, SIR THOMAS, *Castle of Health*, 1539.
ENGLISH, *Fire Saving*, 1766.
Family Dictionary, 1695.
FISHER, A. T., *Saddle Room notes*, 1890.
GEDDE, W., *Booke of Sundry Draughts*, 1615.
GERVES, *Wheel Buckets*, 1728.
Godly Praiers for Baths, 1575.
Guide to Health, Homoeopathic, 1891.
Guide to Seaside Watery Places, 1876.
HARWOOD, DR., *Obstinate Palsy and Electricity*, 1784.
HARWOOD, *Mineral Waters of Gloucester*, 1815.
HOLME, G., *Penmon Priory*, 1924.
HOLME, R., *Academy of Armoury* (Roxburgh Soc.).
HOLME, S., *Want of Water*, 1845.
Horseman, The (whole series 1827–1891 destroyed in Second World War).
HUNT, R., *West Country notes*, 1881.

HUNTER, A., *Buxton Waters*, 1773.
IZARD, *Medical Proof of Miracles*, 1922.
JONES, DR. JOHN, M.D., *Discourse on Ancient Baths of Buckstones*, 1574.
JONES, J., M.D., *Use of Perchloride of Iron and other salts in treatment of consumption*, 1862.
JORDEN, *Natural Baths*, 1631.
Journals of Arch., Various Counties—Cistercian statutes and special Yorkshire notes reprints from 1256.
KEN, BISHOP, *Prayers for Bathers at Bath*, 1692.
KER, W. P., *The Dark Ages*, 1958.
KNIGHT, S., *Water Baptism*, 1837.
Lodgings and Hotel Guides (various), 1700–1900.
Many trade notices on this subject.
Necessary . . . book on Killing Vermine, A, 1688.
NICHOLS, T., *The Water Cure*, 1856.
NICHOLS, W., *Drinking Water*, 1879.
OZELL, J., *Art of Thinking*, 1717.
OZELL, J., *Rape of The Bucket*, 1737.
PARKS, *Chemistry in Pharmacy*, 1940.
PERKS, *Waterline of London after the Gt. Fire*, 1935.
PRICE, LEO SHERLEY, *Bede, Modern Translation*, 1955.
Relations of the Soape Bussiness, 1641.
RIDER, *Humours of an Inn*, 1768.
RUSSELL, R., *Discussion on Sea Water*, 1752.
RUSSELL, *Sea and Mineral Waters*, 1760.
SCOTT, SIR WALTER, *Letters on Demonology, etc.*, 1830.
SEMPLE, *Building in Water*, 1776.
Sope Makers Complaints, 1650.
TOPSELL, *Beasts*, 1607.
Tunbridge Wells Spa, 1725, 1771, 1786.
TUSSER, 1638.
URE, A., *Art of dyeing cloth.*
WESLEY, J., *Primitive Physick*, 1755.
YOUATT, *The Horse*, 1853.

INDEX